365 ENTRIES FROM SEVEN FIELDS OF KNOWLEDGE

THE
INTELLECTUAL
DEVOTIONAL

AMERICAN HISTORY

Revive Your Mind,

Complete Your Education,

and

Converse Confidently

about Our Nation's Past

★ ★ ★

DAVID S. KIDDER & NOAH D. OPPENHEIM
New York Times Best-Selling Authors of *The Intellectual Devotional*

MODERN TIMES
An imprint of Rodale Inc.

© 2007 by TID Volumes, LLC

Modern Times is a trademark of Rodale Inc.

Rodale books may be purchased for business or promotional use or for special sales. For information, please write to:
Special Markets Department, Rodale Inc., 733 Third Avenue, New York, NY 10017

Printed in the United States of America

Rodale Inc. makes every effort to use acid-free ⊗, recycled paper ◉.

Book design by Anthony Serge, principal designer;
initial interior creative by Nelson Kunkel, The Ingredient

For image credits, see page 378.

Library of Congress Cataloging-in-Publication Data

Kidder, David S.
    The intellectual devotional American history : revive your mind, complete your education, and converse confidently about our nation's past / David S. Kidder and Noah D. Oppenheim.
        p.   cm.
    ISBN-13 978–1–59486–744–6   hardcover
    ISBN-10 1–59486–744–5   hardcover
    1. United States—Civilization—Miscellanea.   2. United States—History—Miscellanea.   3. Devotional calendars.   I. Oppenheim, Noah D.   II. Title.
    E169.1.K485   2007
    973—dc22   2007030593

Distributed to the trade by Holtzbrinck Publishers

2   4   6   8   10   9   7   5   3   1   hardcover

To Virelle and Steve Kidder
To Marcia and Jay Oppenheim
—With our love and gratitude

Contributing Writer

Alan Wirzbicki

Contributing Editor

James Downs, PhD

Introduction

The Intellectual Devotional is a collection of daily readings—in this volume, focused on the fascinating history of the United States. Like our first devotional, these readings offer regular stimulation for the mind, an escape from everyday worries, and an education in critical realms of knowledge. Each entry is a thorough treatment of the subject, easily digestible in a short sitting.

In this edition we have chosen to focus entirely on the rich history of this great country. The study of American history sheds essential light on our world today, provides useful points of reference for intelligent conversation, and will capture the imagination of anyone who simply enjoys a good story. Perhaps, most important, as we face momentous decisions about our future, never has it been more imperative for every citizen to understand this nation's challenges and triumphs since its founding.

The 365 readings that follow are divided into the following fields of knowledge:

POLITICS & LEADERSHIP

A profile of the men and women who have led the United States and its people

WAR & PEACE

A survey of the military conflicts that have defined this nation—why they were fought, how they were won or lost, and what the consequences were

RIGHTS & REFORM

A look at America's journey living up to its philosophical promise

BUSINESS

The innovators and tycoons who have fueled the engine of American industry

BUILDING AMERICA

The infrastructure that is the backbone of the nation

LITERATURE

An introduction to the great writers and their works that have shaped our national identity

ARTS

A review of quintessential American artists, from music to the visual and performance arts

John Smith

In the spring of 1607, a group of English settlers reached North America after almost five months at sea. Exhausted by the long voyage, they landed on a small, uninhabited island in Virginia off the coast of Chesapeake Bay. The small colony they built there—the first permanent English settlement in the New World—they named Jamestown, after King James I of England.

One of the best-known leaders of the Jamestown expedition was Captain John Smith (c. 1580–1631), a twenty-seven-year-old adventurer and soldier of fortune who had fought as a mercenary in several European wars before signing up for the English mission to Virginia. Courageous and headstrong, Smith took charge of the colony for much of the next two difficult years, before an injury from a gunpowder explosion forced him to return to England in 1609.

Conditions for the settlers at Jamestown, who were surrounded by Native Americans, were arduous. During their first winter in Virginia, many of the 108 colonists died from disease or Indian attack. A primitive wooden stockade built around the settlement did not halt the attacks. Smith himself was captured by the Indians that winter and held hostage for about a month before he was released.

For the next year, Smith tried to impose discipline on the dysfunctional colony. Many men in the group, the members of which had come to Virginia seeking riches, considered themselves English "gentlemen" and hadn't expected to labor in the New World; Smith put an end to their pretensions, famously declaring that "he who does not work, will not eat."

After Smith's departure, the colony nearly disbanded without his leadership. After a few more rocky years, and an infusion of more settlers from England, Jamestown recovered. But as more English settlers migrated to the region, other towns soon overtook Jamestown in importance, and the Virginia capital moved to Williamsburg in 1698. Jamestown virtually disappeared, and the site of the original stockade later became a farm before it was rescued by historical preservationists.

ADDITIONAL FACTS

1. *Smith had an unfortunate habit of being taken prisoner. Prior to coming to the Americas, he had been employed as a mercenary in Europe, where he was captured in Hungary and sold as a slave to the Turkish pasha before eventually escaping.*

2. *In a later expedition to North America in 1614, Smith explored the coastline of the region north of Virginia, which he dubbed* New England.

3. *Smith claimed that Pocahontas, the young teenage daughter of the powerful Powhatan chief, saved his life by stopping her father from executing him. Pocahontas married one of the Jamestown settlers, John Rolfe, in 1614 and visited England with him in 1616.*

★ ★ ★

Pequot War

Short and bloody, the Pequot War (1636–1638) was the first major clash between Native Americans and English settlers in the New World. The Pequot were one of the most powerful tribes in the region that is now Connecticut, but they were nearly annihilated in the war. In the wake of the conflict, Native Americans in New England were pushed onto smaller and smaller settlements as their land was taken by white settlers streaming to the New World from Europe.

The first permanent European settlements in Connecticut were founded by the Puritans in 1633. Tensions with the Pequots flared almost immediately. The immediate cause of the war was the massacre of an English ship's crew in 1636, which the Puritans blamed on Pequot warriors. The English launched retaliatory raids and quickly convinced many other Indian tribes in the area to join the war. With their native allies and superior weaponry, the English easily defeated the Pequots. By modern standards, the English war was nearly genocidal. The English soldiers regarded all Native Americans as heathens and a threat to peace in the New England wilderness, and the soldiers indiscriminately killed hundreds of Pequot women and children as well as warriors.

With most of the Pequot leadership wiped out, the Treaty of Hartford in 1638 put a halt to the brutal war. The English, determined to erase even the name of the Pequots, officially abolished the tribe, enslaving some members and distributing the rest as spoils to their Native American allies. Major conflict between Native Americans and the English would resurface, however, during King Philip's War in 1675.

ADDITIONAL FACTS

1. *The name* Connecticut *came from the Mohegan word* Quinnehtukqut, *meaning* long tidal river.

2. *The English outlawed the use of the word* Pequot *after the war, but it entered New England lore anyway and later served as the inspiration for the name of the ship* Pequod *in Herman Melville's masterpiece,* Moby-Dick.

3. *Descendants of the Pequots, confined to a tiny reservation in Connecticut, eventually opened the world's largest casino, Foxwoods, in 1993.*

★ ★ ★

Slavery

Beginning in 1619, when the first group of twenty Africans arrived at Jamestown in chains, thousands of slaves were imported into the British colonies of North America. Within a few generations, slave labor formed the basis of the South's agricultural economy and had spread north to the rest of the original thirteen colonies. By any standard, slavery was an unspeakable human tragedy that caused immeasurable harm to its victims.

Although slavery was part of the economy in both the North and the South, the institution eventually took on distinct guises in the two regions. To describe the differences, historians distinguish between a "slave society" and a "society with slaves." A "slave society" was one in which slavery dominated the major forms of economic production, which was the case in the South by the eighteenth century.

A "society with slaves," in contrast, refers to a society in which slaves did not dominate the economic modes of production and instead provided supplemental labor, such as work conducted within the home. In Massachusetts in the mid-1700s, for instance, only about one in eight households owned a slave, and the typical slaveholder had only two slaves. Rather than toil in the fields, Northern slaves often worked as maids, blacksmiths, coopers, carpenters, and house servants.

Because of the differing roles slavery played in the societies of the North and the South, the extent to which the two regions relied on slavery began to diverge in the eighteenth century. In the South, slavery became more important, while in the North, the institution began to fade. At the time of the American Constitutional Convention of 1787, many of the Founders assumed that slavery would eventually die out. Indeed, after the convention, various states in the North began the process of abolishing slavery, granting slaves their freedom in a given year or at a certain age, depending on the law their state established.

However, just as slavery was ending in the North, the invention of the cotton gin in 1793 guaranteed that the institution would remain integral to the Southern economy—laying the groundwork for widening regional differences in the nineteenth century.

ADDITIONAL FACTS

1. *The 1840 census listed one slave in New Hampshire.*

2. *Slavery was also common throughout Europe's other New World colonies. In the French colony of Haiti, Toussaint-Louverture (1743–1803) led a successful slave revolt in 1793.*

3. *The first twenty African slaves taken to Jamestown aboard a Dutch warship were from the modern-day nations of Congo and Angola.*

★ ★ ★

Tobacco

In 1492, sailors aboard Christopher Columbus's first expedition to the New World were puzzled by the sight of Native Americans in the Caribbean smoking rolled-up tobacco leaves. Several of the crew members took the odd custom back to Europe with them, where it caught on immediately. Within a generation, smoking was the rage in the Old World; the resulting demand for the tobacco leaf helped fuel the subsequent colonization of the Americas.

The importance in American history of the tobacco plant, *Nicotiana tabacum*, can hardly be exaggerated. Tobacco was the driving force behind many European ventures in the New World, the single biggest cash crop of the first English settlements in North America, and the backbone of the economy in Virginia, the largest of the thirteen colonies.

In Virginia, large-scale tobacco growing began almost immediately after the establishment of the Jamestown colony. Indeed, in 1620—the year the Pilgrims arrived at Plymouth—the Virginia colony was already exporting 119,000 pounds of tobacco back to England. In Virginia, thousands of English settlers established tobacco farms clustered in the Tidewater region near the present-day city of Norfolk. By the end of the seventeenth century, Europe was importing more than 25 million pounds of tobacco.

Many of the workers on tobacco farms were slaves. However, because of the way tobacco was farmed and cured, the crop was not typically associated with large-scale plantations. After the invention of the cotton gin in 1793, cotton surpassed tobacco as the biggest cash crop in the South. Although no longer the country's agricultural mainstay, tobacco remains a significant part of the American economy today, despite the major health risks associated with smoking.

ADDITIONAL FACTS

1. *A definitive link between smoking and cancer was not proven until the twentieth century, but the intuitive danger of inhaling smoke was grasped much earlier; King James I (1566–1625), the namesake of the Jamestown colony, hated smoking and published a notorious pamphlet attacking the "filthie noveltie."*

2. *Nicotine, the addictive element in tobacco, is so toxic it is also used as an insecticide.*

3. *Jamestown's first major tobacco farmer was John Rolfe (1585–1622), the husband of the legendary Native American princess Pocahontas (c. 1595–1617).*

★ ★ ★

Pueblo Civilization

Some of the oldest known structures in North America, the stone houses and ceremonial sites of the ancient Pueblo civilization were built around 850 AD in the parched canyons of the present-day southwestern United States. Archeologists believe that the cliffside complexes, each a stupendous feat of prehistoric engineering, were in use for about 400 years before they were abruptly abandoned. The ancient cliff dwellers who lived in them were the ancestors of modern-day Native American tribes including the Pueblo, Hopi, and Zuni.

The ancient Pueblo civilization existed for about 2,000 years in the Four Corners region where modern-day Arizona, New Mexico, Colorado, and Utah meet. Sometimes known as the Anasazi, the tribes began carving their famous sandstone structures into canyon walls during a period of explosive population growth beginning about 700 AD. Historians believe the buildings were used for housing, storage, and religious rites.

Set amid the arid mesas and canyons of the Southwest, the empty cliff dwellings dazzled the white settlers who first encountered them in the nineteenth century. Archeologists have spent decades debating whether drought, civil war, religious turmoil, or a combination of factors caused the Pueblo to abandon their elaborate complexes around 1250 AD. Whatever the cause, the ancient Puebloans eventually resettled near present-day Albuquerque and Santa Fe, New Mexico.

Today, thousands of abandoned Pueblo sites are scattered throughout the Four Corners region of the Southwest. The best known are found at Mesa Verde National Park in Colorado and Chaco Canyon in northwestern New Mexico.

ADDITIONAL FACTS

1. *The sandstone formations in the Pueblo region are believed to be about 250 million years old.*

2. Anasazi, *meaning* ancestral enemy *in Navajo, though not considered a politically correct term, remains in widespread use.*

3. *Archaeologists exploring ancient Pueblo sites have unearthed many discarded tools, including wooden flutes almost 1,500 years old.*

★ ★ ★

Anne Bradstreet

Anne Bradstreet (c. 1612–1672) authored the first book of poetry published in the British colonies of North America. The wife of a leading Puritan official, Simon Bradstreet, she arrived in Massachusetts in 1630, aboard the first ship carrying Puritans to the New World. Although she began writing early in life, Bradstreet's poetry was not published until 1650, when her book *The Tenth Muse Lately Sprung Up in America* appeared in print.

The subjects of Bradstreet's poems reflected the difficult lives of the early English settlers, as well as the distinct challenges faced by women in seventeenth-century America. Bradstreet wrote about common problems for the Puritans like sickness and house fires, in addition to more metaphysical poems about her own religious beliefs. The Bradstreets had eight children, and many of Anne's later poems addressed the travails of raising a family amid the difficult conditions of the New World.

Bradstreet's poems, influenced by such English poets as Philip Sidney (1554–1586) and Edmund Spenser (c. 1552–1599), show mastery of formal technique and wide-ranging erudition about subjects ranging from medicine to arcane Puritan theology. Many of her poems are also tender. One of her most well-known verses, "To My Dear and Loving Husband," which was not published until after her death, is a poignant love letter to her husband:

> If ever two were one, then surely we.
> If ever man were lov'd by wife, then thee.
> If ever wife was happy in a man,
> Compare with me, ye women, if you can.
> I prize thy love more than whole Mines of gold
> Or all the riches that the East doth hold.
> My love is such that Rivers cannot quench,
> Nor ought but love from thee give recompense.

Published women poets were a rarity in the seventeenth century, and Bradstreet's poems occasionally hint at some of her fellow Puritans' hostility toward her literary endeavors. For example, in one poem she wrote: "I am obnoxious to each carping tongue / Who says my hand a needle better fits." Many of Bradstreet's most well-known poems were not published until after her death, but she is now considered America's first English-language poet.

ADDITIONAL FACTS

1. Bradstreet's father, Thomas Dudley (1576–1653), also immigrated to Massachusetts and became a leading political opponent of John Winthrop (1588–1649). The two men alternated in the governorship for much of the first two decades of the colony's existence.

2. One of the original Boston Brahmin families, descendents of the Bradstreets include the poet Oliver Wendell Holmes (1809–1894).

3. Bradstreet's husband became governor of Massachusetts after her death.

★ ★ ★

John Singleton Copley

The leading painter of colonial-era America, John Singleton Copley (1738–1815) won acclaim for his big, detailed portraits of many of the most prominent citizens in his native Boston, including Revolutionary War leaders Samuel Adams (1722–1803) and Paul Revere (1734–1818). Although Copley himself left Boston in 1774, never to return, he continued painting in London and won election to Britain's prestigious Royal Academy of Art, a rare honor for an American-born painter.

Copley was born in Boston to a poor Irish immigrant family, and his father died when he was a young boy. At the time, the thirteen colonies lacked the great art schools of Europe, and Copley largely taught himself to paint.

Despite his lack of formal training, Copley's portraits showed remarkable technical sophistication. Borrowing from the European rococo style, Copley used light and shadow much more than other American painters of his day. Another distinctive feature of Copley's portraits is the objects he placed in the hands of his subjects to convey elements of their personalities. For instance, his portrait of Paul Revere, a silversmith, shows him holding a silver teapot.

In addition to the merchant class of Boston—bankers, artisans, and traders—Copley also painted portraits of two future US presidents, the Massachusetts-born John Adams (1735–1826) and his son, John Quincy Adams (1767–1848).

After moving to Europe, Copley toured Italy and France and began experimenting with paintings on historical themes. His single most famous painting, *Watson and the Shark*, shows a shark attacking a swimmer, based on an actual event that took place in Havana, Cuba, in 1749. However, his Boston portraits remained more popular than his later historical paintings. Although Copley never returned to the United States, he is remembered today as the most important artist of the colonial period and the first American painter to achieve a modicum of global renown.

ADDITIONAL FACTS

1. *A large plaza and a subway stop in Boston are named after Copley.*

2. *In art terminology, the telltale objects Copley that painted in the hands of his subjects are called* portraits d'apparat.

3. *The Museum of Fine Arts in Boston has the country's largest collection of Copley's paintings, including portraits of John Adams, John Quincy Adams, Paul Revere, Samuel Adams, and John Hancock.*

★ ★ ★

John Winthrop

John Winthrop (1588–1649) led the first group of Puritan settlers who founded the colony of Massachusetts in 1630. Winthrop and his followers, despite the poor farming conditions in the rocky New England soil and bloody clashes with Native Americans, established a successful colony that quickly grew in population as a "great migration" of Puritans fled persecution in England for a fresh start in the New World.

The Puritans, a splinter sect of the official Church of England, sought to "purify" the church and wanted to break from the ornate and ostentatious customs that the Anglican Church began to adopt in the mid-sixteenth century. Fleeing England, John Winthrop thought, provided the only alternative for Puritans to practice their religion.

Winthrop, a Cambridge-educated native of England's Suffolk County, landed in Salem, Massachusetts, aboard a ship called the *Arbella*. Before going ashore, Winthrop gave one of the most famous sermons in American history, urging his followers to remain true to their religious beliefs as they built a new community in the new continent and to always behave as if the entire world were watching their "city on a hill."

In the years that followed, Winthrop was repeatedly elected governor of Massachusetts by his fellow Puritans. His cherished "city on the hill," however, proved shortlived. As word of Winthrop's successful colony made it back to England, thousands more immigrants departed for Massachusetts's shores, many of whom were not Puritans. Within a century of Winthrop's death in 1649, Puritanism was no longer the dominant faith in New England, but the legacy of the Puritans' industriousness and high sense of moral purpose has echoed through the region's history.

ADDITIONAL FACTS

1. *Winthrop's son, also named John Winthrop (1606–1676), would later become one of the first governors of the neighboring colony of Connecticut.*

2. *Although Winthrop was a devoted Puritan, he was also a personal friend of Roger Williams (c. 1603–1683), the Puritan dissenter who founded neighboring Rhode Island after his banishment from Massachusetts—a banishment Winthrop supported.*

3. *Although Puritanism lost its hold on the New England mind, it did not vanish entirely. The faith of the first settlers evolved into modern-day Congregationalism, which remains relatively common in New England.*

★ ★ ★

King Philip's War

King Philip's War (1675–1676) was the last serious threat to the survival of English settlements in North America. Native American warriors led by Metacom, better known as King Philip, the chief of the Wampanoag tribe, scored a string of victories at the beginning of the war that seriously endangered the future of the New England colonies. However, the colonists eventually turned the tide on the Wampanoag, and the war ended with the near obliteration of the tribe.

The Wampanoag, who inhabited the forests of eastern Rhode Island and the Cape Cod area of Massachusetts, were the first indigenous people to greet the Pilgrims when they arrived on the *Mayflower* in 1620. For a few decades, the two communities lived side by side in relative harmony.

Two developments in the 1650s and 1660s caused tensions to heighten. Native American leaders were increasingly alarmed by the aggressive efforts of Christian missionaries to convert them, and the insatiable English appetite for more land was robbing them of their traditional tribal territories.

The event that triggered the war in 1675 was the hanging of several Wampanoag warriors who had been convicted of murder in an English courtroom. The men were executed because they allegedly killed a member of the Wampanoag tribe who had informed English settlers that the tribe was planning an attack. King Philip, enraged by the killing of his men, organized attacks on outlying English settlements across New England.

The Native Americans, however, lacked an overall strategy for defeating the colonists, and their hesitancy gave the settlers time to regroup. In the spring of 1676, English soldiers began to destroy Native American villages, sending Philip on the run. He was finally cornered and killed in August 1676, and his warriors were executed or sold into slavery.

The war left New Englanders badly shaken. The Native Americans had wiped out many frontier English settlements, and some Puritans interpreted the war as divine retribution for the sins of the settlers. Although it would take decades for New England to recover from King Philip's War, for the Native Americans it marked a disaster that ended their military power in New England.

ADDITIONAL FACTS

1. *After winning the war, the vindictive settlers beheaded King Philip and put his head on a pike in Plymouth, where it remained for decades as a decomposing warning to would-be enemies.*

2. *The war devastated Philip's Wampanoag tribe, which nearly disappeared but rebounded in the twentieth century and received federal recognition in 1987.*

3. *During the war, the city of Boston passed a law forbidding Indians from entering the city. Although the rule had not been enforced for centuries, it remained on the books until its repeal in 2005.*

★ ★ ★

Anne Hutchinson

One of the first prominent female religious leaders in American history, Anne Hutchinson (1591–1643) was expelled from the Massachusetts Bay Colony in 1638 after defying orders from Puritan authorities to stop holding religious meetings in her home. Although Hutchinson thought of herself as a devout Puritan, her refusal to bow to the wishes of the male-dominated Massachusetts clergy turned her into a feminist heroine and major figure in the history of American dissent.

Born in England, Hutchinson had arrived in Boston in 1634 with her wealthy husband, William, and their eleven children. Initially, the family was well liked, and they were accepted into the city's leading church. Hutchinson's skills as a nurse and midwife made her a valuable member of the young colony.

Within a few years, however, Hutchinson began holding meetings on Mondays to give Boston women an opportunity to discuss the previous day's sermons. She also offered her own religious opinions at the meetings, which were often highly critical of leading Puritan ministers. By assuming a role of religious leadership, Hutchinson threatened the authority of the Puritan church. The colony's governor, John Winthrop (1588–1649), warned her to stop holding the meetings, which he said were "not tolerable nor comely in the sight of God, nor fitting for your sex." When she refused, Hutchinson was excommunicated and forced to leave the colony.

The Hutchinsons first moved to neighboring Rhode Island, where they were greeted by Roger Williams (c. 1603–1683), the colony's founder. From Rhode Island, Hutchinson waged a long-distance war of words over various points of theological doctrine with the Boston religious authorities. Fearful that Massachusetts would invade Rhode Island, Hutchinson later moved to the Dutch colony of New Netherland (which later became the English colony of New York), where she was killed in an attack by Native Americans.

ADDITIONAL FACTS

1. *In an era when women frequently died during childbirth, Hutchinson had fifteen children.*

2. *One of Hutchinson's followers was Mary Dyer, who later converted to Quakerism and was hanged by the Puritans in 1660.*

3. *A monument to Hutchinson, praising her as a "Courageous Exponent of Civil Liberty and Religious Toleration," was erected in Boston in 1922.*

★ ★ ★

Joint-Stock Companies

By allowing large groups of investors to pool their resources, joint-stock companies—the forerunners of modern-day corporations—revolutionized the English business world in the seventeenth century and helped spur British settlement in North America. Many of the first English colonies in the New World, including Jamestown, were founded by profit-seeking ventures that hoped to export American tobacco back to English smokers.

Corporations first emerged in Europe during the late Middle Ages as a way of financing large-scale business ventures that were too big or risky for any one merchant. England was the first European country to embrace corporations on a large scale. In essence, a corporation is a legal structure that allows investors to combine their assets—"incorporate"—into a single legal body.

By the seventeenth century, English corporations already resembled their modern counterparts in some respects, with stockholders and an elected board of directors, but were much more difficult to create and usually required a charter from the monarch. For instance, the Virginia Company, which built the Jamestown settlement, was chartered by King James I (1566–1625) in 1606. Early British corporations were often granted exclusive rights to do business in a particular region of the British Empire, giving them enormous power.

Although taken for granted now, the corporation was one of the single most influential concepts in the history of finance. After the American Revolution, states relaxed their incorporation laws one by one, allowing groups of investors to form corporations without an individual charter from the legislature. By the late nineteenth century, the corporation in the United States had evolved into roughly its current form.

ADDITIONAL FACTS

1. *North Carolina was the first state to offer an incorporation law, in 1795.*

2. *The Plymouth Colony was founded by the same corporation as Jamestown was.*

3. *Officially, the settlers at Jamestown and Plymouth were employees of the Virginia Company.*

★ ★ ★

St. Augustine

The city of St. Augustine, Florida, is the oldest continuously occupied settlement established by Europeans in the United States. Founded by Spanish explorer Pedro Menéndez de Avilés (1519–1574) in 1565, the city changed hands several times before becoming American territory in 1821. St. Augustine, which today retains much of its Spanish architecture and colonial ambience, is home to some of the oldest structures in the United States as well as the oldest surviving military fortifications built by Europeans.

The first European to explore Florida was Juan Ponce de León (c. 1460–1521), who arrived in the area in 1513 and claimed the region for Spain, naming it *La Florida*, meaning "flowery." At the time, most European settlement was focused on the Caribbean and South America, and the Spanish paid little attention to Florida for the next fifty years. In the 1560s, French Huguenots (Protestants) fleeing religious persecution briefly established a settlement on the east coast of Florida, but it was destroyed by Menéndez de Avilés. The Spaniards were Roman Catholics.

Menéndez de Avilés, along with 800 settlers, founded the city on the feast day of Saint Augustine and named the colony in his honor. Founded forty years before Jamestown, St. Augustine was already a thriving trading outpost by the time the first English ships arrived in Virginia. As the British presence in North America grew, St. Augustine became a flashpoint for tensions between the two empires. The English privateer Sir Francis Drake (c. 1543–1596) burned and looted the city in 1586, and the British attempted to invade in 1740.

The British finally won control of the city at the end of the French and Indian War in 1763, but British rule was short-lived. During the American Revolution, Spain sided with the Americans and were given Florida back as part of the 1783 treaty ending the war. With the Spanish Empire in serious decline during the nineteenth century, the United States got Florida under the terms of the Adams-Onis Treaty ratified by the US Congress in 1821.

ADDITIONAL FACTS

1. *St. Augustine's Castillo San Marcos, the oldest fort in the United States, was in active military use through the Spanish-American War in 1898.*

2. *Like many European settlements in the New World, the isolated and almost completely womanless St. Augustine was a dreaded assignment for Spanish soldiers; some were deployed there as punishment for desertion.*

3. *The arrival of Europeans in Florida was devastating to the region's American Indian population; between 1614 and 1617, an overwhelming number from Florida's Timucua tribe died of disease.*

★ ★ ★

Phillis Wheatley

The first African-American author to publish a book, Phillis Wheatley (c. 1753–1784) was a literary sensation in colonial-era Boston for the volume of poetry she wrote in 1773 titled *Poems on Various Subjects, Religious and Moral.* Although raised as a slave, Wheatley learned to read and write and was freed by her owners following the book's publication. Wheatley's work astonished whites, many of whom refused to believe an African-American was capable of writing such elevated poetry. Wheatley never published again, however, and died in poverty ten years after the book's appearance.

Wheatley's verse, heavily influenced by the English poets Alexander Pope (1688–1744) and John Milton (1608–1674), often took the form of traditional heroic couplets. A heroic couplet, one of the oldest kinds of poetry in the English language, is composed of two rhyming lines. For instance, in a poem called "On the Death of a Young Lady of Five Years of Age," addressed to grieving parents who have just lost a young daughter named Nancy, Wheatley wrote:

> *From dark abodes to fair etherial light*
> *Th' enraptur'd innocent has wing'd her flight;*
> *On the kind bosom of eternal love*
> *She finds unknown beatitude above.*
> *This known, ye parents, nor her loss deplore,*
> *She feels the iron hand of pain no more.*

Many of Wheatley's poems revolve around religious themes and imagery that reflected her Christian faith. Only a few of her poems refer to Wheatley's own status as a slave, and even those references are usually oblique.

The reception to Wheatley's book reflected the backward beliefs about black people in eighteenth century America. Amid disbelief that a slave had written the poems, Wheatley was forced to appear before a group of leading citizens to prove she had written the poems. When her book was published, it included a preface signed by leading Boston citizens attesting to the fact that an "uncultivated Barbarian from Africa" had actually penned the verses. Wheatley is now considered one of the founders of African-American literature and a lasting influence on poets of all races.

ADDITIONAL FACTS

1. *One of the signers who attested to her authorship was John Hancock, later a leader of the American Revolution.*

2. *Her name was assigned to her by her owner, Boston merchant John Wheatley, who bought her in 1761.*

3. *She married once, to a freed black man named John Peters, but he abandoned her after his grocery business failed.*

★ ★ ★

Monticello

In 1769, the Virginia politician Thomas Jefferson (1743–1826) began construction of Monticello, a forty-three-room mansion on a stately, 1,000-acre plantation he had just inherited. The mansion, which Jefferson designed himself, would take nearly forty years to complete. Jefferson used stone quarried from his own land and expensive glass imported from Europe. By the time the house was finished, Monticello was one of the most distinctive and influential architectural landmarks in the United States.

 Indeed, in addition to his celebrated political accomplishments, Jefferson also emerged as one of the foremost architects of his day. His designs for Monticello and the University of Virginia in nearby Charlottesville are among the finest examples of classic American architecture of the eighteenth and early nineteenth centuries. Heavily influenced by Greek and Roman forms, Jefferson's designs embodied the hopes of the generation of Americans who dreamed of re-creating a modern Roman republic in the New World.

Jefferson inherited the property in 1757 and named it *Monticello,* meaning *little mountain* in Italian. In 1768, at age twenty-five, he began teaching himself architecture so he could design the house. In his studies, Jefferson was influenced by the sixteenth-century Italian architect Andrea Palladio (1508–1580), who gave his name to the Palladian architectural style of domes, porticos, and columns. (The White House was also designed in the Palladian style, though not by Jefferson.)

In addition to Monticello, Jefferson also designed the Rotunda at the University of Virginia, the centerpiece of the campus that bears many similarities to the Pantheon in Rome, a famous ancient temple. By popularizing classical design, Jefferson helped inspire the Federal style, which became the predominant American architectural form of the early nineteenth century. Federal buildings—replete with symmetrical columns and stately facades—expressed the optimistic, revolutionary spirit of the early years of the young Republic.

ADDITIONAL FACTS

1. *A portrait of Monticello was featured on the back of the nickel from 1938 until 2003 and then reinstated in 2006.*

2. *Jefferson grew thirty-one kinds of fruit in his orchards at Monticello, including figs, peaches, cherries, and grapes.*

3. *After Jefferson's death, the site was saved from destruction by Uriah Levy (1792–1862), a Jewish American naval officer who admired Jefferson's views on religious toleration.*

★ ★ ★

William Bradford

Thirteen years after John Smith and the Jamestown settlers arrived in Virginia, a group of 102 English settlers who became known as the Pilgrims landed in the New World in 1620 aboard the *Mayflower*. They established the Plymouth Colony along the New England coast of Cape Cod Bay at the site of present-day Plymouth, Massachusetts. Their leader was William Bradford (1590–1657), who governed the colony for most of the next thirty years and wrote the first definitive history of early English settlement in the area.

Bradford was born in the town of Austerfield, Yorkshire, England. As a young man, he joined the Separatists, an illegal Puritan group that broke away from the national Church of England. Bradford fled to Holland in 1608 with a small band of fellow religious dissidents. Holland provided a haven from persecution for fourteen years, but the congregants struggled economically. In 1620, the Pilgrims voyaged to North America, first arriving in Provincetown and then ultimately settling in Plymouth. Unlike the English settlers in Virginia, who were mostly interested in turning a profit in the lucrative tobacco trade, the first settlers in New England came to the New World primarily to practice their religion in peace.

The Pilgrims' first winter in New England was harrowing and nearly destroyed the colony. Half the population of settlers died. The next year, the desperate colonists made contact with the nearby Wampanoag tribe, whose members helped them survive on the new continent. Their harvest festival that autumn inspired the modern holiday of Thanksgiving. The Plymouth Colony generally maintained peaceful relations with local Native Americans and avoided involvement in the Pequot War (1636–1638).

The mythology surrounding the voyage of the *Mayflower* and the first Thanksgiving often inflates the historical importance of the Pilgrims. Unlike the Puritans guided by John Winthrop (1588–1649), who settled a few miles north of Plymouth in Boston in 1630, the Pilgrim colony never prospered and was eventually absorbed into the Massachusetts Bay Colony in 1691, seventy-one years after its founding. The final years of Bradford's diaries bemoan the declining fortunes of his colony.

Still, the Pilgrims and Bradford left their mark on American culture, and the story of their triumph over hardship in their first winter in Plymouth has resonated with many generations of immigrants arriving in the United States.

ADDITIONAL FACTS

1. *Bradford's wife, Dorothy, drowned in Provincetown Harbor just days before the Pilgrims reached Plymouth.*

2. *The menu at the famous first Thanksgiving, held in the fall of 1621 for fifty-one surviving Pilgrims and about ninety Wampanoags, included turkey, deer, and corn.*

3. *Bradford's famous history of early New England,* Of Plimouth Plantation, *was not published until 1856, nearly 200 years after his death, but it became one of the leading historical sources on early New England.*

* * *

French and Indian War

The French and Indian War (1754–1763) was the largest armed conflict in North America in the era before the American Revolution. The war, called the Seven Years' War in Europe and Canada, pitted Great Britain and its thirteen colonies against France and its Native American allies. Many Americans, including Major George Washington (1732–1799), fought for Britain during the war, gaining valuable military experience.

The British eventually won the war, but at a staggering financial cost. After the war ended, Britain's enormous war debt would force King George III (1738–1820) and Parliament to levy taxes on the colonies, a move that outraged the American colonists and helped fuel demands for independence.

The roots of the war stretched back to the early 1600s, when French fur traders began arriving in North America. Although prosperous, the Canada colony in the empire of New France—including the present-day Canadian province of Quebec— never rivaled the British colonies in population, partly because the Roman Catholic French king did not allow French Protestants to settle in the colony.

Still, the two empires fought several large, inconclusive colonial wars in the seventeenth and eighteenth centuries. Because their Canada colony was so small, the French frequently enlisted Native Americans as military allies.

The French and Indian War started in 1754 over a border dispute in western Pennsylvania, but the fighting quickly spread across North America and soon involved French and British armies and their allies across the globe. In the Americas, most of the battles took place in Canada, culminating in the surrender of Montreal to the British in 1760. At the end of the war in 1763, the British formally gained control of French colonies in North America under the terms of the Treaty of Paris.

The war ended the official French presence in Canada and strengthened the worldwide power of the British Empire. But it would have many unintended consequences. War had forced the British colonials to work together in response to the external threat. Instead of thirteen disparate colonies, many Americans began to think of themselves as a single, united country.

ADDITIONAL FACTS

1. *As a young British officer in the French and Indian War, Washington surrendered Fort Necessity to the French in 1754—the first and only time in his military career Washington would be forced to capitulate to the enemy.*

2. *Under the terms of the treaty, the French were allowed to retain only two tiny islands off the coast of Canada, Saint-Pierre and Miquelon.*

★ ★ ★

Roger Williams

The founder of Rhode Island, Roger Williams (c. 1603–1683) was an early champion of religious freedom who was banished from Massachusetts for his beliefs. In Rhode Island, Williams established a colony where religious dissenters, Quakers, Baptists, and Jews were permitted to practice their religion free from government interference, a rarity in the world of the seventeenth century.

A Puritan minister born in London, Williams fled to America in 1630 to avoid persecution by the official Church of England. However, he quickly discovered that his new home of Massachusetts was no more tolerant of dissent than England. Although a believing Puritan, Williams sympathized with dissidents and supported the separation of church and state, a heretical opinion that quickly got him banished from theocratic Massachusetts.

To avoid deportation to England, Williams fled south, and with land provided by the Narragansett Indians established the city of Providence on Narragansett Bay in 1636. Other religious exiles from Massachusetts, including Anne Hutchinson, quickly joined his colony, which was formally chartered with a secular government in 1644.

Rhode Island was the first English colony in the New World to allow freedom of conscience, a concept the Founding Fathers would later enshrine in the Bill of Rights. Whereas Quakers were hanged in Massachusetts, Williams welcomed them in Rhode Island. Although he stepped down from the colony's presidency in 1657, he remained active in its affairs for the rest of his life. His famous book *The Bloudy Tenet of Persecution* (1644) explains his beliefs about religious freedom.

When the future of Rhode Island was threatened by King Philip's War in 1675, Williams came out of retirement to lead the Providence militia in defending the city. After his death, he was buried in the city and is today celebrated as an early proponent of secular democracy and religious freedom.

ADDITIONAL FACTS

1. *Rhode Island is not actually an island. It got its name when an Italian explorer remarked that an island in Narragansett Bay looked like the Greek island of Rhodes. Williams himself gave the name* Rode Island, *which he said meant* Isle of Roses, *to what is now called Aquidneck Island, in Narragansett Bay.*

2. *To this day, the official name of Rhode Island is State of Rhode Island and Providence Plantations— ironically, the longest official name for the smallest of the fifty US states.*

3. *Williams published a sequel to his book in 1652 titled* The Bloudy Tenet Yet More Bloudy.

★ ★ ★

Mercantilism

In American history, the term *mercantilism* refers to the set of stifling economic rules imposed on the thirteen colonies by the British government before the Revolution. Mercantilist policy was designed to squeeze every penny of revenue out of the colonies to enrich the Crown and expand the British Empire. However, by taxing and restricting American trade, mercantilism contributed to the growing discontent of many middle-class American merchants in the decades preceding the Revolution.

The British Empire of the eighteenth century included not just the thirteen North American colonies but also parts of India, Africa, and the Caribbean. From the perspective of policymakers in London, one of the primary purposes of this colonial archipelago was to generate profit. Seeking to keep wealth within the empire, the British restricted imports. At the same time, other European powers pursued similar policies in their own empires.

For colonial Americans, British mercantilism had many negative everyday consequences, including higher prices for many consumer goods. For example, the price of tea in colonial America was artificially inflated due to taxes that protected British-controlled tea suppliers in India from foreign competition.

Two documents published in 1776 mounted a systemic challenge to British mercantilism. The first was the Declaration of Independence, which, among other things, denounced the Crown "for cutting off our Trade with all parts of the world." The second major document was *The Wealth of Nations*, by Adam Smith (1723–1790). Smith, a Scottish economist who is considered the intellectual founder of capitalism, attacked mercantilism as shortsighted and ultimately ineffective and called instead for "free trade" of goods across international borders.

In the nineteenth and twentieth centuries, the impact of *The Wealth of Nations* in Britain, the United States, and the rest of the world would be profound. Although in practice trade remains fettered by tariffs and taxes today, the explicitly mercantilist British system of the colonial era was dismantled by the Revolution and American independence.

ADDITIONAL FACTS

1. *Smith popularized the word* mercantilist *as a scornful term to criticize British economic policies of his day.*

2. *For his role in creating modern capitalism, Smith's portrait was put on the British £20 banknote in 2007.*

★ ★ ★

Colonial Boston

Founded by Puritan settlers in 1630, the city of Boston quickly became the political, intellectual, and economic capital of the British Empire's North American colonies. Perched on a narrow peninsula jutting into the Atlantic Ocean, Boston was the most influential urban center in colonial America and is sometimes called the Cradle of Liberty for the role its citizenry played in fomenting the American Revolution.

By modern standards, colonial Boston was never very large. As of 1700, seventy years after its founding, the city's population was only about 7,000; it was still under 20,000 at the time of the Revolution. However, as the capital of Massachusetts, Boston was home to many of the most important institutions of colonial America, including Harvard University and most of the biggest banks in the colonies. Additionally, Boston's excellent port enabled the city to grow into a major center for fishing, shipbuilding, and Atlantic commerce during the eighteenth century.

The rise of Boston, however, led to tension with the city's old guard of Puritan clergymen. To the Puritans, Boston was the anchor of a religious community, a "city on a hill" whose religious unity should be enforced by any means necessary. As late as 1692, supposed witches were hanged in Massachusetts. Puritan ministers of the early eighteenth century like Cotton Mather (1663–1728) fought unsuccessfully to preserve the city's vanishing Puritan character.

The new class of merchants that replaced the Puritans would play a crucial role in agitating against British rule in the 1760s. Two Bostonians, John Hancock (1737–1793) and Samuel Adams (1722–1803), were the leaders of the patriot cause and masterminds of the Boston Tea Party in 1773. By the end of the Revolution, Boston remained a major commercial center but had ceded its place as the nation's largest city to New York.

ADDITIONAL FACTS

1. *Boston was named after a town in Lancashire, England, where many Puritan ministers were born.*

2. *After the American Revolution, the old guard of Protestant Bostonians were sometimes referred to—ironically, in light of later baseball revalries—as* Yankees.

3. *Boston was originally referred to as* Shawmut, *the American Indian name for the peninsula on which it was built.*

★ ★ ★

Noah Webster

Before Noah Webster (1758–1843) published his famous dictionary in 1828, American spelling and grammar were notoriously chaotic. Even a refined American of the eighteenth century like Abigail Adams usually spelled words however she wished, with little regard for consistency. For example, in one 1774 letter hectoring her husband for not writing more often, Adams wrote, "I judg you reachd Phylidelphia last Saturday night . . ."

Webster, a Connecticut-born teacher and a stickler for rules, was horrified by the anarchic writing habits of his compatriots. A milestone in the maturation of American English, his dictionary and grammar for the first time imposed some discipline on the language by standardizing spelling, grammar, and capitalization.

A veteran of the American Revolution, Webster had graduated from Yale in 1778 and finished his first book, *A Grammatical Institute of the English Language*, in 1783. The book, like all of Webster's works, had an explicitly nationalistic purpose. Deeply patriotic, Webster believed the new nation needed a truly American language, free from the influence of British aristocrats. It was Webster who pruned the *u* from *colour* and changed the British spelling of *theatre* to the American (and therefore correct) spelling *theater*.

In 1806, Webster published his first dictionary, *A Compendious Dictionary of the English Language*, but it was merely a prelude to his masterpiece, the two-volume *American Dictionary of the English Language* published twenty-two years later. For the dictionary—which contained 70,000 entries, including never-before-seen words like *chowder* and *squash*—Webster learned 26 languages and modernized the spelling of hundreds of words.

Twenty years of labor on the dictionary nearly bankrupted Webster, and the volume was a commercial disappointment in his lifetime. However, over the years his dictionary became recognized as the most authoritative manual of American English and has been in print in revised form ever since.

ADDITIONAL FACTS

1. *Not all of Webster's changes caught on; for instance, he proposed to change the spelling of tongue to tung.*

2. *Webster was a fervent Federalist and edited two party newspapers in New York City, the* American Minerva *and the* Herald.

3. *Webster also had a brief political career, representing New Haven in the Connecticut state legislature for five years beginning in 1800.*

★ ★ ★

"The Star-Spangled Banner"

"The Star-Spangled Banner," the national anthem of the United States, was written in 1814 by Maryland lawyer Francis Scott Key. Set to the melody of an English drinking song, the patriotic tune was an instant hit, and Congress officially decreed it the national anthem in 1931.

Key, a prominent attorney and amateur poet, wrote the anthem's lyrics under peculiar circumstances. During the War of 1812 (which actually lasted into December 1814), the British attacked Washington, DC, sacking the city and burning down the White House. Next they targeted Baltimore, about forty miles north of the capital, and its imposing fortress, Fort McHenry, which guarded the city's harbor.

Before the beginning of that battle in September 1814, Key had been selected to meet the British commander aboard his warship in Baltimore harbor to discuss the release of a prisoner of war. The British agreed to release the prisoner but insisted that Key remain at sea aboard a neutral ship behind the British fleet until after the battle to prevent him from sharing information with the Americans about British preparations.

Forced to watch the fighting from eight miles out at sea, the lyrics to "The Star-Spangled Banner" describe Key's impressions of the battle as it unfolded. The British bombardment—"the rockets' red glare, the bombs bursting in air"—would last for twenty-five hours before the invaders gave up. As the smoke cleared, Key excitedly peered through the haze over Fort McHenry to see the red, white, and blue flag still fluttering in the morning breeze—a sign of American victory.

The British, unsuccessful in their attack on the fort, allowed Key to return to shore that day, and his poem was immediately published in local newspapers. It was reprinted nationally and for the next century would be played at many patriotic events. Major League Baseball made it the de facto national anthem by selecting the song to be played before baseball games, and Congress later made the selection official.

ADDITIONAL FACTS

1. *Author F. Scott Fitzgerald (1896–1940) was a distant relative of Francis Scott Key.*

2. *The lyrics to the original song, "To Anacreon in Heaven," begin "To Anacreon in Heav'n / Where he sat in full glee."*

3. *Fort McHenry's original flag, sewed by Baltimore seamstress Mary Pickersgill, is in the custody of the Smithsonian Institution in Washington, DC.*

★ ★ ★

Mayflower Compact

Days before the Pilgrims landed in Plymouth in 1620, they gathered on the deck of the *Mayflower* to draft the Mayflower Compact, a rudimentary statement of the rules they would follow in the New World, which ultimately became an early landmark in the development of American participatory democracy.

William Bradford (1590–1657), the founder and chronicler of the Plymouth Colony, said the compact was deemed necessary because some of the passengers on the *Mayflower* were suspected of making plans to "use their own liberty" once they reached land by abandoning their shipmates, posing a threat to the unity of the tiny group.

In the short document, the forty-one signers pledged to remain loyal to King James I of England—and, more importantly, to one another. They would not go their own way in the New World but would instead "covenant and combine ourselves together into a civil body politic," the document read, forming a community of shared obligations in the Plymouth Colony.

The Mayflower Compact was not a constitution, since it did not establish a form of government. Rather, it was a statement of shared vision and a blueprint for the sort of colony the Pilgrims wished to build. Like the Puritans, the Pilgrims came to the New World not to make money but to build a particular sort of disciplined religious community.

The communitarian vision expressed in the compact, as Bradford noted in his *Of Plimouth Plantation*, often clashed with the individualistic impulses of some of the settlers. How to strike the right balance between individual desires and the obligations to the larger community has proved an agonizing debate for Americans ever since.

ADDITIONAL FACTS

1. *The Pilgrims had originally intended to settle in Virginia, but they stayed in Massachusetts after getting lost during their difficult trip across the Atlantic.*

2. *According to legend, the Pilgrims first landed at a large boulder along the coast called Plymouth Rock, although their records made no mention of the celebrated landmark.*

3. *The first actual constitution in the English colonies was signed in Connecticut in 1639, thereby earning the region the nickname of the Constitution State.*

★ ★ ★

Boston Massacre

British soldiers shot and killed five Americans who had pelted them with rocks and snowballs on March 5, 1770, in an infamous event dubbed the Boston Massacre. The shooting of unarmed civilians enraged Bostonians and helped turn public opinion in the city against the mother country. For the next five years, until the start of the American Revolutionary War, Boston would be at the forefront of American opposition to British rule.

The British government had sent soldiers to Boston in 1768 to enforce the Townshend Act, a series of taxes on tea, paint, paper, and other goods that it had imposed on the colonies the previous year. Many Bostonians resented the presence of the troops, and crowds regularly harassed British soldiers.

On the night of the massacre, a mob of about sixty protestors accosted a squad of troops near the Boston customs office. Jeering and chanting slogans against the British, they began throwing ice and snowballs at the men and daring them to fire. Unfortunately, one of the soldiers did. In the melee that followed, three of the protestors were killed. Two more later died of their wounds.

Patriot leaders in Boston, in particular Samuel Adams (1722–1803), immediately branded the event a "massacre" and seized on the shootings to inflame public opinion against the British. The British soldiers were arrested and tried for murder. At their trial, however, evidence presented to the jury made it clear that they had been provoked, and none of the soldiers were imprisoned.

Despite the verdicts at trial, the Boston Massacre became a potent rallying cry for the patriot cause. A famous etching of the event made by silversmith Paul Revere (1734–1818), whose workshop was only a few blocks from the site of the shootings, circulated throughout the thirteen colonies and made the colonists increasingly disillusioned with British rule.

ADDITIONAL FACTS

1. *John Adams (1735–1826), the future signer of the Declaration of Independence and second president of the United States, was the defense attorney for the commander of the British troops.*

2. *In the months before the Boston Massacre, Bostonians often taunted the British troops patrolling their city by calling them "lobster-backs," a reference to the floggings the British army inflicted on its soldiers for discipline.*

3. *British officers tried to force American homeowners in Boston to provide housing for their troops, a move that angered landowners. After the Revolution, sour memories of the British occupation inspired the Third Amendment in the Bill of Rights, which made it illegal for the new government to force citizens to "quarter" soldiers.*

* * *

Mary Dyer

On June 1, 1660, a Quaker woman named Mary Dyer was hanged by the Puritans at the gallows on Boston Common for her religious beliefs. She offended the Puritans by preaching in the streets of Boston and loudly defending her Quaker faith. Dyer's execution was part of a spree of hangings in Massachusetts around 1660, marking one of the worst outbreaks of religious persecution in early American history.

The Quakers were members of a small Christian sect called the Religious Society of Friends that was founded by George Fox (1624–1691) of England in about 1647. Fox traveled widely, and Quakerism spread quickly. Dyer, who had immigrated to Massachusetts in 1635, converted during a return visit to England. Quakerism stresses personal faith in the "Inner Light" of Christ rather than formal creeds and sacraments. The Puritan authorities considered Quakers heretics and ordered them banished from Massachusetts. Dyer refused to obey the edict, proclaiming her faith publicly in Boston.

From the standpoint of the Puritans, the Quakers posed a dire threat to Massachusetts. The whole purpose of the colonial experiment in the New World, from their point of view, was to build a religiously unified community of Puritan believers. Allowing religious dissenters like Dyer to challenge the church's teachings, they felt, would destroy the soul of Massachusetts.

In total, four Quakers were executed by the Puritans for defying orders to leave the colony. Most other British colonies in North America, including neighboring Rhode Island, accepted Quaker immigrants. Pennsylvania was founded specifically as an enclave for members of the faith. The Massachusetts theocracy that had condemned Dyer ended in 1686 when King James II (1633–1701) terminated the colony's Puritan charter, placing the province under direct rule by London.

ADDITIONAL FACTS

1. *Dyer had been imprisoned before, in 1659, but was given a reprieve after her husband begged the governor for her life.*

2. *Dyer's last words on the gallows were "I am not now to repent."*

3. *A statue of Dyer was erected in front of the Massachusetts State House near Boston Common.*

★ ★ ★

Cotton Gin

In 1793, the year Eli Whitney (1765–1825) invented the cotton gin, farmers in the United States produced about 10,000 bales of cotton—a relatively modest harvest. For planters, cotton growing was often a laborious and unprofitable business due to the high cost of handpicking the seeds out of the plant fiber, which was then made into fabric. In the late eighteenth century, tobacco remained the most popular crop in much of the agricultural heartland in the South.

However, Whitney's invention changed the economics of cotton almost overnight. The hand-cranked machine, which Whitney patented in 1794, made it possible to remove the seeds from the fiber much more easily. With his invention, the New England native removed the single greatest impediment to the commercial success of the cotton crop.

The cotton gin had an immediate impact on the American economy. Only eight years after the gin's invention, the quantity of cotton farmed in the United States had risen tenfold, to 100,000 bales; in 1835, it topped 1 million bales. (To put the number in perspective, that's enough cotton for 2.1 billion pairs of boxer shorts.) The United States became one of the world's leading cotton exporters, and "King Cotton" became the leading big business of pre–Civil War America.

The cotton gin's social impact, however, was tragic. Many historians believe that the invention of the cotton gin had the unintended consequence of prolonging the institution of slavery in the southern United States. Prior to 1793, many Americans expected the "peculiar institution" to wither away and eventually disappear in the South, as it had in the North; the explosion of cotton farming, and the sudden demand for unskilled labor to plant and harvest the cotton it created, shattered this hope and exacerbated the differences between the North and the South.

ADDITIONAL FACTS

1. Gin *is short for engine; the alcoholic beverage of the same name comes from an unrelated Dutch word.*

2. *After inventing the cotton gin, Whitney went into business selling arms to the US government.*

3. *Despite the enormous popularity of the cotton gin, Whitney felt he was swindled out of his fair share of the profits, and he left the South for good in 1804.*

★ ★ ★

Harvard

In 1636, a group of Puritan ministers founded Harvard, the first institution of higher learning in the New World. Opened in 1638 and named for John Harvard (1607–1638), an English benefactor who donated money and more than 400 books for Harvard's first library, the institution had as its primary purpose the training of new clergymen for the pulpits of New England. Located in Cambridge, Massachusetts—at the time of its founding a distant Boston suburb called Newtowne—the old Puritan academy has grown into one of the world's richest and most prestigious universities.

In its historical context, the decision to build a university in the New World reflected the spiritual priorities of the Puritan immigrants. Unlike the Jamestown farmers in Virginia—or, for that matter, Spanish settlers farther south—the Puritans wanted to build their version of a religious utopia in the New World. To produce the next generation of Puritans, Harvard's founders modeled the university on Cambridge University in England, where many of them had studied.

Religious instruction remained the most important part of a Harvard education well into the eighteenth century. Many leading Puritan theologians and Massachusetts politicians, including Increase Mather (1639–1723), his son Cotton Mather (1663–1728), and the chief judge at the Salem witch trials, were all educated at Harvard. Still, by the early 1700s many ministers were upset with what they perceived as Harvard's liberal drift, and they created a more conservative rival, Yale, in 1701. Harvard began to broaden its curriculum in the 1870s. Under an agreement with nearby Radcliffe College for women, Harvard allowed women into its classrooms for the first time in 1943. Radcliffe merged with Harvard in 1999.

The Harvard campus along the Charles River now forms the nucleus for the country's largest concentration of colleges and universities. More than forty universities operate in the greater Boston area, making it the center of American higher education.

ADDITIONAL FACTS

1. *The country's second-oldest university, the College of William and Mary, was founded in 1693 and named after the king and queen of England at that time.*

2. *All but one of the books bequeathed by John Harvard to the university's library were lost in a subsequent fire.*

3. *Cambridge University was a stronghold of Puritanism in the early seventeenth century and had educated several Massachusetts luminaries, including John Winthrop (1588–1649) and John Harvard himself.*

★ ★ ★

Washington Irving

Diplomat, essayist, and short story writer Washington Irving (1783–1859) was one of the first Americans to earn international literary acclaim. Writing in the early nineteenth century, Irving served as an inspiration and mentor to many early American writers and is considered one of the founders of the American literary tradition. Several of his most famous short stories, including "The Legend of Sleepy Hollow" and "Rip Van Winkle," are still read and taught today.

Irving was born in New York City shortly after the Revolutionary War and named after George Washington. He was trained in law and employed as an American diplomat in Europe for much of his life. Irving spoke Spanish fluently, and in addition to his fiction, he wrote well-received books about Christopher Columbus and fifteenth-century Spanish history.

The author's most well-known short stories were first published in 1819. "The Legend of Sleepy Hollow" tells the tale of the gloomy schoolteacher Ichabod Crane, who is chased by a headless horseman in the New York village of Tarrytown. In "Rip Van Winkle," a "a simple, good-natured man" in the Catskill Mountains of New York falls into a twenty-year coma after drinking a mysterious liquor and is shocked by how much American society has changed when he finally awakes.

Irving continued to publish fiction between his diplomatic stints, and he wrote several well-received Western adventure novels in the 1830s. He also wrote a lengthy biography of his namesake, *Life of George Washington.*

In the history of American literature, Irving is notable as one of the earliest writers to be able to earn a living from his writing. Irving, along with James Fenimore Cooper (1789–1851), proved that American writers could compete with Europeans and laid the groundwork for nineteenth-century American literature.

ADDITIONAL FACTS

1. *Appropriately, Irving is buried in the Sleepy Hollow Cemetery in Sleepy Hollow, New York.*

2. *Tim Burton directed a movie version of "The Legend of Sleepy Hollow," titled* Sleepy Hollow, *in 1999.*

3. *Irving coined many words associated with New York City, including* Knickerbocker, *now the name of the city's NBA team.*

★ ★ ★

John J. Audubon

Painter John James Audubon (1785–1851) loved birds. His enthusiasm for winged creatures was so great that he once had to beg his long-suffering wife, Lucy, "not to be troubled with curious ideas such as my liking birds better than thee."

Lucy, however, may have been on to something. For Audubon, birds were a lifelong passion bordering on obsession. Born in Haiti, Audubon moved to France as a child but fled to the United States in 1803 to avoid being drafted into Napoleon's army. He married Lucy in 1808. In the United States, he started a number of failed businesses in Kentucky and Pennsylvania, all the while drawing his famous watercolors of the continent's birds on the side.

Audubon pursued his hobby with meticulous zeal. Over several decades he trapped and killed thousands of birds, then posed their bodies in simulated natural settings for his life-size paintings. However, no American publishers were interested in Audubon's painstaking drawings.

Finally, Audubon found a publisher in England for his seminal work, *Birds of America,* which was released in 87 parts from 1827 to 1836. The book, containing 435 engravings made from his original watercolors, was unlike anything seen before— or since. A dazzling feat of artistic accomplishment, each page of *Birds of America* was nearly two feet by three feet in size, because Audubon insisted on accurate, life-size pictures of the birds.

In England, Audubon's exotic watercolors were a huge sensation among those wealthy enough to afford them. In the years afterward, he composed several more successful volumes of wildlife drawings. Although Audubon was not a painter in the conventional sense, his art remains hugely popular and influential among both artists and scientists. After his death, the Audubon Society was formed to encourage the study of birds and safeguard the artist's legacy.

As for Audubon himself, his ornithological passion lasted for the rest of his life. His last word, reportedly, was "ducks."

ADDITIONAL FACTS

1. *Audubon's original watercolors are on permanent display at the New York Historical Society.*

2. *The original volume of* Birds of America *cost about $1,000 and was delivered in batches of five pages at a time. Only about 200 were made, and first editions now sell for $2 million and up.*

3. *Subscribers to Audubon's first edition included the queen of England and the American statesmen Daniel Webster (1782–1852) and Henry Clay (1777–1852).*

★ ★ ★

Thomas Paine

Born to a poor family in England, journalist Thomas Paine (1737–1809) moved to Philadelphia in 1774 and almost immediately became a supporter of the revolutionary cause. He wrote several enormously influential pamphlets urging colonists to join the Revolution. Paine's direct, incendiary writing style was so effective that George Washington (1732–1799) ordered some of Paine's articles read to his troops before battle.

Paine's most famous pamphlet, *Common Sense*, published anonymously in early 1776, called on Americans to recognize the absurdity that a hereditary king of a faraway island would govern the thirteen colonies. "There is something exceedingly ridiculous in the composition of monarchy," Paine wrote. Paine's inflammatory prose contrasts with the measured, legalistic rhetoric of his comrade Thomas Jefferson (1743–1826). While Jefferson aimed at the minds of the colonists, Paine's propaganda appealed to their hearts in simple, clear language that everyone could understand.

Paine's popularity after the Revolution, however, was short-lived. Paine was an ardent idealist and a believer in worldwide revolution against monarchs. He traveled to France to support the French Revolution in 1789, putting him at odds with a significant number of his former allies in the United States. Paine also published attacks on organized Christian religion, another unpopular stance.

In France, Paine became a member of one of the revolutionary assemblies that ruled the country after deposing King Louis XVI (1754–1793). After Louis was captured, Paine argued against beheading him. His quixotic opposition to the death penalty again alienated him from his erstwhile allies. Shortly afterward, Paine was himself condemned to the guillotine. While in prison, he began one of his most famous works, *The Age of Reason*, which summed up his philosophy of universal human rights. Paine was finally released after the American ambassador, future US president James Monroe (1758–1831), pressed the French authorities for his release.

Returning to New York in 1802, Paine lived the remainder of his life in poverty, reviled by his compatriots for his anti-Christian views.

ADDITIONAL FACTS

1. *Paine's famous pamphlet* Common Sense *cost two shillings and sold about 120,000 copies within three months, at a time when the entire population of the thirteen colonies was just over 2 million.*

2. *After the war, the grateful New York legislature awarded Paine a farm in New Rochelle that had been confiscated from a Loyalist.*

3. *Paine was one of the few Revolutionary War participants officially convicted of treason in Britain, a verdict passed in December 1792 after he wrote a pamphlet urging the English to overthrow King George III (1738–1820).*

★ ★ ★

Boston Tea Party

In the aftermath of the Boston Massacre in 1770, the city of Boston teetered on the brink of outright rebellion. The city's wharves and cobblestone streets seethed with anti-British resentment. Opponents of British rule, including many of the city's richest and most prominent citizens, organized a shadowy patriot group called the Sons of Liberty that met regularly in the city's taverns and established contacts with other disgruntled Americans across the thirteen colonies.

After the Boston Massacre, Parliament cut some of the controversial taxes on the colonies—but not the duty on tea. Outraged, the patriots launched a successful boycott that resulted in huge losses for the British East India Company, the major exporter of tea to the colonies.

In 1773, in response to the boycott, the British passed the Tea Act. The Tea Act gave the East India Company, which had long-standing ties to the British government, special permission to bring tea directly to the colonies without paying taxes, thus undercutting local merchants. The Tea Act provoked instant outrage across the thirteen colonies. So great was the opposition that when ships carrying the tea arrived at the port of Boston, no buyer was willing to unload them.

For several weeks, the tea sat unsold on three ships in Boston Harbor until the chilly night of December 16, 1773, when members of the Sons of Liberty disguised as Mohawk Indians boarded the ships and dumped 342 crates of tea into the Atlantic Ocean, one of the most famous acts of civil disobedience in American history.

When news of the Boston Tea Party reached London, King George III (1738–1820) was furious. Parliament retaliated by closing Boston's port until the cost of the tea was repaid and dispatching more redcoats to the unruly city. For the next year, until the outbreak of the Revolutionary War, the city was a virtual armed camp—a tinderbox waiting for the spark that would soon come in the spring of 1775 at Lexington and Concord.

ADDITIONAL FACTS

1. *Ships carrying East India tea also arrived in Philadelphia and New York in 1773, but both captains returned their cargo to England rather than risking the wrath of local patriot mobs.*

2. *The British East India Company, one of the largest corporations in England, traded dozens of goods in addition to tea, including opium.*

3. *The American tea boycott was so successful that in 1773, the East India Company recorded 17 million pounds of unpurchased tea piling up in its warehouses in England.*

★ ★ ★

William Penn

William Penn (1644–1718), a convert to Quakerism whose father was a prominent English admiral, established the colony of Pennsylvania in 1681 as a sanctuary for persecuted Quakers. As governor of the colony, Penn guaranteed religious freedom and adopted a far more enlightened stance toward Native Americans than other English colonists, forbidding Pennsylvanians from taking native lands.

Born in London and raised as an Anglican, Penn attended Oxford, where he was first exposed to Quaker preachers. He converted in 1667, at age twenty-three. At the time, Quakers were routinely imprisoned in England for their beliefs and had also been subject to harassment and even execution in other North American colonies.

However, Penn had one advantage that other Quakers didn't: the king, Charles II (1630–1685), owed Penn's prominent father £16,000. After his father's death, Penn convinced the king to trade him a huge tract of land in North America in partial repayment of the debt. About 1,300 Quakers were released from prison in England at Penn's request and immigrated to the new colony.

Despite Penn's idealistic impulses, the colony he founded was no democracy. Not only did Penn name the land after his own father, but as the royally appointed proprietor of the colony he wielded enormous power over his fellow settlers, even designing the street grid for the city of Philadelphia.

Penn eventually suffered financial problems and spent the last years of his life in England fending off his creditors. Still, his ideals of individual liberty and toleration would serve as an inspiration to the authors of the American Revolution.

ADDITIONAL FACTS

1. *Penn's family remained a powerful force in Pennsylvania for decades after his death, appointing top officials in the colony. One of Penn's grandsons, John Penn (1725–1795), was lieutenant governor of Pennsylvania at the outbreak of the Revolution.*

2. *Penn also controlled Delaware, which had originally been settled by Dutch and Swedish explorers before the English seized the area in 1664.*

3. *Before his death, Penn was briefly imprisoned for failure to pay his debts.*

★ ★ ★

Slater's Mill

In 1793, the same year that Eli Whitney invented the cotton gin, Samuel Slater (1768–1835) opened his first mill in Pawtucket, Rhode Island. The mill, perched next to the raging Blackstone River, was a milestone in the history of American industry. Inside its brick walls, the mill was capable of turning large amounts of cotton into spools of cloth by harnessing the power of the nearby river. Slater's mill—which would remain operational until the twentieth century—was the prototype for thousands of factories constructed over the next century during a period of American history known as the Industrial Revolution.

Slater was born in England and was apprenticed to a mill owner at age fourteen. He moved to the United States in 1789 after memorizing the blueprint of the mill, hoping to get rich in the fledgling American textile industry. Slater selected a rural spot along the rocky Blackstone River, with its numerous falls and gushing rapids, as the ideal setting for his factory.

In addition to the factory, Slater built a village called Slatersville, which included a town green, a church, housing for workers, and a company store. His so-called Rhode Island System would become a model for industrialists across New England, where much of the early Industrial Revolution unfolded.

The combination of the cotton gin and Slater's mill provided an enormous boost to the textile industry. For the first time, Americans had the capability of turning cotton into finished cloth on a large-scale basis. The textile industry grew rapidly in the early nineteenth century and became a pillar of the economy in the northern United States. Although many of the stately redbrick New England mills closed in the twentieth century, many remain standing across the region as monuments to the first wave of American industrialization.

ADDITIONAL FACTS

1. *Slater has often been referred to as the Father of the American Industrial Revolution.*

2. *Slater employed children as young as seven years old at his mill, for wages of less than $1 a week, an exploitative labor practice that was not outlawed until the twentieth century.*

3. *The Blackstone River, site of the earliest American industries, drops 430 feet over 50 miles in Massachusetts and Rhode Island, a feature that made it attractive to nineteenth-century factories that depended on hydropower.*

★ ★ ★

Colonial New York City

New York, the largest city in the United States and the nation's economic and financial capital, was founded in 1625 by Dutch settlers on the southern tip of Manhattan Island. Originally called New Amsterdam, the city was renamed in honor of the Duke of York when England seized the Dutch colony in 1664. By the time of the American Revolution, New York had surpassed Boston as the nation's largest city, a distinction it has retained ever since.

A combination of geographic and historical factors accounted for New York's rapid growth in the colonial era. The Dutch built the city at the mouth of the Hudson River, which became one of the most important waterways in colonial America. After the British took control of New York, its central location between the British colonies in New England and Virginia made the city a natural trading center. In addition, the lingering Dutch influence gave New York a cosmopolitan atmosphere that would prove attractive to generations of new immigrants.

Boston, however, remained the financial center of the colonies until the Revolution. During the war, New York was occupied by the British despite a strong patriot faction in the city. General George Washington (1732–1799), wary of Manhattan's defenses, made a strategic decision not to try to retake the city, and New York was one of the last parts of the United States liberated from the British in 1783.

As the most populous city in the new nation, New York briefly served as the first national capital. Washington, the first president, took his oath of office in 1789 on a balcony overlooking Wall Street. The selection of Washington, DC, as the new capital in 1790 did little to stop New York's growth. By the early nineteenth century, the opening of the New York Stock Exchange and the construction of the Erie Canal had transformed the Dutch trading post into the nation's unchallenged economic powerhouse.

ADDITIONAL FACTS

1. The Hudson River was named for Henry Hudson, an English sailor who explored the region on behalf of the Netherlands in 1609.

2. The Dutch briefly retook New York in 1673 and renamed it New Orange in honor of the Dutch royal family's color.

3. New York City included only the borough of Manhattan until the five boroughs of Manhattan, Brooklyn, the Bronx, Queens, and Staten Island were unified in an 1898 reorganization.

★ ★ ★

James Fenimore Cooper

Virtually no literary tradition existed in the United States before the 1820s, when Washington Irving (1783–1859) and James Fenimore Cooper (1789–1851) first began publishing fiction with American settings and characters. During the course of his career, Cooper wrote dozens of adventure novels set on the American frontier and at sea, including his most famous work, *The Last of the Mohicans*, published in 1826.

Cooper, born to a prosperous New Jersey family, had started writing fiction at age thirty to raise money when his farm fell on hard times. His first novel, *Precaution*, was published in 1820, the year after Irving's seminal first collection of American stories. *Precaution* was a failure, but Cooper's next book, *The Spy* (1821), an espionage novel set during the American Revolution, was a success.

Through the course of the 1820s, Cooper authored a series of popular frontier novels called the Leatherstocking Tales, starring the buckskin-clad trapper Natty Bumppo and his American Indian sidekick, Chingachgook. The most famous of these tales, *The Last of the Mohicans*, followed Bumppo's adventures fighting the Huron Indians in the area around Lake Champlain.

In the 1830s, Cooper began to alienate critics and some of his readers by injecting more pointed social commentary into his writing. He wrote a book defending himself, *A Letter to His Countrymen*, in 1834. His critical reputation, however, never recovered, and Mark Twain (1835–1910) memorably skewered Cooper's overwrought writing style in an 1895 essay titled "Fenimore Cooper's Literary Offenses." To modern readers, Cooper's novels seem extremely slow-paced and turgid for adventure stories. Apart from *The Last of the Mohicans*, they are rarely read.

Still, Cooper's influence on the development of American literature has been lasting and pervasive. Many American literary traditions—the Western, the sea romance, the author who moves to Europe to get a better perspective on his own country—can be traced back to Cooper's pioneering career.

ADDITIONAL FACTS

1. *Although born in New Jersey, Cooper lived most of his life in Cooperstown, New York, a town named after his family.*

2. *Cooper went to Yale but was expelled. He then served briefly in the US Navy before moving to New York to farm.*

3. *Uncas, one of the characters in* The Last of the Mohicans, *was based on an actual historical figure. The real Uncas, however, was a member of the Mohegans, not the Mohicans.*

★ ★ ★

Hudson River School

In the early nineteenth century, a handful of painters began drawing big, dramatic landscape portraits of the rugged American outdoors, an artistic movement that became known as the Hudson River school. The daring, unusual paintings were extremely popular, drawing packed audiences at major galleries, and reflected a major shift in the way Americans thought about both art and nature.

Prior to 1825, when painter Thomas Cole (1801–1848) founded the movement with his first paintings of the splendid Hudson River valley, most American artists depicted nature as cold, dangerous, and foreboding. Dating back to the first Puritans, many Americans instinctively associated the wilderness with evil and believed that nature should be tamed, not admired.

But Cole, an English-born painter and newspaper illustrator, was enraptured by the natural beauty of the lakes, mountains, and foliage of the Hudson valley. His paintings, awash in sunlight and brilliant colors, celebrated the mountains, cliffs, and animals of the region. Cole was influenced by the English romanticists, who tended to see nature as inherently good.

Cole died in 1848, at age forty-seven, but several of his students continued to paint landscapes in his epic style. Two of them, Frederick Edwin Church (1826–1900) and Albert Bierstadt (1830–1902), became hugely popular and sold their paintings for then unprecedented sums.

At first, the artists mostly concentrated on the Hudson River, the Adirondack Mountains, and the White Mountains of New Hampshire. In the 1850s, however, as the nation expanded westward, so did the artistic horizons of the Hudson River painters. Bierstadt, in particular, made landscape paintings of the West that fired the imagination of Americans with their grand, sweeping depiction of the then unspoiled wilderness.

The lasting legacy of the Hudson River school was twofold. First, Cole and his followers helped shift American attitudes toward greater appreciation for the environment, arguably leading to the conservation movement that developed later in the nineteenth century. Second, in artistic terms, they helped establish a distinctively American art that did not rely on imported European styles.

ADDITIONAL FACTS

1. *The largest collection of Hudson River school paintings can be found at the Wadsworth Atheneum in Hartford, Connecticut.*

2. *One of Cole's more famous paintings,* The Last of the Mohicans, *was inspired by the best-selling James Fenimore Cooper novel published in 1826.*

3. *Church's 1859 painting* Heart of the Andes *was such a sensation that more than 10,000 New Yorkers lined up at a gallery on Broadway and paid twenty-five cents each to see it.*

* * *

Benjamin Franklin

At the time of the American Revolution, scientist, inventor, and journalist Benjamin Franklin (1706–1790) was by far the most internationally famous American. Simply by endorsing the Declaration of Independence in 1776, Franklin lent instant credibility on the world stage to the cause of American independence.

Born in Boston, Franklin started his writing career at the age of fifteen, lampooning Puritan ministers in a newspaper owned by his older brother, James. Hoping to start his own newspaper, Ben Franklin ran away to Philadelphia in 1723, where he eventually became a successful printer. His famous annual pamphlet, *Poor Richard's Almanac,* a collection of witticisms and advice, established him as a best-selling author in the colonies.

His international reputation, however, stemmed from the amateur scientific experiments Franklin began conducting after reaching middle age. At the time, electricity was a new and poorly understood concept. Franklin famously proved that lightning was a form of electricity, and he invented the lightning rod. He toured Europe and was a sensation in France, where he was introduced to King Louis XV (1710–1774).

Franklin spent much of the 1760s in London as a lobbyist for the American colonies. He returned to Philadelphia in 1775 and, despite some misgivings, endorsed the Revolution. Ever the wit, when he signed the Declaration of Independence, tantamount to treason against King George III (1738–1820), he advised his colleagues, "We must all hang together, or assuredly we shall all hang separately."

Franklin was already seventy years old at the time of the drafting of the Declaration of Independence—the oldest delegate at the Second Continental Congress in Philadelphia—but his service to the new nation was not done. He returned to Europe to serve as the American ambassador to France, the most important American ally in the Revolution, and later helped negotiate with Britain the treaty that ended the war.

Returning home for the last time, Franklin participated in the 1787 Constitutional Convention in Philadelphia and penned several antislavery essays before his death in 1790.

ADDITIONAL FACTS

1. *Franklin had an illegitimate son, William, who split with his father during the Revolution by remaining loyal to the British Crown.*

2. *Franklin is the only American who signed all three of the key founding documents of the United States: the Declaration of Independence, the Treaty of Paris that ended the Revolution, and the Constitution.*

3. *In 1751, Franklin founded the University of Pennsylvania, one of the nation's most prestigious universities.*

★ ★ ★

Battles of Lexington and Concord

The first shots of the American Revolution were fired on April 19, 1775, in the small Massachusetts towns of Lexington and Concord, just outside of Boston. After years of growing tension between the thirteen colonies and the British Crown, the opening of hostilities on the little village green at Lexington was later dubbed "the shot heard round the world."

In the wake of the Boston Tea Party, Parliament had imposed martial law on the city of Boston. In early 1775, the British commander in the city, General Thomas Gage (1721–1787), received orders from London to crack down on dissenters and arrest the city's two leading anti-British agitators, Samuel Adams (1722–1803) and John Hancock (1737–1793).

Adams and Hancock, however, were tipped off to their arrest warrants and hastily fled to the small town of Lexington, located a few miles northwest of Boston. Determined to catch the two men, Gage prepared a force of about 700 British soldiers to hunt them down and also to seize ammunition the patriots had stockpiled in Concord.

On April 18, under cover of darkness, the British marched on Lexington. Two Boston patriots, Paul Revere (1734–1818) and William Dawes (1745–1799), quickly rode out of the city on separate routes to warn Adams and Hancock. A third patriot, Samuel Prescott (c. 1751–1777) joined the ride outside Lexington and made it all the way to Concord after Revere was captured and Dawes turned back. Tipped off, the local Massachusetts militia known as the minutemen were ready and waiting when the redcoats arrived at the Lexington green at dawn on April 19.

A tense standoff ensued, but at first, no shots were fired. The British officer, John Pitcairn (1722–1775), angrily ordered the rebels to disperse. Then, unexpectedly, a single shot rang out. Unsure who had fired, Pitcairn ordered his troops to attack. Eight minutemen died in the battle at Lexington, but no British soldiers did.

The British pressed on to Concord and destroyed military supplies stored in the town. But Adams and Hancock had vanished. The British then encountered another minuteman contingent at the Old North Bridge in Concord, where patriots scored a victory and forced the British troops back toward Boston in disarray. During their retreat, the British were attacked mercilessly by minuteman sharpshooters and lost 73 men.

ADDITIONAL FACTS

1. *The anniversary of the battles, April 19, is marked in Massachusetts as Patriots' Day and celebrated with the running of the Boston Marathon and a Red Sox home game starting at 11:00 a.m.*

2. *As a prosperous businessman after the war, Revere owned a mill that produced the copper plating for the hull of the famous warship USS* Constitution.

3. *The 1861 poem "Paul Revere's Ride," by Henry Wadsworth Longfellow (1807–1882), exaggerated Revere's importance in the battles but established him overnight as a national hero.*

★ ★ ★

First Great Awakening

Starting in the 1720s, a major religious revival called the First Great Awakening swept through the isolated farming communities of rural New England. The movement, which soon spread across North America and lasted until the 1740s, rejuvenated the Puritan religion, which had slipped into serious decline. More important, by challenging established religious authority figures, the Great Awakening helped lay the intellectual groundwork for the American Revolution.

The Great Awakening had its roots in a crisis in New England Puritanism. By the early eighteenth century, less than 100 years after the founding of Boston, the Puritans were beset by theological divisions and a widespread fear that the community was in the midst of "declension," or spiritual decay. Squabbles over theology had led to the founding of Yale in 1701 as a more conservative alternative to Harvard.

One of Yale's graduates, Jonathan Edwards (1703–1758), emerged as the key figure in the Great Awakening. As a young preacher in the Connecticut River valley town of Northampton, Massachusetts, Edwards delivered a series of sermons that urged a return to the strict tenets of the first Puritans.

To arouse his congregation, Edwards used vivid, intimate language in his sermons, a sharp contrast with the staid and impersonal lectures delivered by "Old Light" ministers of the mainstream church. Edwards's most famous sermon, "Sinners in the Hands of an Angry God," was a masterpiece of fire-and-brimstone oratory that reportedly left some of its listeners in 1741 in tears:

> The God that holds you over the pit of hell, much as one holds a spider, or some loathsome insect, over the fire, abhors you, and is dreadfully provoked; his wrath towards you burns like fire; he looks upon you as worthy of nothing else, but to be cast into the fire; he is of purer eyes than to bear to have you in his sight; you are ten thousand times so abominable in his eyes as the most hateful venomous serpent is in ours. You have offended him infinitely more than ever a stubborn rebel did his prince . . .

The First Great Awakening, although urging a return to orthodoxy, was rebellious in its mind-set. According to historians, the atmosphere of opposition to clerical authorities helped embolden the colonists for the ultimate break with their political masters.

ADDITIONAL FACTS

1. *One of Edwards's grandsons was Aaron Burr (1756–1836), who killed Alexander Hamilton (1755–1804) in a famous duel.*

2. *George Whitefield (1714–1770), another prominent Great Awakening preacher, toured the colonies extensively and received a donation from Benjamin Franklin (1706–1790), who attended a sermon in Philadelphia.*

3. *A Second Great Awakening in the early 1800s featured large-scale, outdoor revival meetings with charismatic Christian preachers who urged Americans to improve their society and thereby earn salvation.*

★ ★ ★

Report on Manufactures

Alexander Hamilton's famous *Report on Manufactures,* published in 1791, was one of the earliest blueprints for the American economy after the Revolutionary War. As George Washington's treasury secretary, Hamilton (1755–1804) was responsible for establishing the new government's fundamental economic policies. Hoping to build a firm economic foundation for the Republic, Hamilton favored an aggressive federal effort to build canals and roads, as well as protective tariffs to help fledgling American industries compete in the international marketplace. Although rejected during his lifetime, Hamilton's far-reaching vision would be highly influential in the nineteenth century for politicians like Henry Clay (1777–1852) and Abraham Lincoln (1809–1865).

After the Revolution, the new country had encountered many difficulties in establishing an economic system independent of Britain. Many of the states were deeply in debt after the war. The United States had little domestic industry, and most manufactured goods had to be imported. American ships, no longer sailing under the British flag, were suddenly prone to attack by pirates in the Mediterranean.

Under Hamilton's leadership as treasury secretary, the United States assumed the debt of the individual states, established the Coast Guard to prevent smuggling, and opened a mint to issue American currency. The program outlined in the 1791 report, however, was far more ambitious. By instituting a high tariff and government-subsidized infrastructure improvements, Hamilton wanted to turn his rural, relatively backward country into a major industrial power.

The *Report on Manufactures* was a major source of controversy in the early federal period, and disagreements over the proper governmental role in the economy became one of the defining issues in American politics. Federalists generally backed Hamilton's vision, while the Democratic-Republican Party of Thomas Jefferson (1743–1826) opposed it. Later, in the mid-nineteenth century, leaders like Henry Clay (1777–1852) would revive Hamilton's plan, renaming it the American System.

ADDITIONAL FACTS

1. *One of Hamilton's policies, a tax on whiskey used to pay down debts from the Revolution, was so unpopular it sparked the Whiskey Rebellion.*

2. *Hamilton opened the first United States mint in 1792 in Philadelphia.*

3. *For his role in creating the modern American economy, Hamilton's face is on the $10 bill.*

★ ★ ★

New Orleans

The city of New Orleans, located in the marshes near the mouth of the Mississippi River, was founded by a French trading company in 1718. As the importance of river commerce grew in the eighteenth century, the outpost grew into one of the major trading centers of North America, a role the city still plays today. In a measure of the port's growing strategic value, it changed hands three times in the hundred years after its founding, first to Spain in 1763, then back to France in 1800, and finally to the United States in 1803 as the crown jewel of the Louisiana Purchase.

The mixture of foreign influences produced a famously cosmopolitan culture that has made New Orleans unlike any other city in the United States. Creole and Cajun cuisine, music, and language are unique to Louisiana. The city is famous for its raucous Mardi Gras celebration and historic French Quarter neighborhood, both legacies of the city's French roots.

Because of its distinctive culture and economic importance, New Orleans has always occupied a prominent role in American society. In the nineteenth century, the city nicknamed the Big Easy was famous (or infamous) as a den of gambling, prostitution, and loose morals; later, the city's bohemian atmosphere nurtured many writers, including William Faulkner (1897–1962) and Tennessee Williams (1911–1983). The first jazz artists emerged from the sweaty, swinging nightclubs and Mississippi riverboats of New Orleans.

Hurricane Katrina, the worst natural disaster in American history, dealt a devastating blow to New Orleans when it hit the city on August 29, 2005. As of 2007, New Orleans was still rebuilding amid an uncertain future.

ADDITIONAL FACTS

1. *The city's namesake, "old" Orleans, is located in central France about an hour outside of Paris.*

2. *Before the Civil War (1861–1865), New Orleans was the nation's third-biggest city, after New York and Baltimore.*

3. *One of Faulkner's first novels,* Mosquitoes *(1927), takes place on a New Orleans riverboat and parodies the city's art aficionados.*

★ ★ ★

Lydia Maria Child

One of the first commercially successful female authors in the United States, Lydia Maria Child (1802–1880) emerged as a leading antislavery voice in pre–Civil War America and was the author of dozens of widely read novels, short stories, and magazine articles. Child's deeply held belief in racial equality was a recurring theme in her work, beginning with her first book, *Hobomok*, published in 1824, a sympathetic novel about discrimination against American Indians.

Born Lydia Marie Francis in Medford, Massachusetts, the author became a literary star at the age of twenty-two upon the publication of *Hobomok*, which was an instant success. Over the next ten years, she wrote a stream of historical novels, children's books, and nonfiction about the mistreatment of Native Americans. In 1826, she founded the first children's magazine in the United States, *Juvenile Miscellany*. While still in her twenties, she became one of the first women inducted into Boston's Athenaeum, an exclusive writers' club. In 1828, at the age of twenty-six, she married David Child (1794–1874), a Boston lawyer and abolitionist.

Beginning in the 1830s, Lydia Marie Child increasingly focused her energy on the incipient abolition movement. Inspired by the abolitionist editor William Lloyd Garrison (1805–1879), an acquaintance of her husband's, Child wrote *An Appeal in Favor of That Class of Americans Called Africans* in 1833. For her then-radical stance in favor of immediate abolition of slavery, Child was forced to resign as editor of *Juvenile Miscellany* after some pro-slavery readers canceled their subscriptions and the magazine faced a loss of readership in the South.

In 1841, with her career in Boston stymied by the controversy, Child moved to New York City, where she edited the *National Anti-Slavery Standard* for several years. An extremely prolific writer, she also continued to write novels, nonfiction, biographies, and poetry on other subjects as well. Her most famous poem, "A Boy's Thanksgiving," written in the mid-1840s, is known for its opening lines: "Over the river, and through the wood, / to Grandfather's house we go."

During the Civil War (1861–1865), Child led an effort to teach reading to escaped slaves who had been denied an education in the South. She continued writing after the war, championing equality for women, freed slaves, and American Indians, before retiring with her husband to Medford.

ADDITIONAL FACTS

1. *Child's father was a baker.*

2. *In addition to all her other books, Child wrote a best-selling cookbook,* The Frugal Housewife, *in 1829.*

3. *Child helped Harriet Jacobs, an escaped slave, write her 1861 autobiography,* Incidents in the Life of a Slave Girl, *a widely read book about the hardships of slavery for women.*

★ ★ ★

Sea Chanteys

One of the earliest forms of indigenous American music, sea chanteys (pronounced "*shan*-tees") developed in the nineteenth century as work songs for sailors aboard whaling ships. Derived from the French word *chantez,* meaning *sing,* chanteys grew out of European, African-American, and West Indian musical traditions—an early example of the eclectic mix of styles that produced American music.

In the age of sail, life at sea was full of backbreaking manual labor. The purpose of a sea chantey, first and foremost, was to set the tempo for the grueling tasks that sailors were required to perform every day, such as weighing anchor, hoisting sails, or lading cargo. The beat and structure of a chantey varied depending on the task for which it was needed. For instance, the famous song "Blow the Man Down" was a "hauling" chantey used for lengthy chores like raising a sail. A separate kind of chantey was reserved for gutting whales and boiling down their blubber.

One of the most famous sea chanteys, "Drunken Sailor," was intended specifically for "hand over hand" tasks, such as raising small sails. One sailor, a chanteyman, sang the first line, while the others answered in the chorus:

> SOLO: What shall we do with a drunken sailor?
> CHORUS: What shall we do with a drunken sailor?
> What shall we do with a drunken sailor?
> Early in the morning.

Chanteys were meant to serve specific work purposes and were not intended to be sung for fun. Richard Henry Dana Jr. (1815–1882), in his famous book *Two Years Before the Mast* (1840), called them "as necessary to sailors as the drum and fife to a soldier." However, the songs eventually spread to land in the 1870s and became popular, since they were associated with the alleged romance of the seas. The invention of steamships gradually made heavy manual labor unnecessary, and chanteys disappeared by the early twentieth century.

ADDITIONAL FACTS

1. A *"chanteying" festival is held every June in Mystic, Connecticut.*

2. The *famous folksinger Woody Guthrie recorded a collection of chanteys,* Deep Sea Chanteys and Whaling Ballads, *in 1941.*

★ ★ ★

Patrick Henry

Patrick Henry (1736–1799), a leading Virginia lawyer and politician, is remembered today almost entirely for a single, electrifying speech he gave in March 1775, demanding an end to British rule in the thirteen American colonies. "I know not what course others may take; but as for me, give me liberty or give me death!" he exclaimed at the close of his famous oration before the Virginia legislature, a rousing battle cry at a crucial moment that moved opinion in Virginia decisively for independence. After the Revolution, Henry led with equal vehemence the opposition to the United States Constitution, which he said reminded him too much of the hated British monarchy. Henry believed the Constitution, written and signed in 1787, gave far too much power to the federal government at the expense of the states, and he bitterly opposed its ratification in Virginia.

Born near Richmond, Henry began studying law after failing as a farmer. He proved an able attorney and was elected to the Virginia legislature, the House of Burgesses, while still in his twenties. Henry's uncompromising defense of colonial rights impressed the young Thomas Jefferson (1743–1826), who would later cite Henry as a political mentor.

Henry's reemergence as the leading Virginia anti-Federalist after the Revolution, however, pitted him against his old friend Jefferson, who backed the Constitution. For Henry, the Constitution dangerously expanded federal power and also threatened the institution of slavery. The Constitution, he warned his fellow Virginians, "squints toward monarchy" and would allow the government to "liberate every one of your slaves."

In the end, Henry's objections did not prevent Virginia from ratifying the Constitution in 1788, but they had lasting influence in the South. Seventy years later, Virginia and other Southern states echoed many of his objections to federal power as they seceded from the Union in the name of states' rights and the preservation of slavery.

ADDITIONAL FACTS

1. *At the start of the Revolution, Henry briefly served as the commander of Virginia's first rebel militia, but he proved to be an inept military man and soon returned to politics.*

2. *Henry was elected the first independent governor of Virginia in 1776 and was succeeded by Jefferson in 1779.*

3. *In his later years, Henry rejected invitations from President George Washington (1732–1799) to become secretary of state and, later, chief justice of the Supreme Court.*

★ ★ ★

Battle of Bunker Hill

After the battles of Lexington and Concord in April 1775, the patriot army was impatient to drive British troops out of Boston once and for all. From farms and villages across New England, patriot militiamen streamed into Massachusetts, short on ammunition and training but eager to attack the redcoats. That June, unwilling to wait any longer for much-needed supplies to arrive, they struck. The Americans seized two strategic hilltops north of Boston, Bunker Hill and Breed's Hill, both of which had commanding views of Boston Harbor.

About 1,200 Americans had taken over the hills on the night of June 16. By the time the sun rose the next morning, the soldiers had finished digging fortifications into the hillsides. The British commander in Boston, General William Howe (1729–1814), immediately recognized the danger of allowing the rebels to hold the hills, and he ordered his troops to attack.

In the subsequent Battle of Bunker Hill on June 17, 1775, British soldiers retook the two hilltops in the first major battle of the Revolutionary War. About 400 American soldiers were killed in what would be among the bloodiest clashes of the entire war. In a narrow sense, the battle was a defeat for the undisciplined, overeager Americans. However, the British also suffered massive casualties—about half of their 2,000 soldiers were killed or wounded.

Unlike the Lexington and Concord battles—which, in reality, had been more like small skirmishes—Bunker Hill was a protracted bloodbath for both sides. Although they lacked ammunition and were poorly organized, the Americans proved surprisingly resilient. William Prescott (1726–1795), an American officer, famously instructed his soldiers not to fire at the advancing British soldiers "until you see the whites of their eyes!" This advice was sound; the patriots had so few bullets that they needed to save them for when they would be most effective. In all, it would take three charges up the hill before the British finally dislodged the patriots.

After the battle, George Washington (1732–1799) arrived in Massachusetts to take command of the patriot army. After nine more months of the siege, the British abandoned Boston in March 1776.

ADDITIONAL FACTS

1. *Some patriot leaders opposed sending the militia to seize Bunker Hill before more supplies arrived, since their entire arsenal consisted of eleven barrels of gunpowder.*

2. *One of the American casualties was Dr. Joseph Warren (1741–1775), a patriot leader and member of the Sons of Liberty.*

3. *The battle of Bunker Hill exposed the poor discipline of many American soldiers, who deserted in droves as the battle raged. One of George Washington's first acts as general was to fire a number of officers for "cowardly behavior" during the battle.*

★ ★ ★

Zenger Trial

A colonial-era newspaper publisher in New York City, John Peter Zenger (1697–1746), helped create the American concept of freedom of the press by successfully defending himself against a libel accusation in 1735.

Born in Germany, Zenger came to New York City with his family as a child. His parents apprenticed him to a well-known printer, where he learned to operate presses. In 1733, after finishing his apprenticeship, he started his own newspaper, the *New-York Weekly Journal*.

Like many early American newspapers, the *Journal* was openly partisan. Its mission, Zenger proclaimed in the first issue, was to be a platform for invective against the British-appointed governor, William Cosby (c. 1690–1736).

Cosby, an aristocrat who was widely disliked in New York, was not amused. After Zenger printed some particularly critical articles and poems, Cosby ordered him arrested. Zenger continued to publish the newspaper from behind bars for ten months by passing instructions to his wife during prison visits.

At trial, Zenger was represented at no charge by a well-known Philadelphia lawyer, Andrew Hamilton (1676–1741). The jurors faced enormous pressure from the government—and from the Cosby-appointed judge—to return a guilty verdict. But in a much-acclaimed argument to the jury, Hamilton convinced jurors that since the law was unjust, they should acquit Zenger despite the judge's instructions.

By the end of the trial, Zenger had won the sympathy of many New Yorkers, and the memory of his trial helped inspire the First Amendment to the Constitution protecting free speech fifty years later.

ADDITIONAL FACTS

1. *Zenger's wife, Anna, and his son, John, continued printing the* Journal *after Zenger's death until the paper folded in 1751.*

2. *The offending articles were likely not written by Zenger himself, whose grasp of English was incomplete, but by James Alexander, a political opponent of Governor Cosby who helped finance the* Journal.

3. *The jurors depended on the controversial concept of "jury nullification," by which juries can choose not to enforce laws they consider unjust, to acquit Zenger. Although rarely used, American juries still have this prerogative.*

★ ★ ★

Wall Street

Wall Street, a narrow alley in downtown Manhattan, has been the nation's financial capital ever since a group of twenty-four stockbrokers set up the first American stock exchange there under a buttonwood tree in 1792. At its inception, only five equities were traded on Wall Street. As the exchange grew in the early nineteenth century, lower Manhattan became a magnet for dozens of banks and speculators who moved to the neighborhood and made the words *Wall Street* a synonym for American capitalism.

Initially, the only two types of equities traded on Wall Street were bonds, which the federal government issued beginning in the 1790s to repay its Revolutionary War debts, and stocks in bank companies. Over time, manufacturers, insurance companies, and railroads also began listing their stocks on Wall Street. As the American economy surged in the late nineteenth century, the New York Stock Exchange (NYSE) on Wall Street surpassed European financial capitals in importance and became the world's largest stock exchange in 1918. By 2007, a total of 2,764 corporations were listed on the NYSE, where billions of dollars are now traded daily.

Even by the mid-nineteenth century, the growing power of the stock exchange concerned some Americans. Traders on Wall Street wielded enormous clout over the corporations whose stock they owned, and critics accused them of using that power to encourage rapacious corporate behavior. In addition, Wall Street's cycles of boom and bust could put millions of Americans out of work by depriving companies of needed capital. The panic of 1873 and, most famously, the stock market crash of 1929 illustrated the devastating effects of stock downturns on the overall American economy.

As the symbol of American capitalism, the street itself became a target of violence in 1920, when anarchists attempted to blow up the exchange and surrounding buildings. The bank J. P. Morgan & Company, located across the street from the NYSE at 23 Wall Street, decided not to fix the shrapnel damage to its headquarters as a monument to the blast's thirty-nine victims. Pockmarks are still visible in the building's facade today.

ADDITIONAL FACTS

1. *A Chinese gong was originally used to signal the end of the trading day instead of the now-familiar closing bell.*

2. *The second major American stock exchange, NASDAQ, now trades more shares per day than the NYSE, although its companies have a smaller overall market capitalization.*

3. *Until 1836, members of the stock exchange actually traded in the streets outside the building.*

★ ★ ★

Washington, DC

During the American Revolution, the Continental Congress met in five different cities and even convened briefly in the small town of York, Pennsylvania, while Philadelphia was under British occupation. After the war, the nomadic governing continued, with a half dozen different cities serving as the nation's capital.

In the late 1780s, the Founding Fathers began looking for a more permanent seat of government. Many members of Congress favored a major commercial center like New York or Philadelphia, but southerners wanted the capital built in the agricultural South. In 1790, northern politicians finally agreed to build the permanent capital between the borders of Virginia and Maryland, in exchange for southern votes on a separate bill backed by northerners.

The result of this compromise is the federal city of Washington, which was named after the first United States president and has been the official home of the US government since 1800. A French born American architect, Pierre L'Enfant (1754–1825), was hired to design the city's blueprint, making Washington one of the first examples of a modern planned city.

A relatively small town until the mid-twentieth century, Washington with its surrounding area is now one of the most heavily populated regions in the country and a global center of commerce and diplomacy. Many national landmarks, including the Smithsonian Museum, the White House, and the United States Capitol building, are located within the original boundaries sketched out by Congress in 1790.

Washington's legal status remains unique in American government. Although carved out of the states of Maryland and Virginia, the District of Columbia that Washington occupies is not itself a state. Its citizens have no vote in Congress (although they must pay federal taxes and may be conscripted in wartime), and Congress—rather than elected city council members—retains ultimate say over most laws within the district's borders.

ADDITIONAL FACTS

1. *In 1961, the Constitution was amended to give residents of the District of Columbia the right to vote in presidential elections.*

2. *George Washington himself was too modest to accept the name of the city, and he referred to the capital as the Federal City.*

3. *During the 1790s, while the city of Washington was under construction, Philadelphia was the nation's capital.*

★ ★ ★

Edgar Allan Poe

In 1845, a newspaper in New York City published on its back page a poem by Edgar Allan Poe (1809–1849) titled "The Raven." The poem began with a stanza that is now one of the most instantly recognizable verses in American literature:

> Once upon a midnight dreary, while I pondered, weak and weary,
> Over many a quaint and curious volume of forgotten lore,
> While I nodded, nearly napping, suddenly there came a tapping,
> As of some one gently rapping, rapping at my chamber door.
> "'Tis some visitor," I muttered, "tapping at my chamber door—
>   Only this, and nothing more."

The poem, one of Poe's most well-known works, is typical of the author's bewitching style. Poet, short story writer, and literary critic, Poe specialized in phantasmagoric tales of the supernatural.

Although "The Raven" is Poe's single most famous work, he wrote mostly short stories, including such macabre classics as "The Tell-Tale Heart," "The Fall of the House of Usher," and "The Murders in the Rue Morgue." Poe's tales are often dark, morbid, and suspenseful, full of strange deaths in exotic lands. For instance, in one of Poe's most notorious horror stories, "The Cask of Amontillado," a murderer chains an Italian nobleman up in a basement and walls him in to die a slow death.

As one might guess, Poe's disturbing tales were the product of a deeply troubled soul. During much of his lifetime, Poe struggled with alcoholism, debt, and gambling problems. He was devastated by the death of his wife, Virginia, from tuberculosis in 1847, and he died at age forty after a drinking binge in Baltimore.

In terms of influence, few nineteenth-century American writers rival Poe. Among his other distinctions, he was the first American mystery writer and one of the inventors of the science fiction genre. His work was widely read abroad and has been arguably even more influential in France than in the United States. Nearly every American horror writer, from H. P. Lovecraft (1890–1937) to Stephen King (1947–), owes a direct debt to Poe's pioneering fiction.

ADDITIONAL FACTS

1. *Although born in Boston and raised in Virginia, Poe is most closely associated with his adopted hometown of Baltimore, where the NFL team is named the Ravens in honor of Poe's famous poem.*

2. *Poe is mentioned in the famous 1967 Beatles song "I Am the Walrus," in which an "elementary penguin singing Hare Krishna" is kicking Edgar Allan Poe for an unspecified reason.*

3. *In a little-known 1848 book,* Eureka, *Poe baffled readers by insisting that the universe began in "one instantaneous flash"—forecasting the big-bang hypothesis more than a century before astronomers made the same claim.*

★ ★ ★

Stephen Foster

The leading songwriter of the nineteenth-century United States, Stephen Foster (1826–1864) penned hundreds of American standards, including "Oh, Susanna," "Swanee River" (originally titled "Old Folks at Home"), "My Old Kentucky Home," and "Beautiful Dreamer," but died with thirty-eight cents in his pocket at a New York City hospital.

Foster was born in Pittsburgh, where he was taught music by Henry Kleber, a German immigrant. When he was only eighteen, Foster published his first song, "Open Thy Lattice." In an era before recorded music, composers like Foster made most of their income from the sale of sheet music. In 1848, Foster sold "Oh, Susanna," one of the most popular songs in American history, to a publisher for $100—his first major success.

Foster's style was heavily influenced by so-called plantation music, and some modern detractors accuse Foster, who was white, of beginning the inglorious American tradition of stealing from African-American musicians. Many of Foster's songs were sentimental and highly unrealistic odes to plantation life in the South, and they use racial terminology now considered offensive.

In the context of the 1850s, however, the casual racism in Foster's songs was hardly unusual. Minstrel shows, performed by whites in blackface, were one of the era's most popular forms of entertainment, and several of Foster's most famous songs, including "Camptown Races" and "Swanee River," became staples of minstrel performances.

For Foster, however, the prosperity of the 1850s was short-lived. In 1860, after the collapse of his marriage, he moved to New York City and promptly descended into alcoholism and poverty. He continued to write music, but found little success after abandoning minstrel music. He died at the age of thirty-seven in a public hospital in January 1864. Foster's last song, the poignant ballad "Beautiful Dreamer," was published shortly after his death and became one of his greatest, most beloved hits.

ADDITIONAL FACTS

1. *Two of his songs are official state anthems: "Swanee River" in Florida and "My Old Kentucky Home" in Kentucky.*

2. *Foster was born July 4, 1826, the same day that Thomas Jefferson and John Adams died.*

3. *He wrote his ballad "Jeannie with the Light Brown Hair" in 1854 for his wife, Jane Denny McDowell. The couple separated later that year.*

★ ★ ★

John Hancock

Boston merchant and banker John Hancock (1737–1793) emerged as a leading financier of opposition to British rule in Massachusetts in the decade before the American Revolution. Outraged by taxes imposed on his lucrative businesses, Hancock used his profits to fund the Sons of Liberty, the clandestine radical group responsible for the Boston Tea Party. In recognition of his contributions to the patriot cause, Hancock became the first person to sign the Declaration of Independence in 1776.

In the turbulent years leading up to the Revolution, Hancock and Samuel Adams (1722–1803) were the most vocal critics of the British in Boston, organizing the merchant class of the city to oppose the series of taxes imposed by the British Parliament. The British taxes and trade restrictions hit Hancock's shipping, whale oil, and real estate interests particularly hard. The two men were a constant thorn in the side of the Boston colonial authorities, who were eventually ordered to arrest them in 1775.

The British raid to capture Hancock and Adams led directly to the first battles of the Revolution, at Lexington and Concord, in April 1775. The two men evaded capture by hiding in the countryside near Boston. Hancock, who became a national hero for his defiance of the British, was elected president of the Continental Congress in Philadelphia the next month. His position as president entitled him to sign the Declaration of Independence first.

Once the Revolution began, however, Hancock was sidelined by his comrades. Despite his undeniable dedication to the cause and his deep pockets, Hancock was not popular with his fellow revolutionaries, who tired of his pomposity. His gigantic, curlicued signature on the Declaration of Independence is a fitting reflection of a man deeply dedicated both to American liberty and to himself.

ADDITIONAL FACTS

1. *The tallest building in modern Boston, the glass-paneled John Hancock Tower, is named after the John Hancock insurance company, which in turn named itself after the famous Boston patriot.*

2. *Slavery was still legal in Massachusetts until 1780. Although himself a slave owner, Hancock supported the state constitution that abolished the institution.*

3. *Hancock graduated from Harvard and before that from Boston Latin School, the first public high school founded in the British colonies.*

★ ★ ★

General George Washington

"I heard Bullets whistle and believe me there
was something charming in the Sound."
—George Washington

On June 15, 1775, the Continental Congress chose a wealthy Virginia planter and surveyor, George Washington (1732–1799), to command the patriot army camped near Boston. A veteran of the French and Indian War (1754–1763), Washington accepted the commission as commander in chief of the newly established Continental army and rode to Massachusetts to take charge of his army the next month.

By the time General Washington arrived, the ragtag patriot force had already fought one large battle against the British at Bunker Hill and had encircled the city of Boston. In his first campaign of the war, Washington directed a successful siege of the city, leading the British to evacuate in March 1776.

The army Washington led, however, bore little resemblance to the well-trained British enemy. Drawn from colonial militia regiments, his soldiers often had little or no training, lacked uniforms, deserted regularly, and were accustomed to electing their own officers.

As the commander of the Continental army, Washington's most urgent task at the beginning of the war was to bring discipline to the unruly force. In the early years, he desperately sought to avoid pitched battles with the British, preferring instead to harass the enemy in small skirmishes. The arrival of several European advisors, including the Marquis de Lafayette (1757–1834) from France and Baron von Steuben (1730–1794) from Prussia, helped transform the army into a professional fighting force.

An officer of great bravery, Washington often led the army into battle himself, miraculously avoiding any serious injury for the course of the war. Immensely popular by the end of the war, Washington was the unanimous choice as the first president of the United States in the election of 1789.

ADDITIONAL FACTS

1. *When he agreed to lead the Continental army in 1775, Washington declined a salary, asking only that Congress reimburse his expenses.*

2. *Washington was the first of twelve US presidents to hold the rank of general.*

3. *According to biographer Joseph Ellis, the general had a soft spot for theater and had a performance of his favorite play,* Cato, *staged for his soldiers.*

★ ★ ★

Slave Trade

Millions of Africans were forcibly transported to the Americas in the international slave trade that flourished in the eighteenth century. The horrible conditions aboard the slave ships during the notorious Middle Passage killed as many as a third of the enslaved Africans before they even landed.

The first African slaves in the British colonies of North America arrived in Virginia in 1619, shortly after the establishment of the Jamestown colony. However, the mass forcible importation of human beings into the British colonies would not begin in earnest for another century. Most of the slaves had been kidnapped or taken prisoner by local chiefs during military struggles in western Africa, sold to European traders, and chained together in floating dungeons for the months-long journey to the Americas.

The vast majority of African slaves were taken to Spanish and Portuguese colonies in South America and the Caribbean to toil on sugar plantations. A relatively smaller number ended up in British North America. Initially, all of the thirteen colonies allowed slavery, but it was much more common in the agricultural South.

Some eighteenth-century Americans were well aware of, and ashamed by, the horrors of the Middle Passage. In the first draft of the Declaration of Independence, Thomas Jefferson (1743–1826), who himself owned slaves, assailed King George III (1738–1820) for allowing the importation of slaves: "He has waged cruel war against human nature itself, violating its most sacred rights of life & liberty in the persons of a distant people who never offended him, captivating & carrying them into slavery in another hemisphere, or to incur miserable death in their transportation thither."

The United States Congress outlawed the international slave trade in 1808, and the British Navy began arresting slavers in the 1830s. However, the Atlantic slave trade continued until 1888, when Brazil became the last American country to outlaw slavery. Even after the end of the international slave trade, however, domestic slave auctions continued in the United States until the Civil War (1861–1865).

ADDITIONAL FACTS

1. *Most of the slaves taken to the United States came from the modern-day nations of Ghana, Benin, Togo, Nigeria, and Sierra Leone.*

2. *Homelands for liberated slaves who wanted to return to Africa were established by the British in Sierra Leone in 1808 and by the Americans in Liberia in 1821.*

3. *The Royal Navy hastened the end of the Middle Passage by declared slave trading a form of piracy, which exposed slave traders caught by the British to the death penalty.*

★ ★ ★

Erie Canal

Prior to 1825, the year the Erie Canal opened for business, transporting cargo from the Midwest to the East Coast was a slow and arduous task. Mule-drawn carts carrying grain or whiskey from the Ohio River valley to New York might take months to cross the Appalachian Mountains on rough, muddy paths through terrain that was still mostly wilderness.

The Erie Canal, which at the time of its construction was the most significant feat of engineering in United States history, made transportation drastically cheaper and faster, giving an enormous boost to the economy of the Midwest. The canal, which connected the Great Lakes region with the Hudson River, allowed farmers in Ohio or upstate New York to ship their wares to New York City in about two weeks for about one-tenth the cost of overland shipping.

New York State, led by Governor DeWitt Clinton (1769–1828), sponsored the construction of the 363-mile canal at the cost of $7 million—one of the most profitable investments in the state's history. The canal solidified New York City's place as the busiest port in the United States, making it the principal departure point for American products shipped to Europe. The canal also led to more settlement in Michigan, Ohio, Indiana, and Illinois, regions that suddenly had easy access to eastern ports and European markets.

The enormous success of the Erie Canal spawned a boom of canal construction in the United States, including several feeder canals in New York. However, the popularity of canals waned after the introduction of the railroads in the 1830s, which were even faster. Still, the Erie Canal remained a lucrative business for decades. Many remnants of the original canal remain in upstate New York, and parts are still used for commercial shipping.

ADDITIONAL FACTS

1. The canal rose a total of 420 feet in elevation on its route westward and required 82 locks.

2. Originally, barges on the Erie Canal had no source of power and had to be pulled by horses or oxen that walked alongside the canal on a strip called a towpath.

3. Many New Yorkers were skeptical of Clinton's plan, and they derisively referred to the canal as Clinton's Folly until it proved a spectacular success.

★ ★ ★

Pierre L'Enfant

Engineer Pierre L'Enfant (1754–1825) designed the blueprint for the nation's capital, an influential milestone in urban planning that was largely ignored in L'Enfant's time but later became the basis for the layout of modern Washington, DC. In L'Enfant's plan, he sought to translate the democratic aspirations of the United States into urban form and create a city that would win international respect for the young nation.

Born in France, L'Enfant traveled to America to enlist in the patriot army at age twenty-two, following in the footsteps of his compatriot, the Marquis de Lafayette (1757–1834). He eventually rose to the rank of major and befriended General George Washington (1732–1799). After the Revolutionary War, L'Enfant Americanized his first name to Peter and found work designing houses and furniture in his adopted homeland. In 1790, Congress decided to build a new capital city and gave Washington control over the details. Washington, in turn, asked L'Enfant to prepare a design for the city.

L'Enfant's elegant plan attempted to give physical form to the nation's revolutionary ideals. He envisioned two great buildings, the Capitol and the White House, which would be physically separate to symbolize the concept of separation of powers that is enshrined in the Constitution. L'Enfant's plan also called for a system of grand avenues, each of which would be named after a state in recognition of the importance of federalism.

Because of L'Enfant's prickly personality and the high cost of his plan, Washington removed the Frenchman from the project less than a year later. By the nineteenth century, relatively little of his blueprint had become reality. City planners in Washington, DC, revived the L'Enfant Plan in 1901, however, and finally implemented many of his ideas—a testament to L'Enfant's visionary accomplishment.

ADDITIONAL FACTS

1. *Every state has an avenue in Washington, DC, named in its honor.*

2. *L'Enfant was never paid for his work, and he died in Maryland in poverty.*

3. *Thomas Jefferson (1743–1826), who had opposed the L'Enfant plan because of its cost, was the first US president inaugurated in Washington, DC, in 1801.*

★ ★ ★

Ralph Waldo Emerson

"Whosoever would be a man, must be a nonconformist."
—Ralph Waldo Emerson

Massachusetts writer, poet, and philosopher Ralph Waldo Emerson (1803–1882) is among the most influential literary figures in American history, and he played a crucial role in encouraging the development of American fiction and poetry in the mid-nineteenth century. In one of his most famous works, an 1837 lecture titled "The American Scholar," Emerson called on his compatriots to cast off foreign influences and create a distinctively national literature, a clarion call that inspired many American writers. "We have listened too long to the courtly muses of Europe," Emerson intoned in the lecture.

Emerson's own poetic output was modest. His most famous poem is probably "Concord Hymn," a short patriotic verse about the Battle of Concord in 1775.

As a lecturer and essayist, however, Emerson was far more prolific. In addition to "The American Scholar," he wrote the highly influential essay "Self Reliance" (1841), which called on writers to develop their own intellect rather than rely on hidebound convention and tradition. The truly inventive mind, Emerson explained, would often contradict itself, but so what? "A foolish consistency is the hobgoblin of little minds," he famously wrote.

Emerson's criticism was largely rooted in the transcendentalist philosophy that he helped shape and define. Although trained as a Unitarian minister, Emerson stopped preaching in the 1830s. The transcendentalists—a movement with religious, literary, and philosophical dimensions—for the most part rejected organized religion in favor of a highly individualistic, optimistic view of the world and of human nature.

Written with elegance and occasional pungency, Emerson's essays in the pages of *The Dial*, the leading Transcendentalist journal, were extremely influential and would inspire Henry David Thoreau (1817–1862), Herman Melville (1819–1891), and Walt Whitman (1819–1892), among others. Whitman is said to have been directly inspired by one of Emerson's articles, "The Poet" (1844), in which the critic lamented the absence of a true American poet. Thoreau, meanwhile, owed a more literal debt to Emerson, who had allowed the writer to build a cabin on his land next to Walden Pond.

ADDITIONAL FACTS

1. *Emerson attended Harvard on a scholarship that required him to wait tables for other students.*

2. *The poem "Concord Hymn" was written for the dedication of a monument to the minutemen in the writer's hometown of Concord, Massachusetts.*

3. *Emerson preferred to be called Waldo, rather than Ralph, by his friends.*

★ ★ ★

Mathew Brady

The first nationally famous photographer in American history, New York-born Mathew Brady (c. 1823–1896) shocked his viewers by documenting the gruesome bloodshed of the Civil War (1861–1865). Thanks to Brady and his crew of assistants, who toted primitive camera equipment from battlefield to battlefield, . Americans for the first time saw accurate pictures of the death and devastation of war. Brady also snapped many iconic portraits of leading generals and political leaders of the nineteenth century, including President Abraham Lincoln (1809–1865) and General Ulysses S. Grant (1822–1855).

Photography had been invented in France in the 1820s and 1830s and imported to the United States in the early 1840s. Brady, one of the first artists to make use of the new technology, opened his photography studio in New York City in 1844.

In its early years, taking and developing pictures was a cumbersome, time-consuming process. Cameras of the 1860s were the size of microwave ovens, and few photographers ventured outside of their studios.

Brady was among the first photographers to realize the journalistic potential of the primitive technology. Although unable to capture actual snapshots of battle, Brady and his men were often the first to arrive on the scene afterward, taking haunting photos of scorched buildings, destroyed bridges, and the bloated corpses of the dead.

In 1862, Brady mounted his first exhibit of war photos, displaying a collection of pictures from the Battle of Antietam. The photos were hailed for their raw realism, and Brady would take more than 10,000 pictures over the course of the war at huge cost.

Unfortunately for Brady, his investment never paid off. After the end of the Civil War, Americans had little interest in graphic reminders of the conflict. Brady's business collapsed, and he died thirty years later after being hit by a streetcar in New York City.

ADDITIONAL FACTS

1. *Congress granted Brady $25,000 in 1875 in recognition of his Civil War service, but Brady used the entire gift to pay off some of his crushing debts.*

2. *During the war, Brady employed a primitive photographic process known as albumen printing, which used paper coated with dissolved egg whites to produce a print.*

3. *He also photographed several Confederate generals after the war, including Robert E. Lee (1807–1870).*

★ ★ ★

King George III

The Declaration of Independence issued by the American colonies in 1776 reserved its angriest invective for one man: King George III (1738–1820), the much-loathed monarch of Great Britain. Although Britain was evolving into a parliamentary democracy in the eighteenth century, the hereditary king still wielded considerable power in the overseas colonies, and many Americans held King George personally responsible for the oppressive British policies that had driven them to rebellion.

George inherited the throne in 1760 after the death of his grandfather, King George II. He faced a budget crisis within a few years because Britain had gone heavily into debt to win the Seven Years' War—or the French and Indian War, as it was known in North America.

The king, like many other British politicians, viewed the American colonies primarily as a source of revenue. To the British leadership, taxing the colonies to repay the war debt made perfect sense—after all, they believed, that's what colonies were for. The colonists, however, chafed at the numerous heavy taxes and other restrictive measures the British government imposed on them.

The Declaration of Independence attacked the king's treatment of the colonies in uncompromising tones:

> He has plundered our seas, ravaged our Coasts, burnt our towns, and destroyed the lives of our people.
> He is at this time transporting large Armies of foreign Mercenaries to compleat the works of death, desolation and tyranny, already begun with circumstances of Cruelty & perfidy scarcely paralleled in the most barbarous ages, and totally unworthy the Head of a civilized nation.

Back in England, George III had a reputation as a conservative family man, an anomaly in the scandal ridden British royal family. But the loss of the thirteen colonies forever tarnished his legacy. The king remained on the throne until 1820, although he went blind and insane in 1810 and was incapacitated for the last ten years of his reign. As the last king of America, George III played his greatest political role in this country's history in acting as a lightning rod, the personification of the oppressive reign the colonies hoped to overthrow.

ADDITIONAL FACTS

1. *King George's great-great-great-great-granddaughter is Elizabeth II, the current queen of the United Kingdom.*

2. *When he became monarch in 1760, George III was the first native English speaker to rule Britain in fifty years. His father and grandfather both spoke German as their first language.*

3. *In 2003, scientists in England tested strands of the king's hair and found extremely high levels of the poison arsenic, leading some to believe that the seizures he had may have been caused by bad nineteenth-century medicine (given as treatment for insanity) and not by madness.*

★ ★ ★

Battle of Saratoga

The victory of patriot forces at the Battle of Saratoga (1777) marked the crucial turning point of the American Revolution. Prior to Saratoga, the patriots had managed only a few triumphs in small skirmishes against British forces. They had lost the largest pitched battle of the war up to that point, the Battle of Bunker Hill (1775).

But Saratoga, located in upstate New York near Albany, was a massive victory that quickly echoed across the globe. An entire British army—six generals and 5,500 men—was forced to surrender. European powers were so impressed by the military wherewithal of the Americans that the French government officially recognized the United States when it received the news of Saratoga, becoming the first foreign power to accept the independence of the colonies.

The British commander at Saratoga was General John "Gentleman Johnny" Burgoyne (1722–1792), an English officer who believed the British would make short work of the American rebels. Burgoyne entered New York from Canada with about 8,000 troops. His troops seized Fort Ticonderoga and then marched slowly in the direction of Albany. Americans under the command of General Horatio Gates (c. 1728–1806) caught up with Burgoyne near the town of Saratoga in September 1777.

The American hero of the battle was none other than Benedict Arnold (1741–1801), the man whose name later became synonymous with *traitor*. Despite arguments with Gates over strategy, Arnold led the first frontal attack on Burgoyne. After the battle, the British found themselves boxed in by the Americans, cut off from their supply lines to Canada.

His situation hopeless, Burgoyne surrendered on October 17, 1777. The British Empire, the most powerful nation on earth, had been humbled by the ragtag American rebels. Indeed, the Americans were nearly as surprised by the outcome as the British were. Completely unprepared to take prisoners, American commanders let Burgoyne and his troops return to England, as long as they promised not to come back. Benjamin Franklin (1706–1790), the American ambassador in Paris, used the victory at Saratoga to convince King Louis XVI (1754–1793) to formally recognize the United States. With official French recognition on February 6, 1778, the revolutionaries gained a crucial military and diplomatic ally. French ships and troops began aiding the American cause, providing a decisive counterweight to the British navy.

ADDITIONAL FACTS

1. *Arnold was so loathed after his betrayal of the Americans in 1780—when, as commander of West Point, he plotted to surrender it to the British but was caught before doing so—that his monument on the Saratoga battlefield does not mention him by name.*

2. *After the battle, some members of the Continental Congress briefly considered replacing George Washington with the hero of Saratoga, Gates, as leader of the Continental army.*

3. *The British commander at Saratoga, Burgoyne, had made a rash bet at a club in London that he would return home, victorious, by the end of 1777.*

★ ★ ★

Declaration of Independence

The immediate purpose of the Declaration of Independence, signed in Philadelphia in 1776, was to "declare the causes" that impelled the thirteen colonies to revolt against British rule. To that end, the famous document contains long passages detailing the "abuses and usurpations" suffered by the colonies at the hands of King George III (1738–1820).

But the declaration, written by the brilliant Virginia delegate Thomas Jefferson (1743–1826), was more than a laundry list of complaints. It was also a taut philosophical argument against monarchy and in favor of republican government, which was still considered a radical and dangerous concept in the eighteenth century.

While most European nations at the time were still governed by autocratic monarchies, the Declaration of Independence made the then-controversial assertion that it was "self evident" that "all men are created equal." Every citizen, Jefferson wrote, has an equal right to "Life, Liberty, and the pursuit of Happiness."

Furthermore, Jefferson argued, only governments that protect those basic rights could be considered legitimate. If a government tramples individual rights, he wrote, "it is the right of the people to alter or abolish it." Based on this logic, the colonists declared they had a right and a duty—to overthrow the British.

Jefferson's eloquent words, which were heavily influenced by the English philosopher John Locke (1632–1704), have had enormous influence on American politics and society in the two centuries since the framing of the declaration. Although the Declaration of Independence is not a law, and its promises of "life, liberty, and the pursuit of happiness" have no legal force, to many Americans the declaration represents the ideological foundation of the American polity.

Indeed, while many of the particular grievances against Britain listed in the declaration have been forgotten, civil rights movements have continued to cite Jefferson's philosophical arguments to justify expansions of individual rights and liberties.

ADDITIONAL FACTS

1. *The original copy of the Declaration of Independence is now preserved in a fireproof vault at the National Archives building in Washington, DC.*

2. *Fifty-six men signed the Declaration of Independence, including two future US presidents: Jefferson and Massachusetts delegate John Adams (1735–1826).*

3. *In order to garner support from southern delegates, the declaration dropped denunciations of the king for allowing slavery that Jefferson had included in his original first draft.*

★ ★ ★

Lowell, Massachusetts

The city of Lowell, Massachusetts, was founded as a planned industrial community in 1826 and grew into one of the largest manufacturing cities in the United States in the decades before the Civil War (1861–1865). Internationally famous for its sprawling factories and employment of women laborers, Lowell in its heyday produced up to one-fifth of the nation's textiles.

After the opening of Slater's Mill in 1793, the Industrial Revolution had spread quickly across New England. A group of Boston businessmen, believing they could improve on Slater's model by creating a town entirely dedicated to manufacturing, began searching for a site in the 1810s. They picked Lowell for its proximity to a steep drop in the Merrimack River that provided ample hydropower.

At the time Lowell opened for business, its population was less than 2,500 people. Within twenty-five years, the city had grown to more than 33,000 and become the state's second-biggest city after Boston. Huge, redbrick factories stretched for almost a mile along the river, astonishing foreign visitors who hailed the city as a modern wonder of the world.

For workers at Lowell, hours were long, but conditions and pay often offered an appealing alternative to farm life. Unlike the first mill owners like Slater, who depended heavily on child labor, the Lowell owners recruited young, single women from rural New England to work at the looms. An early experiment in planned communities and social engineering, Lowell included churches, schools, a newspaper, and company boardinghouses specifically for workers.

Although the original workers at Lowell were mainly Yankee farm girls, the demographics of Lowell changed over the years as more immigrants arrived in the United States. The city lost business after the Civil War, and many of the mills became obsolete in the twentieth century. Today many of the gigantic mill buildings have been recycled for other uses, and the Lowell National Historical Park was created to commemorate America's foremost industrial center of the nineteenth century.

ADDITIONAL FACTS

1. *Beat generation author Jack Kerouac (1922–1969) was born in Lowell in 1922; one of his first novels,* The Town and the City *(1950), is partially about growing up in Lowell.*

2. *The typical workday at Lowell was from 4:50 a.m. to 7:00 p.m., with a few breaks for meals.*

3. *The city of Lowell was named after Francis Cabot Lowell (1775–1817), a Boston industrialist who died before the planned town opened.*

★ ★ ★

Northwest Ordinance

Under the terms of the Treaty of Paris, the peace treaty that ended the American Revolution in 1783, Great Britain ceded to the new United States huge tracts of land west of the Appalachian Mountains. At the time, this vast forested area— now the states of the American Midwest—was largely untouched by whites as a result of a deliberate British policy of restricting colonial expansion in North America. With the British suddenly gone, however, land-hungry Americans streamed into the Great Lakes region.

How to manage the sprawling "northwest territories" presented Congress with one of the most serious challenges of the 1780s. Several of the original thirteen states claimed portions of the land for themselves, based on their original royal grants. Massachusetts, for instance, dusted off its 1629 charter and declared that its western border was the Pacific Ocean. Connecticut, Virginia, and several other states also asserted claims to major swathes of the vast territory.

In 1787, in an effort to resolve the territorial disputes, Congress passed the Northwest Ordinance, one of the most crucial pieces of legislation in the history of the early Republic. Instead of adding land to existing states, Congress decreed, territories in the Northwest could join as completely new states, thus avoiding an endless argument over borders and setting an important legal precedent. The law also barred slavery in the entire region, ensuring that midwestern territories would enter the Union as free states.

By ending the debates over borders, the Northwest Ordinance removed a major source of tension among the thirteen original states. According to some historians, the goodwill generated by the law helped convince some states to ratify the new Constitution, which was written in Philadelphia the same year.

In the long term, the Northwest Ordinance had an unexpected impact on the slavery debate that its authors could not have foreseen. By outlawing slavery in the Midwest, Congress helped shift the long-term geographic balance of power against the institution. In the nineteenth century, six new free territories—Ohio, Indiana, Illinois, Michigan, Wisconsin, and Minnesota—were admitted into the Union as free states, adding to the strength of the antislavery bloc in Congress.

ADDITIONAL FACTS

1. *The law also required the territories to protect civil liberties, a provision that some scholars see as a forerunner to the Bill of Rights.*

2. *Connecticut did not give up its last claims to the vicinity of present-day Cleveland, Ohio, until 1800, a region briefly dubbed New Connecticut.*

3. *Even after the act, border disputes flared up occasionally in the Midwest; Michigan and Ohio nearly came to blows in 1835 for control of Toledo.*

★ ★ ★

Nathaniel Hawthorne

The bane of generations of high school English students, Nathaniel Hawthorne (1804–1864) wrote many of the most important American novels of the nineteenth century, including *The Scarlet Letter* (1850) and *The House of the Seven Gables* (1851). A key figure in the literary scene of his day, Hawthorne's novels and short stories, infused with the history of his native New England, influenced many contemporaries like Herman Melville (1819–1891) and Henry David Thoreau (1817–1862).

 Hawthorne was born in Salem, Massachusetts, and attended Bowdoin College, where his classmates included the poet Henry Wadsworth Longfellow (1807–1882) and future US president Franklin Pierce (1804–1869), who became a lifelong friend. Hawthorne graduated in the middle of his class and returned to Salem, where he began publishing short stories in local magazines. Several of his most well-known stories, including the dark tale "Young Goodman Brown," date from this early period in Hawthorne's career.

Despite the success of his stories, Hawthorne needed money, and so he took a job in 1846 as surveyor at the Custom House in Salem. The customhouse would provide a setting for his most well-known novel, *The Scarlet Letter*. Like "Young Goodman Brown," *The Scarlet Letter* is set in Puritan-era New England. It tells the story of a woman who gives birth to an illegitimate child and is forced to wear a scarlet *A* (for *adultery*) as punishment. Considered risqué when published in the mid-1800s, the book is now one of the standards of American literature.

Hawthorne was a friend to many leading literary figures of the 1840s and 1850s, including Melville, Thoreau, and Ralph Waldo Emerson (1803–1882), and is considered a key figure in New England transcendentalism. Although Hawthorne sympathized with the transcendentalists, he also wrote one of the most pointed satires of the movement, his comic 1852 novel *The Blithedale Romance*.

When Hawthorne's college pal Pierce ran for president in 1852, Hawthorne wrote the candidate's official campaign biography and was appointed to a diplomatic posting in England as a reward. Distracted by his diplomatic duties, Hawthorne would publish only one more novel, *The Marble Faun* (1860), during his lifetime. He died in 1864 while vacationing with Pierce in New Hampshire.

ADDITIONAL FACTS

1. *One of Hawthorne's ancestors was a judge at the Salem witch trials in 1692.*

2. *Hawthorne was so ashamed of the first novel he wrote,* Fanshawe *(1828), that he never publicly acknowledged his authorship.*

3. *The* House of the Seven Gables *was inspired by an actual house in Salem, Massachusetts, which was begun in 1668 and is now a museum open to the public.*

★ ★ ★

Winslow Homer

At the outbreak of the Civil War in 1861, *Harper's* magazine sent a twenty-five-year-old freelance illustrator to the front to sketch scenes from the battlefield. A precocious artist, Winslow Homer (1836–1910) traveled with the Union army for months, sending his powerful etchings of tired soldiers and bucking warhorses back to the magazine in New York. Homer's bold, dramatic Civil War drawings, published in the one of the era's most well-respected magazines, instantly established his national reputation.

Homer had moved to New York at age nineteen to seek his fame and fortune. After his war drawings in *Harper's* made him famous, however, Homer gradually gave up commercial illustration to concentrate on the watercolor paintings that would become his lasting legacy to American art.

In 1883, Homer left New York and moved to a lonely corner of Maine, where he would live for the rest of his life. The fishermen, driftwood, and storms of the rocky coastline area provided inspiration for some of Homer's best-known work. His maritime paintings of storm-battered shores conveyed the power and beauty of the sea, but also the awful fury of nature.

Homer was an artistic loner, and his distinctive style of painting does not fit easily into any category. Unlike the artists of the Hudson River school, Homer did not sentimentalize nature. And while he was familiar with French impressionism and had toured Europe, Homer's watercolors were distinctively American in their subject matter and forceful representation of the natural landscape.

During Homer's lifetime, his reputation was based largely on the Civil War illustrations he drew while still in his twenties. After his death, however, the watercolors of his beloved Maine shore emerged as extremely influential landmarks in the evolution of American art.

ADDITIONAL FACTS

1. *To support himself, Homer turned part of his Maine property into a resort, which is still in existence today.*

2. *Homer reportedly learned to draw by copying photographs, at the time a new and novel medium.*

3. *Many of his Civil War drawings can now be seen at the Cooper-Hewitt museum in New York City.*

★ ★ ★

Lord Dunmore

John Murray, also known as the fourth Earl of Dunmore (1732–1809), was the last British colonial governor of Virginia. A descendent of Scottish kings, Lord Dunmore was dispatched to the colonies in 1770, an appointment that was considered a plum assignment for a young British aristocrat at the time. During the governor's rocky tenure in Williamsburg, however, he clashed repeatedly with the colony's unruly legislature, the House of Burgesses. After the outbreak of war in 1775, Lord Dunmore unsuccessfully tried to suppress the rebellion by offering freedom to Virginia slaves who fought for the British, but he was defeated and forced to flee to England in 1776.

At the time of Lord Dunmore's arrival in Virginia, members of the House of Burgesses included brilliant patriot luminaries like Thomas Jefferson (1743–1826), Patrick Henry (1736–1799), and George Washington (1732–1799). The governor first tangled with this group of notables in 1773 and took the unpopular step of dissolving the house in 1774 after legislators proposed a day of fasting in solidarity with Boston after the British closed that city's port in retaliation for the Boston Tea Party.

In late 1774, Lord Dunmore led a successful expedition to the western frontier against the Shawnee Indians. However, by the time he returned to the capital, Virginia was in nearly open revolt against him. Henry, a constant thorn in the governor's side, gave his famous "give me liberty or give me death" speech on March 23, 1775. The Revolution began in Boston a few weeks later. Lord Dunmore, sensing it was unsafe for him to remain ashore, fled to a British warship off the Virginia coast that June.

From aboard the *Fowey,* Lord Dunmore made a famous and highly unusual proclamation. He offered to free any American slaves who joined the British army fighting the Revolution. The offer incensed Virginia slaveholders, but it was the first large-scale emancipation offered to slaves in the South. The earl, however, never made good on his promise, and was forced to leave Virginia for good in 1776.

ADDITIONAL FACTS

1. *In his native Scotland, Lord Dunmore may be best remembered for a bizarre building he constructed on his country estate in 1761, the so-called Dunmore Pineapple. The building features a cupola shaped like a pineapple, a fruit that was considered an extremely rare delicacy in the eighteenth century.*

2. *A county in northern Virginia was named in Lord Dunmore's honor in 1772 but was quickly renamed Shenandoah County during the Revolution.*

3. *After the colonials drove him out of Virginia, Lord Dunmore later served a more peaceful stint as British governor of the Bahamas from 1787 to 1796.*

★ ★ ★

Valley Forge

In December 1777, the exhausted army of General George Washington (1732–1799) arrived in the small town of Valley Forge, Pennsylvania. With the British occupying nearby Philadelphia, Washington picked the town, already under six inches of snow, for the army's winter quarters. The winter at Valley Forge proved hellish, the most difficult stretch of the war for Washington and his troops. As the British stayed warm and comfortable in Philadelphia, more than 2,000 of the approximately 10,000 American soldiers died from cold, disease, and hunger in the snows of Valley Forge.

The months at Valley Forge were, in the words of Thomas Paine (1737–1809), "times that try men's souls." Typhoid fever and pneumonia were rampant in the camps. The men lacked blankets, clothing, even shoes. Rather than face death and disease, many soldiers simply deserted—a fairly common problem in Washington's army.

However, the soldiers who survived Valley Forge emerged in 1778 as a hardened and battle ready force. A Prussian officer named Friedrich von Steuben (1730–1794) joined the army at Valley Forge and helped Washington impose discipline on the troops. As the snows melted, von Steuben drilled the army, molding them into a more professional force.

The army remained at Valley Forge into June 1778, when the British commander in Philadelphia suddenly decided to transfer his troops to New York. Washington's forces attacked the British columns at the Battle of Monmouth in central New Jersey. Although the battle was inconclusive, the results showed the value of von Steuben's drills. In open battle against the best troops of the British army, Washington's army held its own.

The awful months at Valley Forge represented the worst period of the war for Washington's troops but created an army that would eventually drive the British out of America.

ADDITIONAL FACTS

1. *Many men who would later become famous—or infamous—suffered through the winter at Valley Forge, including both Alexander Hamilton (1755–1804) and his eventual killer, Aaron Burr (1756–1836).*

2. *Historians believe that the hardships of American soldiers at Valley Forge were partly caused by the greedy profiteering of Pennsylvania farmers, who sold their crops to the British at Philadelphia instead of to Washington's army.*

3. *Washington's army at Valley Forge was multiracial, including freed slaves and a handful of Oneida Indians. Washington had openly disobeyed the Continental Congress by allowing black soldiers to reenlist.*

★ ★ ★

Three-Fifths Compromise

At the Constitutional Convention in Philadelphia in 1787, the framers struggled to reach consensus on the contentious issue of slavery. Although declining in the North and regarded as a moral evil by many of the delegates, slavery was a major part of the South's economy, and Southern representatives at the convention insisted on protecting their "peculiar institution."

Eventually, rather than allowing disputes over slavery to derail the whole convention, the framers made the fateful decision to set the whole issue aside for future generations. Instead of banning the slave trade, as many delegates had hoped, the delegates wrote a clause into the document allowing Congress to outlaw the practice—but not until 1808.

The delegates also faced a related question: Would slaves count as people in determining the number of seats each state received in the new House of Representatives? Southerners, not surprisingly, wanted representation based on their total population, which would have increased their influence in the House. Northern delegates objected, arguing that if slaves were not to be treated as citizens, why should they have representation in Congress?

After heated argument, the delegates agreed on the notorious three-fifths compromise. For the purposes of congressional representation, the compromise said, a slave would count as three-fifths of a person. A million slaves, in other words, would count as 600,000 people under the formula.

In the short term, the three-fifths compromise made the Constitution possible. In the long term, by dealing so inconclusively with the slavery issue, the framers planted the seeds of the Civil War (1861–1865). The compromise also had the effect of giving Southern whites hugely disproportionate power in early Congresses, which they used to fend off challenges to slavery. And in the eyes of abolitionists, the tacit acceptance of slavery by the delegates in Philadelphia made the North complicit in Southern slavery.

ADDITIONAL FACTS

1. *The three-fifths compromise was officially repealed by the Fourteenth Amendment to the Constitution, which based congressional representation on the total number of citizens in a state.*

2. *The compromise was proposed by Pennsylvania delegate James Wilson (1742–1798), who later became one of the original Supreme Court justices appointed by President George Washington (1732–1799).*

3. *Several ratios were considered before the delegates agreed on three-fifths.*

★ ★ ★

Whaling

Whale hunting was one of the most important parts of the economy before the Civil War (1861–1865), with more than 700 ships from American ports sailing the Atlantic and Pacific oceans in search of right whales and sperm whales. Whaling expeditions often lasted years, and a single tall-masted ship might catch hundreds of the giant mammals. Once a whale was harpooned, its blubber was boiled down to produce oil, which was prized in nineteenth-century America as a source of fuel for lamps. The whale's bones, meanwhile, were used as a component in buggy whips, umbrellas, and certain kinds of women's clothing.

In the early nineteenth century, the major centers of American whaling were New Bedford, Massachusetts; the island of Nantucket; and New London, Connecticut. Later, after the Civil War, the industry migrated to San Francisco. Crews aboard American whaling ships tended to be international in nature, with Africans, Asians, and Caribbean Islanders joining American-born sailors; a high percentage of these ships' crew members emigrated from the small African island nation of Cape Verde.

Even during its heyday, whalers enjoyed a reputation as romantic adventurers on the high seas. In *Moby-Dick* (1851), the most famous whaling novel, Herman Melville (1819–1891) observed that "scores of green Vermonters and New Hampshire men" poured into the whaling ports of Massachusetts in the mid-nineteenth century, "all athirst for gain and glory." The grueling routine of life at sea, however, was hardly romantic.

The tapping of oil in Pennsylvania in 1859 and the start of the Civil War dealt a serious blow to the whaling industry. During the war, dozens of Union whaling ships were sunk by the Confederacy. Although the whale fishery resumed after the war, it never regained either its economic prominence or its place in the national consciousness. The last whaling ship sailed out of New Bedford in 1924. To protect endangered species, whaling is now illegal in the United States, but the rich cultural heritage of the whaling fleet remains central to American literature.

ADDITIONAL FACTS

1. *In recognition of its importance to the state's economy in the nineteenth century, the sperm whale is the state animal of Connecticut.*

2. *Art made from whale bones is called* scrimshaw, *and a scrimshaw artist is referred to as a* scrimshander.

3. *A whale yielded an array of products, including ambergris, a substance from its intestine that was treasured as a source of perfume. In* Moby-Dick, *Melville noted the irony of rich Americans spritzing themselves with whale guts: "Who would think, then, that such fine ladies and gentlemen should regale themselves with an essence found in the inglorious bowels of a sick whale!"*

★ ★ ★

Louisiana Purchase

President Thomas Jefferson's purchase of the Louisiana Territory from France in 1803 nearly doubled the size of the United States. For the bargain price of $15 million, Jefferson (1743–1826) purchased 800,000 square miles of land stretching from New Orleans to the foothills of the Rocky Mountains. About one-quarter of the current United States, including all or part of fifteen states, joined the nation as a result of the deal with the French ruler Napoleon Bonaparte (1769–1821).

Originally, the diplomats Jefferson sent to Paris in 1803 wanted to buy only the key city of New Orleans in order to protect American shipping on the Mississippi River. Napoleon, however, had other ideas. The soon-to-be emperor insisted on including the rest of France's territory in North America as well, famously declaring, "I renounce Louisiana." At the time, Napoleon was planning war with Great Britain, and he needed the proceeds from the sale of Louisiana to finance his army.

For Jefferson, the treaty with France presented a personal and political dilemma. During the 1790s, Jefferson had been a scathing critic of the expansion of the government's power under the presidency of George Washington (1732–1799), but the Louisiana Purchase would be the most brazen application of federal power yet. Many critics considered the deal illegal, since the Constitution did not give the government the authority to acquire new territory. In the end, however, Jefferson decided the opportunity was simply too good to allow principle to get in his way. Setting aside his own scruples, Jefferson sent the treaty to Congress, where it was approved in the fall of 1803.

The Louisiana Purchase was the first major territorial expansion in American history, and it set a fateful precedent. To an American at the time of the Revolution, it was neither obvious nor necessarily desirable that the country would expand at all—much less reach the shores of the Pacific Ocean. But in the nineteenth century, in the wake of the Louisiana Purchase, the nation began to look increasingly westward. The dream of "manifest destiny" took hold among many Americans and helped drive the waves of territorial purchase and conquest that would build the modern United States.

ADDITIONAL FACTS

1. *One of Jefferson's diplomats in Paris was James Monroe (1758–1831), later the fifth president of the United States.*

2. *The deal with Napoleon was opposed by the leaders of the Federalist Party, who feared it would alienate the British.*

3. *Louisiana was actually owned by Spain at the time Napoleon negotiated the treaty with Monroe. However, the Spanish had already agreed to relinquish control to France later in 1803.*

★ ★ ★

Henry Wadsworth Longfellow

Among the most popular American literati of the nineteenth century, Henry Wadsworth Longfellow (1807–1882) wrote many of the classics of the American canon, including his famous poem "Paul Revere's Ride." Longfellow's poetry expressed the nationalism and optimism of his age and helped create the self-image of the United States as a beacon for freedom and tolerance in the world.

Longfellow was born in Portland, Maine, and attended Bowdoin College, where he befriended the novelist Nathaniel Hawthorne (1804–1864). Longfellow traveled widely in Europe in the 1820s and 1830s and was appointed to a Harvard professorship of modern languages in 1836. Longfellow began writing poetry after moving to Cambridge, and he published one of his best-known epic poems, *Evangeline: A Tale of Acadie,* in 1847. The poem tells the story of the Acadians, a group of French-speaking Canadians who were expelled from Nova Scotia in 1755 by the British and found refuge in Louisiana.

Other works by Longfellow included *The Song of Hiawatha* (1855) and *The Courtship of Miles Standish* (1858). Like *Evangeline,* these long poems were accounts based loosely on actual episodes from American history, burnished into patriotic myth.

His most well-known historical poem, "Paul Revere's Ride," was first published in 1860, on the eve of the Civil War (1861–1865). Although the poem is based on the real events preceding the Battles of Lexington and Concord in 1775, it severely exaggerates the role of Boston silversmith Paul Revere (1734–1818). Still, to a nation thirsty for heroes at the beginning of the Civil War, the poem was an instant hit. Its opening lines are among the most famous in all of American verse:

> Listen, my children, and you shall hear
> Of the midnight ride of Paul Revere,
> On the eighteenth of April, in Seventy-five;
> Hardly a man is now alive
> Who remembers that famous day and year.

Although based only very loosely on the facts, Longfellow's poems struck a nerve with the American public and have remained popular ever since.

ADDITIONAL FACTS

1. *Longfellow was the first American translator of Dante's* Divine Comedy.

2. *Longfellow's son, Charley, ran away from home to join the Union army in 1863 against his father's orders.*

3. *Longfellow was traumatized by the death of his wife, who accidentally set herself on fire at their Cambridge home in 1861. Longfellow was injured trying to put out the flames and later wrote, "how I am alive after what my eyes have seen, I know not."*

★ ★ ★

Thomas Nast

The most famous and influential cartoonist of American journalistic history, Thomas Nast (1840–1902) lampooned the rich and powerful of the nineteenth-century United States and popularized the Democratic donkey and the Republican elephant still used to symbolize the two major American political parties.

Born in Germany, Nast immigrated to the United States in 1846 with his mother, settling in New York City. Ironically, despite his own foreign background, anti-immigrant stereotypes would form a large part of Nast's later work.

After briefly attending art school, Nast began working during the Civil War (1861–1865) at *Harper's*, the same prestigious magazine that also employed the young Winslow Homer. An ardent Republican and supporter of President Abraham Lincoln (1809–1865), during the war Nast drew cartoons attacking slavery and the copperhead Democrats who favored negotiating a peace settlement with the Confederacy.

Nast achieved his lasting fame after the war, however, with his caricatures of Boss Tweed. Nast depicted Tweed, the head of New York's corrupt Tammany Hall political organization and a behind-the-scenes power broker in city politics, as fat and greedy. Published in *Harper's* between 1869 and 1871, Nast's cartoons are widely credited with bringing down the Tammany organization.

The Tammany cartoons, however, also exposed Nast's darker side. The Tweed ring derived much of its support from newly arrived immigrants, especially the Irish, and Nast blamed the Irish as a whole for the ring's crimes. In his cartoons, Nast often portrayed Irishmen as apes, a testament to the deep ethnic prejudices of nineteenth-century America.

In recognition of his services to the Republican Party, President Theodore Roosevelt in 1902 appointed Nast to a diplomatic posting in Guayaquil, Ecuador, where he died shortly thereafter in a yellow fever outbreak.

ADDITIONAL FACTS

1. *In 1862, Nast drew the first version of the modern American depiction of Santa Claus, an image that contributed to the commercialization of the once-religious holiday in the late 1800s.*

2. *Nast chose the elephant to represent the Republican Party for its size, strength, and intelligence, in implicit contrast to the Democratic jackass.*

3. *Nast is buried at Woodlawn Cemetery in Brooklyn, a massive graveyard that is also home to the remains of author Herman Melville (1819–1891), jazz trumpeter Miles Davis (1926–1991), and composer Irving Berlin (1888–1989).*

★ ★ ★

Constitutional Convention

The United States Constitution was written over the summer of 1787 at a convention in Philadelphia. Fifty-five delegates from twelve states eventually signed the document that created the modern American government, but its main author was Virginia delegate James Madison (1751–1836), who later became the nation's fourth president. Madison's plan created the basic institutions of American government—the Supreme Court, the US Congress, and the presidency—that have remained essentially unchanged ever since.

By the time the delegates gathered in Philadelphia, it had become painfully clear to many Americans that the national government created during the Revolution was utterly dysfunctional. Under the Articles of Confederation adopted in 1777, the government lacked the authority to collect taxes. It also granted each of the thirteen states an equal say in national policy, which bigger states like Virginia and New York considered grossly unfair.

Small states, while aware of the iniquities in the Articles of Confederation, were wary of ceding too much power to their neighbors. Indeed, the smallest of the thirteen, Rhode Island, refused to even participate in the convention. Eventually, a delegate from medium-size Connecticut, Roger Sherman (1721–1793), proposed his famous compromise: the new Constitution would create a House of Representatives, where seats would be allotted by population, and a Senate, where each state would have equal representation.

The so-called Connecticut compromise removed the greatest obstacle to the success of the convention. Still, many contentious questions remained for the delegates, including the thorny issue of slavery. The debates over slavery eventually resulted in the three-fifths compromise, which stated that a nonfree person would be considered three-fifths of a person for tax reasons and in determining representation in Congress. Barricading themselves in Independence Hall, the delegates sweated through the hot Philadelphia summer until finally agreeing to the final draft in September. After a public relations blitz orchestrated by Madison and Alexander Hamilton (1755–1804), the required number of states ratified the document and it went into effect in 1789.

ADDITIONAL FACTS

1. *The state of Rhode Island boycotted the Philadelphia convention and was the last of the thirteen states to ratify the new Constitution.*

2. *After the ratification of the Constitution, Sherman was elected to the First Congress but also continued to serve as mayor of New Haven at the same time.*

3. *Delaware was the first state to ratify the Constitution on December 7, 1787; Pennsylvania and New Jersey followed suit later that month.*

* * *

Benedict Arnold

The American general Benedict Arnold (1741–1801) acquired eternal infamy by betraying his compatriots during the Revolution and joining the British. Arnold, a Connecticut native, believed that he should have earned a promotion and more of the glory for his role in the American victory at the Battle of Saratoga in 1777. Disgruntled by his treatment in the patriot army and deeply in debt, Arnold negotiated a secret deal with the British in 1781 to switch sides in exchange for the enormous sum of £20,000.

Arnold's betrayal shocked his former comrades. When the Revolution broke out, Arnold had joined the fight with gusto, leading the first Connecticut regiment to enter the war. He fought bravely with the Green Mountain Boys in Vermont and New York, participating in the seizure of Fort Ticonderoga, a British outpost on Lake Champlain, in 1775. His heroism at the Battle of Saratoga, although it did not win him the promotion he thought he deserved, was widely praised.

The secret plot that Arnold hatched with the British could have turned the tide of the war. In exchange for the cash, Arnold promised to hand over the key Hudson River fort of West Point to British forces. However, Arnold's plot was discovered, and as a result he never got the full £20,000 he had been promised.

After switching sides, Arnold received a command in the British army. In 1781, now in the red uniform of a British officer, he led raids on the Connecticut coastline, pillaging his own home turf.

After the Revolution, Arnold became a kind of founding national villain, and his name continues to be used as a synonym for *traitor*. The legacy of his treason against the United States at a time of war, in the eyes of most historians, far outweighs his earlier military contributions to the patriot cause.

ADDITIONAL FACTS

1. *Arnold's heroism at the Battle of Saratoga happened despite orders from his annoyed superiors that he not leave his quarters.*

2. *The British agent who arranged Arnold's betrayal, Major John André, was captured by the Americans and hanged in 1780. His remains were eventually returned to Britain, where he was reburied as a hero in Westminster Abbey.*

3. *Having backed the losing side in the war, Arnold ended up in London, where he died debt-ridden and disgraced in 1801 at the age of sixty.*

* * *

Bill of Rights

Shortly after the ratification of the United States Constitution in 1789, Congress added ten amendments to the document guaranteeing American citizens a long list of basic rights and liberties. The Bill of Rights, as it became known, was written largely by James Madison (1751–1836) to address the concerns of many Americans that the original Constitution, as written at the 1787 Philadelphia convention, did not explicitly protect individual liberties.

The Bill of Rights defined the basic legal protections for American citizens, including:

★ The right to free speech
★ Freedom of religion
★ The right to bear arms
★ Protection from unreasonable search and seizure by the government
★ Trial by jury
★ Freedom from cruel or unusual punishment

Ratification of the ten amendments was swift, although some Americans, including Alexander Hamilton (1755–1804), argued that they were unnecessary. With ratification by three-fourths of the states, the Bill of Rights became official in 1791.

Initially, the amendments applied only to the federal government, and individual states could still restrict individual liberties if they wished. For instance, in Massachusetts, Congregationalist churches were supported by taxpayers until the nineteenth century, even though the Bill of Rights forbade "an establishment of religion."

Over time, however, and especially after the passage of the Fourteenth Amendment to the Constitution in 1868, the Supreme Court has ruled that individual states also must abide by most provisions of the Bill of Rights. Madison's ten short amendments now form the bedrock of American civil rights.

ADDITIONAL FACTS

1. *The absence of a bill of rights in the original Constitution was a major reason anti-Federalists like Patrick Henry (1736–1799) opposed its ratification.*

2. *Vermont and Kentucky became the fourteenth and fifteenth states to join the Union in the midst of the ratification process. Both approved the Bill of Rights.*

3. *In 1987, historians uncovered a handwritten draft of the Bill of Rights by Roger Sherman (1721–1793), the father of the Connecticut Compromise. It was Sherman who proposed adding the Bill of Rights as amendments to the Constitution rather than trying to rewrite the text of the original document at the last minute.*

★ ★ ★

Tariff

For most of the nineteenth century, the single biggest source of revenue for the United States government was the tariff, a tax on foreign products imported from abroad. All cloth, iron, and agricultural goods unloaded at American ports were subject to the tariff, which sometimes exceeded 50 percent of the underlying value of the import. How high to raise the tax was the single most divisive economic issue of the early nineteenth century, and disagreements over the tariff triggered one of the country's gravest political crises in the era before the Civil War (1861–1865).

The Constitution approved in 1789 gave Congress the power to impose a tariff, but political leaders immediately disagreed over how high the rate should be pegged. Many Southerners wanted the tariff set as low as possible—just enough to fund the government. Their objection was partly ideological and partly out of self-interest: the Southern economy was dependent on selling raw cotton to British textile mills, and the powerful cotton producers did not want a tax in place that would discourage trade with Britain.

In the North, however, the tariff was regarded not just as a source of revenue for the government but also as an economic tool to protect fledgling northern industries from European competition. In the early years of the Industrial Revolution, politicians in the North were concerned that without the protection of the tariff, their markets would be swamped with cheap European goods. A high tariff was a key part of the American System envisioned by senator and Whig Party member Henry Clay (1777–1852) to encourage the growth of domestic industry.

The controversy reached a peak in 1828, after Whigs in Congress imposed a particularly high rate known as the Tariff of Abominations. Southerners were outraged. Led by John C. Calhoun (1782–1850), the state of South Carolina refused to obey the law, prompting the "nullification crisis" that ended only when Congress gave President Andrew Jackson (1767–1845) the power, in 1833, to enforce the tariff by military force.

In the early twentieth century, the income tax replaced the tariff as the biggest source of federal revenue. However, the dispute between advocates of free trade and protectionism remains a perennial political issue in national elections.

ADDITIONAL FACTS

1. *In the nineteenth century, as today, politicians frequently switched sides on the tariff issue. During the War of 1812, Daniel Webster (1782–1852) opposed a high tariff while Calhoun supported it; in the 1830s, they had reversed positions and argued strongly against their old views.*

2. *Most of the tariff disputes involved trade with Great Britain, which was the biggest trading partner of the United States in the early nineteenth century.*

3. *The nullification crisis is seen as a precursor to the Civil War, and it caused the first open discussions of secession in states of the future Confederacy.*

★ ★ ★

Lewis and Clark Expedition

After acquiring the Louisiana Purchase from France in 1803, President Thomas Jefferson (1743–1826) dispatched army officers Meriwether Lewis (1774–1809) and William Clark (1770–1838) to chart the vast new territory. The three-year Lewis and Clark expedition, one of the most famous exploits in the history of American exploration, traversed thousands of miles of rugged wilderness and marked one of the first steps in the nation's westward expansion.

Lewis, the main organizer of the expedition, was the son of a Continental army officer who had died during the Revolution. The young Lewis joined the army at age twenty, served on the frontier, and was eventually appointed Jefferson's secretary. Impressed by the young officer's courage and knowledge of Native Americans, Jefferson selected Lewis to lead the Louisiana expedition. Lewis, in turn, picked Clark as his cocaptain.

The purpose of the Lewis and Clark expedition was partly geographical and partly political. Jefferson wanted the two men to search for a (nonexistent, as it turned out) all-water route to the Pacific Ocean that would be suitable for commerce, and also to establish contact with Native American tribes in the interior. On the expedition, Clark took charge of mapping their progress while Lewis handled the diplomatic tasks and catalogued the strange plants and animals encountered by the men.

Along with their thirty-three-man crew, dubbed the Corps of Discovery by historians, Lewis and Clark followed a route that began in St. Louis, Missouri, and followed the Missouri River north to its headwaters in Montana. From there, they crossed the Rocky Mountains into present-day Idaho, Washington, and Oregon. The group finally reached the Pacific Ocean. Clark's journal entry for November 7, 1805, captures the exhilaration of the moment: "Great joy in camp we are in View of the Ocian, this great Pacific Octean which we been So long anxious to See. and the roreing or noise made by the waves breaking on the rockey Shores (as I Suppose) may be heard distictly. Ocian in View! O! the joy."

ADDITIONAL FACTS

1. *Lewis committed suicide in 1809.*

2. *Clark's older brother, George Rogers Clark (1752–1818), was a Revolutionary war hero and frontiersman who helped pry the Northwest Territory away from the British.*

3. *Although he had been promised a promotion in exchange for participating in the expedition, Clark was not promoted to captain until 2001—posthumously, of course.*

★ ★ ★

Henry David Thoreau

The most well-known book by Henry David Thoreau (1817–1862) is *Walden*, published in 1854, a chronicle of the writer's experiment living a simple life in the woods next to Walden Pond in Massachusetts. Thoreau moved to his hut at Walden on Independence Day of 1845 and lived there intermittently for the next two years. Separated from mainstream society, Thoreau wrote a searing cultural critique, decrying the monotony and soul-crushing routine that he believed characterized American life in the nineteenth century. "The mass of men," he famously wrote from his perch in the forest, "lead lives of quiet desperation."

Nature, politics, and the individual's relationship to society were recurring themes in Thoreau's writing. In addition to *Walden,* Thoreau is well known for his fiery essay "Civil Disobedience" (1849), which argued that an individual has both the right and the responsibility to defy unjust laws. Thoreau wrote the essay after he was thrown in prison for refusing to pay taxes to support the Mexican War (1846–1848), a conflict that he considered unjust.

> Must the citizen ever for a moment, or in the least degree, resign his conscience to the legislator? Why has every man a conscience, then? I think that we should be men first, and subjects afterward. It is not desirable to cultivate a respect for the law, so much as for the right.

In the twentieth century, Thoreau's meditation on the rights and power of the individual would be a source of inspiration for the Indian nationalist Mohandas K. Gandhi (1869–1948) and the American civil rights leader Martin Luther King Jr. (1929–1968), who wrote that he was "fascinated by the idea of refusing to cooperate with an evil system" that he found in Thoreau's writings.

At the time, however, the publication of "Civil Disobedience" and *Walden* brought Thoreau little income, and he struggled to support himself with his nature writing. A lifelong opponent of slavery, Thoreau became one of the few public supporters of the controversial antislavery militant John Brown (1800–1859) and gave a speech titled "A Plea for Captain John Brown" before Brown's execution in 1859. Thoreau's health collapsed after a bout of tuberculosis, and he died at age forty-four after several years of sickness.

ADDITIONAL FACTS

1. *Thoreau is buried at Sleepy Hollow Cemetery in Concord, Massachusetts, in a section of the graveyard referred to as Authors' Ridge because so many other great writers, including Ralph Waldo Emerson (1803–1882) and Nathaniel Hawthorne (1804–1864), are also interred there.*

2. *To make ends meet, Thoreau worked at his family's pencil factory on and off for much of his life.*

3. *Thoreau's Walden hideaway was built on land owned by Emerson, his friend and mentor.*

★ ★ ★

Statue of Liberty

"Give me your tired, your poor,
Your huddled masses yearning to breathe free,
The wretched refuse of your teeming shore;
Send these, the homeless, tempest-tost to me,
I lift my lamp beside the golden door!"

—Plaque on the pedestal of the Statue of Liberty

The most famous monument in American history, the Statue of Liberty was built by France and dedicated in 1886 as a gift of friendship to the United States. Erected on an island in New York Harbor at enormous cost, the 305-foot copper colossus has greeted generations of immigrants arriving in the United States seeking a better life and the promise of freedom.

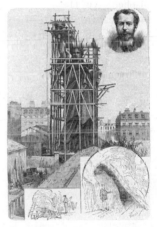

Designed by the French sculptor Frédéric-Auguste Bartholdi (1834–1904), the Statue of Liberty took ten years to build. Bartholdi based his idea on the Colossus of Rhodes, a giant statue in Greece that was one of the Seven Wonders of the World before its destruction in an earthquake in 226 BC. Bartholdi raised private donations from French citizens to build the statue, which was originally intended to commemorate French assistance during the American Revolution.

To make the statue structurally sound, Bartholdi enlisted the help of French engineer Alexandre Gustave Eiffel (1832–1923), the same architect who later built the famous Eiffel Tower in Paris. Eiffel designed Lady Liberty's "skeleton," a system of steel girders that keeps the thin copper shell in place. Bartholdi and Eiffel also built a smaller replica that stands in Paris.

Immediately hailed as a national landmark after its opening, the Statue of Liberty suffered gradual damage as its fragile copper shell deteriorated throughout the twentieth century. A major renovation in the 1980s restored the colossus. The statue reopened in 1986 to national fanfare. Sadly, the inside of the statue has been closed to visitors since the September 11, 2001, terrorist attacks in New York City.

ADDITIONAL FACTS

1. *The statue's official name is* La liberté éclairant le monde, *or Liberty Enlightening the World.*

2. *Liberty Island was named Bedloe's Island until 1956, when the name was officially changed.*

3. *The gold-plated torch held aloft in the statue's hand has an open-air platform that was originally open to visitors, but it was closed in 1916.*

★ ★ ★

First Presidency

In August 1788, the happily retired George Washington (1732–1799) received a letter at his sprawling estate of Mount Vernon from an old war buddy, Alexander Hamilton (1755–1804). In the letter, Hamilton politely urged Washington to accept the office of the United States presidency. For the newly formed government to succeed, Hamilton wrote, it needed a strong and respected leader, and the great war hero from Virginia was the natural choice. "I take it for granted, Sir, you have concluded to comply with what will no doubt be the general call of your country in relation to the new government," Hamilton wrote.

Washington, however had little interest in returning to power, and in his reply to Hamilton, he expressed his ambivalence about the presidency. In the five years since resigning from the army, Washington had been content to tend his fields at Mount Vernon, playing little role in the government. Although he served as the titular president of the 1787 Constitutional Convention in Philadelphia, Washington did not play a significant part in the deliberations that created the new system of government. "My great and sole desire," Washington wrote to Hamilton a few days after receiving the letter, was "to live and die, in peace and retirement on my own farm."

Eventually, however, after several more pestering letters to Mount Vernon, Hamilton finally prevailed on Washington to accept the office. In 1789, Washington rode to the national capital, then located in New York, where he took the oath of office on a balcony overlooking Wall Street.

The creation of a presidency by the new Constitution had been controversial in the thirteen states. Many Americans, such as the Virginia patriot leader Patrick Henry (1736–1799), feared it would simply turn into a new kind of monarchy. To assuage their fears, Washington deliberately avoided the sort of ostentatious displays of power associated with European crowns. He insisted on the modest, democratic title of "Mr. President" instead of "His Majesty." He wore ordinary civilian clothes rather than a military uniform. Most important, Washington left office voluntarily after two four-year terms, a precedent observed until 1940.

ADDITIONAL FACTS

1. *In the election of 1789—largely a formality, since the whole country backed Washington—North Carolina and Rhode Island did not participate because they had not formally joined the Union yet by ratifying the Constitution.*

2. *Washington's inauguration, scheduled for March 4, 1789, was delayed by several weeks because the House and Senate lacked a quorum.*

3. *Washington gave the shortest inaugural address on record, a mere 133 words, at his second inauguration in 1793.*

* * *

Shays's Rebellion and Whiskey Rebellion

Burdened by crushing war debts from the American Revolution, the now-independent state of Massachusetts was forced to impose heavy taxes on its citizens after the war. Farmers in the central part of the state revolted in protest, leading to a small uprising called Shays's Rebellion (1786–1787). Under the direction of Daniel Shays (c. 1747–1825), a Revolutionary War veteran, the farmers seized the armory in Springfield, Massachusetts, before the state militia put down the rebellion and executed several of the conspirators.

Although suppressed relatively quickly, Shays's Rebellion exposed the impotence of the American government under the old Articles of Confederation. The national government had been a mere spectator in the rebellion, which had been stopped entirely with Massachusetts state militia. From his home at Mount Vernon, George Washington (1732–1799) was appalled that a small gang of Massachusetts farmers could threaten the country he had fought to establish. Shays's Rebellion provided added urgency for the delegates who met in Philadelphia later in 1787 to replace the Articles of Confederation with a stronger central government under a new Constitution.

When the Whiskey Rebellion broke out in western Pennsylvania in 1794, Washington was determined to show that the new federal government could now defend itself. Like the revolt in Massachusetts, the Whiskey Rebellion arose from opposition to taxes, this time a nine-cents-a-gallon levy on whiskey producers.

As president, Washington assembled a huge army of 13,000 soldiers to suppress the revolt. By the time this massive force arrived in Pennsylvania, the rebels had dispersed. The army managed to locate two conspirators and they were tried and condemned to death for treason, but Washington pardoned both.

The distinct contrast between the national government's meek response to Shays's Rebellion in 1786 and its zealous suppression of the Whiskey Rebellion in 1794 showed that under the new Constitution, the federal government had both the power and the will to protect itself.

ADDITIONAL FACTS

1. *The army of 13,000 soldiers dispatched to quell the Whiskey Rebellion was derisively referred to as the "watermelon army" for the supposedly untrained New Jerseyans in the force.*

2. *At the time of Shays's Rebellion, the national capital was in New York. Before permanently settling in the new city of Washington, DC, the capital had also been located in Philadelphia; Annapolis, Maryland; Trenton, New Jersey; and Princeton, New Jersey.*

3. *After his revolt was quashed, Shays fled to Vermont, which was an independent republic until it joined the Union in 1791.*

★ ★ ★

Washington's Letter on Toleration

In August 1790, President George Washington (1732–1799) wrote a letter to the Jewish congregation of about 300 members in Newport, Rhode Island. Washington had a personal connection to the congregation and had visited their synagogue during the Revolution. His letter—written in uncharacteristically eloquent language for Washington—promised Rhode Island's small Jewish community that the newly formed government of the United States would treat Jews no differently than other Americans.

> The citizens of the United States of America have a right to applaud themselves for having given to mankind examples of an enlarged and liberal policy— a policy worthy of imitation. All possess alike liberty of conscience and immunities of citizenship.
>
> It is now no more that toleration is spoken of as if it were the indulgence of one class of people that another enjoyed the exercise of their inherent natural rights, for, happily, the Government of the United States, which gives to bigotry no sanction, to persecution no assistance, requires only that they who live under its protection should demean themselves as good citizens in giving it on all occasions their effectual support.

Washington's famous letter, and its promise to give "bigotry no sanction," has historical significance in both the American and global contexts. In the late eighteenth century, persecution of Jewish communities was the norm in most European countries. Virtually no other leader could have guaranteed the "enlarged and liberal policy" towards Jews promised by Washington.

The letter was also significant because it expanded the American definition of "religious toleration" to include non-Christians. For even the most open-minded colonial settlers, religious toleration meant only a respect for the differences between different versions of Christianity. Their understanding of toleration rarely extended to Native American religions, Judaism, or other non-Christian denominations.

Like Jefferson's letter to the Danbury Baptists, which was written about a decade later, Washington's letter to Newport's Jewish community became a key document in the evolution of modern American concepts of religious tolerance.

ADDITIONAL FACTS

1. *Rhode Island was the destination for the first Jewish immigrants to America in the 1650s, described in Henry Wordsworth Longfellow's poem "The Jewish Cemetery at Newport."*

2. *The center of the Jewish community in Newport, Touro Synagogue, was completed in 1762 and is now the oldest synagogue in the nation.*

3. *Washington's statement came in response to a letter from Moses Seixas, the warden of the congregation, who had written to the president earlier that summer congratulating Washington on his election.*

★ ★ ★

Panic of 1837

The panic of 1837 was a devastating economic crisis triggered by a sudden shortage of gold and silver at American banks. The panic cast the banking system into disarray, and the resulting turmoil soon rippled across the national economy. Thousands of businesses were destroyed during the panic, which did not lift until the 1840s.

The panic had its roots in the metals-based currency system of the nineteenth century. By law, only gold and silver coins were officially recognized as money. However, the two precious metals were rare, and relatively few coins were produced at the government's mint in Philadelphia.

Instead, many Americans used paper money issued by private banks. Unlike today, when only the United States government prints paper money, many individual banks in the 1830s issued their own notes.

In theory, private banknotes were redeemable in gold or silver at the institution that issued them. In practice, however, most banks printed much more currency than they could actually back up. Initially, the resulting flood of "soft" money provided a major economic stimulus, fueling the construction of railroads, canals, and factories in the 1830s.

However, President Andrew Jackson (1767–1845) distrusted banks and paper money and regarded the whole arrangement as a scam. In 1836, his administration issued an order instructing federal agents to refuse banknotes and accept payment for federal land only in "hard" money—gold or silver. In effect, with a stroke of the pen, Jackson declared the paper money used by most Americans worthless. Predictably, many rushed to their bank to trade in paper money for gold and silver, provoking a shortage that overwhelmed the banking system early in the presidency of Martin van Buren (1782–1862). Van Buren refused to intervene in the crisis and was punished at the polls in 1840 when William Henry Harrison (1773–1841) defeated him in his bid for a second term.

ADDITIONAL FACTS

1. *In economic parlance, when gold and silver are used as currency, they are referred to as* specie—*from the Latin in kind. Thus, Jackson's 1836 order was known as the* specie circular.

2. *The crisis was exacerbated by the lack of a federal bank, which might have lent money to the insolvent private banks; Jackson had taken away its charter in 1836.*

3. *The specie circular was rescinded in 1838, but the effects of the panic did not lift until after van Buren's defeat.*

★ ★ ★

Mississippi River

For most of the nation's history, the Mississippi River has been the most economically important waterway in the United States, stretching about 2,320 miles from the Midwest to the Gulf of Mexico. If its main tributary, the Missouri River, is included, the Mississippi is the third-longest river in the world, trailing only the Nile and the Amazon. Thanks to its size and historical importance, "Old Man River" also looms large in American literature, culture, and music.

Acquiring control over the Mississippi was a key goal of President Thomas Jefferson (1743–1826) when he authorized American diplomats to buy the Louisiana Territory from France in 1803. American farmers wanted safe access to the river to ship their goods to New Orleans and from there onward to Europe. Steamboats, which were first built in the United States in 1809, made river navigation easier and replaced hand-powered keelboats as the main form of transportation on the Mississippi in the early nineteenth century. During the Civil War, the Battle of Vicksburg in 1863 delivered control of the Mississippi to the Union, a key victory that split the Confederacy in two.

The lore of the Mississippi owes much to one of the steamboat pilots, Samuel Clemens. Writing under the pseudonym Mark Twain, Clemens (1835–1910) set many of his tales along the river, including his most famous work, *The Adventures of Huckleberry Finn* (1884). The river also figures prominently in the blues, a musical style that developed in the Mississippi Delta region. River commerce is still a major source of traffic on the Mississippi and, measured in tons of goods, New Orleans remains one of the busiest ports in the world.

ADDITIONAL FACTS

1. *Spanish explorer Hernando De Soto (c. 1500–1542) was the first European to discover the Mississippi in 1541.*

2. *The first steamboat to travel the Mississippi was the New Orleans, which was built in Pittsburgh in 1811 and cost $40,000.*

3. *Although up to four miles wide in some sections, most of the Mississippi is less than ten feet deep.*

★ ★ ★

Moby-Dick

When it was first published in 1851, the novel *Moby-Dick or, The Whale* by Herman Melville (1819–1891) disappointed many of the author's fans. Unlike his previous works, swashbuckling nautical thrillers like *Typee* (1846) and *Omoo* (1847), *Moby-Dick* was long, complex, and dark. The novel received terrible reviews—the London *Atheneum* called it an "absurd book"—and it was a commercial failure that dealt a severe blow to Melville's budding literary career.

About seventy years later, however, literary scholars rediscovered Melville's brilliant, inventive novel, which had been gathering dust in libraries. Most modern critics now consider *Moby-Dick* and Mark Twain's *The Adventures of Huckleberry Finn* (1884) the two greatest American novels of the nineteenth century.

Moby-Dick follows the voyage of the *Pequod*, a whaling ship based on Nantucket Island in Massachusetts. At the beginning of the novel, the main character, a crew member named Ishmael, expects that the voyage will be an ordinary whaling expedition. After the *Pequod* leaves port, however, Ishmael discovers that Captain Ahab has something else in mind, he wants to kill Moby Dick, a legendary white whale that had crippled him on a previous trip.

Moby-Dick is laden with allegory and symbolism, starting with the elusive white whale itself. In one of the most famous chapters in the book, "The Whiteness of the Whale," Melville describes the combination of awe and terror the "ghastly whiteness" of the beast provokes aboard the *Pequod*. The whale's pale hue, Melville writes, seems to symbolize the "nameless horror" of nihilism:

> in essence whiteness is not so much a color as the visible absence of color, is it for these reasons that there is such a dumb blankness, full of meaning, in a wide landscape of snows—a colorless, all-color of atheism from which we should shrink?

Ahab's obsessive quest for the whale, which grows over the course of *Moby-Dick* as the ship sails across the Atlantic and Pacific Oceans, can be interpreted in a variety of ways. The pursuit for the whale is often seen as an allegory for humankind's search for truth—an object, like the great white whale, that seems to recede the harder one looks.

ADDITIONAL FACTS

1. The book was dedicated to author Nathaniel Hawthorne (1804–1864), a friend of Melville's who had encouraged him to write Moby-Dick.

2. The Starbucks coffee chain was named for Starbuck, Ahab's levelheaded first mate on the Pequod.

3. One of the inspirations for Moby-Dick was the real-life story of the American whaling ship Essex, which was attacked by a sperm whale in 1820.

★ ★ ★

H. H. Richardson

Famous for his arched doorways and graceful brownstone trim buildings, architect H. H. Richardson (1838–1886) set a new standard for American design in the nineteenth century with the elegant train stations, courthouses, and churches he built in cities and towns across the United States.

Henry Hobson Richardson was born on a Louisiana plantation and attended Harvard, where he was a classmate of author Henry Adams (1838–1918). After graduation, Richardson traveled to Paris for architecture school, missing the Civil War (1861–1865). Richardson returned to the United States in 1866 and opened an office in New York City.

Although he died young, during Richardson's brief career he built a stunning number of well-regarded buildings, including department stores, college halls, jails, libraries, and private homes. Many of his buildings feature rounded facades and mud-toned coloring, a style sometimes referred to as Romanesque Revival for its similarities to European buildings of the Middle Ages.

Boston's Trinity Church, one of the most architecturally significant buildings in the United States, is Richardson's most famous work. Made out of granite and brownstone and constructed in the shape of a cross, the giant church took five years for Richardson to complete in 1877. Home to the city's Episcopalian congregation—known by wags for many decades as "the Republican Party at prayer"—the church remains in everyday use.

Designing at a frantic pace, Richardson worked himself to death at age forty-eight. Several of his students went on to become famous architects in their own right, including two of the founders of the architectural firm McKim, Mead, and White, Charles F. McKim (1847–1909) and Stanford White (1853–1906). Many of Richardson's buildings are now considered historic sites, although his famous Marshall Field's department store in Chicago was torn down during the Great Depression of the 1930s.

ADDITIONAL FACTS

1. *Richardson worked mostly in Chicago or on the East Coast, but he also designed a monument in rural Wyoming to the Ames family, major financiers of the transcontinental railroad.*

2. *The jail Richardson designed in Pittsburgh was in operation until 1995.*

3. *Highlights of the first Romanesque period, around the eleventh and twelfth centuries AD, include the Cathedral and Leaning Tower in Pisa, Italy.*

★ ★ ★

John Adams

John Adams (1735–1826), a Massachusetts lawyer and politician, was elected the second president of the United States in 1796, succeeding George Washington (1732–1799). Adams served a single difficult term before Thomas Jefferson (1743–1826), a lifelong friend and political adversary, defeated him in the 1800 election.

By his own description, Adams was an unattractive, dislikable man. A graduate of Harvard, he parlayed his quick intelligence and unpleasant personality into a thriving legal practice in colonial-era Boston. Along with his cousin, the radical orator Samuel Adams (1722–1803), John Adams became involved with revolutionary politics in the 1760s, penning attacks on the Stamp Act and other British colonial policies.

In 1774, in recognition of his influential writing on colonial rights, Adams was chosen as one of the representatives from Massachusetts to the Continental Congress, where he collaborated with Jefferson on the drafting of the Declaration of Independence. Returning to Massachusetts, he wrote the state's constitution in 1780, a document that remains in force today. He also served as the American ambassador successively to France, Holland, and Great Britain before becoming vice president of the United States under President George Washington (1732–1799) in 1789.

The 1796 presidential election was the first seriously contested presidential race in American history after the unanimous choosing of Washington in 1789 and 1792. Adams ran as a Federalist, pledging to continue Washington's policies, against Jefferson, who led a faction concerned by the growing power of the new federal government.

Adams narrowly won the election, but his term was marked by foreign policy divisions and deepening partisanship between the two factions. Britain and France were at war during Adams's term, and the United States was divided into the Federalists, who sided with Britain, and the Republicans, who sympathized with France.

Embittered by his defeat in the rematch with Jefferson in 1800, Adams returned to Massachusetts and retired from politics. In his old age, however, he resumed his friendship with Jefferson. The two men died on the same day, July 4, 1826, exactly fifty years after the adoption of the Declaration of Independence.

ADDITIONAL FACTS

1. *A precocious child, Adams entered Harvard at the age of fifteen.*

2. *The Massachusetts state constitution that Adams wrote served as an inspiration for James Madison (1751–1836), who incorporated similar language protecting individual freedoms into the Bill of Rights.*

3. *Adams was painfully aware of his shortcomings, and he asked Jefferson to write the Declaration of Independence because, he said, "I am obnoxious, suspected and unpopular. You are very much otherwise."*

★ ★ ★

Isolationism

In 1796, as George Washington (1732–1799) prepared to depart the presidency after thirty years of overall service to his country, he began writing a farewell address to the American public. The address, published as an essay in numerous American newspapers later that year, would become an important milestone in American politics and foreign policy.

In the text, Washington advised his fellow citizens to avoid any alliances with foreign nations, or even excessive "affection" for them. "History and experience prove that foreign influence is one of the most baneful foes of republican government," he wrote. Better to focus on the well-being of the United States, Washington wrote, than to get involved in the endless intrigues of European countries.

> Excessive partiality for one foreign nation and excessive dislike of another cause those whom they actuate to see danger only on one side, and serve to veil and even second the arts of influence on the other. Real patriots who may resist the intrigues of the favorite are liable to become suspected and odious, while its tools and dupes usurp the applause and confidence of the people to surrender their interests . . . Why, by interweaving our destiny with that of any part of Europe, entangle our peace and prosperity in the toils of Euro-pean ambition, rivalship, interest, humor, or caprice?

Washington's clarion call to avoid foreign entanglements reflected, and helped to shape, an enduring aversion to international affairs among the American public. Heeding Washington's advice, the United States would not sign a formal foreign "alliance" for the next 150 years. But the American commitment to isolationism began to fray after World War I (1914–1918), and especially after the genocidal horrors of World War II (1939–1945), which forced the country to ask searching questions about its role in the world. Although isolationism still has its supporters, American foreign-policy makers of the post–World War II era have largely abandoned Washington's recommendations.

ADDITIONAL FACTS

1. *The United States did not enter a permanent foreign alliance until the signing of the North Atlantic Treaty Organization (NATO) pact in 1949.*

2. *Washington's farewell address was so influential that it is still read aloud every year in Congress.*

3. *The isolationist America First Committee was founded in 1940 with the goal of keeping the United States out of World War II. It disbanded on December 11, 1941, four days after the Japanese attack on Pearl Harbor.*

★ ★ ★

Second Great Awakening

The Second Great Awakening, about a century after the First Great Awakening revival movement, was a period of intense religious fervor in early nineteenth-century America that energized Protestant churches and helped fuel many important social reform movements, including abolitionism. Charismatic preachers of the era like Charles Grandison Finney (1792–1875) and Henry Ward Beecher (1813–1887) challenged American Protestants to perfect society as a way of earning their own eternal salvation.

Historians point to a camp meeting in Cane Ridge, Kentucky, as the first major event of the Second Great Awakening. Leading Christian ministers from several denominations—including Baptist, Presbyterian, and Methodist—preached to 20,000 people over several days of services. Large-scale, outdoor revival meetings, an incredibly powerful experience for nineteenth-century Americans, quickly spread across the country.

Unlike the First Great Awakening of the eighteenth century, which emphasized a return to the religious orthodoxy of the Puritans, the Second Great Awakening was liberal in both its theology and its outlook, stressing the possibility of Christians earning God's forgiveness. The optimistic atmosphere of the Second Great Awakening gave rise to many utopian communities that reflected a belief in the perfectibility of humankind.

Initially, the Second Great Awakening had no explicit political agenda. Soon, however, Finney and Beecher, the brother of the influential antislavery writer Harriet Beecher Stowe, began to inject criticisms of slavery and alcohol into their sermons. "The churches by their silence and by permitting slaveholders to belong to their communion have been consenting to it," Finney wrote.

In theological terms, the Second Great Awakening asked American Protestants to take an active role in their own salvation. This message helped awaken the abolitionist movement, which would deepen the sectional differences in the United States in the years before the Civil War (1861–1865).

ADDITIONAL FACTS

1. *So many revival meetings were held in western New York during the Second Great Awakening that Finney referred to the region as the "burned-over district."*

2. *One of the most popular preachers of the Second Great Awakening was William Miller (1782–1849), who attracted tens of thousands of followers with his prediction that the apocalypse would come on October 22, 1844. It didn't. However, Miller's supporters later formed the Seventh-Day Adventist Church.*

3. *Several other permanent additions to the American religious landscape, including Unitarianism and Mormonism, also date to the period of the Second Great Awakening.*

* * *

Baltimore and Ohio Railroad

In the spring of 1830, a thirteen-mile railroad connecting the city of Baltimore with neighboring suburbs opened to great fanfare. Initially, the railroad used horses to pull the trains along the line. Later that year, a steam-powered locomotive made its first trip on the railroad, inaugurating the age of steam. Within a few years of the first trip on the Baltimore and Ohio Railroad (the B&O, for short), hundreds of miles of railroad tracks were under construction across the nation, making it practical for the first time to ship unprecedented amounts of freight and providing a key impetus for the Industrial Revolution.

At the time of the railroad's opening, Baltimore was the second-largest city in the United States. However, its port was rapidly losing business to New York City, thanks to the success of the Erie Canal. The builders of the railroad hoped to build tracks across the Appalachian Mountains to connect Baltimore with the Ohio River valley, allowing the city to compete with New York for access to western markets.

The technology behind the steam locomotive had been invented in England in the early 1800s. However, many Americans were skeptical until an infamous race between a horse and the first American-built locomotive, Tom Thumb, on the B&O. Although the horse actually won, the locomotive performed well enough to convince Americans that steam locomotion was a practical alternative to draft animals.

In the short term, the B&O was a commercial success, eventually expanding into one of the leading East Coast railroads. More important, by demonstrating that steam railroads were feasible, the line inspired an immediate wave of imitators. Another railroad opened in South Carolina later that year; in 1835, Boston was connected with the industrial city of Lowell. By the end of the decade, total trackage had gone from 23 miles to 2,818 miles; at the outbreak of the Civil War in 1861, more than 30,000 miles of steel crisscrossed the United States, becoming the arteries of industrial America.

ADDITIONAL FACTS

1. *The first stone of the B&O was laid by Charles Carroll (1737–1832), the last living signer of the Declaration of Independence, on July 4, 1828.*

2. *The original B&O route is still operated by the CSX railroad company.*

3. *Although called the Baltimore and Ohio, the railroad did not actually reach the Ohio River until 1852, when it connected to Wheeling, Virginia, which is now part of West Virginia.*

★ ★ ★

Utopian Communities

Amid the religious revival of the Second Great Awakening, thousands of Americans joined short-lived utopian communities that formed across the United States in the 1830s and 1840s. Although many of these communes, which were often linked to a particular Christian religious sect, closed down after only a few years, others survived well into the twentieth century. Perhaps more important, the founding of villages in places like Oneida, New York, and Harmony, Indiana, reflected a particularly American strain of utopianism that attempted to infuse the nation's growth with religious and political idealism.

One of the most famous utopian communities was founded in 1848 in upstate New York by preacher John Humphrey Noyes (1811–1886). Like many other American utopian villages of the era, members of the Oneida community embraced an unorthodox Christian theology; in their case, they believed that the Second Coming of Christ had already occurred in 70 AD, thus making it possible for his followers to achieve perfection on Earth. In practice, Noyes preached that all members of the community were married to one another and could have sex with whomever they wished without committing a sin. The community lasted for several decades, until Noyes's death.

Other communes, like Brook Farm, established in Massachusetts in 1841, were more secular in their outlook. Inspired by the transcendentalist movement and European socialism, the founders of Brook Farm sought to create a community whose members would pool their finances, share in the labor needed to run the farm, and discuss literature around the dinner table. The experiment folded after six years.

The flourishing of utopian communities in the 1840s reflected both the religious enthusiasm of the Second Great Awakening and the pioneer mentality of the age. Many of the communities have been preserved as monuments to the optimism and zealotry of Americans living in pre–Civil War times.

ADDITIONAL FACTS

1. *Noyes was arrested once for adultery and fled to Canada to avoid arrest for statutory rape.*

2. *The longest-lasting utopian movement of the nineteenth century may have been the Shakers, a Christian sect that still has a handful of members in New England. Their resilience is somewhat ironic, since one of the religion's principles is total celibacy.*

3. *After Noyes's death, the Oneida community evolved into a corporation that made the world-famous Oneida silverware.*

★ ★ ★

Uncle Tom's Cabin

Uncle Tom's Cabin, an 1852 novel dramatizing the evils of slavery written by abolitionist Harriet Beecher Stowe (1811–1896), was the best-selling book of the nineteenth century in the United States. By portraying the human consequences of slavery in vivid fashion, Stowe outraged northern audiences and hardened opposition to slavery in the decade before the Civil War (1861–1865). The novel's impact was so great that when President Abraham Lincoln (1809–1865) was introduced to Stowe during the war, he remarked, "So you're the little woman who wrote the book that started this great war."

The novel tells the story of a group of slaves in Kentucky. Their owner, George Shelby, falls into debt and is forced to sell two of the slaves, Uncle Tom and Eliza. Rather than be separated from her baby, Eliza escapes to the North, crossing the Ohio River in one of the most well-known and suspenseful passages of the novel. Tom, however, accepts his fate and is eventually sold to a cruel new master, the evil Simon Legree.

As a work of literature, *Uncle Tom's Cabin* is highly sentimental and sometimes even mawkish in tone. However, the melodramatic tale had an enormous impact on the American reading public at that time, as it powerfully described the brutality of slavery and the threat of slave families being separated by the domestic slave trade. Hundreds of thousands of copies of the book were sold in its first year alone. Southerners, meanwhile, were outraged.

By galvanizing antislavery sentiment, *Uncle Tom's Cabin* accomplished Stowe's political goal and assured the book's lasting historical importance. The novel's afterlife, however, has been complicated. Since the Civil War, and especially since the civil rights movement of the twentieth century, literary critics have pointed out the book's many shortcomings. Even while criticizing the institution of slavery, Stowe's writing often reinforced negative stereotypes of African-Americans. The title character of Uncle Tom has been especially controversial. Stowe intended Tom as a positive example, someone who bore his hardship with Christian grace. But the label *Uncle Tom* is now often used as an extremely insulting epithet for African-Americans seen as complicit in racism.

ADDITIONAL FACTS

1. *Stowe based parts of the novel on stories related to her by escaped slaves she encountered while living in Ohio.*

2. *After the success of* Uncle Tom's Cabin, *Stowe and her husband moved into a big house in Hartford, Connecticut. Their next-door neighbor was author Mark Twain (1835–1910).*

3. *Most of the novel was written while Stowe lived in Brunswick, Maine, where her husband was a professor at Bowdoin College.*

★ ★ ★

John Philip Sousa

Composer and United States Marine Band conductor John Philip Sousa (1854–1932) wrote many of the best-loved patriotic marches in American history, including "Semper Fidelis" (1888), "Washington Post March" (1889), and his masterpiece, "Stars and Stripes Forever" (1897). Immensely popular in his own day, Sousa's upbeat, brassy music is still routinely performed on the Fourth of July, at patriotic events, and at football games nationwide.

Born in Washington, DC, Sousa was a musical prodigy at a young age and enlisted in the Marine Corps at the age of thirteen to begin his apprenticeship in its band. After learning to play all the instruments in the band, he became director when he was only twenty-six.

During Sousa's tenure, he turned the Marine Band into the nation's premier brass band, earning the group the nickname "The President's Own" that is still used today. Sousa wrote many of his best-known marches during this time, including "Washington Post March." Sousa himself became known as the March King.

Hoping to reach a wider audience, Sousa left the military in 1892 to form a touring civilian band and spent much of the rest of his life on the road, performing at bandstands in towns and cities across the nation. A national celebrity, Sousa's arrival almost invariably created a sensation wherever he went.

Sousa's signature style—crashing cymbals, staccato piccolos, and thumping bass lines—pulses with energy and excitement. Marches, Sousa believed, were "for the feet, not for the head," and, indeed, audiences still find it virtually impossible to remain seated during the bombastic finale to "Stars and Stripes Forever."

In addition to his marches, Sousa wrote operettas, an autobiography titled *Marching Along* (1928), and several novels. Although Sousa lived well into the twentieth century, recordings of his performances are extremely rare, since he disdained radio and phonographs and almost never allowed his shows to be recorded. Appropriately, the March King died in a hotel while on tour, after conducting "Stars and Stripes Forever" that morning.

ADDITIONAL FACTS

1. *Sousa invented the sousaphone, a tuba-like instrument that can be carried in a marching band.*

2. *A Sousa march entitled "Liberty Bell" (1893) was used for the opening credits of the classic British TV comedy show* Monty Python's Flying Circus.

3. *Congress declared "Stars and Stripes Forever" the national march of the United States in 1987.*

★ ★ ★

Thomas Jefferson

Widely regarded as the most intellectual American president, Thomas Jefferson (1743–1826) wrote the Declaration of Independence and acquired the vast Louisiana Territory for the United States. He was also an expert in a stunning range of human endeavor, with interests ranging from politics to botany to architecture.

After receiving a classical education at the College of William and Mary, Jefferson entered Virginia politics at age twenty-five. Jefferson was an awkward speaker but a brilliant writer. Recognizing his abilities, Virginia leaders sent Jefferson to represent them at the Continental Congress in Philadelphia in 1774. At the convention, the thirty-three-year-old Jefferson was given the job of composing the text of its famous declaration:

We hold these truths to be self-evident, that all men are created equal, that they are endowed by their Creator with certain unalienable Rights, that among these are Life, Liberty and the pursuit of Happiness.—That to secure these rights, Governments are instituted among Men, deriving their just powers from the consent of the governed,—That whenever any Form of Government becomes destructive of these ends, it is the Right of the People to alter or to abolish it, and to institute new Government, laying its foundation on such principles and organizing its powers in such form, as to them shall seem most likely to effect their Safety and Happiness . . .

Politically, Jefferson believed that individual farmers such as the tobacco planters in his native Virginia were the backbone of the nation, and he distrusted big government and grand economic schemes embraced by Federalists like Alexander Hamilton (1755–1804). Worried by the Federalist Party's policies and sympathy for the British, Jefferson ran for president in 1796 against John Adams (1735–1826), George Washington's vice president and favored successor. The election was surprisingly close, but Jefferson lost. He bided his time in the vice presidency, returning four years later to defeat Adams.

Jefferson himself did not consider his years in the White House a major accomplishment, and he left the presidency off of his epitaph. The importance of Jefferson's purchase of Louisiana from France, which contradicted his ideas of limited federal power, would not be fully appreciated until decades after his death in 1826.

ADDITIONAL FACTS

1. *Among his many other pursuits, Jefferson was also an oenophile who tried, unsuccessfully, to grow wine grapes at his Monticello estate.*

2. *In 1998, DNA evidence suggested that Jefferson had fathered a child with one of his slaves, Sally Hemings, a finding that confirmed rumors prevalent during Jefferson's lifetime.*

3. *Of his many accomplishments, Jefferson was proudest of his authorship of the Declaration of Independence and his role as a founder of the University of Virginia in 1819.*

★ ★ ★

Barbary Pirates

President Thomas Jefferson (1743–1826) waged the first foreign war of the United States in 1804 against gangs of pirates known as *corsairs* who preyed on American ships in the Mediterranean Sea. By attacking the home base of the so-called Barbary pirates in northern Africa, the United States was able to stop their harassment of American merchant ships. The war substantially boosted the international prestige of the young nation and its military. In particular, the performance of the US Navy demonstrated to the rest of the world that the United States, just twenty years after achieving its independence, was now a legitimate military power.

The Barbary pirates, based in the African port cities of Algiers, Tunis, and Tripoli, had for hundreds of years plundered European ships that failed to make tribute payments. When the United States became independent, its ships lost the protection of the British Royal Navy and were suddenly vulnerable to the pirate attacks. The first two American presidents, George Washington (1732–1799) and John Adams (1735–1826), grudgingly agreed to pay ransoms and tribute to the pirates in exchange for peace. By the time Jefferson took office, the United States had spent an astonishing sum on pirate tribute.

Jefferson detested tribute, and shortly after taking office, he sent the navy to Africa to teach the pirates a lesson. The American fleet, led by the USS *Constitution*, arrived off the shores of Tripoli in 1804. Thanks to the exploits of naval hero Stephen Decatur (1779–1820), who captured several enemy vessels and led a daring nighttime raid on Tripoli, the city's corsairs were forced to stop attacking American shipping.

The United States would fight several other battles with other gangs of Barbary pirates, and the tribute payments did not cease completely until after the War of 1812. However, the expedition to Africa proved to the Europeans—and Americans—that the United States was capable of fighting and winning a war.

ADDITIONAL FACTS

1. *The expedition against the Barbary pirates was the first overseas deployment of the US Marines, inspiring the phrase in the famous opening stanza of the "Marine's Hymn," "to the shores of Tripoli."*

2. *The Barbary pirates, contrary to myth, did not make their prisoners walk the plank, a practice that is thought to have originated in the 1820s in the Caribbean.*

3. *By the time of the war, the Barbary pirates had been raiding ships in the Mediterranean for centuries. In the seventeenth century, one of their hostages was Miguel de Cervantes (1547–1616), the author of* Don Quixote.

★ ★ ★

Separation of Church and State

In 1801, members of the small Baptist church in Danbury, Connecticut, wrote a letter to President Thomas Jefferson (1743–1826) congratulating him on his recent election. At the time, the Baptists were a minority religion in overwhelmingly Congregationalist New England. In their letter, the Baptists expressed concern that the state of Connecticut would trample the rights of religious minorities and force them to support the Congregationalists.

A few months later, Jefferson mailed a response to the Danbury Baptists. In his now famous letter, Jefferson said, in effect, that they had nothing to worry about. The First Amendment to the Constitution, Jefferson argued, had erected a "wall of separation" between church and state that meant Connecticut could not interfere with the Baptists' religious freedom.

> Believing with you that religion is a matter which lies solely between Man & his God, that he owes account to none other for his faith or his worship, that the legitimate powers of government reach actions only, & not opinions, I contemplate with sovereign reverence that act of the whole American people which declared that their legislature should 'make no law respecting an establishment of religion, or prohibiting the free exercise thereof,' thus building a wall of separation between Church & State.

Jefferson's metaphor of the wall between church and state became enormously influential and has been cited by many American political and religious leaders in the two centuries since. Although not part of the Constitution, Jefferson's metaphorical wall has been recognized by the Supreme Court as a guiding concept in the relationship between church and state.

Jefferson's letter, however, has also led to controversy. Courts have relied on Jefferson's concept of the wall to ban prayer and religious instruction in public schools, which some religious leaders believe goes too far in separating religion from government. Still, more than 200 years after its writing, Jefferson's letter to the Danbury Baptists remains an influential interpretation of the First Amendment's establishment clause and a cornerstone of religious liberty in the United States.

ADDITIONAL FACTS

1. *At the time, Jefferson had already alienated New Englanders by inviting Thomas Paine (1737–1809) to return to the United States from France despite his anti-Christian writings.*

2. *On the same day he mailed the letter, Jefferson accepted a 1,235-pound cheese produced by parishioners at a Baptist Church in Cheshire, Massachusetts.*

3. *Anticipating a negative public reaction to his letter, Jefferson began a ttending church services in Washington, DC, two days after sending it, preempting the inevitable charges that he was an atheist.*

★ ★ ★

Samuel Morse

The construction of the first telegraph line in the United States by Samuel Morse (1791–1872) in 1844 sparked a technological revolution that changed the way Americans communicated and, for the first time, allowed nearly instantaneous transmissions across vast distances. Morse's line, a forty-mile wire next to the railroad tracks between Baltimore and Washington, was the prototype for a network of telegraph lines that quickly sprawled across the pre–Civil War United States.

A painter by training, Morse was born in Massachusetts and traveled widely in Europe in pursuing of his artistic career. However, he became fascinated by electricity, a concept that was still poorly understood in the early nineteenth century, and gradually gave up on art to concentrate on his new interest.

Whether Morse truly deserves credit for "inventing" the telegraph is subject to great historical debate. He did not invent the concept. Many scientists in Europe had envisioned using electric pulses transmitted through a metal wire as a form of communication. But Morse through a combination of technological innovation and salesmanship, was able to turn the theoretical idea into reality. After returning to the United States, he began lobbying Congress to fund an experimental line between Washington and Baltimore in the 1830s, and he finally received a $30,000 grant in 1843. Morse also developed Morse code, the system of dots and dashes used to transmit numbers and letters along telegraph wires. Anticipating the huge impact the telegraph would have on the world, the first message tapped along the line in 1844 was a famous quote from the Bible: "What hath God wrought!"

Morse's patent on the telegraph made him a wealthy man. By 1872, the year of his death, wires had been strung from coast to coast and across the Atlantic Ocean, huge feats of engineering that suddenly closed the gap between cities, nations, and continents.

ADDITIONAL FACTS

1. Europeans had built versions of the telegraph as early as 1774, but many of the designs were highly impractical; one used twenty-six wires, one for each letter of the alphabet.

2. By 1854, ten years after the first forty-mile section was built by Morse, about 23,000 miles of telegraph wire were in operation in the United States.

3. The first words transmitted on the transcontinental telegraph line, which was completed in 1861, were anticlimactic: "Line just completed."

★ ★ ★

Five Points

Even the English novelist Charles Dickens (1812–1870)—no stranger to urban decay—was stunned by what he saw at the Five Points, New York City's worst slum of the early nineteenth century. Visiting in 1842, Dickens was disgusted by the neighborhood's filthy alleys and seedy buildings. "Debauchery has made the very houses prematurely old," he wrote. "See how the rotten beams are tumbling down, and how the patched and broken windows seem to scowl dimly, like eyes that have been hurt in drunken frays."

To Americans of the nineteenth century, the Five Points area was synonymous with urban poverty, violence, and disease. Thousands of poor New Yorkers—many of them recently arrived immigrants—were crammed into decrepit buildings near the convergence of Park, Worth, and Baxter streets in Manhattan. At a time of massive immigration, the notorious Five Points represented the dark, threatening side of American urbanization.

Indeed, only forty years before Dickens's visit, the Five Points did not exist. In 1800, the area was covered by a pond that was a popular destination for fishermen. As New York's population multiplied in the early nineteenth century, however, all vestiges of the area's rural past were quickly obliterated to make way for development. By the 1830s, the neighborhood had acquired its seedy reputation and resident population of prostitutes and hooligans.

The slum grew with immigration in the 1840s and became notorious for gang violence and ethnic tension. Although many of the residents were Irish immigrants, the neighborhood was also home to freed blacks and poor Protestant whites. Under pressure from reformers, the city of New York tore down the neighborhood later in the nineteenth century, which merely displaced the poor to other parts of the teeming city.

ADDITIONAL FACTS

1. *According to historians, tap dancing was invented in the Five Points in the 1840s.*

2. *The center of the Five Points was the "old brewery," a large abandoned brewery that had been converted into tenement housing and is depicted in Martin Scorsese's 2002 movie* Gangs of New York.

3. *Most of the area once known as the Five Points was torn down in a slum clearance program throughout the late nineteenth century and replaced with a courthouse and the notorious Tombs prison.*

★ ★ ★

Walt Whitman

Leaves of Grass, an enormously influential book of risqué, exuberant poems celebrating American life by Walt Whitman (1819–1892), provided the foundation for much of nineteenth- and twentieth-century American verse. The book, which Whitman expanded and revised throughout his lifetime, featured an unorthodox poetic style different than that of any of Whitman's contemporaries and inspired American poets from Langston Hughes (1902–1967) to Allen Ginsberg (1926–1997).

When *Leaves of Grass* was first published in 1855, Ralph Waldo Emerson (1803–1882) was one of the few critics to grasp the volume's importance. "I find it the most extraordinary piece of wit and wisdom that America has yet contributed," he wrote in a letter to Whitman encouraging the young poet.

During the Civil War (1861–1865), Whitman left New York to volunteer as a nurse in army hospitals in Washington, DC. After the Union victory, he published a book of war poems, *Drum Taps* (1865).

In general, Whitman's poems celebrate individualism, democracy, nature, and the beauty of the human body. His poems dealt frankly and positively with homosexuality and masturbation, highly unusual topics in the United States during the Victorian era. One of Whitman's most famous free verse poems, "I Hear America Singing," exemplifies Whitman's characteristic style and subject matter:

> *I hear America singing, the varied carols I hear,*
> *Those of mechanics, each one singing his as it should be blithe and strong,*
> *The carpenter singing his as he measures his plank or beam,*
> *The mason singing his as he makes ready for work, or leaves off work,*
> *The boatman singing what belongs to him in his boat, the deckhand singing on*
> *   the steamboat deck,*
> *The shoemaker singing as he sits on his bench, the hatter singing as he stands,*
> *The wood-cutter's song, the ploughboy's on his way in the morning, or at noon*
> *   intermission or at sundown,*
> *The delicious singing of the mother, or of the young wife at work, or of the girl*
> *   sewing or washing,*
> *Each singing what belongs to him or her and to none else,*
> *The day what belongs to the day—at night the party of young fellows, robust, friendly,*
> *Singing with open mouths their strong melodious songs.*

ADDITIONAL FACTS

1. *Original editions of* Leaves of Grass *are among the most sought-after books for American collectors.*

2. *In a telltale indication of its high literary quality,* Leaves of Grass *was banned in Boston in 1882.*

3. *Whitman considered Abraham Lincoln a personal hero and wrote one of his few rhyming poems, "O Captain! My Captain!" after the president's assassination in 1865.*

★ ★ ★

Augustus Saint-Gaudens

In 1905, President Theodore Roosevelt (1858–1919) decided that American money was too boring. A great nation, he thought, should have beautiful coins, like the ancient Greeks and Romans did. So Roosevelt asked the most famous sculptor of the day, Augustus Saint-Gaudens (1848–1907), to design new ones.

Although dying of cancer at his home in New Hampshire, Saint-Gaudens gladly accepted the president's commission, and two years later, the mint issued $10 and $20 gold coins based on his designs. The coins, which circulated for the next twenty-five years, are widely considered the most beautiful in American history.

For Saint-Gaudens, an Irish-born sculptor whose parents immigrated to the United States when he was an infant, the coins were a fitting end to his long career in the public spotlight. Trained in classical sculpture, Saint-Gaudens first achieved commercial success in the United States after the Civil War (1861–1865), when the demand for monuments to the war dead created a thriving market for sculptors.

In his moving statues of war heroes, Saint-Gaudens managed the difficult feat of pleasing both art critics and the public at large. Several of his monuments, including a statue of President Abraham Lincoln in Chicago and his memorial to Colonel Robert Gould Shaw and the Fifty-Fourth Massachusetts Infantry Regiment in Boston, are considered among the finest works of public art in American history.

In addition to the plaudits from critics, his Civil War monuments also made Saint-Gaudens rich. In 1885, he purchased his hilltop mansion in New Hampshire, which he nicknamed Aspet after the village where his father was born. Saint-Gaudens soon inspired other artists to move to New Hampshire, and his hometown of Cornish became a popular artists' colony around the turn of the twentieth century.

Stylistically, Saint-Gaudens managed to combine classical sculpture with cutting-edge European trends. His $20 coin, for instance, recalls Greek antiquity but at the same time is distinctively modern in its bold and expressive design. In a fitting tribute, the government resurrected the design in 1986 and continues to mint high-value gold coins designed by one of the greatest American sculptors.

ADDITIONAL FACTS

1. *The design for the $20 coin did not originally include the motto "In God We Trust," but Congress forced the mint to add the four words in 1908 after an outcry.*

2. *Saint-Gaudens was a friend of Winslow Homer (1836–1910), and both belonged to the Tile Club, a New York-based art salon.*

3. *Saint-Gaudens labored for fourteen years on the Gould memorial, which was finally dedicated on Boston Common in 1897.*

★ ★ ★

James Madison

James Madison (1751–1836), the fourth president of the United States, was elected in 1808 and served two rocky terms before leaving office in 1817. During his presidency, the United States fought the War of 1812 against Great Britain. During the war, the first major foreign conflict fought by the young United States, Madison earned the distinction of becoming the last American president to command the US Army in the field, directing the retreat from Washington, DC, after British forces ransacked the capital.

Like his mentor and fellow Virginian Thomas Jefferson (1743–1826), Madison found the presidency an unsatisfying coda to his political career. Madison hadn't wanted war with Britain, but the "war hawks" in Congress cajoled him into the confrontation, which they hoped would end the British navy's harassment of American shipping. In an era when Congress was the strongest branch of the federal government, Madison ended up having little choice but to go along with the hawks.

Twenty-five years earlier, by contrast, Madison's political debut at the Constitutional Convention had made him a national hero. Madison wrote much of the document and was dubbed "Father of the Constitution" for his patient work reconciling the various factions at Philadelphia. In particular, Madison stressed the need for the system of checks and balances that was incorporated into the Constitution. He also drafted the Bill of Rights that was later added to the document.

The son of a wealthy Virginia slaveholder, Madison studied law and philosophy at Princeton before entering politics during the Revolution. In the Virginia legislature he was an ally of Jefferson and later became his secretary of state.

Like Jefferson, Madison left the presidency after two terms. Madison retired to his estate in Virginia, an elegant mansion named Montpelier. He died in 1836, as the sectional tensions that would eventually lead to the Civil War (1861–1865) were intensifying. In one of his last letters, he pleaded with his compatriots to revive the national unity he had helped create at Philadelphia. "The advice nearest to my heart and deepest in my convictions is that the Union of the States be cherished and perpetuated," he wrote.

ADDITIONAL FACTS

1. *Madison's draft version of the Bill of Rights initially comprised seventeen amendments but was whittled down to twelve by Congress and then to ten by the states.*

2. *Madison's face is on the rarely seen $5,000 bill, which is no longer in circulation.*

3. *Madison's charismatic wife, Dolley Payne Madison (1768–1849), created the hostess role of the First Lady and became famous for carrying the portrait of George Washington out of the White House when the British torched the building in 1814.*

★ ★ ★

USS *Constitution*

The most famous vessel in the history of the United States Navy, the USS *Constitution* won numerous battles in the War of 1812 and remains on duty today as the navy's oldest warship.

Launched in Boston in 1797, the *Constitution* first saw action chasing pirates in the Caribbean. When President Thomas Jefferson (1743–1826) ordered the navy to North Africa to attack the Barbary pirates, the *Constitution* served as flagship of the American fleet, bombarding the fortress of Tripoli. In battle during the War of 1812, the *Constitution* captured several British ships and earned its famous nickname, "Old Ironsides," for the way enemy cannonballs seemed to bounce harmlessly off its sides.

In 1830, after more than thirty years of service, the ship was slated for demolition when the poet Oliver Wendell Holmes (1809–1894) wrote a famous poem expressing indignation that such a heroic ship would be decommissioned:

> Her deck, once red with heroes' blood,
> Where knelt the vanquished foe,
> When winds were hurrying o'er the flood,
> And waves were white below,
> No more shall feel the victor's tread,
> Or know the conquered knee;
> The harpies of the shore shall pluck
> The eagle of the sea!
>
> Oh, better that her shattered bulk
> Should sink beneath the wave;
> Her thunders shook the mighty deep,
> And there should be her grave;
> Nail to the mast her holy flag,
> Set every threadbare sail,
> And give her to the god of storms,
> The lightning and the gale!

The poem inspired a wave of protest, forcing the navy to preserve the warship. The *Constitution* went back into active service and served as a training vessel until after the Civil War (1861–1865). The navy continues to maintain the *Constitution* as a floating monument to the nation's maritime tradition, and all crew members are active-duty members of the military. Following long-needed repairs in the 1990s, the ship is again seaworthy.

ADDITIONAL FACTS

1. *The* Constitution *circumnavigated the globe between 1844 and 1846.*

2. *The original figurehead of the* Constitution *was of Hercules, the Greek demigod of strength, but it was lost during the Barbary wars.*

3. *Congress was so thrilled by the* Constitution's *victory over the HMS Guerriere in 1812 that its captain was given a gold medal and the crew a prize of $50,000.*

★ ★ ★

Trail of Tears

In 1838, President Martin van Buren (1782–1862) forced 16,000 members of the Cherokee tribe to leave their ancestral homelands in Georgia and relocate to Oklahoma. The Cherokees' unwilling journey westward—more than 1,200 miles on foot—is often referred to as the Trail of Tears. During the trip, thousands of Cherokees died of dysentery, road accidents, and exhaustion.

Before the arrival of European settlers, the Cherokees were one of the most powerful tribes in the Southeast. At the beginning of the nineteenth century, more than 20,000 Cherokees lived in present-day Georgia, Tennessee, and Alabama.

In the early 1800s, however, the federal government and the state of Georgia decided that the Cherokees should be "relocated" to make room for more white settlers. Cherokee chiefs refused to leave and declared themselves an independent nation. The Supreme Court sided with the Cherokees, but President Andrew Jackson famously dismissed the court's opinion, declaring, "[Chief Justice] John Marshall has made his decision; let him enforce it now if he can."

The final order to evacuate was issued by Van Buren, Jackson's successor, in May 1838. About 7,000 soldiers were dispatched to Cherokee territory that spring to round up the tribe at gunpoint, despite vociferous protests from many Americans who sympathized with the tribe's plight. The brutal march west would kill between 2,000 and 8,000 Cherokees.

The tribe had no connections to Oklahoma, which the federal government had designated as Indian Territory, but those who survived were eventually able to adapt to their new surroundings. According to the 2000 census, the Cherokees are now the largest tribe in the United States, with about 730,000 members.

ADDITIONAL FACTS

1. *Many other Native American tribes were forcibly "evacuated" to Oklahoma in the 1830s, including the Chickasaw, Choctaw, Creek, and Seminole.*

2. *During the roundup of the Cherokees, about 1,000 tribal members managed to evade capture. Their descendents form the Eastern Band of the Cherokee Indians in North Carolina.*

3. *One reason for the sudden federal interest in the Cherokees was the discovery of gold near tribal lands in Dahlonega, Georgia, in 1829, which set off the nation's first gold rush.*

★ ★ ★

Cyrus McCormick

Cyrus McCormick (1809–1884) invented the mechanical reaper, a farming device that simplified the grain harvest and greatly improved the efficiency of American agriculture in the mid-nineteenth century. The company McCormick founded to sell his reaper, headquartered in Chicago, became one of the biggest businesses of the century and one of the catalysts for the city's growth into a major metropolis. The McCormick Company is also historically notable as one of the first American companies to sell its products on credit, which made its reapers available to the average farmer and greatly increased its sales.

McCormick was born in the Shenandoah Valley of rural Virginia. In the early nineteenth century of his childhood, farmers still harvested grain with sickles, scythes, and other handheld tools. McCormick's father, Robert, a farmer and blacksmith, had tried for years to invent a mechanized version of the reaper that could be towed by horses, thus saving labor. After his father's death, McCormick finally perfected a working design, which he unveiled in 1831 and patented three years later.

It took almost two decades, however, for farmers to accept the new invention. The first reapers were made of heavy cast iron, and they exhausted the horses. In 1847, McCormick relocated to Chicago, where he redesigned his reaper to make it more lightweight and efficient. The improved models more than doubled farm efficiency. McCormick's invention helped spark settlement in the West by making farming the vast prairies more practical; by the mid-1850s, he was a millionaire. After his death, his company eventually became International Harvester, which is now part of Navistar, a Fortune 500 manufacturer.

ADDITIONAL FACTS

1. *McCormick's daughter-in-law, Katharine McCormick (1875–1967), was the major backer of Margaret Sanger (1879–1966) and helped fund the research that eventually led to the invention of the birth control pill.*

2. *A portion of Walnut Grove, the 532-acre farm that belonged to McCormick's father, is now preserved as part of Virginia Tech.*

3. *The Great Chicago Fire of 1871 destroyed McCormick's factory; he soon rebuilt.*

★ ★ ★

Chicago

HOG Butcher for the World,
Tool Maker, Stacker of Wheat,
Player with Railroads and the Nation's Freight Handler;
Stormy, husky, brawling,
City of the Big Shoulders:

—"Chicago," by Carl Sandburg

Before it became a reality, Chicago already existed in the nation's imagination. As early as the seventeenth century, French explorers had identified the area of present-day Chicago as a potential site for a canal linking the Great Lakes and the Mississippi River. At the time, however, the site was surrounded by wilderness; the modern city of Chicago would not be founded until 1833, when it had a modest population of 200 residents.

The year 1848 represented a crucial turning point in the city's history. Two events— the arrival of the railroad and the completion of a canal that finally linked the Mississippi River and Lake Michigan—turned the city into the nation's transportation hub. Railroad lines soon converged on the city, bringing livestock from the west, steel from the east, and a steady flow of immigrants from around the world. The closure of the Mississippi to commerce during the Civil War (1861–1865) was a major boost to the city, since it forced many shippers to route their goods by rail through Chicago.

The "City of the Big Shoulders," as Chicago poet Carl Sandburg (1878–1967) dubbed it in 1916, was the engine that would drive American growth in the late nineteenth century. In particular, Chicago's location in the middle of the nation's heartland made it the nexus of grain and livestock. For instance, the majority of the beef eaten in the United States in 1900 was processed in Chicago's sprawling stockyards.

In its early years, the growing city endured considerable hardship, including legendarily filthy streets and sewers, a cholera epidemic that killed 6 percent of its residents in 1854, and the Great Fire of 1871. By the 1890 census, however, it had passed Philadelphia to become the nation's second largest city, a place it would hold for a century.

ADDITIONAL FACTS

1. *When they were first opened in 1864, Chicago's Union Stock Yards covered 320 acres.*

2. *In a feat of environmental hubris, engineers reversed the direction of the Chicago River in 1871 so that the city's sewage would flow into the Mississippi rather than Lake Michigan.*

3. *Illinois was originally claimed by the state of Virginia, based on its colonial borders, but was given up in 1784.*

★ ★ ★

Emily Dickinson

Virtually unknown during her lifetime, Massachusetts poet Emily Dickinson (1830–1886) is now considered one of the leading lights of American literature for the thousands of complex, enigmatic poems that were published after her death.

Dickinson was born to a prominent family in Amherst, Massachusetts, where she remained her entire life. Considered an eccentric by her neighbors, she never married and led an isolated life in the family's home.

Still, through her family connections Dickinson was able to establish contact with many major nineteenth-century literary figures, including Boston minister Thomas Wentworth Higginson (1823–1911), to whom she mailed some of her poems in 1862. Higginson was impressed by her "wholly new" style but discouraged Dickinson from seeking a publisher. In total, only ten of Dickinson's 1,700 poems are known to have been printed during her lifetime.

Dickinson's poetic voice was unusual and alien to the poetry styles of the mid-nineteenth century. Many of her poems are short, mordant, and full of ambiguity; Higginson called them "spasmodic" for their uneven meter and unpredictable punctuation.

One of Dickinson's poems, written in about 1861, provides an example of her morbid, enigmatic style:

> *I like a look of Agony,*
> *Because I know it's true—*
> *Men do not sham Convulsion,*
> *Nor simulate, a Throe—*
>
> *The Eyes glaze once—and that is Death—*
> *Impossible to feign*
> *The Beads upon the Forehead*
> *By homely Anguish strung.*

During her lifetime, Dickinson scribbled her poems whenever the inspiration seized her, and some of her verse was written on discarded wrapping paper or the backs of instruction manuals for kerosene lamps. After her death at age fifty-five, Dickinson's family was astonished to find thousands of poems among her belongings, bundled together with twine. They were published in 1890 to enthusiastic reviews, establishing her reputation as one of her country's most innovative, unusual literary stars.

ADDITIONAL FACTS

1. *Her father, Edward Dickinson, served one term in the House of Representatives as a Whig.*

2. *Many of her poems are written in ballad meter, the same as Samuel Taylor Coleridge's "The Rime of the Ancient Mariner" and many other famous songs and poems.*

3. *Dickinson wrote the bulk of her poems during a sustained spurt of creativity in the midst of the Civil War; between 1862 and 1864, she averaged a poem every two days.*

★ ★ ★

Skyscrapers

A distinctively American contribution to world architecture, the first skyscrapers were built in Chicago and St. Louis in the 1880s and 1890s. Although initially the term *skyscraper* was used for buildings as short as ten stories, within a few decades American builders regularly surpassed forty floors. The nation's tallest skyscraper is currently the Sears Tower, which looms a staggering 110 stories—one-quarter of a mile—above downtown Chicago.

Several nineteenth-century technological innovations made the skyscraper feasible. The invention of the elevator made tall buildings practical. Better techniques for refining steel, which were developed in the 1860s, made them possible. By using lightweight steel girders, engineers were no longer limited by heavy stone masonry.

Chicago's Home Insurance Company building, erected in 1885, is often considered history's first skyscraper. At ten stories, the landmark building proved that taller buildings could be constructed safely. Downtown Chicago, with many empty lots after the Great Chicago Fire of 1871, became the home of the first wave of skyscraper construction. The original Home Insurance Company building, however, was demolished during the Great Depression of the 1930s.

Chicago-based designer Louis Sullivan (1856–1924) is widely considered the first master of the skyscraper. Sullivan built many of Chicago's first tall buildings, and he also designed the influential Wainwright Building in downtown St. Louis, which still stands today.

The most famous skyscrapers of the early twentieth century, however, were built in New York City, the nation's economic capital. The art deco Chrysler Building was constructed in 1930, while the nation's second-tallest building, the Empire State Building, opened in Midtown in 1931. Several very tall buildings are currently being designed in American cities, including the Freedom Tower in New York that will be the city's tallest structure at 1,776 feet if finished as planned.

ADDITIONAL FACTS

1. *A building under construction in the United Arab Emirates is expected to become the tallest structure in the world when it is completed in 2009.*

2. *The Boston-born Sullivan entered the Massachusetts Institute of Technology (MIT) at age sixteen but dropped out after one year, before receiving a degree.*

3. *Architect Frank Lloyd Wright (1867–1959), once a protégé of Sullivan's, always referred to him as Liebermeister, or beloved master in German, even after the two had a falling out.*

★ ★ ★

Abigail Adams

Abigail Smith Adams (1744–1818), the daughter of a Massachusetts preacher, began exchanging love letters with lawyer John Adams (1735–1826) in 1762, when she was a sickly teenager. The long letters between Abigail and John, the work of two tender and playful souls, led to their marriage in 1764, when she was twenty and he was twenty-nine. For the rest of their fifty-four-year marriage, John and Abigail continued to trade thousands of notes and letters. Abigail's letters about politics, gardening, life in the White House, religion, and women's rights form an extraordinary trove for historians and a moving monument to the second First Lady of the United States.

Much like her famous husband, Abigail comes across in her letters as principled, witty, and occasionally sarcastic. Her most famous letter to John Adams was written on March 31, 1776, while he was in Philadelphia working on the Declaration of Independence. After inquiring about the proceedings at Philadelphia, Abigail went on to lambaste her husband and men in general:

By the way in the new Code of Laws which I suppose it will be necessary for you to make I desire you would Remember the Ladies, and be more generous and favourable to them than your ancestors. Do not put such unlimited power into the hands of the Husbands. Remember all Men would be tyrants if they could. If perticuliar care and attention is not paid to the Laidies we are determined to foment a Rebelion, and will not hold ourselves bound by any Laws in which we have no voice, or Representation . . . That your Sex are Naturally Tyrannical is a Truth so thoroughly established as to admit of no dispute . . .

John Adams, in his sarcastic response mailed several days later, accused his wife of being "saucy," and said he planned to ignore her suggestions because they would lead to the "Despotism of the Peticoat."

The letters continued for the next two decades, in huge torrents of loving prose, irate political arguments, and updates on the Adams family. The letters finally cease in 1801, when they retired, together, to Massachusetts.

ADDITIONAL FACTS

1. *John Adams was the first president to live in the White House, which was half-finished in late 1800 when he and Abigail moved in.*

2. *While posted in Europe in the 1780s, John and Abigail hosted the visiting daughter of Thomas Jefferson (1743–1826) along with one of Jefferson's slaves—Sally Hemings.*

3. *Their oldest son, John Quincy Adams (1735–1826), became president of the United States in 1825.*

★ ★ ★

War of 1812

On June 18, 1812, the United States declared war on Great Britain, the most powerful country in the world. In the first decade of the 1800s, the British navy had routinely harassed American shipping in the Atlantic, seizing cargo with little or no justification. The British also frequently stopped American ships to "impress" sailors for forcible service in the Royal Navy. Fed up with the demeaning treatment on the high seas, in 1810 American voters elected a hawkish Congress bent on a confrontation with Britain.

The War of 1812, as it became known, unfolded on two fronts. British and American warships battled in the Atlantic, where the United States Navy, led by the USS *Constitution,* captured several enemy ships. At the same time, American armies wrestled for control of the Great Lakes region, where they faced both the British and their Native American allies under the great Shawnee chief Tecumseh (c. 1768–1813).

After several years of episodic fighting, American forces finally succeeded in controlling the Great Lakes, thanks in large part to the exploits of Oliver Hazard Perry (1785–1819), who defeated the British Navy on Lake Erie. However, at the same time, the British mounted a series of successful attacks on the East Coast of the United States. In 1814, the British army burned Washington, DC, forcing President James Madison (1751–1836) to flee from the city.

With both sides tiring of war, they signed the Treaty of Ghent on December 24, 1814. The treaty restored the status quo, meaning that both sides were able to claim victory. Britain made no concessions and did not agree to stop the impressment of American sailors. Canada remained a British possession. However, in practice the British never again interfered with American shipping.

ADDITIONAL FACTS

1. *The War of 1812 was so unpopular in New England, where trade with the British was a major part of the economy, that the governments of Connecticut and Massachusetts took their state militias out of the fighting.*

2. *The famous Battle of New Orleans, which made a national hero of Andrew Jackson (1767–1845), was fought on January 8, 1815—two weeks after Britain and the United States had signed the treaty ending the war but before the news had crossed the Atlantic.*

3. *Civil War general William Tecumseh Sherman (1820–1891) was named after the defeated Native American leader Tecumseh, whose military acumen was greatly admired even by his US Army adversaries.*

★ ★ ★

William Lloyd Garrison

A ferocious, unrelenting enemy of slavery, journalist William Lloyd Garrison (1805–1879) worked tirelessly starting in 1830 to turn northern public opinion in favor of abolition. Garrison started a newspaper called *The Liberator* in 1831, penning a famous editorial in his first edition promising, "I will be as harsh as truth and as uncompromising as justice . . . I will not retreat a single inch—AND I WILL BE HEARD."

In its heyday in the 1840s, *The Liberator* reached hundreds of thousands of homes across the North. As a writer, Garrison was a master of invective, in the radical tradition of Thomas Paine (1737–1809). The United States Constitution, Garrison wrote in one typically harsh article, was a "covenant with death and an agreement with hell" because it permitted slavery.

A native of Massachusetts, Garrison quickly became popular in the North, but his essays made him an instant villain to many southerners. He was burned in effigy in 1835 in Charleston, South Carolina. Southern lawmakers, led by Senator John C. Calhoun (1782–1850) of South Carolina, sought to prevent copies of *The Liberator* from circulating in the South, on the grounds that they could incite slaves to revolt.

In addition to its nonstop advocacy for abolition, *The Liberator* campaigned for women's rights and against the death penalty. A champion of many causes, Garrison had little patience for politicians. At a time when Abraham Lincoln (1809–1865) was seen as a national hero, Garrison denounced him when he failed to free slaves in the border states in his Emancipation Proclamation of 1863.

After the Civil War (1861–1865) and the December 1865 passage of the Thirteenth Amendment to the US Constitution that abolished slavery, Garrison triumphantly published a final edition of *The Liberator*. But he remained active politically, defending the rights of newly freed African-Americans in the South as well as Native Americans and Chinese immigrants.

ADDITIONAL FACTS

1. *Garrison's father, Abijah, abandoned his family a few years after William's birth by running away to sea.*

2. *In 1830, Garrison was convicted of libel and imprisoned for forty-five days after accusing a Massachusetts merchant of illegally trafficking in slaves.*

3. *Although nominally a pacifist, Garrison endorsed John Brown's raid on the US arsenal at Harpers Ferry, Virginia, in 1859 and enthusiastically backed the Union effort in the Civil War.*

★ ★ ★

California Gold Rush

On January 24, 1848, a lumber mill foreman named James Marshall (1810–1885) noticed a few shiny metallic flakes in a flume near Sacramento, California. Marshall and the mill's owner, John Sutter (1803–1880), tested the specks and were astonished by the results: They had discovered gold.

Within a year of the discovery at Sutter's Mill, a massive stampede of prospectors descended on northern California in a tumultuous chase for riches known as the California Gold Rush. Nearly overnight, the rush changed the face of California, which the United States had seized from Mexico only two years earlier. Swollen with profits from gold mining, Sacramento and San Francisco grew into major cities, and California was admitted into the Union as a state in 1850.

At the time of the gold rush, the metal was not only a valuable commodity but also the basis of the world's economy. The discovery of gold turned California into a nexus of world trade and made San Francisco the major gateway of American commerce with Asia.

For the prospectors who streamed to California by land and by sea, California during the early years of the gold rush was a notoriously dangerous, anarchic environment. Many "claims" to mining territory in the Sierra Nevada were enforced violently, helping to create the popular image of the lawless West. (The cartoon character Yosemite Sam, for instance, is supposed to be a *forty-niner*—a common term used to describe those who traveled to California in search of gold in 1849.) The gold rush also helped inspire the notion of "the American dream," the promise of a country in which anyone could become rich through the right combination of ambition and luck.

Within a few years of the discovery of the mother lode, the most easily accessible gold deposits in California were tapped out, and many forty-niners were ruined. Wealth from the gold rush, however, helped build the transatlantic railroad, and the cities established during the 1850s remained major centers of commerce. The gold rush itself was one of the most important events in the history of California, which is now the nation's most populous state.

ADDITIONAL FACTS

1. *In an homage to its gold-mining history, California's state motto is* Eureka—*a Greek term meaning I have found it!*

2. *San Francisco's NFL team, the Forty-Niners, is named in honor of the 1849 gold rush.*

3. *To handle the immense quantity of gold mined in California, the mint opened a branch office in San Francisco to turn the metal into currency. The facility is still in operation today.*

★ ★ ★

Oregon Trail

Before the completion of the transcontinental railroad in 1869, the most common overland route used by travelers to the West was a long, arduous path known as the Oregon Trail. First mapped in 1810, the route stretched more than 2,000 miles from Missouri to the Pacific Northwest. Although the voyage along the Oregon Trail took months to complete and was fraught with danger, thousands of pioneers crossed the continent on the trail to reach the lush farmlands of the Willamette Valley. The path remained in use for decades, and ruts created by thousands of covered wagons are still visible along many sections of the original trail.

First mapped by fur traders, the Oregon Trail was not widely used until 1836, when a new type of covered wagon was invented that could withstand the long westward journey. At the time, much of the region encompassing present-day Oregon and Washington still belonged to Great Britain, but the availability of cheap farmland was a major lure for Americans. Indeed, the rush of American settlers contributed to Britain's decision to cede its claim in the region to the United States in 1846.

For travelers, the trek across the Great Plains and through the Rocky Mountains was extremely dangerous, and hundreds of settlers died en route. In the mid-1840s, at the peak of the Oregon Trail's popularity, most of the Louisiana Purchase remained a near wilderness, with few outposts along the route. As users of the educational computer game *Oregon Trail* may recall, diseases like dysentery were a frequent affliction for the pioneers, and oxen often died before finishing the trip.

The fact that so many settlers were willing to brave the hardships of the Oregon Trail was a testament to the great enthusiasm for expansion shared by many nineteenth-century Americans. The Oregon Trail reflected and reinforced the widely held belief that the United States had a "Manifest Destiny" to expand its borders all the way to the Pacific Ocean.

ADDITIONAL FACTS

1. *New Yorkers Marcus and Narcissa Whitman, who crossed the continent in 1836, were the first settlers to complete the trip with a covered wagon.*

2. *The trail crossed the Rocky Mountains at South Pass, a famous route across the Continental Divide in Wyoming that was also used by Mormons fleeing to Utah.*

3. *The first trip along the trail took ten months; later, the average time was reduced to about four months.*

★ ★ ★

Mark Twain

Author, satirist, and literary critic Mark Twain (1835–1910) was the most prominent American writer of the late nineteenth century. Born in Missouri, Twain worked as a pilot on Mississippi River steamboats before moving to New England in the 1870s, where he wrote many of his best-known works. Although most famous for his immortal novel *The Adventures of Huckleberry Finn* (1884), Twain also authored *The Adventures of Tom Sawyer* (1876), *The Prince and the Pauper* (1882), *A Connecticut Yankee in King Arthur's Court* (1889), and reams of short stories and essays.

Born Samuel Langhorne Clemens, Twain adopted his pseudonym from a common phrase he heard in his travels along the Mississippi. Boatmen measuring the depth of the river would cry, "By the mark twain," meaning the water was two fathoms deep. Clemens joined the Confederate army in the Civil War, but deserted after his first taste of battle. He fled west, where he spent most of the war and where his first short story, "The Celebrated Jumping Frog of Calaveras County" (1865), was set.

The story, a comic tale of a California gold miner and his pet frog, contains many elements typical of Twain's wry, satirical style. In one passage, Twain describes the miner's earnest efforts to train his frog to "outjump any frog in Calaveras county."

> He ketched a frog one day, and took him home, and said he cal'klated to eder-cate him; and so he never done nothing for three months but set in his back yard and learn that frog to jump. And you bet you he did learn him, too, He'd give him a little punch behind, and the next minute you'd see that frog whirling in the air like a doughnut see him turn one summerset, or may be a couple, if he got a good start, and come down flat-footed and all right, like a cat.

Unlike many authors of his day, Twain wrote in the American vernacular, attempting to render the language as it was actually spoken by the people. Twain's influence on American literature was profound, and he was cited as a role model by authors from William Faulkner (1897–1962) to Ernest Hemingway (1899–1961).

ADDITIONAL FACTS

1. *Twain became politically active toward the end of his life, and he served as vice president of the Anti-Imperialist League formed to oppose the American occupation of the Philippines.*

2. *Always leery of organized religion, Twain targeted, among others, the Christian Science church, which he lampooned in the 1907 book* Christian Science: With Notes Containing Corrections to Date.

3. *Twain was fascinated by the French heroine Joan of Arc (1412–1431) and published a long, fictionalized account of her life in 1896.*

★ ★ ★

Jacob Riis

In 1870, a Danish carpenter named Jacob Riis (1849–1914) arrived in the United States with no friends, no money, and a spotty grasp of English. By the time he died more than forty years later, Riis had become a famed journalist, a trusted confidant of the president of the United States—and a wealthy man.

Riis achieved the American dream, ironically, by documenting the plight of those who didn't. His black-and-white photographs, published in major American magazines and in his seminal 1890 book *How the Other Half Lives*, exposed the violent, dirty conditions in New York City's teeming, dangerous slums.

Riis's concern for the urban poor stemmed, in part, from his own immigrant experience. After his arrival in New York, Riis spent several years living on the streets, sleeping in police stations and squalid flophouses. He finally found a job as a newspaper reporter, where he wrote about the woes of New York's poor that he so recently had experienced firsthand.

For Riis, however, photography proved a far more powerful form of journalism than writing. Technological advances after the Civil War (1861–1865) had made it possible to take candid shots with relative ease, giving Riis's pictures far more immediacy and intimacy than pictures by earlier photographers like Mathew Brady (c. 1823–1896). (More recently, however, scholars have criticized Riis for staging some of his pictures.) Riis was one of the first artists to take advantage of flash photography, which made nighttime and indoor photography possible after its invention in 1887.

For *How the Other Half Lives*, his most famous work, Riis photographed the over-crowded tenements, crime-ridden alleyways, and impoverished children of the slums. At a time when photography was still a relatively new and novel medium, the pictures provoked enormous outrage and helped inspire urban reformers like Jane Addams (1860–1935) in the twentieth century.

ADDITIONAL FACTS

1. *After becoming famous, Riis befriended Teddy Roosevelt (1858–1919), who invented the term* muck-raking *to describe the activities of Riis and his journalistic peers.*

2. *A public housing project on Avenue D on the Lower East Side of Manhattan is named after Riis.*

3. *The most famous picture taken by Riis, "Bandits' Roost," shows thugs standing in an alleyway at 59 ½ Mulberry Street in Manhattan, in a notoriously dangerous neighborhood that was later torn down and replaced by Columbus Park.*

★ ★ ★

John Marshall

One of the most influential judges in American history, John Marshall (1755–1835) served as chief justice of the United States for thirty-four years and wrote many of the most important rulings in the US Supreme Court's history. A Virginia politician, Revolutionary War veteran, and cousin of Thomas Jefferson (1743–1826), Marshall established the Court as an important and powerful force within the federal government. Marshall was one of the last remaining men of the revolutionary generation to remain active in national politics. Fittingly, when Marshall died in 1835, the Liberty Bell in Philadelphia tolled for the last time before cracking irreparably.

As a young officer during the Revolution, Marshall served under George Washington (1732–1799) during the awful winter at Valley Forge. After the war, Marshall entered Virginia politics and was a delegate to the Constitutional Convention in 1787.

Marshall remained active in the Virginia legislature after the convention, but eventually broke with Jefferson, his famous cousin, over national politics. Unlike most other prominent Virginians, Marshall sympathized with the Federalists, the political party of George Washington. Federalist President John Adams (1735–1826) named Marshall to the Supreme Court in 1801, just before the end of his term.

At the time Marshall took office, the Supreme Court was regarded as a backwater in the American government. In the early years of the Republic, it remained an open question whether the president would obey an unfavorable Supreme Court order or simply ignore the justices.

Marshall's first major case, *Marbury v. Madison* (1803), established the right of the Supreme Court to assess the constitutionality of legislation passed by Congress. Although taken for granted now, the principle of judicial review was highly controversial at the time. Thomas Jefferson, for one, thought it gave the Court too much power. Over the next three decades, Marshall consistently enraged Jefferson by expanding the powers of the federal government.

ADDITIONAL FACTS

1. *Thomas Jefferson loathed Marshall, believing that his cousin gave too much power to the federal government. During Jefferson's presidency, Jefferson appointed new justices he hoped would oppose Marshall on the Court, but he was frustrated when the persuasive Marshall talked them into backing his decisions.*

2. *Marshall, who lived in Virginia, was a slave owner and sought to avoid the issue of slavery in the Court.*

3. *In 1807, Marshall presided over the treason trial of Aaron Burr (1756–1836), who had been accused of plotting against the United States government. Marshall found Burr innocent, again enraging Jefferson, an enemy of Burr.*

★ ★ ★

Tecumseh

One of the most feared military leaders in American history, Tecumseh (c. 1768–1813) united dozens of Native American tribes in the Great Lakes region and led a series of wars against the United States before his death in battle during the War of 1812.

Born in Ohio into the powerful Shawnee tribe, Tecumseh grew up during a period of rapid white encroachment on traditional Native American territory. Prior to the American Revolution, British policy had discouraged settlement west of the thirteen original colonies. After American independence, a wave of settlers pushed into the region. Native Americans were defeated in a frontier war in the 1790s, and Ohio officially became a state in 1803.

Like many other Native Americans in the Great Lakes region, Tecumseh regarded the sudden arrival of so many settlers as a mortal threat to his tribe and their way of life. Once-powerful tribes in the East like the Pequot, Tecumseh noticed, had "vanished before the avarice and oppression of the white man, as snow before the summer sun."

In an effort to save his people from a similar fate, Tecumseh and his brother, the religious leader Tenskwatawa (c. 1775–c. 1837), also known as the Shawnee Prophet, assembled a military coalition to battle white expansion. "Let the white race perish," Tecumseh exhorted. "They seize your land, they corrupt your women, they trample on the ashes of your dead."

Emphasizing the need for Native Americans to act together, Tecumseh's following cut across tribal lines. The Sauk, Ojibway, and Miami tribes, among many others, contributed to the army assembled by Tecumseh.

Tecumseh's coalition was an impressive feat of diplomacy. Still, the force was defeated by the army of General William Henry Harrison (1773–1841) in its first major clash with the Americans at the Battle of Tippecanoe in 1811. Tecumseh was forced to flee north to Canada, where he began rebuilding his forces. After the start of the War of 1812, Tecumseh allied himself with the British and participated in the siege of Detroit. A year later, however, Tecumseh was killed at the Battle of the Thames.

ADDITIONAL FACTS

1. *Tecumseh and his followers referred to Americans as the "Long Knives."*

2. *Harrison later capitalized on his fame for defeating Tecumseh during the 1840 presidential race, when he and running mate John Tyler (1790–1862) ran successfully under the slogan "Tippecanoe and Tyler Too."*

3. *Among many other tributes, a starship in the TV series* Star Trek: Deep Space Nine *is named after Tecumseh.*

★ ★ ★

Mormonism

The founder of the Mormon religion, Joseph Smith (1805–1844), was born in a tiny Vermont village and moved to upstate New York as a child. In New York, at age twenty-four, Smith claimed at the direction of an angel to have found, buried in a hillside, gold plates engraved in a form of ancient Egyptian that contained additional books of the Bible. Smith's translation of the plates, first published as the Book of Mormon by Smith in 1830, said that Jesus had come to North America after his resurrection, among other claims. In the fervent atmosphere of the Second Great Awakening, Smith attracted a handful of believers.

For the next several decades, Smith and his growing band of Mormon converts encountered enormous hostility and occasionally violent persecution. Smith himself would be killed by an angry mob in Illinois. Mainstream Christians considered Mormonism either blasphemous or a cult, and they eventually chased Smith's followers out of their settlements in Missouri and Illinois. Under the leadership of Brigham Young (1801–1877), Smith's successor as head of the church, the Mormons eventually fled to Utah.

The persecution of the Mormons exposed, often tragically, the limits of religious tolerance in nineteenth-century American society. Mormon leaders, including Smith, were occasionally tarred and feathered. The governor of Missouri issued an "extermination order" expelling Mormons from the state in 1838, which resulted in the deaths of several adherents. The Mormon belief in "plural marriage," or bigamy, was considered bizarre and repulsive by many Americans.

For decades after moving to Utah—and, arguably, into the present day—Mormons continued to encounter suspicion and hostility. In 1890, Congress refused to admit Utah as a state unless it banned bigamy. The president of the Mormon Church, officially called the Church of Jesus Christ of Latter-Day Saints, had a revelation from God at roughly the same time that the practice should be discontinued. Although Mormons describe themselves as Christians, many other Christian groups continue to regard them as heretical.

ADDITIONAL FACTS

1. *Before their exodus to Utah, the Mormons tried to establish a city in Illinois called* Nauvoo, *after a Hebrew word for* beautiful.

2. *Utah was a Mexican territory when the Mormons first arrived, but it became a part of the United States after the Mexican War (1846–1848).*

3. *The state governments of Missouri and Illinois officially apologized for their earlier harassment of Mormons in 1976 and 2004, respectively.*

★ ★ ★

Cornelius Vanderbilt

"You have undertaken to cheat me. I won't sue you,
for the law is too slow. I'll ruin you."
—Letter from Cornelius Vanderbilt to business associates

Ruthless railroad tycoon Cornelius Vanderbilt (1794–1877) was one of the nineteenth century's most notorious and successful businessmen. Driven and ambitious, Vanderbilt was said to have had few friends but countless enemies thanks to his bare-knuckle business tactics. Vanderbilt significantly expanded the American railroad network and created one of the nation's largest and most profitable railways, the New York Central. He died one of the nation's wealthiest but most despised men.

Born on Staten Island, New York, to a middle-class family of Dutch origin, Vanderbilt attended school only briefly. He was running his own ferry business by age sixteen and eventually made a fortune as a steamship operator. Vanderbilt's famous nickname, "Commodore," dated back to his steamship days.

In the 1840s, Vanderbilt was one of the first businessmen to realize the enormous commercial potential of the railways. By the outbreak of the Civil War in 1861, he had assembled a stable of East Coast railroads, which he eventually merged into the New York Central.

Relentlessly competitive, Vanderbilt's fight with Jay Gould (1836–1892) and Daniel Drew (1797–1879) over ownership of the Erie Railroad, a line between New York City and Buffalo, was one of the most famous business rivalries of the nineteenth century. Although Gould eventually won control of the Erie, the clash strengthened Vanderbilt's reputation as a cutthroat tycoon.

After Vanderbilt's death, the New York Central remained one of the biggest companies in the United States until it went bankrupt in the 1960s and was merged with its major competitor, the Pennsylvania Railroad. Despite his occasional forays into philanthropy, Vanderbilt is known today mostly as a prime example of the nineteenth-century robber baron.

ADDITIONAL FACTS

1. *The Erie Railroad was nicknamed "the scarlet woman of Wall Street" because of the huge financial battles over its ownership in the 1860s and 1870s.*

2. *A Vanderbilt steamship that sank off Connecticut in 1840, the Lexington, was rediscovered in 1983 by divers who found about $100,000 worth of silver amid the wreckage.*

3. *When Vanderbilt died, his estate, worth more than $100 million, exceeded the holdings of the United States Treasury.*

★ ★ ★

Mormon Trail

Between 1846 and 1869, 70,000 Mormons migrated to the barren deserts of Utah seeking religious freedom. The huge exodus, led by church president Brigham Young (1801–1877), had been triggered by the lynching of the church's founder in 1844 and the violent persecution endured by Mormons in Illinois and Missouri. Overcoming significant hardships, the first wagon train of Mormons arrived at the Great Salt Lake in the summer of 1847, where they would establish one of the largest settlements in the West.

The first group of Mormons had departed Nauvoo, Illinois, in February 1846. Headed by Young, the group made slow progress, covering only 300 miles before the next winter. The migrants camped near Council Bluffs, Iowa, where they endured a famously harsh winter. By some estimates, about 15 percent of the pilgrims died of cholera, scurvy, or starvation during the long stay at their winter quarters.

The next spring, Young and 147 other Mormons resumed the westward trek through the wilderness. Much of the Mormon Trail paralleled the Oregon Trail, but it veered south after crossing the Continental Divide. After 111 days, Young and his exhausted followers finally reached the Great Salt Lake.

Back in Nauvoo, meanwhile, the persecution of the Mormons continued unabated, which in turn fueled more migration west. When word spread of Young's successful trek, more wagon trains followed him to Utah. By 1852, about 20,000 Mormons lived in the vicinity of Salt Lake, making it one of the largest cities in the West.

For the initial wave of Mormon settlers, life in Utah was not easy. The region around Salt Lake had been bypassed by Spanish and Mexican settlers because of its inhospitable conditions; the Mormons' first crops nearly failed as the result of an infestation of crickets. Then, in 1857, President James Buchanan (1791–1868) sent federal troops to Utah in the "Mormon War" to rein in Young's control over the territory. Not until 1896, after the Mormons outlawed polygamy, would Utah join the Union.

ADDITIONAL FACTS

1. *Anti-Mormon violence in Illinois had grown so bad that in a single month in 1845, 200 Mormon homes and farms were burned.*

2. *The Mormons wanted to name the area Deseret, after a word in the Book of Mormon; the United States called it Utah instead, after the Ute tribe of Native Americans.*

3. *Knowing it would cause controversy, the Mormons attempted to keep the doctrine of "plural marriage" a secret following Smith's 1843 revelation sanctioning the practice, but word quickly spread, inflaming anti-Mormon sentiment in the Midwest.*

★ ★ ★

The Adventures of Huckleberry Finn

The Adventures of Huckleberry Finn, a novel published by Mark Twain in 1884, is considered one of the single most beloved and influential works of fiction in the American canon. A picaresque, the novel follows the adventures of a young boy, Huckleberry Finn, and an escaped slave, Jim, as they float down the Mississippi River on a raft. Part adventure story and part social satire, Twain's novel is also extremely controversial for its frequent use of racial epithets, its problematic depiction of Jim, and its somewhat bizarre ending.

At the beginning of the novel, the young Huckleberry Finn fakes his own death in order to run away from his abusive father and his caretaker, an old widow. On the run, he eventually meets Jim, a runaway slave owned by the sister of Huck's caretaker, and the two resolve to escape to the North together. Unfortunately for them, the Mississippi River flows south, and unwittingly the two drift farther and farther into the slave states in the course of their wild adventures.

During the trip down the Mississippi, Huck and Jim meet a fantastic array of swindlers, grifters, crooks, impostors, and drunks. Twain's zany, improbable characters—especially two con men, the Duke and the Dauphin, who join the escapees on the raft for several chapters—are among the most memorable in American fiction. Through the course of the novel, Twain uses the adventures of Huck and Jim to lampoon American capitalism, family life, and racial attitudes.

The novel was Twain's most commercially successful book during his lifetime. Today, Twain's admirers interpret his frequent use of racial epithets as an ironic commentary on American racism, rather than an endorsement of those views. However, due to the racial aspects of the book, *The Adventures of Huckleberry Finn* is one of the most frequently banned books in the history of American literature. At any given time, a parent somewhere in the United States is complaining about Twain, a situation that surely would have gratified the great satirist.

Twain himself, as if anticipating the controversy his book would cause a century later, warned against taking anything in the novel too seriously. In the beginning of the book, he offered a famous, tongue-in-cheek disclaimer to his readers: "Persons attempting to find a motive in this narrative will be prosecuted; persons attempting to find a moral in it will be banished; persons attempting to find a plot in it will be shot."

ADDITIONAL FACTS

1. *Disney released a film version of* The Adventures of Huckleberry Finn *in 1993 starring future hobbit Elijah Wood as Huck.*

2. *Although based on Twain's recollections of his Missouri childhood,* The Adventures of Huckleberry Finn *was written after he moved to Hartford, Connecticut.*

3. *In the old French monarchy,* dauphin *was the title used for heir to the throne.*

★ ★ ★

Scott Joplin

In the last decade of the nineteenth century, a popular new musical style called *ragtime* emerged from the saloons and nightclubs of the United States. Ragtime, a precursor to jazz, was characterized by complex, syncopated beats and joyous, lilting piano melodies. Pianist Scott Joplin (c. 1867–1917), the son of a former slave, was the most famous ragtime composer and wrote two of the most well-known rags of the era, "The Entertainer" and "Maple Leaf Rag."

Born in Texas, Joplin later moved to Sedalia, Missouri, where he would spend much of his life. In high school, he took piano lessons from a German classical music teacher who had recognized his exceptional talent. Joplin also learned to play cornet and violin and began performing in brass bands around Sedalia.

Joplin's big breakthrough as a composer came in 1899, with the publication of "Maple Leaf Rag," which went on to sell hundreds of thousands of copies. Over the next three years, as ragtime's popularity peaked, Joplin published many of his most well-known rags in quick succession, including "The Entertainer," "Elite Syncopations," and "The Easy Winners."

Despite his commercial success, Joplin still yearned to be taken seriously as a classical musician, and he began crafting more ambitious compositions. He wrote an opera, *A Guest of Honor*, in 1903, but it flopped commercially, and the score has been lost. Joplin moved to New York in 1907 to find a producer for his second opera, *Treemonisha*. Self-published in 1911, it would never be staged in his lifetime; at the time of his death from syphilis in 1917, Joplin was still seeking a producer for *Treemonisha*.

With the growing popularity of jazz, Joplin's rags fell into obscurity after his death. *Treemonisha* was finally staged in 1972, and the hit movie *The Sting* (1973), which used Joplin's rags in its sound track, revived popular interest in ragtime and Joplin.

ADDITIONAL FACTS

1. *Under the terms of his contract, Joplin got a royalty payment for each copy of "Maple Leaf Rag" sold: one cent.*

2. *Joplin wrote a tribute to President Theodore Roosevelt (1858–1919) in 1902 titled "The Strenuous Life" after Roosevelt became the first president to invite an African-American to dinner at the White House the previous year.*

3. *After his move to New York, Joplin briefly had the same music publisher as the young Irving Berlin (1888–1989); Joplin believed that Berlin stole part of the tune of "Alexander's Ragtime Band" from him.*

★ ★ ★

Alexander Hamilton

Alexander Hamilton (c. 1755–1804), a New York military officer and lawyer, ran the Department of the Treasury during the presidency of George Washington (1732–1799) and used his position to expand the power of the fledgling federal government. Hamilton believed that the new government needed to be strong and centralized to ensure economic prosperity and security, pitting him against Thomas Jefferson (1743–1826) and other skeptics of federal power.

 Hamilton was born in the British island colony of Nevis and moved to New York as a teenager. He attended King's College—now Columbia University—and fought under George Washington during the Revolution, becoming one of the general's trusted aides. After the war, he opened a prosperous law office on Wall Street in New York.

Like many other Americans, Hamilton became frustrated with the disorganized and weak national government created by the Articles of Confederation. Hamilton eagerly joined the New York delegation sent to Philadelphia in 1787 to draft a new Constitution. After the completion of the document, he returned to New York to lobby skeptical state politicians to approve the new plan. Determined to make the new government work, Hamilton played a leading role in convincing Washington to accept the presidency.

During Washington's administration, Hamilton supported internal improvements aimed at fostering the industrial base of the new nation. Hamilton and his supporters became the Federalist Party, the first political party in the Republic's history, while Jefferson, Madison, and their allies coalesced into the opposing Republicans.

One of Hamilton's biggest political rivals was Jefferson's vice president, Aaron Burr (1756–1836), a fellow New Yorker. When Hamilton campaigned against Burr's candidacy for governor of New York, the enraged Burr challenged him to a duel. Hamilton foolishly accepted and was killed by Burr on July 12, 1804.

ADDITIONAL FACTS

1. *Hamilton resigned as secretary of the treasury in 1795, unable to live on his $3,500-a-year government salary. He returned to the private sector and soon tripled his salary as a New York lawyer.*

2. *Hamilton was the only signer of the Constitution from New York State, since the two other delegates refused to sign.*

3. *In 1801, Hamilton was one of the founders of the* New York Post *newspaper, now the oldest continuously published newspaper in the United States.*

★ ★ ★

Nat Turner

The cruelty of southern slavery led to several attempted revolts by enslaved African-Americans against their owners. One of the most famous was Nat Turner's rebellion (1831) in southern Virginia. Turner's band of followers, totaling about fifty slaves, killed dozens of whites and terrorized Virginia slave owners before Turner's eventual capture and execution later that year.

Turner (1800–1831), who believed his actions were directed by God, began planning the revolt in February 1831, after a lunar eclipse that he interpreted as a divine order to mount a rebellion. The revolt itself started August 22, 1831. Turner killed his owner, Joseph Travis, along with the entire Travis family, and then the rebels began moving from house to house killing white men, women, and children.

The Virginia militia eventually quashed the rebellion, and Turner was captured October 30, 1831. After a short trial, he was hanged on November 11, and his body horribly mutilated by Virginia authorities. Many of Turner's followers were also executed. The revolt sent a wave of fear across the South, and hysterical white mobs killed hundreds of blacks in reprisal for Turner's revolt.

Although militarily unsuccessful, Nat Turner's revolt was a profound shock to the South. Fearing another revolt, slave owners became even harsher in their treatment of slaves. They also stepped up their criticism of northern abolitionists like William Lloyd Garrison (1805–1879), whom they accused of fomenting rebellion and chaos.

Some historians argue that Nat Turner's revolt may have derailed a homegrown southern abolitionist movement and hardened pro-slavery sentiment. Prior to Nat Turner's revolt, many Virginians opposed slavery. But those voices were muted after 1831, when southern politicians increasingly portrayed slavery as a necessary institution and portrayed any criticism of slavery as support for revolt.

For the next thirty years, southern slave owners lived in constant fear of revolt. Historians have uncovered evidence of hundreds of small acts of armed resistance to slavery by African-Americans, but none had as immediate an impact on public opinion as Nat Turner's doomed uprising in 1831.

ADDITIONAL FACTS

1. The story of Nat Turner's life was turned into a Pulitzer Prize–winning book, The Confessions of Nat Turner, by author William Styron in 1967.

2. After Nat Turner's revolt, southern politicians successfully lobbied Congress to forbid abolitionists from mailing antislavery publications to the South on the grounds they might incite another uprising.

3. In 1859, white abolitionist John Brown (1800–1859) tried to start another slave revolt in the town of Harpers Ferry, Virginia, but was thwarted by an American officer named Robert E. Lee (1807–1870).

★ ★ ★

Amistad Case

In 1839, fifty-three Africans were kidnapped in Sierra Leone and transported to Cuba to be sold into slavery. In Cuba, the captives were transferred to a small schooner called *La Amistad*, which means *the friendship* in Spanish. A few days later, after the *Amistad* had left Havana, one of the men, Joseph Cinque, led a revolt against the crew, killing the captain and the cook. With the Africans now running the ship, they sailed northward until they eventually reached Long Island, New York, where they were taken into custody by the US Navy.

American authorities imprisoned the Africans in New Haven, Connecticut, while the courts mulled their fate. The Spanish government, which at that point still controlled Cuba, demanded the return of the ship and the slaves. The administration of President Martin van Buren (1782–1862), hoping to avoid an international incident, sided with the Spanish.

With Northern public opinion in the 1830s turning swiftly against slavery, many prominent businessmen and ministers rallied to the defense of the Africans and formed a legal defense committee. To the surprise of the Van Buren administration, a federal judge in Connecticut ruled in favor of the Africans, agreeing that their revolt was lawful and they were free to return to Africa.

The *Amistad* decision outraged both the Spanish government and Southern slaveholders. To placate Spain, Van Buren immediately appealed the decision to the United States Supreme Court, setting up what was to be one of the most memorable cases in the Court's short history. In Washington, DC, the Africans were represented by former president John Quincy Adams (1767–1848). In an eloquent opening argument, Adams criticized Van Buren and argued that the Africans were persons, not cargo, and thus not covered by the treaties with Spain that required the United States to return lost cargo. The Supreme Court ruled in favor of the Africans, who then returned to Sierra Leone in 1842.

ADDITIONAL FACTS

1. *On the day of their revolt, the slaves aboard the* Amistad *spared the lives of two Spanish slave traders, hoping the two could steer the ship back to Africa. Instead, the two men guided the boat toward the United States, and they were later allowed to return to Cuba.*

2. *For the next twenty years, the enraged Spanish government continued to press for compensation from the United States for the Africans aboard the* Amistad, *to no avail.*

3. *Director Steven Spielberg released a movie about the case,* Amistad, *in 1997. A replica of the* Amistad *was built in 2000 and docked in Connecticut near the site of the first* Amistad *trial.*

★ ★ ★

P. T. Barnum

P. T. Barnum (1810–1891) never said "there's a sucker born every minute," a quote widely attributed to the entrepreneur, but he might as well have. As the self-proclaimed "greatest showman on earth," Barnum made millions selling nineteenth-century Americans tickets to see his collection of freaks, midgets, elephants, geeks, mermaids, Siamese twins, bearded ladies, snakes, and other outlandish exhibits. The famous Ringling Brothers and Barnum and Bailey Circus, which still tours the United States today, is the direct descendent of the show devised by the nineteenth century's greatest entertainment mogul.

Born in Connecticut, Phineas Taylor Barnum showed a talent for hucksterism at an early age by selling lottery tickets to neighbors. In 1834, he moved to New York City, where he hired an elderly African-American woman named Joice Heth to pose as the "161-year-old woman." Exhibiting her throughout the Northeast, Barnum made a huge profit off gullible audiences who paid to gawk at the woman Barnum claimed had been George Washington's nurse." He soon hired his most famous midget, the twenty-five-inch-tall Charles Sherwood Stratton (1838–1883), who went by the stage name General Tom Thumb and became so famous that he was summoned to meet Great Britain's Queen Victoria in 1844.

Barnum, who later in life established his first traveling circus, P. T. Barnum's Grand Traveling Museum, Menagerie, Caravan, and Circus, was the first to admit that most of his shows were pure "humbug." As long as audiences had a good time, however, he saw nothing wrong with his far-fetched claims. "I have never been in any humbug business where I did not give full value," Barnum once claimed.

In addition to his shows, Barnum served briefly as the mayor of Bridgeport, Connecticut, his hometown and now the site of the Barnum Museum. An ardent Union supporter during the Civil War (1861–1865), he also served in the Connecticut legislature. In 1881, Barnum merged his circus with another show run by James Bailey. Barnum's last words were reportedly, "Ask Bailey what the box office was at the Garden last night."

ADDITIONAL FACTS

1. *When Barnum was on his deathbed, a New York newspaper published his obituary early so that the showman could enjoy reading it.*

2. *A commemorative half-dollar was minted in 1936, the 100th anniversary of Bridgeport's incorporation, with Barnum's face on the front; he is the only huckster so honored on American currency.*

3. *The slang term* jumbo *comes from the name of one of the elephants in Barnum's circus, Jumbo.*

★ ★ ★

Smithsonian Institution

The Smithsonian Institution—nineteen separate branches that together form the largest museum in the world—was originally founded in 1846 after the federal government received a bequest of $508,318 from the estate of the English chemist James Smithson (1765–1829). From its relatively humble beginnings, the Smithsonian has grown into a collection of more than 136 million items and is nicknamed "the nation's attic" for its role in preserving the American cultural heritage.

Smithson, a scientist best known for his research on zinc, was the illegitimate son of an English nobleman. In his will, he left his fortune to the United States, a country he had never visited, for reasons that remain a mystery. Unsure at first whether it could legally accept the huge inheritance, Congress debated for several years before finally chartering the institution. The Smithsonian Castle, the unusual medieval-style headquarters building that sits on the National Mall in Washington DC, opened in 1855.

Originally, most of the Smithsonian's budget was devoted to scientific research, which still forms a significant part of its mission. By the late nineteenth century, however, public museums had become the institution's face to the world. Today, more than 20 million people visit the museums clustered on the National Mall, which are free of charge. The list of famous artifacts housed at the Smithsonian includes the original star-spangled banner that flew over Fort McHenry in 1814, the Wright Brothers' plane, and the lunar landing craft that took astronauts to the Moon in 1969.

The most recent branch of the Smithsonian, the National Museum of the American Indian, opened on the Mall in 2004.

ADDITIONAL FACTS

1. *The Smithson inheritance was delivered to the United States in the form of eleven boxes of British gold coins, which had to be shipped to Philadelphia and reminted in American currency in 1838.*

2. *Smithson died and was buried in Italy in 1829, but Alexander Graham Bell (1847–1922), the inventor of the telephone, later arranged for his remains to be moved to the United States.*

3. *The Smithsonian includes the 213 books from Smithson's private library.*

★ ★ ★

Henry James

In his long and prolific career, the author Henry James (1843–1916) penned several of the most influential novels in late nineteenth- and early twentieth-century American literature, including *The Portrait of a Lady* (1881), *The Bostonians* (1886), and *The Golden Bowl* (1904). James's graceful, elegant stories frequently explored the collision of free-spirited and naive Americans with cynical and sophisticated Europe. James himself lived most of his adult life in Europe and renounced his American citizenship shortly before his death.

Born to an extremely wealthy New York City family, James traveled widely during his teenage years, an unusual luxury in the nineteenth century. He returned to the United States during the Civil War (1861–1865) and briefly attended Harvard Law School, but he dropped out to devote himself to writing. His first short stories were immediately hailed for their realism and richly detailed characters. He moved back to Europe in the 1870s and set his first successful novel, *Roderick Hudson* (1875), in Rome.

Scholars often divide James's literary career into three distinct periods. His first major works explore the sharp contrasts between American and European society, and specifically the differences between American and European women. *The Portrait of a Lady*, a novel about a naive American girl named Isabel Archer and her travels in Europe, is the most famous example of this early period in James's career. In his next phase, James began to write about politics. One of the most well-known novels of this period, *The Bostonians*, is a wry satire of New England reform movements and the role of women in society and politics. Finally, after the turn of the century, James published a series of lengthy novels that employed a more experimental narrative style with less of the clarity of his earlier works. *The Golden Bowl*, a novel about adultery, is one of the most famous of his later, twentieth-century novels.

Throughout his career, James's exacting attention to characterization was one of the chief distinguishing features in his work. Influenced by the Russian novelist Ivan Turgenev (1818–1883), James believed that characters, not plots, were the essence of great fiction.

ADDITIONAL FACTS

1. *His older brother, William James (1842–1910), was a leading American philosopher and psychology professor at Harvard.*

2. *Henry James became a British subject in 1915, the year before his death, in an act of protest against American neutrality in World War I (1914–1918).*

3. *The famous main character of* The Portrait of a Lady, *Isabel Archer, was based in part on James's own cousin, Minny Temple.*

★ ★ ★

Frank Lloyd Wright

The father of modern American architecture, Frank Lloyd Wright (1867–1959) rejected the traditional, boxy designs of the nineteenth century and created hundreds of houses in his own distinctive "prairie" architecture style. Although Wright himself built few urban buildings and disdained skyscrapers, a generation of architects influenced by his iconoclastic style profoundly reshaped the look of American cities.

Born in Wisconsin shortly after the Civil War (1861–1865), Wright moved to Chicago in 1887 to work for architect Louis Sullivan (1856–1924), the famous designer of skyscrapers. Sullivan and Wright shared a contempt for what they regarded as stale, classical design. An ordinary box-style building, Wright once said, was a "coffin for the human spirit."

Wright grew to loathe skyscrapers, too. Instead, he believed in a concept that he invented called *organic architecture*, the notion that the form and the function of a building were the same. Imposing a style on a building, he felt, made no sense—the design should grow out of the building's use and setting. In practice, Wright's home designs were usually sleek, low-slung bungalows with open floor plans and big windows. Concerned with every detail, Wright sometimes even designed the furniture to be used in his buildings.

Wright was often caustic in his criticisms of other architects, and he immodestly referred to himself as the nation's "greatest living architect." In addition to homes, Wright designed hotels, museums, and churches, including the bulbous Guggenheim Museum in New York City. The Guggenheim, still under construction at the time of his death, has become perhaps his most famous building and the greatest memorial to the most influential architect of the United States.

ADDITIONAL FACTS

1. *In 1915, the emperor of Japan commissioned Wright to build a hotel in Tokyo. Thanks to Wright's ingenious design, the Imperial Hotel was one of the few large buildings in the city to survive a 1923 earthquake, but it was demolished in 1968.*

2. *Raised in a devout Unitarian household, Wright would go on to design a Unitarian church in his home state of Wisconsin that is still in use.*

3. *Private homes designed by Wright are routinely resold on the real estate market, and he is one of the few famous architects whose works are remotely affordable for a middle-class family. Listings can be found at www.savewright.org.*

★ ★ ★

Federalist Papers

The Federalist Papers is the collective name for an extraordinary series of newspaper columns published in 1787 and 1788 aiming to convince Americans to accept the new Constitution. Published in New York under the pseudonym *Publius*, the columns were actually written by three eminent politicians: Alexander Hamilton (c. 1755–1804), James Madison (1751–1836), and John Jay (1745–1829). Hamilton picked the name *Publius* in honor of an ancient Roman statesman, Publius Valerius Publicola, one of the founders of the Roman Republic. The collected columns later were published as a book titled *The Federalist*. The Federalist Papers are still cited by lawyers and scholars today for their insight into how the Founders intended the constitutional system to work.

Under the Constitution, at least nine of the thirteen states had to ratify the document before it would come into force. Several states, led by Delaware, ratified promptly, but New York hesitated. A strong anti-Federalist faction in the state, led by Governor George Clinton (1739–1812), argued that the Constitution took too much power from the individual states, that it failed to protect individual liberties, and that the office of the presidency would replicate the dictatorial monarchy Americans had just overthrown. Critics in Virginia, led by Revolutionary War firebrand Patrick Henry (1736–1799), also publicly argued against the Constitution.

Hamilton, Madison, and Jay began publishing their columns in 1787 to counter these influential critics. Without the Constitution's ratification in New York, they feared, all their work at Philadelphia would go to waste. The Federalist Papers were measured and analytical, setting forth a practical explanation of how the new government would work and why it would benefit the thirteen states. In total, the three men published eighty-five articles over the course of several months.

In the short term, the Federalist Papers accomplished their political goal. After tumultuous debate, New York ratified the Constitution in mid-1788. Almost immediately, however, the papers were recognized as brilliant commentaries on the new Constitution. George Washington (1732–1799), in a 1788 letter to Hamilton, said he would give a printed edition of the Federalist Papers the place of honor in his library at Mount Vernon. Hamilton, Madison, and Jay were unmasked as the authors within months of publication, and their practical, analytical commentaries on the Constitution are still studied today.

ADDITIONAL FACTS

1. *After the columns became famous, Madison and Hamilton both claimed credit for certain essays. It took historians until 1964 to determine that Madison had, in fact, authored the disputed articles.*

2. *Governor Clinton also published a series of anonymous newspaper essays, under the pen name Cato, after a Roman politician.*

3. *Anti-Federalists convinced Congress to add the Bill of Rights to protect individual liberties in 1791.*

★ ★ ★

Mexican War

California, Nevada, Utah, and parts of four other present-day western states were ceded to the United States as a result of the American victory in the Mexican War, fought between 1846 and 1848. In the conflict, American troops occupied Mexico City and forced the Mexican government to hand over vast parcels of land, almost half its entire country, in exchange for peace.

In the fall of 1845, newly elected US President James K. Polk (1795–1849) had sent an envoy to Mexico with an offer that would relieve Mexico of its $3 million debt to the United States. He wanted to buy California for $25 million. The Mexicans rejected the offer, considering it an insult to their national honor. In the spring of 1846, Polk sent thousands of American troops to Texas, ostensibly to guard the area against Mexican attack. After a skirmish between the two nations near the border, Polk asked Congress for a declaration of war.

Even at the time, a war fought simply to expand the size of the United States caused great controversy. The famous writer Henry David Thoreau (1817–1862) went to jail for refusing to pay taxes to support the war. Abraham Lincoln (1809–1865), then a member of the House of Representatives from Illinois, voted against the war declaration.

Militarily, the war was a shining success. The weak Mexican government was incapable of defending itself against invaders commanded by General Zachary Taylor (1784–1850). After American troops took Mexico City, the Mexican government had little choice but to agree to the Treaty of Guadalupe Hidalgo in early 1848. Under the terms of the treaty, Mexico gave up its land in exchange for $15 million—much less than Polk had originally offered back in 1845.

The resounding success of the war made Taylor a national hero and propelled him into the White House in 1848 when Polk decided not to run for a second term.

ADDITIONAL FACTS

1. *Memories of the war remain raw in Mexico, where the loss of half the country's territory to the United States is remembered as "the Mutilation."*

2. *Many of the leaders who later became famous in the Civil War (1861–1865), including both Confederate general Robert E. Lee (1807–1870) and Union general Ulysses S. Grant (1822–1855), fought as comrades in the Mexican War.*

3. *Taylor's opponent in the 1848 election was another Mexican War hero, General Winfield Scott (1786–1866), nicknamed "Old Fuss and Feathers."*

* * *

Dorothea Dix

Nurse and social reformer Dorothea Dix (1802–1887) led numerous campaigns seeking humane treatment for the mentally ill in the 1840s and 1850s and later served as the head Union nurse during the Civil War (1861–1865). Her passionate advocacy for society's outcasts led to the establishment of the first major American mental hospitals.

Born in Maine, Dix became interested in the treatment of people with mental illness after touring England in 1836. In both the United States and England, mentally ill individuals in the nineteenth century were often locked away with criminals under horrific conditions in ordinary prisons. During her trip, Dix met a number of English reformers active in the asylum movement, which sought to build separate facilities for the mentally ill where they could receive treatment.

On her return to the United States, Dix presented a proposal to the Massachusetts legislature in 1843 to build a state mental hospital. She introduced the proposal with a memorably fiery speech: "I come as the advocate of the helpless, forgotten, insane and idiotic men and women," she said. Her proposal was successful, and the Massachusetts campaign served as a template for similar proposals across the Union.

In the 1850s, now a high-profile reformer, Dix devised a national plan to build federally supported hospitals. The proposal passed Congress but was vetoed by President Franklin Pierce (1804–1869), who thought giving such support was an inappropriate role for the federal government to play. Crushed, Dix left the United States for much of the late 1850s, continuing her reform work in England, Scotland, and continental Europe.

At the outbreak of the Civil War, Dix returned home and was appointed superintendent of female nurses for the Union. Although her influence in the job proved minimal, she won plaudits in the South for the compassionate treatment her nurses provided to enemy prisoners.

After the war, Dix resumed her work on behalf of the mentally ill. Unfortunately, after Dix's death in 1887, many of the hospitals she supported fell into decline.

ADDITIONAL FACTS

1. *Although steeped in the same New England liberalism as other contemporary reformers, Dix opposed abolitionism and women's suffrage, which cost her crusades crucial support.*

2. *Her position during the Civil War was unpaid.*

3. *Dix is credited with founding a total of thirty-two mental hospitals during her long career.*

★ ★ ★

Samuel Colt

One of the first American millionaires, Samuel Colt (1814–1862) invented the revolver that bears his name and built the world's largest private armory at his sprawling headquarters in Hartford, Connecticut. Guns manufactured by Colt were standard issue on the Union side during the Civil War, and the famous Colt six-shooter, nicknamed "the Peacemaker," was the most popular handgun for settlers in the West. Thanks to the Crimean War (1853–1856) and the Civil War (1861–1865), Colt amassed an enormous fortune and was thought to be the richest man in the United States at the time of his death.

Born in Hartford, Colt was a mediocre student who loved firearms and explosives as a child. He designed his first revolver prototype at age eighteen and patented his first designs when he was twenty-one. The major advantage of Colt's revolver was that it could be fired repeatedly without reloading, a huge time-saver. Colt received an order for 1,000 revolvers from the US military during the Mexican War (1846–1848), his first major sale.

Colt's business took off during the 1850s, when he sold weapons to both sides during the Crimean War. Brash and pompous, Colt used his sudden wealth to build a highly unusual factory building in Hartford to house his company. The factory, a giant brick building topped with a blue, onion-shaped dome, remained home to the Colt company until 1994 and for many decades was the largest privately owned weapons factory in the world.

Although Colt himself was a Democrat who opposed President Abraham Lincoln's war policies, he reaped a huge profit from the Civil War. However, the stress of running his company during the war took a ruinous toll on Colt's health, and he died in January 1862. Colt's business remained a top American corporation for most of the nineteenth century, but fell on hard times after World War II (1939–1945) and merged with a Texas armory in 1955. The M-16 automatic rifle—currently the standard-issue rifle in the United States military—is produced by one of the direct descendants of Colt's original firm.

ADDITIONAL FACTS

1. *Colt was the first American manufacturer to open a foreign branch, building a factory in London in 1853 to supply the British with weapons during the Crimean War.*

2. *In recognition of Colt's significance in Texas history, Houston's first Major League Baseball team was called the Colt .45s from 1962 until 1965, when it changed its name to the Astros.*

3. *Colt's design for the revolver is said to have been inspired by the wheel of a ship.*

★ ★ ★

San Francisco

The prototypical boomtown of the American West, San Francisco went from small mission pueblo to sprawling metropolis within five years. In 1848, before the discovery of gold in the nearby Sierra Nevada, San Francisco's population was about 1,000. By 1852, the population was 35,000 and San Francisco was the biggest, richest city in California.

Founded by the Spanish in 1776 and named after Saint Francis of Assisi, the town was initially home to little more than an elegant stone mission and a small fortress. The entire area was considered part of Mexico, which declared its independence from Spain in 1821. Mission Dolores, the oldest structure in San Francisco, is one of the few remaining buildings from the city's colonial period.

Along with the rest of California, the city became American territory in 1848 under the terms of the treaty ending the Mexican War. In the same year, gold was discovered in the mountains east of the city, and hundreds of ships rushed to California carrying miners bound for the hills. Many of them got no farther than the foggy streets of San Francisco, where hundreds of shops and banks opened to serve the new arrivals. San Francisco was incorporated as a city in 1850.

In its early years, San Francisco grew too fast for the law to catch up, and the city developed a reputation for lawlessness and corruption. Irish and Chinese immigrants faced harassment, and even lynching, from armed vigilante bands that roamed the city. It took decades for law and order to take root in the city, with corruption remaining a major problem into the twentieth century. The city's rough-and-tumble formative phase ended abruptly with the earthquake of 1906, which destroyed much of the city.

ADDITIONAL FACTS

1. The company Levi Strauss was founded in San Francisco in 1853 to sell pants to miners headed for the Sierra Nevada.

2. Until the 1920 census, San Francisco was larger than Los Angeles. It is now only the fourth-biggest city in the state, after Los Angeles, San Diego, and San Jose.

3. In the early years of its history, San Francisco passed some of the harshest anti-Chinese laws in the country, including ones requiring strict racial segregation in the city's public schools.

★ ★ ★

The Red Badge of Courage

The novelist Stephen Crane (1871–1900) authored a dozen books in his short career. Most of his volumes have slipped into obscurity, with the exception of his crowning masterpiece, *The Red Badge of Courage* (1895), which is regarded as one of the best war novels in American literature and was a precursor to twentieth-century fiction for its gritty, realistic portrayal of battle and its unusual narrative style.

Crane, who was only twenty-four when he published the book and had never seen battle himself, based the novella on his interviews with shell-shocked Civil War veterans. Unlike standard war literature of the nineteenth century, which often depicted battle as a glorious test of manhood, Crane dealt frankly with the fears of his main character, a Union soldier named Henry Fleming, as he prepares for and then fights in his first engagement. The choice of a lowly private as his narrator was exceptional in itself; as contemporary critics pointed out, most war fiction of the day was told from a general's point of view.

The writing technique employed by Crane was also highly unorthodox for its time. Crane did not attempt to capture every twist and turn in the battle. Indeed, the reader has little sense of the overall battlefield or of which side is winning. His subject is the soldier, not the war. The book focuses on Fleming's personal impressions and emotions—the color of the trees, for instance, or the fleeting images that pass through his head as he marches uncertainly into battle.

Reaction to *The Red Badge of Courage* was mostly positive, although some northern veterans complained that Crane was unpatriotic for depicting an American soldier as fearful. The book sold well, and Crane became a minor literary celebrity. Based on his sensitive portrayal of battle, he was hired as a war correspondent by a New York newspaper and sent to cover fighting in Greece. He stayed in Europe for several years and ended up in London, where he contracted tuberculosis and then died at a spa in Germany. *The Red Badge of Courage* has been in print continuously since its publication and has been cited as an influence on Joseph Conrad (1857–1924), Ernest Hemingway (1899–1961), and many other authors.

ADDITIONAL FACTS

1. *The battle in the book is believed to have been modeled on the Battle of Chancellorsville.*

2. *One critic, a former Union general, assumed that Crane was English after reading* The Red Badge of Courage *because, as he explained, "It is only too well known that English writers have had a very low opinion of American soldiers, and have always, as a rule, assumed to ridicule them."*

3. *During his lifetime, according to biographer Linda Davis, Crane earned a total of $1,200 for all twelve of his books.*

★ ★ ★

Ashcan School

In 1896, an aspiring painter named George Luks (1867–1933) from Pennsylvania coal-mining country arrived in New York City seeking to establish his reputation. The art scene in New York, however, quickly disappointed the ambitious young artist. American painting, Luks complained, focused on genteel subject matter or nature scenes and rarely depicted the rough realities of American working-class life that Luks knew from his hardscrabble Appalachian upbringing.

Determined to inject more realism into American painting, Luks and seven colleagues joined a new artistic movement in 1908 called the Ashcan school. Although short-lived, the Ashcan school had an enormous influence on the history of American art. For the first time, Luks and his comrades made it fashionable to paint the gritty, raw reality of an increasingly urban and industrialized United States.

Many of the painters of the Ashcan school had begun their careers as newspaper illustrators, and their paintings often show a journalistic sensibility. Subjects included boxers, subway trains, and grimy urban alleyways. Like the photographer Jacob Riis (1849–1914), the Ashcan painters tried to use art to document and expose the often shocking conditions in American cities. George Bellows (1882–1925), one of the most famous Ashcan school painters, also helped edit a socialist publication, and the movement was avowedly leftist in its political outlook.

Although it fizzled thanks to an invasion of European-influenced modernists, the Ashcan school in its heyday produced dozens of famous paintings, especially Bellow's raw depictions of illegal boxing matches. Twenty years later, social realism roared back into fashion, and the influence of the group can be seen in the work of Edward Hopper (1882–1967) and other Depression-era painters.

ADDITIONAL FACTS

1. *One female member of the Ashcan school, Theresa Bernstein, who died in 2002, was thought to have reached an age of between 111 and 115.*

2. *The founders of the movement referred to themselves as "the Eight."*

3. *The painter Winslow Homer (1836–1910) and the poet Walt Whitman (1819–1892) served as inspirations for the Ashcan artists.*

★ ★ ★

James Monroe

James Monroe (1758–1831) served two terms as president of the United States between 1817 and 1825. He followed his friend, fellow Virginian and occasional rival James Madison (1751–1836), into the White House. Monroe's greatest presidential accomplishments came in the foreign policy arena: his administration acquired Florida from Spain and codified the Monroe Doctrine declaring the Americas closed to further European colonization.

Monroe, like Madison, began his political career in the Virginia legislature as a protégé of the great Thomas Jefferson (1743–1826). After the American Revolution, in which he was seriously wounded, Monroe was elected to the United States Senate in 1790. The three Virginians—Madison, Jefferson, and Monroe—worked together to form the Democratic-Republican Party to oppose what they viewed as the dangerous policies of the ruling Federalists.

After Jefferson's election to the White House in 1800, Monroe was rewarded with a series of diplomatic postings. He was sent to France to help negotiate the Louisiana Purchase, and then to Great Britain as Jefferson's ambassador when tensions between the two countries were rising. Monroe was unable to negotiate an end to British impressment of American sailors, a major cause of the tension, disappointing Jefferson and Madison.

Now estranged, Madison and Monroe ran against each other for the presidency in 1808, and Monroe lost. However, Madison selected him as his secretary of state in 1811, just before the outbreak of the War of 1812 against Britain. In 1816, Monroe easily secured the Democratic-Republican nomination for the presidency and trounced his Federalist opponent, Senator Rufus King (1786–1853) of New York.

Although Monroe is best remembered for his foreign policy, his presidency also marked the first stirrings of regional conflict between the North and the South over the issue of slavery. In 1819, Missouri sought to join the nation as a slave state, but northern lawmakers objected, fearing it would tilt the balance of power in Congress in favor of slavery. Finally, the Missouri Compromise was forged in 1820, under which Missouri would enter the Union along with Maine, a new free state that was carved out of Massachusetts. The Missouri Compromise successfully defused tensions over slavery—if only temporarily.

ADDITIONAL FACTS

1. *Virginians held the presidency for all but four years between 1789 and the end of Monroe's term; in total, eight presidents have been born in Virginia.*

2. *The capital city of the African nation of Liberia, Monrovia, was named after Monroe.*

3. *In 1819, Monroe became the first president to ride aboard a steamship.*

★ ★ ★

Beginnings of the Civil War

During the presidential election campaign of 1860, many Southern states warned that they would secede from the Union if voters elected the Republican candidate, Abraham Lincoln (1809–1865). Lincoln had promised to ban slavery in all new states added to the Union, a proposal that Southern politicians believed would inevitably doom the institution by shifting the balance of power in Congress to the free states. South Carolina became the first state to follow through on the secession threat; delegates to a state convention voted to leave the Union on December 20, 1960.

The secession crisis was the culmination of thirty years of mounting tension over slavery in the United States. After South Carolina, most of the rest of the slave-holding South voted to leave the Union. Only a few of the slave states—Maryland, Kentucky, Missouri, and Delaware—rejected secession.

Initially, Northern politicians were unsure how to respond to the actions by the Southern states. Lincoln and many other Northerners considered secession illegal but hoped the crisis could be resolved peacefully. However, on April 12, 1861, Southerners fired on the Union fortification in the harbor of Charlestown, South Carolina, forcing the small Union force inside Fort Sumter to surrender.

The attack on Fort Sumter created an enormous uproar in the North and dashed hopes for a peaceful reconciliation. In the wake of the incident, both sides began forming armies in preparation for war.

Over the next four years of fighting, more than 600,000 men were killed and many parts of the nation reduced to rubble before the final defeat of the Southern states. Ironically, the skirmish at Fort Sumter that sparked the war was also one of the smallest battles of the conflict: Only one soldier was killed in the fateful attack.

ADDITIONAL FACTS

1. *About 2 percent of the population of the United States died during the Civil War, according to demographic estimates.*

2. *The state of Virginia bore the brunt of the fighting. According to the 1992 PBS documentary* The Civil War, *the town of Winchester, Virginia, changed hands seventy-two times during the war.*

3. *In total, about 185,000 African-Americans fought on the side of the Union, despite the initial reluctance of Northern politicians to accept black soldiers.*

★ ★ ★

Seneca Falls Convention

The Seneca Falls Convention (1848) was one of the earliest gatherings of women's rights advocates in American history and is credited with starting the feminist movement that culminated seventy-two years later with the ratification of the Nineteenth Amendment to the Constitution, guaranteeing women the right to vote.

Delegates to the convention, held in the upstate New York village of Seneca Falls, drafted an ambitious Declaration of Sentiments purposefully modeled on the 1776 Declaration of Independence. It read:

> The history of mankind is a history of repeated injuries and usurpations on the part of man toward woman, having in direct object the establishment of an absolute tyranny over her. To prove this, let facts be submitted to a candid world.
>
> He has never permitted her to exercise her inalienable right to the elective franchise.
>
> He has compelled her to submit to laws, in the formation of which she had no voice.
>
> He has withheld from her rights which are given to the most ignorant and degraded men—both natives and foreigners.

By using the hallowed cadences of the Declaration of Independence, the authors of the Seneca Falls Convention hoped to highlight the hypocrisy of denying women the political rights American men claimed to hold dear. Wherever Thomas Jefferson had referred to King George III, they substituted "all men."

In the short term, the Declaration of Sentiments was either ignored or scorned. But the convention at Seneca Falls started a movement. Signers included Elizabeth Cady Stanton (1815–1902), Lucretia Mott (1793–1880), and Frederick Douglass (1817–1895), all of whom would go on to become prominent fighters for the rights of American women.

ADDITIONAL FACTS

1. *About 300 women and men attended the convention, and 100 people—68 women and 32 men—signed the Declaration of Sentiments.*

2. *Only one of the women who signed the Declaration—Charlotte Woodward—lived to see the passage of the Nineteenth Amendment. But at ninety-two years of age on Election Day 1920, Woodward was too sick to leave her home to vote.*

★ ★ ★

Otis Elevator

The invention of the world's first safe and reliable elevator by Elisha Otis (1811–1861) in 1852 made tall buildings feasible and changed the face of American cities in the nineteenth century by allowing for the construction of skyscrapers. A company founded by Otis, the Otis Elevator Company, today remains the world's largest manufacturer of elevators.

Otis was born on a farm in rural Vermont and moved to New York City in 1845 to work at a factory, taking part in the migration from farm to city prevalent during the Industrial Revolution. In New York, Otis developed an interest in improving the brakes used on railroad trains, a specialty that eventually led him to his most well-known invention.

Primitive elevators had existed for centuries, but were extremely unsafe and generally used only to hoist cargo, not people. Applying some of the same technology he had used for railroad brakes, Otis unveiled his *safety elevator* in 1853. The elevator included a novel mechanism—basically, a ratchet—to prevent the elevator from falling if the pulley snapped. In the event the rope broke, the brake devised by Otis would catch the elevator before it plunged downward.

Although it took several years for Otis to work out the kinks in the system—the doors for the elevator were particularly hard to design—architects began incorporating elevator shafts into their blueprints almost immediately. The invention eliminated one of the single biggest practical obstacles to skyscraper construction. Within twenty years of Otis's invention, 2,000 elevators had been installed in American buildings.

Otis himself died at age fifty, but his two sons built the Otis Elevator Company into a major industrial powerhouse.

ADDITIONAL FACTS

1. *Otis first demonstrated his invention at New York's Crystal Palace in 1854, when he rode an elevator halfway up a shaft and then had an assistant snip the rope. To the crowd's astonishment, the safety mechanism worked, and Otis descended only a few inches before the brake stopped the elevator's fall.*

2. *Through the 1930s, almost all elevators were operated by specially trained attendants. With technological advances, most human-staffed elevators were phased out by the 1950s.*

3. *The Otis Elevator Company later invented the Escalator, which was officially demoted to a generic, lowercase noun by the U.S. Patent Office in 1950.*

★ ★ ★

Gadsden Purchase

In 1854, the United States paid Mexico $10 million for a vast tract of land in the present-day states of New Mexico and Arizona. Named the Gadsden Purchase after the American diplomat who negotiated the sale, the acquisition fixed the borders of the modern continental United States at their present location.

After the Mexican War ended in 1848, Mexico had been forced to relinquish control over most of the Southwest to the United States. However, it retained the area around present-day Tucson, Arizona.

Support for the buying the 29,000-square-mile area was driven mostly by Southerners, who hoped to use it for a transcontinental railroad they envisioned linking the West Coast to the South. President Franklin Pierce (1804–1869), a Northerner, was convinced by his secretary of war, Mississippian Jefferson Davis (1808–1889), to authorize James Gadsden (1788–1858) to negotiate a deal for the territory.

When it was announced in 1853, the sale was controversial in both countries. Mexicans were outraged at the loss of land, and many northern senators feared the purchase was a ploy to strengthen the South's economy and extend slavery westward. The controversy over the purchase illustrated the growing sectional acrimony in Congress in the decade prior to the Civil War (1861–1865).

Eventually, Congress accepted a modified version of Gadsden's deal that included a much smaller area. Had the Southerners been successful, the map of the United States would look much different today, including much of northern Mexico. As it was, Arizona and New Mexico were admitted in 1912, the last two states in the continental United States to join the Union.

ADDITIONAL FACTS

1. *A second transcontinental railroad connecting New Orleans with the West Coast, the Southern Pacific, was built through the Gadsden Purchase lands in the 1880s.*

2. *The Mexican dictator who negotiated the sale, Antonio López de Santa Anna (1794–1876), was deposed the next year.*

3. *Davis went on to be president of the Confederacy during the Civil War.*

★ ★ ★

Henry Adams

One of the leading historians of the nineteenth-century United States, Henry Adams (1838–1918) is better known today for his brilliant autobiography, *The Education of Henry Adams*, which was not widely published until after his death.

Adams was born in Quincy, Massachusetts, into the illustrious Adams family. Both his grandfather, John Quincy Adams (1767–1848), and great-grandfather, John Adams (1735–1826), were presidents of the United States, and all of his brothers would go on to distinguished business or literary careers.

Following the family tradition, Adams enrolled in Harvard in 1854, but he detested his college experience. He found Harvard suffocating and would later try out innovative teaching techniques when he returned there as a history professor in the 1870s.

After his graduation in 1858, Adams spent the Civil War (1861–1865) in London, where he was a secretary for his father, the American ambassador to Great Britain. Adams returned to the United States after the war and moved to Washington, DC. Although an ardent Republican, he became disillusioned by the corrupt administration of President Ulysses S. Grant (1822–1885). In 1870, Adams accepted a professorship at Harvard but could endure it for only seven years. He returned to Washington, where he wrote his best-known historical work, the nine-volume *The History of the United States of America* (1889–1891), a painstaking reconstruction of the administrations of Thomas Jefferson (1743–1826) and James Madison (1751–1836).

Near the end of his life, Adams began writing his autobiography, intending to circulate it only to close friends. It was first published in a private edition in 1907. The book is both an amazing chronicle of the nineteenth century and a work of literary art. *The Education of Henry Adams* won the Pulitzer Prize for biography in 1919. Since its publication, critics have marveled at Adams's lapidary prose and sharp insights into his times, and in 1999 the Modern Library named *The Education* the greatest nonfiction work of the twentieth century.

ADDITIONAL FACTS

1. *His wife, Marian Hooper, committed suicide in 1885. Adams left the entire time period of his marriage out of* The Education.

2. *Adams wrote biographies of Albert Gallatin (1761–1849), the treasury secretary under presidents Thomas Jefferson and James Madison, and John Randolph (1773–1833), an early nineteenth-century Virginia politician.*

3. *Adams edited the prestigious* North American Review *from 1870 to 1876.*

★ ★ ★

McKim, Mead, and White

A legendary architecture firm responsible for some of the grandest public buildings in the United States, the partnership of McKim, Mead, and White designed and built significant parts of the skylines of Boston, New York, and Chicago in the late nineteenth and early twentieth centuries.

Originally made up of three architects— Charles Follen McKim (1847–1909), William Rutherford Mead (1846–1928), and Stanford White (1853–1906)—the firm went into business in New York City in 1878. McKim and White were former students of the renowned architect H. H. Richardson (1838–1886). Breaking with Richardson's famous Romanesque, however, the firm's monumental style took its major inspiration from Italian Renaissance palaces of the sixteenth century.

The Boston Public Library, begun in 1887, is characteristic of the firm's signature style. The giant building, which sits on Copley Square across from Richardson's Trinity Church, resembles an Italian palazzo, with huge windows on its facade and an interior courtyard ringed by an arcade. The imposing granite edifice conveys an overwhelming sense of strength and solidity.

Over the next three decades, the firm also built the huge Farley Post Office in New York, the West Wing of the White House, and several buildings at Columbia University in New York City.

In the view of many architecture critics, however, the single greatest building designed by the partners was the soaring Pennsylvania Station in midtown New York City. The great railway station, which took five years to reach completion in 1910 and was modeled on an ancient Roman ruin, served hundreds of trains daily on the busy Pennsylvania Railroad. The building was torn down in 1964 to make way for Madison Square Garden, a shortsighted demolition lamented today as a huge loss to the architecture of the United States and the world.

ADDITIONAL FACTS

1. *The city of New York occasionally announces plans to turn the Farley Post Office into a new Pennsylvania Station, but the project still had gone nowhere as of 2007.*

2. *The annual Boston Marathon, one of the most prestigious long-distance running events in the United States, ends just beyond the steps of the Boston Public Library.*

3. *Although its three namesake partners were all dead by 1928, the firm remained in business until 1950.*

★ ★ ★

John Quincy Adams

The eldest son of a Founding Father, John Quincy Adams (1767–1848) grew up in a world of privilege and power. As a ten-year-old boy, he accompanied his famous father, John Adams (1735–1826), on diplomatic missions to Europe. In 1797, when the elder Adams was elected president, he appointed his thirty-year-old son the American ambassador to Prussia. Like his father, John Quincy Adams attended Harvard and briefly practiced law before devoting himself to politics.

 Following in his father's footsteps, John Quincy Adams ran for president in 1824. In a close four-way race, he defeated Henry Clay (1777–1852), Andrew Jackson (1767–1845), and William Crawford (1772–1834). His presidency, however, lasted only a single rocky term. Jackson had won the popular vote, and many of his supporters considered him the rightful president. While in the White House, Adams was unable to muster congressional support for his agenda of internal improvements such as roads and canals.

In the 1828 election, even many of Adams's own cabinet officers supported Jackson, who won their rematch in a landslide. Again following in his father's path, an embittered Adams returned to Massachusetts.

However, instead of simply fading from the political scene, Adams then embarked on one of the most successful political careers of any ex-president. In 1830, he returned to Washington, DC, as a member of the House of Representatives from Massachusetts, and he continued to represent the state until his death. In Congress, Adams emerged as a leading critic of slavery. He also resumed his law practice, and he represented the prisoners who had overthrown their captors on the *Amistad* before the Supreme Court, winning their release in 1841. After his death, Adams was buried alongside his father at the family's home in Quincy, Massachusetts.

ADDITIONAL FACTS

1. *The patrician Adams hated his opponent Jackson and wrote a letter of protest to Harvard University when it awarded Old Hickory an honorary degree, calling the seventh president "a barbarian who could not write a sentence of grammar and hardly could spell his own name."*

2. *Since Adams, only one other son of a president, George W. Bush, has been elected to the White House.*

3. *John Adams and John Quincy Adams are the only two presidents not to attend the inauguration of their successor.*

★ ★ ★

Battle of Bull Run

The Battle of Bull Run on July 21, 1861, was the first major clash of the American Civil War. Nearly a thousand men lost their lives at Bull Run, a victory of the South that was a grim beginning to the most savage of American conflicts.

Before Bull Run, many leading politicians in the North confidently predicted the Union would crush the Southern rebels within a few months. But the unexpected Confederate victory at Bull Run signaled to the world that the Southern army was a fighting force to be taken seriously.

After the secession of the Southern states and the subsequent attack against Union troops at Fort Sumter on April 12, 1861, it was only a matter of time before the North went on the offensive. In Washington, DC, President Abraham Lincoln (1809–1865) and enraged Union politicians prodded the US Army to attack the Confederacy immediately. The Union general in charge, Irvin McDowell (1818–1885), hesitated, arguing that his men were unprepared to confront the rebels. Eventually, he gave in to pressure to move against the South. Union forces crossed into northern Virginia on July 16, 1861, meeting the Southerners near a creek called Bull Run in the crossroads town of Manassas, Virginia.

The battle that ensued was a debacle for both sides, but especially for the North. The two armies had similar-looking uniforms and flags, and confused soldiers often fired at their own comrades. Discipline among the Union ranks was poor, and many Northern soldiers fled back to Washington in a disorganized retreat after the battle.

The Confederate victory was a major shock to the Union leadership and the country at large. Lincoln immediately replaced McDowell, the first of the many generals the president would fire. Talk of a quick victory faded, and Union politicians realized they had a real fight on their hands. Pictures taken by Mathew Brady (c. 1823–1896), the famous war photographer, made the public aware of the awful realities of the new war.

In the South, meanwhile, Bull Run was a huge psychological lift for the rebels, who had proved they could hold their own against the Union army.

ADDITIONAL FACTS

1. *The term* skedaddle *was coined after the Battle of Bull Run by Union soldiers who fled back to Washington, DC, after the carnage.*

2. *A second battle of Bull Run, also resulting in a Confederate victory, took place at almost exactly the same spot in 1862.*

3. *Bull Run took its name from a small creek that ran near the battlefield.*

★ ★ ★

Underground Railroad

As opposition to slavery grew in the North starting in the 1830s, abolitionists organized a clandestine network that helped smuggle escaped slaves to freedom. Between 30,000 and 100,000 slaves are estimated to have escaped from the South thanks to the efforts of the Underground Railroad, an informal term that referred to the web of secret escape routes organized by abolitionists rather than to an actual railroad.

For most escapees, the ultimate destination was Canada, where slavery was illegal and fugitives could not be extradited back to the United States. Fugitives relied on local abolitionists, code-named "conductors," to aid them on their way north. William Still (1801–1892), the free son of an escaped slave, was one of the most successful conductors. His home in Philadelphia served as a safe resting place for escaped slaves en route to Canada. Harriet Tubman (c. 1820–1913), herself an escaped slave, famously ventured back into the South to help arrange escapes for hundreds of slaves. The white abolitionist Levi Coffin (1798–1877) helped more than 3,000 slaves reach freedom, providing his home in Indiana as a way station along three escape routes.

By the early 1850s, many northern churches and individuals were quietly participating in the Underground Railroad. In many parts of the North it operated more or less in the open, as sympathetic authorities looked the other way.

Still, by helping slaves escape to freedom, abolitionists took a significant legal risk. Congress had outlawed assisting fugitive slaves in 1793, and it greatly strengthened the Fugitive Slave Act in 1850. The law, however, was widely ignored, in what historian Fergus M. Bordewich called "first great movement of mass civil disobedience after the American Revolution."

After the war, Still published his copious notes as a book called *The Underground Rail Road* (1872), one of the most important records of resistance to slavery. Many stations along the railroad have been preserved as monuments to the popular resistance to slavery in the North.

ADDITIONAL FACTS

1. *The Fugitive Slave Act of 1850 was widely despised in most of the North. When Anthony Burns (1834–1862), a fugitive slave, was arrested in Massachusetts under the act in 1854, protests were so large that 1,000 soldiers had to be sent to Boston to escort the slave back to Virginia.*

2. *Recently, some historians have questioned the true extent of the Underground Railroad, suggesting that some Northerners may have exaggerated or invented their roles in the network after the war.*

3. *In the 1850s, Southern slave owners often hired bounty hunters to chase down their escaped slaves in the North, which provided the historical inspiration for the Pulitzer Prize–winning Toni Morrison novel* Beloved *(1987).*

★ ★ ★

Transcontinental Railroad

The first transcontinental railroad across the Rocky Mountains, completed in 1869, drastically reduced the cost of moving goods and people between the coasts and opened the West for a massive wave of white settlement. Crossing the Rockies was one of the greatest engineering challenges in the nation's history, requiring hundreds of bridges and tunnels and thousands of miles of track. Countless workers died in avalanches, explosions, and train collisions while building the railroad, which is considered one of most significant industrial milestones in the nation's history.

Since the invention of the railroad in the early nineteenth century, Americans had dreamed of forging a route to the Pacific. The first serious plan was submitted to Congress in 1845. With the nation paralyzed by sectional strife, the proposal went nowhere. During the Civil War (1861–1865), however, the administration of Abraham Lincoln (1809–1865) made construction of the transcontinental railroad a national priority. In 1862, Congress chartered two railroads to build the route, the Central Pacific and the Union Pacific, and offered them enormous cash incentives: $48,000 and 12,800 acres of land for every mile of track they built.

From its inception, the transcontinental railroad represented an uneasy collaboration between the federal government, which wanted the railroad built, and railroad corporations more concerned with turning a profit. The Central Pacific and Union Pacific employed dubious and unsafe labor practices to build the railroad cheaply and financial chicanery to inflate their already vast profits. The Crédit Mobilier scandal, which broke in the 1870s after the railroad's completion, exposed how the Union Pacific had bilked the federal government and provided kickbacks to influential politicians.

Nevertheless, the ultimate goal of crossing the continent was achieved, an accomplishment as far-reaching as the completion of the Erie Canal a generation before. On May 10, 1869, the two railroads met at Promontory Point, Utah, setting off a national celebration. Trade between the coasts exploded, as the travel time between New York and San Francisco plummeted from six months to less than a week. By 1880, the railroads were carrying millions of dollars worth of cargo and thousands of white settlers migrating to the newly accessible towns of the West.

ADDITIONAL FACTS

1. *Chinese laborers dominated the Central Pacific workforce.*

2. *Although much of the original transcontinental railroad has been abandoned, travelers can still ride along some of the line on the Amtrak route California Zephyr.*

3. *The Central Pacific was one of the first American companies to make use of nitroglycerin, a dangerous explosive that had been invented in Europe in 1864.*

★ ★ ★

Central Park

New York City's Central Park was one of the first public parks in the United States when it opened in 1859. Designed by famed landscape architect Frederick Law Olmstead (1822–1903), the 843-acre preserve amid New York's urban bustle would be a model for hundreds of public spaces built in cities across the United States in the late nineteenth century.

The city of New York had grown dramatically in the 1840s, thanks to a wave of immigration from overseas. With this growth came many urban problems, including overcrowding, noise, and crime. City elders struggling to cope with New York's explosive growth envisioned Central Park as an oasis of calm in the city, and they spent $5 million in the 1850s buying mostly uninhabited land north of Fifty Ninth Street.

At the time, the idea of such a big public space was itself unusual. While Paris and London had large public parks, no American city had ever constructed anything like Central Park. The city sponsored a design competition in 1857, which was won by Olmstead and a collaborator, Calvert Vaux (1824–1895). Their design, full of ponds and hills and stately granite bridges, was heavily influenced by parks Olmstead had toured in Europe in the early 1850s.

The construction of Central Park stimulated a wave of park building in cities across the United States. Olmstead designed parks in Buffalo, Boston, Chicago, and elsewhere. Like Central Park, many nineteenth-century parks were built on the fringes of cities but have since been surrounded on all sides by urban growth.

ADDITIONAL FACTS

1. *Although Central Park is probably the most famous park in the United States, it was not the first; that distinction belongs to Boston Common, which opened in roughly 1634.*

2. *The park was built on swampy terrain, and most of its soil had to be imported from New Jersey.*

3. *More than 1,400 plant species live in Central Park.*

★ ★ ★

Upton Sinclair

Muckraking journalist Upton Sinclair (1878–1968) published his most well-known book, *The Jungle*, in 1906 to draw attention to the dangerous working conditions for and poor wages of slaughterhouse workers in Chicago. As Sinclair intended, the book created an uproar—but not for the reasons he expected. To many readers, Sinclair's graphic descriptions of the unsanitary slaughterhouses were horrifying, and they led to major new food safety regulations. "I aimed at the public's heart," Sinclair complained, "and by accident I hit it in the stomach."

 Sinclair was born in Baltimore, Maryland, and wrote a successful novel about the Civil War at age twenty-four. A lifelong devotee of left-wing politics, he used the considerable proceeds from *The Jungle* to indulge in various socialist causes, including a short-lived commune in New Jersey. During this time, Sinclair also made the first of what would be dozens of unsuccessful runs for public office, losing a New Jersey congressional race by an overwhelming margin.

As a writer, Sinclair's style was often dramatic, sincere, and emotional, unlike the arch cynicism of his contemporary H. L. Mencken (1880–1956). *The Jungle* was written to create sympathy for the poor and oppressed, and modern readers expecting a tirade against injustice are sometimes surprised by the book's sentimentalism.

Nevertheless, the book was a runaway success and perhaps the most well-known example of muckraking journalism in the early twentieth century. President Theodore Roosevelt (1858–1919) read it, summoned Sinclair to a meeting in the White House, and dispatched aides to investigate his allegations. The result, later that year, was the Food and Drug Administration, established to assure the purity of American food.

Sinclair continued to write for the next six decades, championing dozens of progressive causes from workers' rights to vegetarianism in the ninety books he published. He also ran for office several more times, coming closest to victory in the 1934 California governor's race, in which he ran as a left-wing Democrat in the midst of the Depression and came within 200,000 votes of victory.

ADDITIONAL FACTS

1. *In 1943, he won the Pulitzer Prize, his only major award, for* Dragon's Teeth, *a novelization of the Nazi takeover of Germany in the 1930s.*

2. *Sinclair resigned from the Socialist Party in 1917 over his support of American involvement in World War I (1914–1918) but later rejoined the party when President Woodrow Wilson (1856–1924) supported intervention in the Soviet Union.*

3. *A lifelong civil libertarian, Sinclair was a board member of the American Civil Liberties Union (ACLU) and founded the organization's Southern California branch.*

★ ★ ★

The Birth of a Nation

Even by the standards of 1915, the year of its initial release, the silent film *The Birth of a Nation*, produced and directed by D. W. Griffith (1875–1948), was considered racist. The three-hour epic tells the story of the creation of the Ku Klux Klan in the post–Civil War South—and portrays the white-hooded Klansmen as the heroes. In one of its first-ever publicity campaigns, the National Association for the Advancement of Colored People (NAACP) called for a national boycott of the controversial film immediately after its release.

Despite its overt bigotry, however, *The Birth of a Nation* was a huge sensation among both the public and critics because of Griffith's innovative use of new film techniques. In the opinion of many film historians, *The Birth of a Nation* virtually created modern cinematography by inventing such film basics as establishing shots, close-ups, flashbacks, and quick cuts between different scenes.

When it hit theaters, *The Birth of a Nation*, which starred the actress Lillian Gish (1893–1993), was far more exciting than anything audiences had ever seen before. For Hollywood's first two decades, most silent movies were slow and plodding—basically stage plays performed in front of an unmoving camera. In his fast-paced and dramatic epic, Griffith was the first to explore the true possibilities of the new technology.

In the history of film, *The Birth of a Nation* is considered an important milestone, despite its offensive subject matter. In the broader history of the United States, however, the movie played a far darker role. By portraying the Ku Klux Klan as heroic, *The Birth of a Nation* helped inspire the Klan's resurgence in the early twentieth century. Nearly extinct by 1915, the Klan enjoyed a huge revival in both the South and the North, with the movie acting as an invaluable recruiting tool. Griffith tried to atone for the movie the next year with another historical epic called *Intolerance*, which criticized bigotry and racism, but *The Birth of a Nation* has forever marred the pioneering director's legacy.

ADDITIONAL FACTS

1. *The movie, based on a book by Thomas F. Dixon, was originally titled* The Clansman.

2. *Many of the African-American characters in the movie were actually whites wearing blackface makeup, a common practice in Hollywood in the early twentieth century.*

3. *Born in Kentucky, Griffith's father was a Confederate officer during the Civil War (1861–1865).*

★ ★ ★

Andrew Jackson

The election of General Andrew Jackson (1767–1845) to the White House in 1828 marked an earthquake in national politics. Unlike his aristocratic predecessors, Jackson was a self-made man from Tennessee who had been born in poverty. To his many detractors, Jackson was a tyrant, a half-wit, and a barbarian unfit for the august office of the presidency, but his election as a "man of the people" signaled the beginning of a more democratic age in American politics.

Jackson joined the patriot army at age thirteen during the Revolutionary War and was taken prisoner by the British. After the Revolution, he worked as a lawyer in the frontier state of Tennessee. He returned to military service for the War of 1812 and became a national hero after defeating the British at the Battle of New Orleans, but to some he became known as the "Butcher of New Orleans" for his ruthlessness.

Jackson ran for president against the Massachusetts patrician John Quincy Adams (1767–1848) in 1824 but lost the election despite winning the popular vote. Outraged, Jackson began plotting his 1828 campaign almost immediately. His rematch with Adams was the most vicious campaign up to that point in American history, but the result was not close: Jackson won handily, sweeping the South and Midwest.

From the moment he took office, Jackson made it clear that he was a different sort of politician than previous chief executives. On the day of his inauguration, he opened the White House to the public. A drunken mob ransacked the mansion, forcing Jackson to flee to a nearby hotel.

During his two terms in office, Jackson aggressively expanded the power of the presidency. He was the first president to make frequent use of his constitutional veto power, vetoing more bills than all his predecessors combined. In particular, Jackson worked to destroy the national bank, which he and many of his supporters believed was a tool of Eastern financial elites. In the South, Jackson insisted on evicting the Cherokee from their tribal homelands to make way for white settlers.

Enormously popular, Jackson retired to his Nashville, Tennessee, estate in 1837 but continued to exert considerable influence on his party.

ADDITIONAL FACTS

1. *Jackson despised paper money and believed that gold and silver should be the only forms of American currency. Ironically, his face now appears on the $20 bill.*

2. *During the 1828 presidential campaign, Jackson's supporters used hickory leaves and hickory poles to show their support for their candidate, who was nicknamed "Old Hickory."*

3. *In 1999, scientists tested two strands of Jackson's hair and determined that lead poisoning, likely the result of a bullet lodged in his shoulder from an 1813 gunfight, caused many of the president's chronic health problems.*

★ ★ ★

Robert E. Lee

Robert E. Lee (1807–1870) commanded the Confederate army during the Civil War (1861–1865). Although ultimately defeated by the Union, Lee was considered a brilliant military tactician and inspiring leader by his troops. Gallant even in defeat, Lee became a symbol of Southern pride and a near-religious figure to may Southerners after the war's end.

Born in Virginia to a prominent family, Lee attended the West Point military academy. He was extremely successful in school and later fought with distinction for the United States in the Mexican War (1846–1848). Lee opposed secession and considered slavery immoral, but he agreed to lead the Confederate forces out of loyalty to his home state of Virginia.

As a general, Lee faced overwhelming odds. At the beginning of the war, the Confederacy had a smaller population, fewer miles of roads and railroads, and a far smaller industrial base than the North.

Still, Lee's Army of Northern Virginia proved surprisingly able. He won several battles in Virginia in 1862 before mounting the ill-fated invasion of Maryland that ended in the defeat of his forces at Antietam. He tried invading the North again in 1863 but was again stopped, this time at Gettysburg.

In 1864, Ulysses S. Grant (1822–1885) took command of the Union army. For the first time, a Union general effectively attacked Lee on his own turf. By the spring of 1865, the Confederate army, exhausted and starving, was in a state of collapse. Lee surrendered to Grant on April 9, 1865.

After the surrender, Lee urged his fellow Southerners to accept defeat graciously. In the years after his death, Lee's sense of duty and honor made him a hero to Southerners and a central figure in the "lost cause" romanticism of the Confederacy. Hundreds of streets and bridges across the South still bear the name of the war's greatest Confederate hero.

ADDITIONAL FACTS

1. *Military service was in Lee's blood. He was the son of Henry "Lighthorse Harry" Lee (1756–1818), a famed hero of the American Revolution.*

2. *Lee graduated second in his class at West Point in 1829 and is the only student in the history of the institution to graduate without a single demerit on his record.*

3. *After the war, Lee was indicted for treason against the United States but never tried.*

★ ★ ★

Harriet Tubman

One of the most famous "conductors" on the Underground Railroad, escaped slave Harriet Tubman (c. 1820–1913) personally smuggled hundreds of fugitives into the North and later served as an important Union spy during the Civil War (1861–1865).

Born Araminta Ross in Maryland, Tubman escaped from slavery in 1849 and settled in Philadelphia. She worked as a servant and cook, and she used her meager salary to finance trips back to the South to help members of her family escape.

In the 1850s, most Underground Railroad volunteers remained in the relative safety of the North, waiting for fugitives to come to them. Tubman was one of the few abolitionists who actually ventured into the South to help slaves escape. A woman of extreme courage and ingenuity, she ran enormous personal risks by crossing the Mason-Dixon line into slave territory.

In total, Tubman is credited with helping about 300 slaves escape in her nineteen covert trips into the hostile territory of the South. For her bravery, she was nicknamed "Moses." Said one fellow Underground Railroad conductor of Tubman: "She seemed wholly devoid of personal fear . . . her like . . . was never known before or since."

After the outbreak of the Civil War, Tubman volunteered to serve as a spy for the Union army. Posing as a slave, she slipped past the Confederate lines on numerous occasions to scout military fortifications in South Carolina and Georgia, intelligence that contributed to a successful Union raid of Combahee River, South Carolina, in 1863.

Tubman's heroic actions in the war came at huge peril: the penalty for espionage was death. After the war, however, the United States government never fulfilled its promises to pay Tubman for her spying.

Tubman spent the rest of her life in Auburn, New York, where she founded a home for the poor and elderly. She later slipped into poverty and was eventually forced to sell vegetables door-to-door for a living. She died in 1913 and was buried with military honors in belated recognition of her Civil War service.

ADDITIONAL FACTS

1. *Tubman was so hated by Southern slave owners that they reportedly offered a $60,000 reward—more than $1.3 million in 2007 dollars—for her capture.*

2. *Although she has been the subject of countless children's books, no serious biography of Tubman existed until 2005, when Catherine Clinton published* Harriet Tubman: Road to Freedom.

3. *The Combahee River raid enabled about 750 slaves to escape from South Carolina.*

★ ★ ★

Leland Stanford

Philanthropist and railroad mogul Leland Stanford (1824–1893) hammered in the golden spike that completed the transcontinental railroad at Promontory Point, Utah, in 1869 and later used his enormous fortune to found Stanford University. In many respects, Stanford's career reflected the unusual contradictions of the Gilded Age: although Stanford and his partners cut corners, mistreated employees, and corrupted politicians, they constructed a railroad that helped build the United States, and Stanford used the proceeds to found one of the world's most prestigious universities.

Stanford was born into a prosperous New York family and moved to California shortly after the beginning of the 1848 gold rush. A shrewd entrepreneur, Stanford realized he could make more money selling supplies to miners than looking for gold himself; he opened a store and made a killing. Soon after, he formed a partnership with three other businessmen, creating a group that became known as the Big Four, to construct the California section of the planned transcontinental railroad. He also got involved with Republican politics and was elected governor of California in 1861.

While serving as governor, Stanford remained one of the Big Four, using his political influence and connections to grease the wheels for the Central Pacific Railroad because he believed that it would ultimately benefit the citizens of California. Immediately after leaving the governorship, Stanford resumed his position as the president of the line, a position he would hold for the rest of his life. The Central Pacific was notorious for mistreating the Chinese American laborers who built the vast majority of the route, paying them less than whites and forcing employees of all races to work under unsafe conditions in the avalanche-prone Sierra Nevada.

By 1884, fifteen years after the opening of the transcontinental railroad line, Stanford had accumulated an enormous fortune of around $100 million. That year, however, his fifteen-year-old son died, a major blow to the tycoon. In his son's memory, Stanford endowed Stanford University in Palo Alto, California, in 1885. Still the president of the Central Pacific, Stanford was appointed the same year by the California legislature to the United States Senate, where he served until his death.

ADDITIONAL FACTS

1. *Technically the university is named after Stanford's deceased son, Leland Jr., and not the mogul himself.*

2. *Stanford was a delegate to the 1860 Republican National Convention that nominated Abraham Lincoln (1809–1865) for president.*

3. *Although Chinese immigrants built most of the railroad that made Stanford rich, he referred to them as "the dregs of Asia" in his 1862 inaugural address as governor of California and supported discriminatory policies against Chinese-Americans.*

★ ★ ★

Homestead Act

The Homestead Act of 1862 was a massive federal program that provided huge parcels of free land in the West to settlers. Under the act, which was designed to encourage Americans to populate the territory acquired sixty years earlier in the Louisiana Purchase, about 8 percent of the entire United States landmass was transferred from federal to private ownership. In total, about two million homesteaders claimed a tract of free land under the program, which remained in effect until 1986.

Providing land to settlers was a key goal of Abraham Lincoln's Republican Party. Indeed, along with containing the expansion of slavery, "free soil" was a key plank in the party's original platform. Southern Democrats had opposed free soil, but when they left Congress during the Civil War (1861–1865), the Republicans suddenly had the votes to enact their agenda. The Homestead Act was passed in the same year as the law subsidizing the construction of the transcontinental railroad, another major impetus for migration to the West.

Under the law, any person over the age of twenty-one who was the head of a family and either a US citizen or an "alien" who intended to become a US citizen could file a claim for a 160-acre plot of federally owned land, as long as he or she built a home on the parcel and lived there for five years. As the Republicans hoped, the allure of free farmland prompted a mass migration to the West, which accelerated in the late nineteenth century and crested in 1913. The flow of settlers into the region allowed Congress to admit dozens of new western states after the Civil War.

Naturally, the biggest victims of the Homestead Act were Native Americans, whose ancestral lands the government was giving away to newcomers. The crush of white settlers, along with the completion of the transcontinental railroad in 1869, led to increasing tension with tribes on the Great Plains and in the Southwest that culminated in a series of wars in the 1870s and 1880s. By the early 1890s, most Native Americans had been forced onto reservations, and the "frontier" was officially declared closed in 1890.

With the obvious exception of the Civil War, the Homestead Act is often considered one of Lincoln's most important accomplishments. By the time the program ended, the government had given away 270 million acres of land and successfully populated the western wilderness with white settlers.

ADDITIONAL FACTS

1. *The last homestead deed was awarded in 1988 to Kenneth Deardorff, a Vietnam veteran who in 1974 filed a claim for 80 acres in southern Alaska.*

2. *For most homesteaders, the entire cost of their 160 acres was an $18 application fee.*

3. *Many applications were rejected because the applicant did not fulfill the law's building and residence requirements.*

★ ★ ★

Edith Wharton

Pulitzer Prize–winning author Edith Wharton (1862–1937) grew up in a wealthy family in New York City and chronicled the habits of the wealthy in her elegant, urbane novels of Manhattan life. A trailblazing female author, Wharton wrote three of the best-known books of the early twentieth century: *The House of Mirth* (1905), *Ethan Frome* (1911), and her masterpiece, *The Age of Innocence* (1920).

Edith Newbold Jones was born when polite society in Manhattan was still ruled by "Old New York," an aristocratic elite ensconced in stately mansions along Fifth Avenue. A product of this cloistered culture, she was a debutante at age seventeen, took her sailing vacations in Newport, traveled widely in Europe, and married a wealthy heir, Edward Wharton, in 1885.

Although she began writing in her teens, she did not publish her first poems and stories until after her marriage, when her work began to appear in *Scribner's Magazine* and the *Atlantic Monthly*, the leading popular journals of the late nineteenth century. Edith Wharton's first book, an interior decorating manual called *The Decoration of Houses*, was published in 1897.

Wharton's debut novel, *The House of Mirth*, was published in 1905, and it was the biggest literary sensation of the year. In the novel, main character Lily Bart struggles to find a sufficiently rich husband among New York's elite. *The House of Mirth* is often referred to as a "book of manners," a literary genre distinguished by its detailed, even sociological attention to the customs and traditions of the characters.

After divorcing her husband in 1913, Wharton moved to France, where she hobnobbed with author Henry James (1843–1916) and other famous writers and artists and continued her successful writing career. Although Wharton spent the last three decades of her life in Europe, her American upbringing remained a major inspiration. In *Ethan Frome*, a short novel set in rural Massachusetts, Wharton explored the themes of sexual repression and the stunted intellectual life of rural New England. Her most famous book, the Pulitzer-winning novel *The Age of Innocence*, was set in the Manhattan of Wharton's privileged youth, a time she wistfully remembered as an "age of innocence" before World War I (1914–1918) and the great social upheavals of the twentieth century.

ADDITIONAL FACTS

1. *The title of* The House of Mirth *comes from the King James version of a verse in the Bible, Ecclesiastes 7:4: "The heart of the wise is in the house of mourning; but the heart of fools is in the house of mirth."*

2. *Wharton volunteered to help war refugees during World War I and was awarded the French Legion of Honor in recognition of her efforts.*

3. *Wharton's "country house"—a palatial estate she built in 1902 near Lenox, Massachusetts—is now a museum open to the public.*

★ ★ ★

Isadora Duncan

Considered the first modern American ballet dancer and the mother of American choreography, Isadora Duncan (1877–1927) spent most of her tumultuous career in Europe but had a huge and lasting influence on dance in her native country.

Born in San Francisco, Duncan moved to New York at age eighteen but soon tired of the roles offered to her and moved to London in 1899 seeking more challenging work. Lithe, beautiful, and temperamental, Duncan quickly became a sensation in the ballet halls of Europe, performing in Paris, Budapest, Vienna, Munich, and St. Petersburg.

In addition to her critical acclaim, Duncan became notorious for her unorthodox beliefs about politics and sexuality. A lifelong atheist, she sympathized with communism and briefly moved to the Soviet Union. She also disdained the institution of marriage and had high-profile affairs with several rich men who helped bankroll her extravagant lifestyle. She had two children by different fathers. A free spirit in every way imaginable, Duncan famously ended one of her shows by baring her left breast to the audience, defiantly rejecting the conventional standards of modesty demanded of women.

Duncan's personal life, always turbulent, suffered a terrible blow in 1913, when her children drowned in the Seine River in Paris after their car slid over the bank. Later in life, after her return to Paris from the Soviet Union, Duncan became an alcoholic, and her dance career faltered. She published her autobiography, *My Life*, in 1927, and died later that year in an infamous automobile accident when her long, flowing scarf became entangled in a wheel and broke her neck.

Although Duncan did not allow her performances to be recorded, her bold, impulsive style liberated dance from its traditional styles and influenced the development of modern ballet in both Europe and the United States.

ADDITIONAL FACTS

1. *One of her beaus was Paris Singer, the heir to the Singer Sewing Machine Company fortune, who offered to buy her Madison Square Garden for performances.*

2. *Duncan's family had an unfortunate tendency for unusual deaths; her father died at sea in a shipwreck.*

3. *Duncan legally adopted six female dancers, nicknamed* les Isadorables, *who carried on her legacy after her death.*

★ ★ ★

James K. Polk

James K. Polk (1795–1849) served only a single term in the White House, but he made an enormous impact in his four years as president by winning the Mexican War (1846–1848) and adding huge new swathes of land in the West to the United States. A Democrat who patterned himself after President Andrew Jackson (1767–1845), Polk enjoyed high popularity for winning the war but was in poor health and declined to seek a second term. In the era of weak chief executives between Jackson and Abraham Lincoln (1809–1865), Polk was the only president of the period who left office with a significant record of accomplishment.

Born in North Carolina, Polk entered the 1844 presidential race against Henry Clay (1777–1852) as a distinct underdog. Clay's Whigs, dominant in the Northeast, expected to ride Clay's personal popularity to victory. Clay was undone, however, by two unexpected developments. First, his running mate, Theodore Frelinghuysen (1753–1804), made disparaging remarks about Catholics, who retaliated by voting for Polk en masse. Second, Polk touched a nerve among the electorate by calling for a more aggressive stance toward Mexico.

Within months of taking office, Polk had triggered the Mexican War, which resulted in the acquisition of California, Arizona, and New Mexico. Polk also negotiated an end to a border dispute with Great Britain in the Pacific Northwest, clearing the way for the creation of Oregon and Washington and fixing the northern border of the United States at the forty-ninth parallel.

Polk captured the mood of a country enchanted by the notion of westward expansion. In total square miles, his administration added more territory to the United States than any other, surpassing even the Louisiana Purchase. Disputes over whether to allow slavery in these new territories, however, helped trigger the Civil War a decade after Polk's death.

ADDITIONAL FACTS

1. Polk's wife, Sarah, was the daughter of former president Andrew Jackson.

2. Although he had served as Speaker of the House, Polk was virtually an unknown when he ran for president in 1844. Democrats coined the nickname "Young Hickory" to capitalize on the popularity of the former Democratic president Andrew "Old Hickory" Jackson.

3. The term dark horse originated in the 1844 election, which Polk won unexpectedly over the heavy favorite, Clay.

★ ★ ★

Thomas "Stonewall" Jackson

Confederate war hero Thomas "Stonewall" Jackson (1824–1863) led Southern troops in several brilliant campaigns early in the Civil War (1861–1865) before he was killed in a "friendly fire" accident at the Battle of Chancellorsville. Intelligent, courageous, and devoted to the Confederacy, Jackson was an important leader whose death was a heavy blow to the Southern cause. "I know not how to replace him," wrote the despondent Confederate general Robert E. Lee (1807–1870) after learning of Jackson's death.

Born into a poor family, Jackson was orphaned as a child and raised by his uncle. He won admission to the US military academy at West Point and later served in the Mexican War (1846–1848). Jackson left the US Army in 1851 to teach artillery tactics at the Virginia Military Institute in Lexington, Virginia.

But at the start of the war, Jackson was virtually unknown outside Lexington. In the midst of the Battle of Bull Run, another Confederate general spotted Jackson's well-trained men resisting a Union onslaught and famously yelled, "There is Jackson standing like a stone wall!" His legendary performance made Jackson an instant Southern hero, although he would later insist that the nickname properly belonged to his troops, not to him.

In the spring of 1862, Jackson was put in charge of Confederate forces in the Shenandoah Valley, an agricultural area west of Washington, DC. His Shenandoah campaign showcased Jackson's tactical genius. His fast-moving army of 16,000 Confederate soldiers outfoxed a much larger Union force, keeping them pinned down in western Virginia, away from the main front.

Jackson was a peculiar man, dogged by rumors that he was insane. To his critics, Jackson was needlessly reckless with the lives of his soldiers, but he enjoyed Lee's full support. Jackson's death in 1863 came during another daring maneuver, as he prepared to attack a Union force near Fredericksburg, Virginia. So great was the impact of his death on the South that he lay in state at the Confederate capital of Richmond, Virginia, before his burial in Lexington.

ADDITIONAL FACTS

1. *One of Jackson's opponents during the Shenandoah campaign was a Union major named Rutherford B. Hayes (1822–1893), who went on to become the nineteenth president of the United States in 1877.*

2. *Deeply religious, Jackson disliked fighting on Sundays, but did so anyway.*

3. *The Confederate general who gave Jackson his nom de guerre, Barnard Bee (1824–1861), died several hours later at the Battle of Bull Run.*

★ ★ ★

Frederick Douglass

Born into slavery, civil rights leader Frederick Douglass (c. 1817–1895) was separated from his mother as a child and grew up in Maryland. After several attempts, he managed to escape by boat to Philadelphia and from there made his way to New Bedford, Massachusetts. He made contact with leading New England abolitionists and quickly became one of the most prominent antislavery speakers and organizers of the pre–Civil War period.

On the lecture circuit, Douglass impressed and awed Northern audiences not only with his personal accounts of slavery, but also with his poise and stature. His famous biography, *Narrative of the Life of Frederick Douglass,* published in 1845, exposed a large international readership to the hardships of slavery. He traveled to Europe to lecture on the evils of slavery and started his own abolitionist newspaper, *The North Star.*

In addition to his antislavery work, Douglass was a supporter of the women's suffrage movement and was one of the few male signatories of the Declaration of Sentiments at the Seneca Falls Convention in New York in 1040. By the time the Civil War began in 1861, Douglass was regarded as one of the leading African-American civil rights leaders of his day and was consulted by President Abraham Lincoln (1809–1865) for his advice during the Civil War. At Lincoln's urging, Douglass helped the Union army recruit black soldiers after 1863.

After the war ended, Douglass was an advocate for ex-slaves, urging swift passage of the postwar amendments to the Constitution that officially extended citizenship and voting rights to freed slaves. A charismatic speaker and eloquent moral authority, he remained prominent in national politics for the rest of his life. His commitment to reform causes was unflagging; Douglass attended a women's suffrage convention on the morning of the day he died in 1895.

ADDITIONAL FACTS

1. *In 1889, Douglass was appointed ambassador to Haiti.*

2. *Douglass broke with some of his colleagues in the women's sufferage movement by backing the Fifteenth Ammendment to the Constitution, even though it only exteded voting rights to black men and ignored women.*

3. *Douglass's given name was Frederick Augustus Washington Bailey, but he changed it after his escape to throw slave catchers off his trail. Douglass formally bought his freedom in 1847.*

★ ★ ★

Gilded Age

Author Mark Twain (1835–1910) coined the term the *Gilded Age* to refer to the period of American history between the end of the Civil War (1861–1865) and roughly 1900. The Gilded Age was characterized by massive immigration from abroad, ostentatious displays of wealth by the affluent, and rising tensions between rich and poor. The term was not intended as a compliment: Twain and other social critics used it to suggest that underneath the era's gaudy excess and superficial prosperity was a country in crisis.

The industrialization of the United States, which had begun before the Civil War, rapidly intensified after the conflict. Within a few years, the rates of railroad and factory construction passed their prewar levels, and the United States surpassed France and Great Britain as the world's leader in industrial production.

At the same time, a wave of consolidation merged smaller companies into giant national conglomerates like Standard Oil. Consolidation made industries more efficient and generated enormous wealth for their owners. Corporate executives—the era's robber barons like Cornelius Vanderbilt—collected paychecks so large they had no precedent in American history and used them to build lavish mansions in wealthy enclaves like Newport, Rhode Island.

However, during this period, wages for workers stagnated or even declined, and widespread dissatisfaction with the economic system led to calls for reform. The labor movement gained steam during the Gilded Age in response to the low pay and long hours expected of American workers. Beginning in the 1880s, labor unrest spread to many major industries.

The government, still under the sway of the laissez-faire philosophy of staying out of economic affairs in the marketplace, initially rebuffed calls to interfere with business during the Gilded Age. However, over time, the excesses of the tycoons became too great to ignore. Starting in the 1880s, the government incrementally increased the regulation of major industries and moved to rein in the power of the robber barons.

ADDITIONAL FACTS

1. *The phrase Gilded Age was derived from the play* King John *by William Shakespeare: "To gild refined gold, to paint the lily . . . is wasteful and ridiculous excess."*

2. *Twain first used the phrase in* The Gilded Age: A Tale of Today *(1873), a book he cowrote with Charles Dudley Warner that was one of his few literary collaborations.*

3. *Industrialists welcomed the roughly ten million immigrants who came to the United States during the last half of the nineteenth century, since the huge supply of labor meant they could keep wages low.*

★ ★ ★

Land-Grant Act of 1862

One of the most farsighted pieces of federal law ever approved by the United States Congress, the Morrill Act, or Land-Grant Act of 1862, allotted large tracts of free land to each state to build public universities. By the twentieth century, nearly every American state had taken advantage of the law, leading to the establishment of many of the nation's leading institutions of higher education.

The act was the brainchild of Justin Morrill (1810–1898), a representative from Vermont in the US Congress. Morrill wanted to encourage states to build universities that would be open and affordable to the general public, not just the privileged elite. Congress hoped they would teach practical subjects like agriculture and military tactics in addition to the classic curriculum of older private schools like Harvard and Yale.

Almost immediately, states began opening land-grant universities on their allotments of 30,000 acres per congressional representative. Kansas State University was the first school founded under the act, in 1863; dozens more soon followed. Today, 105 colleges and universities are beneficiaries of the act, including major institutions like Texas A&M, the University of Florida, and the Massachusetts Institute of Technology (MIT).

By creating the system of public universities, the Land-Grant Act has had a major impact on both the American landscape and its education system. The act ensured that every state, no matter how small, would have its own center for higher learning. By democratizing access to higher education, the act also gave milllions of students a chance at economic advancement. Today more Americans have access to a liberal arts education than citizens of most other developed countries do, in large part thanks to Morrill's legacy

ADDITIONAL FACTS

1. *Many of the land-grant colleges were founded as coeducational institutions, greatly expanding higher education opportunities for women.*

2. *The original act, passed during the Civil War, excluded the South. An 1890 revision to the law, however, provided a way for Southern states to qualify for land-grant support.*

3. *One of the eight Ivy League universities, Cornell was founded as a land-grant college in 1865.*

★ ★ ★

Robert Frost

Robert Frost (1874–1963), a four-time winner of the Pulitzer Prize for poetry and one of the most popular American writers of the twentieth century, was the author of many beloved poems, including "Birches," "The Gift Outright," "Fire and Ice," and "The Road Not Taken." Many of Frost's best-known poems were set in rural New England, and he is particularly known for his lyrical descriptions of people's relationship with nature. In a reflection of Frost's immense popularity, he was asked to read at the inauguration of President John F. Kennedy (1917–1963) in 1961, where he recited "The Gift Outright" from memory.

Frost was born in San Francisco but moved to New England as a child. He published his first poem in a Massachusetts newspaper in 1894. Many of Frost's poems are set in the rocky fields and rolling hills of New Hampshire and Vermont, the rural region where he lived for most of his adult life. In his poems, Frost often used images from nature as metaphors for deeper philosophical observations. For instance, in "The Road Not Taken," Frost uses the image of a crossroads in the middle of the woods to evoke an important decision in his life:

> Two roads diverged in a wood, and I—
> I took the one less traveled by,
> And that has made all the difference.

Unlike many of his contemporaries, Frost wrote in plain, easy-to-understand language that made his work more accessible to the general public. Still, his poems were often deceptively complex. Frost was a master of formal rhyme and meter, even at a time when many other American poets were putting less emphasis on traditional forms in favor of free verse. Frost was held in high regard by academic readers and the public at large, a rare feat for American poets in the twentieth century.

ADDITIONAL FACTS

1. *At President Kennedy's request, the eighty-seven-year-old Frost traveled to Russia to meet with Soviet Premier Nikita Khrushchev (1894–1971) in 1962 on a goodwill mission at the height of the Cold War.*

2. *Frost attended Dartmouth and Harvard but failed to graduate from either college.*

3. *Frost's first child, Elliott, died in 1900 at age four. Frost's heartbreaking poem "Home Burial" describes the family's grief and the difficulty of moving on from such a loss.*

★ ★ ★

Jazz

The historic city of New Orleans, with one face to the Caribbean and the other to Dixie, was a mélange of races and ethnicities in the early twentieth century: part French, part English, and part African-American. Out of this eclectic heritage grew a hybrid, improvisational musical style known as jazz, the greatest indigenous American contribution to world music.

The first prominent performers of jazz were cornetist Buddy Bolden (1877–1931) and bandleader Ferdinand "Jelly Roll" Morton (1885–1941), African-American musicians who began performing in New Orleans nightclubs in the first two decades of the 1900s. They were influenced by blues and ragtime as well as by European folk songs and balladry, synthesizing these styles into a new genre unlike anything heard before.

After World War I (1914–1918), jazz emanated outward from New Orleans and became enormously popular during the Roaring Twenties, a decade sometimes referred to as the Jazz Age. White audiences flocked to hear African-American performers like trumpeter Louis Armstrong (1900–1971) and pianist Duke Ellington (1899–1974), two of the greatest jazz stars of the decade.

The music itself is famously difficult to describe. As Louis Armstrong once said, "If you have to ask what it is, you'll never know." Jazz is ordinarily performed with trumpet, clarinet, trombone, string bass, and drums, with piano and guitar often added to the ensemble. Jazz is built on solo improvisation, allowing for almost endless variety.

Since its birth in New Orleans, jazz has influenced nearly every other American musical style of the twentieth century, from swing and bebop to rock and funk.

ADDITIONAL FACTS

1. *The term Jazz Age was introduced by author F. Scott Fitzgerald (1896–1940), who titled a 1922 collection of short stories* Tales of the Jazz Age.

2. *Jazz heavily influenced composer George Gershwin (1898–1937), who incorporated many elements of jazz into his famous 1924 work* Rhapsody in Blue.

3. *Although often lumped together, jazz and blues are separate genres. Unlike improvised jazz, blues is almost always played with a repeating, twelve-bar chord progression.*

★ ★ ★

John C. Calhoun

A staunch defender of slavery, John C. Calhoun (1782–1850) represented South Carolina in the US Senate for decades and also served as vice president of the United States under two presidents. Calhoun, along with Henry Clay (1777–1852) and Daniel Webster (1782–1852), belonged to the so-called Great Triumvirate of prominent senators who dominated Congress in the decades leading up to the Civil War (1861–1865).

Of the three, Calhoun remains the most controversial for his unabashed support of slavery. Unlike many other Southerners, who claimed that slavery was a "necessary evil," Calhoun insisted that it was, in fact, a "positive good." In an infamous 1837 speech on the Senate floor, Calhoun claimed that the institution of slavery had actually helped blacks. "Never before has the black race of Central Africa, from the dawn of history to the present day, attained a condition so civilized and so improved, not only physically, but morally and intellectually," he said.

Although his justifications for slavery sound appalling to modern ears, Calhoun was by far the most eloquent and powerful voice for the South in Congress at a time when Northern opinion, prodded by the abolitionist movement, was beginning to turn decisively against slavery. Calhoun tenaciously opposed efforts to limit slavery. Indeed, the main purpose of Calhoun's 1837 speech was to attack the Northern abolitionists, whom Calhoun dismissed as "fanatics" blind to slavery's alleged benefits.

Calhoun was born in South Carolina and graduated from Yale in 1804. In his early political career, which began with his election to Congress in 1810, he did not show any particular interest in slavery. Not until the 1830s, with sectional differences over slavery deepening, did Calhoun mount the zealous defense of the institution for which he is now remembered.

ADDITIONAL FACTS

1. *John Caldwall Calhoun was named after an uncle who was murdered by British Loyalists during the American Revolution.*

2. *In 1840, Calhoun successfully passed a law prohibiting abolitionists from mailing their pamphlets to the South.*

3. *Calhoun resigned as President Andrew Jackson's vice president in 1832, one of only two vice presidents to resign from office. (Spiro Agnew became the second in 1973.)*

★ ★ ★

Battle of Antietam

The Battle of Antietam, fought on September 17, 1862, was the single bloodiest day of the American Civil War and remains the deadliest day in the history of American warfare. Total Union and Confederate casualties at Antietam, a small creek in Maryland about fifty miles northwest of Washington, DC, exceeded 23,000 men. The battle, a Union victory, halted a planned Confederate invasion of Maryland.

On September 3, 1862, Confederate general Robert E. Lee (1807–1870) decided to invade Maryland, a border state where slavery was still legal. Lee and Confederate president Jefferson Davis (1808–1889) hoped that a Southern victory on Northern soil would deal a crippling blow to Union morale before the 1862 midterm elections.

However, the warm welcome from Marylanders that Lee expected never materialized, and US President Abraham Lincoln (1809–1865) immediately sent Union general George McClellan (1826–1885) with troops to repel the invasion. The Union troops caught up with Lee near the town of Sharpsburg on the evening of September 16.

The battle the next day lasted twelve ferocious hours. Nearly 100,000 soldiers participated in the battle—a force of greater size than the entire army that had fought the American Revolution seventy years earlier.

Although both armies suffered awful casualties, it was Lee who decided to withdraw from the fight, retreating back to Virginia. Lincoln, sensing an opportunity to finish off Lee's army once and for all, ordered McClellan to pursue Lee into Virginia, but McClellan enraged Lincoln by dragging his feet. For the Union, McClellan's failure to follow Lee into Virginia was one of the great lost opportunities of the war.

ADDITIONAL FACTS

1. *In the South, the clash was known by a different name, the Battle of Sharpsburg.*

2. *Six generals were killed—three on each side—during the battle.*

3. *The dead were buried hastily after the battle in shallow graves, many of which soon became exposed; not until 1867 did the army finally establish a cemetery on the site and give its fallen proper burials.*

★ ★ ★

Know-Nothings

Starting in 1845, hundreds of thousands of Irish peasants immigrated to the United States to escape a deadly famine devastating their homeland. The Irish, most of them Roman Catholics who settled in the big cities of the Northeast, formed the first mass influx of immigrants in US history. But the sudden arrival of so many poor, uneducated immigrants provoked a wave of hysteria among the area's Protestant population and led to a vicious backlash against Catholics and foreigners in the 1850s.

Prior to the Irish famine, the population of the United States was almost exclusively Protestant. Anti-Catholic prejudice, moreover, was strong. Beginning with the Puritans, many Americans regarded the Roman Catholic Church and the pope with deep suspicion and perceived Catholicism as a threat to democratic government.

The sudden arrival of so many Catholics, combined with centuries-old hatred, made friction inevitable. Anti-Irish riots erupted in Philadelphia. In Massachusetts, several Catholic churches and convents were looted by Protestant mobs. In 1854, at the height of the backlash, opponents of immigration formed a political party, the Know-Nothing Party, that swept the Massachusetts elections that fall and polled well across the Northeast and Midwest. The Know-Nothing platform promised to limit future immigration from Catholic countries, make it more difficult for immigrants to acquire American citizenship, and teach Protestantism in public schools.

Religious tensions subsided after the Civil War (1861–1865), and subsequent waves of Catholic immigrants arrived from Italy, Poland, and Germany. However, prejudice against the Irish would linger for decades.

ADDITIONAL FACTS

1. *Despite a rather auspicious start in politics, the Know-Nothings had dissolved by the election of 1860, with the new Republican Party absorbing their antislavery contingent.*

2. *The 2002 movie* Gangs of New York, *directed by Martin Scorsese, is loosely based on religious strife between Catholics and Protestants in New York City during the 1840s.*

3. *The Know-Nothings began as a clandestine organization. They acquired their name from the reply members were supposed to give—"I know nothing"—when asked about their secret meetings.*

★ ★ ★

Panic of 1873

One of the first global economic downturns, the Panic of 1873 started in Vienna, Austria, and spread to the United States several months later, where it sparked a five-year depression that ruined thousands of businesses, depressed wages, and sent the unemployment rate skyrocketing. The Panic of 1873 temporarily slowed the massive growth in manufacturing that had followed the end of the Civil War (1861–1865) and greatly crippled the progress of Reconstruction in the South.

In early 1873, the national economy showed few outward signs of vulnerability. Indeed, in the eight years after the Civil War, tens of thousands of miles of railroad track had been constructed, thousands of factories opened, and the stock market surged upward. Even in the South, which bore the brunt of the devastation from the war, agriculture was on the rebound.

Many of the railroads, however, were built with borrowed money. In June 1873, the Vienna Stock Exchange crashed. Turmoil in the European markets spread to the United States on September 18, 1873, when one of the biggest bankers for the American railroad industry, Jay Cooke and Company, declared bankruptcy. Cooke's bankruptcy was a major blow to the railroads, which lost their biggest source of cash; 89 of 364 American railroads would go bankrupt during the panic, and railroad stocks lost a third of their overall value.

For American workers, the Panic of 1873 was a crippling blow. Unemployment shot up to 14 percent of the labor force, and average wages declined sharply. While railroad stocks recovered by the end of the 1870s, it would be decades before wages would return to their pre-1873 levels.

The Panic of 1873 also exposed the hapless incompetence of the administration of President Ulysses S. Grant (1822–1885). Although a war hero and military genius, Grant proved incapable of responding to the nation's sudden onset of economic woe. Indeed, in the view of some historians, the Grant administration may have exacerbated the panic by deflating the money supply, a policy that made credit relatively scarce and hastened bankruptcy for some firms.

ADDITIONAL FACTS

1. *At the time of the panic, Cooke was hoping to finance a second transcontinental railroad to compete with the line opened in 1869; the Northern Pacific would not be completed until 1883.*

2. *The stock market crash on September 19, 1873, the day after Cooke declared bankruptcy, became known as Black Friday.*

3. *The average daily wage dropped from $1.46 in 1872 to $1.12 in 1879 before beginning to inch back up.*

★ ★ ★

Atlanta

The flag of Atlanta shows a phoenix rising from the ashes, a fitting symbol for a city that recovered from greater devastation than perhaps any other major American metropolis. Burned to the ground in 1864 by Union troops, the city was quickly rebuilt into one of the largest and most prosperous cities in the South.

Founded in 1837 at the end of a railroad line, the city was originally named Terminus. It became Marthasville in 1843—in honor of the then-governor's daughter—and finally Atlanta in 1845. By the beginning of the Civil War in 1861, Atlanta had grown into one of the leading rail hubs in the South, with four lines converging on the city and a population of about 10,000 residents.

During the war, the city was a major supply center for the Confederacy, dispatching trainloads of ammunition and food from its foundries, mills, and carriage shops to Southern troops at the front. In an effort to destroy the Confederacy's war-making ability, Union general William Tecumseh Sherman (1820–1891) attacked Atlanta during his famous "March to the Sea" on September 2, 1864, and set the city ablaze two weeks later—a fire famously portrayed in the movie *Gone with the Wind* (1939).

Sherman's attack reduced Atlanta to blackened ruins, but the city vowed to rebuild. In the decades after the Civil War, Atlanta became the capital for proponents of the so-called New South, a generation of Southerners who wanted to rebuild their region and forget about the tainted past. Within two decades, Atlanta had far surpassed its prewar population number. Many major businesses, including the famous soft drink maker Coca-Cola, moved to the newly resurgent city, which has become one of the biggest metropolitan areas in the United States.

ADDITIONAL FACTS

1. *The word Atlanta has no historical meaning; it was derived from Atlantic.*

2. *The city was built on land vacated by the Cherokees who were forced to move to Oklahoma on the Trail of Tears in 1837.*

3. *Only 400 buildings were left standing in Atlanta at the end of 1864.*

★ ★ ★

H. L. Mencken

The leading man of letters in the early twentieth century, sharp-witted Baltimore journalist and critic H. L. Mencken (1880–1956) held American society up for ridicule in his powerful essays and helped popularize a generation of iconoclastic novelists like Theodore Dreiser (1871–1945) and Sinclair Lewis (1885–1951).

Henry Louis Mencken, the son of a successful Baltimore cigar maker, got his first newspaper job at the *Baltimore Morning Herald* when he was eighteen. He rose quickly through the ranks at the newspaper and in 1906 moved to the rival *Baltimore Sun*, which would remain his journalistic home on and off for the remainder of his life.

Even as a young reporter, Mencken took an active interest in the American literary scene, and he authored his first book in 1905, *George Bernard Shaw—His Plays*. Mencken was an extremely prolific writer, sometimes penning dozens of letters a day in addition to his journalistic endeavors.

In 1908, Mencken began his association with *The Smart Set*, an irreverent magazine that gave the young writer a national audience and space to hone his trademark, snarling style. In his writing about culture and politics, Mencken lampooned American society with his caustic, savage wit, often referring contemptuously to ordinary Americans as the "Boobus Americanus." Hypocrisy and religious fundamentalism particularly annoyed Mencken, who reserved some of his harshest invective for President Woodrow Wilson (1856–1924).

Smart Set went out of business after World War I (1914–1918), but in 1924 it was resurrected as a new publication called *American Mercury*. In *American Mercury*, one of the most popular magazines of the decade, Mencken continued his attacks on American "boobs," and he achieved notoriety for his coverage of the Scopes trial in 1925, in which he relentlessly ridiculed William Jennings Bryan (1860–1925) and the fundamentalist Christian opponents of evolution. Mencken also used the magazine to praise up-and-coming writers like Lewis, whose famous Babbitt character Mencken cited as an archetypal American boob.

A proud, lifelong Baltimore resident, Mencken died in his sleep at age seventy-five in the same house he had lived in with his parents since age two.

ADDITIONAL FACTS

1. *Mencken was married once, at age fifty, to Baltimore writer Sara Haardt in 1930, but she died five years later.*

2. *A conservative, Mencken was a committed opponent of the New Deal and ridiculed the economic recovery programs of President Franklin Delano Roosevelt (1882–1945) in his column.*

3. *Over a lifetime in print, Mencken produced thousands of articles, memorabilia, and ephemera affectionately known to collectors and admirers as "Menckeniana."*

★ ★ ★

Charlie Chaplin

In 1936, Charlie Chaplin (1889–1977) released his most famous motion picture, *Modern Times*. The movie's title was a deliberate misnomer. Chaplin, a star of silent films who hated the newfangled "talkies," never spoke in the movie, which was the last hurrah of the silent film era. The movie also marked the last appearance of Chaplin's beloved Little Tramp character, the biggest star of Hollywood's formative years.

 The British-born Charles Spencer Chaplin had moved to California in 1913 and was soon acting in dozens of silent films every year. His famous, unnamed Little Tramp dressed in comically oversize pants, a tiny jacket, and a black bowler hat. Within a few years, Chaplin had become a major star and was directing most of his own films. Along with fellow movie stars Mary Pickford (1893–1979) and Douglas Fairbanks Sr. (1883–1939) and the famous director D. W. Griffith (1875–1948), he founded the United Artists studio in 1919.

For the most part, Chaplin's films were whimsical and comical. The Little Tramp was an endearing naïf, always in the wrong place at the wrong time. For instance, in *The Kid*, released in 1921, the Tramp finds a baby who has been abandoned by his mother and ends up trying to raise the child himself. Chaplin, who had been trained on the vaudeville stage, was able to master the art of the silent film, communicating the emotions of his character through gestures alone.

The invention of the talkie made the Little Tramp obsolete. Chaplin, however, saved his best effort for last. *Modern Times*, appropriately enough, tells the story of the Little Tramp struggling to survive in an increasingly impersonal, technological society. In one famous scene, the Tramp is ground between the gears at a factory, a metaphor for the dehumanizing effect of modern industry on the human spirit.

Chaplin finally spoke in his 1940 film *The Great Dictator*, a pointed satire of Nazi Germany. In that film, Chaplin played Adenoid Hynkel, the dictator of the fictional country of Tomania, who bore a striking resemblance to Adolf Hitler (1889–1945). Chaplin continued to act in occasional films and also wrote the music for many movies, but he went into self-imposed exile in Switzerland in 1952 and died there in 1977.

ADDITIONAL FACTS

1. *Chaplin never acquired United States citizenship, and he was knighted by Queen Elizabeth II (1926–) in 1975, shortly before his death.*

2. *Chaplin's fourth wife, eighteen-year-old Oona O'Neill (1926–1991), whom he married when he was fifty-four, was the daughter of playwright Eugene O'Neill (1888–1953).*

3. *Chaplin won two honorary Oscars—one at the first Academy Awards in 1929 and the other in 1972—but only one ordinary award: the 1973 Best Original Score Oscar for his music for* Limelight.

* * *

Henry Clay

For the better part of fifty years, Henry Clay (1777–1852) dominated the United States Congress, first as the most powerful Speaker of the House in the history of the office and then as a leading senator from Kentucky. Clay entered Congress at age twenty-nine and remained in national government for most of the remainder of his life. Eloquent and ambitious, Clay ran for president five times, on the ticket of three different political parties, but was never able to achieve his ultimate goal. Nicknamed the "Great Compromiser," Clay's canny, pragmatic deal making helped preserve the Union and advanced his own favorite cause, the construction of federally funded canals and roadways connecting the cities of the growing nation.

A lawyer by training, Clay was only thirty-four years old when his colleagues in Congress elected him Speaker of the House. Up until then, the position was regarded as an undesirable and largely ceremonial job. But the Kentuckian transformed the office into a powerhouse. Clay cajoled Congress into declaring war on Great Britain in 1812, supporting his "American System" of costly infrastructure projects, and agreeing to the Missouri Compromise, which averted a crisis over slavery.

In 1824, Clay made his first run for the presidency but finished in fourth place. He entered the Senate in 1831 as one of the founders of a new political party, the Whigs. Clay ran against Democrat Andrew Jackson (1767–1845) in 1832, again promising to build roads, railroads, and canals, but was soundly defeated by the popular Tennessean.

On the great issue of the day, slavery, Clay closely followed his Senate colleague and fellow Whig Daniel Webster (1782–1852). Like Webster, Clay opposed slavery personally but was willing to compromise with pro-slavery forces to preserve the Union. With the deaths of these two men in 1852, a new generation of uncompromising politicians took power in Washington, DC, and within a decade the North and South were at war.

ADDITIONAL FACTS

1. *In 1986, a poll of history professors ranked Clay as the greatest-ever United States senator, narrowly edging out second-place Hubert Humphrey (1911–1978) and third-place Daniel Webster, according to the* New York Times.

2. *Although Clay never became president, a peak in the Presidential Range in New Hampshire is named in his honor.*

3. *Nicknames for Clay included "Harry of the West," "Prince Hal," and the "Great Compromiser."*

★ ★ ★

Battle of Gettysburg

The Union victory at the Battle of Gettysburg (1863) was the decisive turning point of the Civil War. The gruesome three-day battle, which resulted in 51,000 casualties, stopped an attempted Confederate invasion of Pennsylvania. After the battle, Confederate general Robert E. Lee (1807–1870) was forced to retreat to Virginia. His army, battered by superior Union firepower, would never again mount an invasion of the North.

Gettysburg, located in central Pennsylvania on the road to the state capital of Harrisburg, was a sleepy college town in 1863. The town held little strategic value, but it was where the Union cavalry pursuing Lee's invaders happened to catch up with him on the morning of July 1, 1863.

The plan for the Confederate invasion, hatched that spring, was simple. Lee and the Confederate president, Jefferson Davis (1808–1889), hoped to resupply their famished army in the rich Pennsylvania farmland. Additionally, Lee and Davis hoped that a successful strike on the North would demoralize the enemy and strengthen the antiwar faction in the North before the 1864 presidential election.

The significance of Gettysburg to American history can hardly be overstated. For three days, both armies fought out of desperation. Union troops, more accustomed to fighting on Southern soil, were suddenly called on to defend their home turf. Southern leaders understood that the Pennsylvania campaign was a last-ditch effort and that if the invasion failed, the Confederacy would probably be doomed.

On the third day, with the Union winning the battle, Lee ordered one of the most famous actions of the war, a massive assault of 13,000 infantry soldiers against the Union lines known as "Pickett's charge" after its leader, General George E. Pickett (1825–1875). The charge was a failure, and thousands of Confederate soldiers were killed or taken prisoner. Pickett's charge would go down in Southern lore as the last, best effort of the Confederate army to overcome the Northerners.

ADDITIONAL FACTS

1. *The Gettysburg Address, President Lincoln's famous speech defending the Union cause, was delivered five months after the battle at the dedication of a cemetery for 3,500 Union soldiers killed there.*

2. *The* New York Times *reporter who covered the battle, Sam Wilkeson, reported on the death of his own son, a Union soldier.*

3. *Hundreds of miles from Gettysburg, another Union general, Ulysses S. Grant (1822–1885), took the city of Vicksburg, handing a double victory to the Union on Independence Day 1863.*

★ ★ ★

Emancipation Proclamation

On January 1, 1863, President Abraham Lincoln (1809–1865) issued the Emancipation Proclamation that freed the slaves in the Southern states. Unlike many of Lincoln's famous speeches, the proclamation was inelegant, even verbose. It resembled a legal pleading, not a landmark document in the history of civil rights:

> . . . on the 1st day of January, A.D. 1863, all persons held as slaves within any State or designated part of a State the people whereof shall then be in rebellion against the United States shall be then, thenceforward, and forever free; and the executive government of the United States, including the military and naval authority thereof, will recognize and maintain the freedom of such persons and will do no act or acts to repress such persons, or any of them, in any efforts they may make for their actual freedom.

Prior to the Emancipation Proclamation, the legal status of Southern slaves in Union camps during the Civil War (1861–1865) was the subject of considerable debate and confusion. Some Union generals set slaves free, defying orders from Washington, DC, while others considered slaves taken from Confederate landowners as "contraband," meaning they legally remained slaves but could not be returned to their owners.

The proclamation, issued by Lincoln in his capacity as commander in chief, applied only to the Southern states in rebellion, a loophole that raised the ire of abolitionists like William Lloyd Garrison (1805–1879). Slavery remained legal in the border states loyal to the Union until the Thirteenth Amendment was added to the US Constitution in 1865.

In the long term, the Emancipation Proclamation changed the complexion of the Civil War from a dispute over the integrity of the Union to a fight over the fundamental moral issue of slavery. The proclamation redefined the Northern cause: the North was no longer fighting only for the somewhat abstract goal of preserving the Union, but also to free an oppressed people.

ADDITIONAL FACTS

1. *One provision of the proclamation also allowed blacks to join the Union army, leading to the creation of all-black units like the Fifth-Fourth Massachusetts Regiment.*

2. *The last slaves to be liberated were in Delaware and Kentucky, two states that had remained loyal to the Union.*

3. *Lincoln waited until after the Union victory at the Battle of Antietam (September 17, 1862) to issue the proclamation, so that it would appear to have been announced from a position of strength.*

★ ★ ★

Laissez-Faire

Laissez-faire, an economic doctrine that calls for minimal government inter-ference with the marketplace, was dominant in the United States during the nineteenth century and remains a strong intellectual tradition in American political thought. In general, supporters of laissez-faire believe that allowing the market to function unfettered by regulation will result in economic prosperity for all. However, critics of laissez-faire have argued successfully since the Gilded Age that some government regulation is needed to prevent corporate abuses.

French for *leave alone,* laissez-faire had its roots in the backlash against mercantilism that started in the late eighteenth century. Beginning in 1776, Adam Smith (1723–1790) and a growing number of his fellow economists rejected mercantilism and began to argue against government interference with trade. If the government stepped aside and left private industry to its own devices, they believed, the laws of supply and demand would ultimately create a more efficient economy for everyone.

Across Europe and the United States, the mid-nineteenth century represented the zenith of laissez-faire. Labor laws were generally nonexistent, and corporate tycoons wielded unchecked power over their employees. Railroads could set prices as high as they wanted. Several large companies, such as John D. Rockefeller's Standard Oil, began to develop monopolies that squeezed out their competition. In historical usage, the term *laissez-faire* is sometimes used to refer specifically to the lax economic policies of this period in American history.

The reaction against the excesses of laissez-faire began to gain force in the 1880s. One of the first regulatory bills, the Interstate Commerce Act, was passed in 1887 to limit the clout of railroad corporations. In the beginning of the twentieth century, President Theodore Roosevelt (1858–1919) campaigned strongly against corporate power. Finally, the Great Depression of the 1930s was a major catalyst for the passage of stringent new government regulations on industry, banks, and utilities.

More recently, supporters of laissez-faire have made a minor comeback. Since the 1970s, Congress has wholly or partially deregulated several major industries, including airlines, banks, and railroads. In general, however, the modern regulatory state would be unrecognizable to the robber barons whose abuses and excesses led to its creation.

ADDITIONAL FACTS

1. *The term* laissez-faire *was coined by a group of eighteenth-century French economists known as* physiocrats.

2. *To the widespread confusion of both Europeans and Americans, the word* liberal *has very different definitions on the two continents. In Europe, a liberal generally supports free market economics and minimal government regulation; in the United States, people who identify themselves as liberals generally believe just the opposite.*

3. *The leading journal for laissez-faire supporters, the* Economist, *was founded in 1843 in Britain and is still published today.*

* * *

Great Chicago Fire of 1871

Destroying thousands of homes and killing hundreds of people, the Great Chicago Fire of 1871 was one of the worst disasters in the nineteenth-century United States. The inferno, which raged for two days before it finally died out, obliterated much of downtown Chicago and forced the city to rebuild almost entirely from scratch.

The fire started on the city's West Side at the home of Catherine (Mrs. Patrick) O'Leary, an Irish immigrant, on October 8, 1871. Thanks to high winds that night, the flames spread quickly to neighboring wooden structures, and by the next morning the whole city was ablaze. A newspaper reporter made up an infamous story that the fire had been started when Mrs. O'Leary's cow kicked over a kerosene lamp. In reality, however, the exact cause of the blaze at the O'Leary home still remains unknown.

At the time of the fire, the city of Chicago was less than forty years old and had undergone fantastic growth since its founding. The 1870 census placed the city as the fifth largest in the nation, with 298,977 residents, up from only 4,470 in 1840. Many of the new arrivals were immigrants from Poland, Ireland, and Germany who were crammed into hastily built wooden houses.

Although the fire devastated downtown Chicago, the death toll of about 300 was considered surprisingly light. The fire left acres of space in prime downtown locations vacant, which in turn attracted many of the nation's leading architects, including Daniel Burnham (1846–1912) and Louis Sullivan (1856–1924). Several of the world's first skyscrapers were built in Chicago on parcels of land left empty by the famous blaze.

ADDITIONAL FACTS

1. *The O'Leary house survived the fire with relatively light damage; it was later demolished.*

2. *The Chicago Fire of 1871 was the inspiration for national Fire Prevention Week, which is marked every year in early October.*

3. *An estimated 70,000 buildings were destroyed in the blaze, along with 73 miles of streets, which at that time were made of wooden planks.*

★ ★ ★

T. S. Eliot

Poet T. S. Eliot (1888–1965) was born in St. Louis and educated at Harvard. He moved to England in his twenties and eventually became a British subject. Although most of his best-known poetry was published while he lived abroad, Eliot's ties to his home country remained deep, and he is considered one of the leading modernists of twentieth-century American verse.

Thomas Stearns Eliot published his first poems as a college student and wrote one of his most famous, "The Love Song of J. Alfred Prufrock," while still in his twenties. Published in 1917, the poem established his reputation in literary circles and introduced the public to Eliot's highly abstract, dense writing style. Eliot's poems are not easy to read. He sprinkled obscure allusions and foreign phrases throughout his verse; "The Love Song of J. Alfred Prufrock," for instance, begins with six lines of untranslated Italian.

Still, the poem was hailed for its striking imagery and stream-of-consciousness narration. The narrator of the poem is a balding, middle-aged man named Prufrock, a timid, sexually frustrated nebbish who, in one famous passage, asks himself if he dares "to eat a peach."

The Waste Land, a long poem considered Eliot's masterpiece by many critics, was published in 1922. Although difficult to summarize, *The Waste Land* expressed the deep spiritual malaise of the post–World War I generation in the United States and Europe. Eliot himself referred to the early 1920s as a particularly rough period in his own life, due to an unhappy marriage. A demanding poem, *The Waste Land* was not intended for the faint of heart or feeble of vocabulary; in addition to English, parts of the poem are in Latin, Greek, German, French, Italian, and Sanskrit. The themes and imagery in the poem are borrowed heavily from a book called *The Golden Bough* (1890, expanded 1907–1915) by the Scottish anthropologist James George Frazer (1854–1941), which many of Eliot's readers would also have read, making the poem slightly more accessible to them.

Later in life, Eliot found religion and converted to Anglicanism. His later poems, including "Ash Wednesday" (1930) and *Four Quartets* (1936–1942) are heavy with Christian symbolism. In recognition of his highly influential poetry, Eliot won the Nobel Prize for Literature in 1948.

ADDITIONAL FACTS

1. *The hit musical* Cats, *by Andrew Lloyd Webber, was based on Eliot's 1939 book* Old Possum's Book of Practical Cats.

2. *Eliot and his friend and fellow anti-Semite Ezra Pound (1885–1972) both feature in the Bob Dylan song "Desolation Row," in which they are said to be "fighting in the captain's tower."*

3. *A heavy smoker, Eliot died of emphysema.*

★ ★ ★

George Gershwin

A prodigy whose early death robbed the nation of one of its greatest musical talents, George Gershwin (1898–1937) became the most famous composer of the 1920s and 1930s with his wild, inventive melodies in classics like *Rhapsody in Blue* and the opera *Porgy and Bess*. Along with his older brother, lyricist Ira Gershwin (1896–1983), he wrote dozens of American standards, including the songs "Summertime," "Someone to Watch Over Me," "Embraceable You," and "I Got Rhythm."

Born in Brooklyn to Russian Jewish immigrant parents, Gershwin took piano lessons as a boy and sold his first song, "When You Want 'Em, You Can't Get 'Em," on Tin Pan Alley—the nickname for an area in New York City where many music publishers had their offices—in 1916. His first hit, published in 1919, was the song "Swanee," inspired by Stephen Foster's classic "Swanee River."

While composing popular tunes for Tin Pan Alley, Gershwin also began writing classical music in an effort to establish himself as a serious musician. His best-known classical composition, *Rhapsody in Blue*, debuted in 1924. One of the most famous pieces of instrumental music by an American, the rhapsody represented an exuberant "kaleidoscope of America," mixing jazz, blues, and classical styles into a unique seventeen-minute composition.

In 1931, the Gershwin brothers won a Pulitzer Prize for *Of Thee I Sing* the first musical comedy to win the prestigious award. They wrote their most ambitious Broadway work, *Porgy and Bess*, in 1935. The racial aspects of the opera, which was intended for an all-black cast but has been criticized for perpetuating negative racial stereotypes, have been controversial, but it produced several classic songs, including "Summertime."

Porgy and Bess, however, would be Gershwin's last major work. While in Hollywood working on a movie in 1937, Gershwin fell ill and died of a brain tumor.

ADDITIONAL FACTS

1. *The great Russian composers Sergey Rachmaninoff (1873–1943) and Igor Stravinsky (1882–1971) were in the audience at the 1924 premier of* Rhapsody in Blue *at New York's Aeolian Hall.*

2. *Gershwin's popular musical comedies include* Lady, Be Good *(1924),* Funny Face *(1927), and* Strike Up the Band *(1930).*

3. *Parts of* Rhapsody in Blue *are used by United Airlines in its television commercials.*

★ ★ ★

Daniel Webster

Daniel Webster (1782–1852) was the most famous orator of the first half of the nineteenth century, a person capable of drawing tens of thousands of spectators to his captivating speeches. As a lawyer and politician, Webster used his gift to successfully argue several landmark cases before the United States Supreme Court and then won election to the US Senate from Massachusetts. In his long Senate career, Webster reached the pinnacle of his fame as an unceasing supporter of the Union during acrimonious debates over slavery in the 1830s and 1840s.

Webster graduated from Dartmouth College in his home state of New Hampshire. He later moved to Boston to open a law office. As a lawyer, he represented his alma mater in a precedent-setting Supreme Court case, *Dartmouth College v. Woodward* (1819). In the case, justices ruled that the state of New Hampshire couldn't seize Dartmouth and turn it into a public university, as they had planned. Webster also argued *McCulloch v. Maryland* (1819), a crucial case upholding the federal government's right to charter a national bank.

Elected to the Senate from Massachusetts in 1827, Webster emerged as one of the foremost opponents of Southern separatism and the doctrine of states' rights. Webster believed in a strong federal government and opposed efforts by Southern states to opt out of tax laws they disliked. He ended an 1830 speech on the Senate floor with a famous refrain that would be repeated by Webster's admirers for decades: "Liberty *and* Union, now and forever, one and inseparable!"

On the issue of slavery, Webster's personal views favored the abolitionists. Slavery, he felt, was "a great moral and political evil." But Webster cared more about preserving the Union than about ending slavery, and he alienated many abolitionists with his willingness to compromise with pro-slavery southerners. Abolitionists denounced Webster for supporting the controversial Compromise of 1850, which they felt gave too much ground to pro-slavery forces; Webster, sensing that both sides would not budge, acridly declared in the middle of the debate that he wanted to "beat down the Northern and Southern follies, now raging in equal extremes."

Like Henry Clay and John C. Calhoun, Webster achieved greatness as a senator but never realized his ultimate ambition, the presidency. He ran several times without success. Webster was on the ticket in 1852, but he died a few weeks before the election.

ADDITIONAL FACTS

1. *In an 1825 speech marking the fiftieth anniversary of the Battle of Bunker Hill, 20,000 Bostonians listened to Webster's oration, which he gave without the assistance of a microphone.*

2. *Webster's last words, as he lay dying of cirrhosis, were "I still live."*

3. *A fantastical 1937 short story, "The Devil and Daniel Webster," by Stephen Vincent Benét (1898–1943), was made into an opera of the same title by Douglas Stuart Moore (1893–1969) in 1939.*

* * *

Fifty-Fourth Massachusetts Infantry

Although the Union attack on Battery Wagner on July 11, 1863, had little military impact on the Civil War (1861–1865), it marked a significant milestone in the history of civil rights and American warfare. The 600-man unit that led the assault on the small Confederate fortress in Charleston, South Carolina, was the Fifty-Fourth Massachusetts Infantry Regiment, the first all-black unit in the history of the United States Army.

African-Americans had fought in the American Revolution, but at the outset of the Civil War, the military strongly resisted accepting black volunteers as regular soldiers. Only in March 1863, with the war raging and manpower short, did President Abraham Lincoln (1809–1865) sign the Emancipation Proclamation allowing black soldiers to enlist in segregated regiments.

Not surprisingly, many African-Americans in the North, eager for a chance to help crush slavery, rushed to join the fight against the Confederacy, including two sons of the prominent abolitionist Frederick Douglass (1817–1895). Within months of Lincoln's order, the Fifty-Fourth Massachusetts was ready for combat.

Even before entering the battlefield, the soldiers in the regiment endured a series of humiliations from their own leadership. Initially, the War Department in Washington, DC, offered to pay black privates only $10 a month, rather than the $13 paid whites of the same rank. Outraged, the soldiers of the Fifty-Fourth Massachusetts fought without pay, rather than accept less than whites. Originally, the army also refused to allow blacks to become officers. The commander of the Fifty-Fourth Massachusetts was Colonel Robert Gould Shaw (1837–1863), a prominent white antislavery activist from Boston.

The heroics of the soldiers during the attack on Battery Wagner made the Fifty-Fourth Massachusetts nationally famous. The assault itself, ironically, was a failure, and about a third of the regiment, including Shaw, died in battle. However, the bravery of the soldiers of the Fifty-Fourth Massachusetts impressed the nation and put pressure on Congress to equalize pay for black and white soldiers, which it finally did in June 1864.

ADDITIONAL FACTS

1. *A member of the Fifty-Fourth Massachusetts Infantry, Sergeant William H. Carney, became the first African-American to win the Medal of Honor, the nation's highest military decoration, for his heroism at Battery Wagner in 1863.*

2. *In 1897, the city of Boston erected a monument designed by Augustus Saint-Gaudens (1848–1907) in memory of the regiment, in a place of honor across the street from the Massachusetts state capitol.*

3. *The 1989 movie Glory, starring Matthew Broderick and Denzel Washington, was based on the exploits of the Fifty-Fourth Massachusetts. Washington's performance in the film won him an Academy Award for Best Supporting Actor.*

★ ★ ★

Draft Riots

On July 13, 1863, in the midst of the Civil War, deadly riots erupted in New York City in protest of the North's military draft. Most of the rioters were poor, white, unskilled immigrants, many of them newly arrived from Ireland. The rioters burned and looted hundreds of buildings in New York and killed dozens of African-Americans in one of the country's deadliest outbreaks of racial violence.

Economic competition between immigrants and African-Americans formed the backdrop for the riots. The Emancipation Proclamation not only freed the slaves, overnight it created a vast new potential source of labor for American industry. Irish immigrants, who occupied the lowest rung on the nation's economic ladder, feared they would lose their jobs to ex-slaves, and they deeply resented the draft that forced them to fight for a cause many feared would lead to their own economic ruin. Rioters also objected to the unfairness of the draft, which allowed the rich to avoid service by paying a $300 fee.

Over the course of three days, the mob took over the city's Second Avenue Armory, ransacked the homes of prominent abolitionists, looted the headquarters of a leading Republican newspaper, burned down a black orphanage, and hanged or drowned in the East River scores of African-Americans. According to historian Eric Foner, the riots were the second-worst rebellion against federal authority in the nation's history—after only the Civil War itself.

In response to the outbreak of violence, President Abraham Lincoln (1809–1865) responded forcefully. Battle-hardened Union troops were diverted from Gettysburg and quickly marched to New York, where they killed more than 100 of the protesters. Estimates of the total death toll range as high as 1,000. Although suppressed within a few days, the riots exposed seething racial tensions in the North.

ADDITIONAL FACTS

1. *New York was a stronghold for "copperheads," or Democrats who opposed the Civil War. The label, coined by Republicans, comes from the name of a poisonous snake.*

2. *At the time of the riots, the New York police force numbered 800 poorly equipped officers; the mayhem prompted the formation of the modern New York City police department.*

3. *The mob, perhaps making a fashion statement, also burned down the Brooks Brothers clothing store.*

★ ★ ★

Thomas Edison

Inventor Thomas Edison (1847–1931) developed scores of new technologies at his famous laboratory in Menlo Park, New Jersey, including the incandescent lightbulb, the phonograph, and many of the advances that made movies possible. An entrepreneur, Edison also founded the company that eventually became General Electric, which is today among the nation's largest corporations. One of the keys to Edison's huge success was his ability to combine technological genius with a practical understanding of the desires of the American consumer.

Edison was born in Ohio and first learned about electricity while working for telegraph companies in the Midwest in the 1860s. Many of his first patents were improvements to the telegraph. Edison eventually moved to New Jersey, where he would establish his national reputation after his invention of the phonograph in 1877.

The first phonograph was a primitive device that recorded sounds onto a fragile metal disk. Its invention made Edison famous, it seemed so magical that he became known as the Wizard of Menlo Park for his ingenuity. After the phonograph, Edison was able to attract investments from major financiers, including the finance mogul J. P. Morgan (1837–1913), to begin work on developing an electric lightbulb. Many other scientists had attempted to build such a device, but Edison was the first to succeed. He produced the first practical incandescent lightbulb in 1879.

During the 1880s, the electricity company Edison founded to power the bulbs was locked in a battle with its main competitor over how to transmit electricity. The competition pitted Edison's direct current (DC) transmission system against the alternating current (AC) system devised by rival George Westinghouse (1846–1914). After decades of bitter rivalry, the AC system won out as a means of delivering power to homes, although Edison's DC is still used for other applications, including the third rail on subway lines.

Edison continued to invent during the 1880s and 1890s. In 1891, he patented the kinetoscope, a motion picture projector that was an early predecessor to modern motion picture technology. In 1892, Morgan arranged to combine Edison's business with several others to form General Electric.

ADDITIONAL FACTS

1. *Edison opposed capital punishment but inadvertently invented the electric chair. Seeking to disparage AC power as too dangerous, he facetiously suggested it should be used for executions; state authorities took him seriously and began electrocuting criminals in the 1890s.*

2. *Edison did not invent the telephone, but he is sometimes credited as the person responsible for popularizing the practice of answering the phone with the word "hello."*

3. *In 1954, the New Jersey town that included Menlo Park renamed itself Edison in honor of the inventor.*

★ ★ ★

Brooklyn Bridge

At the time of its opening on May 24, 1883, the Brooklyn Bridge was the longest suspension bridge in the world and a marvel of modern construction. Spanning the East River, the bridge connected Manhattan with Brooklyn, which at that time were separate cities in New York. Iconic as an engineering milestone, the Brooklyn Bridge also reflected the rapid growth of American cities in the decades after the Civil War (1861–1865).

Prior to the bridge's construction, travelers had to take a ferry between the two cities, which were the first and third largest in the nation as of 1880 (Philadelphia occupied second place). The East River at that point widened to nearly a half mile across, far too great a distance for traditional bridges. The difficulty of crossing the river was both an everyday annoyance to New Yorkers and a drain on the city's economy.

Engineer John Roebling (1806–1869), a German immigrant, finally devised a way to cross the river in 1870. Suspension bridges were not a new idea; they had been constructed by the ancient Roman and ancient Incan civilizations, among others. But Roebling added a new element. Instead of using rope woven from hemp, his design called for thick steel wires to hold up the bridge's span.

The construction of the bridge took thirteen years and exacted a major toll on Roebling's family. Roebling himself died from tetanus following an accident in the early stages of construction; his son, Washington Roebling (1837–1926), took over the project but was crippled for life after contracting decompression sickness on a visit to the underwater section of one of the bridge's piers. Although Washington Roebling remained nominally in charge of the bridge's construction, his wife, Emily Warren Roebling (1843–1903), handled most of rest of the project.

When it finally opened, the Brooklyn Bridge surpassed any other structure in the world. More than a mile long, it was a thousand feet longer than any other span. Additionally, its towers were believed to be the tallest in the world. Despite fears that the fantastic structure would collapse, thousands crossed the bridge on its first day, and it has continued to dazzle visitors to New York City ever since.

ADDITIONAL FACTS

1. *The Brooklyn Bridge once carried elevated trains in addition to cars; a pedestrian walkway is now in the space once occupied by train tracks.*

2. *Manhattan and Brooklyn, along with the Bronx, Queens, and Staten Island, were formally joined into one city, Greater New York, in 1898.*

3. *Two other suspension bridges built later, the Manhattan Bridge (1909) and the Williamsburg Bridge (1903), now connect Manhattan and Brooklyn.*

★ ★ ★

Sinclair Lewis

The first American writer to win the Nobel Prize for Literature, Sinclair Lewis (1885–1951) was recognized in 1930 for his books *Main Street* (1920) and *Babbit* (1922), which lampooned American materialism and provincialism and earned the author his reputation as an acerbic cultural critic.

Lewis was born in Minnesota in 1885 and graduated from Yale in 1908. He spent most of his twenties as a struggling writer, working at various magazines and publishing houses, including a brief stint as an editor at a magazine for teachers of the deaf.

Main Street, published when Lewis was thirty-five, was an enormous success, aided by the enthusiastic reviews of H. L. Mencken (1880–1956). The book chronicled the life of Carol Milford, a young woman in Minneapolis who marries a doctor and moves to his small hometown of Gopher Prairie, Minnesota. Expecting a bucolic country village, she instead finds an ugly, conservative backwater.

By satirizing small-town customs, Lewis challenged one of America's favorite beliefs about itself—namely, the inherent virtue of rural life. Lewis himself described the reaction to the book's message with his characteristic droll sarcasm. "One of the most treasured American myths," he wrote, "had been that all American villages were peculiarly noble and happy, and here an American attacked that myth. Scandalous."

Babbitt, a wry satire on conformity and civic boosterism, followed two years later. Set in the fictional city of Zenith, which Lewis modeled on Cincinnati, the novel's main character is the selfish real estate salesman George Babbitt, one of the most memorable characters in American fiction.

After winning the Nobel Prize, Lewis's career quickly slid downhill, lubricated by large amounts of alcohol. He wrote one more well-received novel, a satire on fascism called *It Can't Happen Here* (1935), and died in Rome of health problems related to his alcoholism at age sixty-five.

ADDITIONAL FACTS

1. *In 1906, Lewis worked briefly as a janitor at a utopian community founded by the author Upton Sinclair (1878–1968), with whom he is often confused because of their similar names.*

2. *Lewis was born in the town of Sauk Centre, Minnesota, the model for Gopher Prairie.*

3. *His oldest son, Wells Lewis, was killed in France during World War II (1939–1945).*

★ ★ ★

Irving Berlin

One of the twentieth century's most popular and prolific songwriters, Irving Berlin (1888–1989) composed "White Christmas," "God Bless America," "Puttin' On the Ritz," and dozens of other tunes that lifted spirits during World War II (1939–1945) and have become permanent parts of the nation's songbook.

Originally named Israel Baline, Berlin was born to a large Jewish family in a tiny Siberian village called Tyumen. After a pogrom, the family fled to the United States in 1893 and wound up in the Lower East Side neighborhood of Manhattan, where many newly arrived Jewish immigrants first settled.

Growing up on the rough-and-tumble streets of New York, the young Berlin worked as a newspaper vendor, street busker, and even a singing waiter in Chinatown. Forced to support his family after the death of his father in 1896, Berlin completed only about two years of school.

Despite a lack of formal musical training, Berlin began writing songs in his spare time when he was eighteen and published his first score in 1907. His first major Tin Pan Alley hit, the unforgettably catchy "Alexander's Ragtime Band," was released in 1911.

A rising musical star, Berlin's career was put on hold when he was drafted into the US Army during World War I (1914–1918). After his return, Berlin wrote a spate of hits in the 1920s, including "Remember" and "Always," and embarked on a high-profile courtship of a wealthy Irish Catholic heiress, Ellin Mackay. In a drama worthy of one of his own songs, Berlin convinced Mackay to marry him and then gave her the royalty rights to the romantic song "Always" after her father disowned her for marrying a lowly Jewish immigrant.

In 1938, at the peak of his career, Berlin wrote the patriotic song "God Bless America" for the singer Kate Smith (1909–1986); it was an instant hit. "White Christmas," Berlin's single most successful song, was released in 1942.

After World War II, Berlin continued writing at a prodigious clip. By the time he retired in the late 1960s, he had composed 1,500 songs, 19 Broadway shows, and the sound tracks to 18 movies. In the last decades of his life, Berlin became somewhat of a recluse at his Manhattan townhouse, but he lived to see a huge Carnegie Hall party for his 100th birthday in 1988, a celebration of America's best-loved songwriter. He died at age 101.

ADDITIONAL FACTS

1. *The Willie Nelson hit "Blue Skies" was originally composed by Berlin in 1927.*

2. *Berlin wrote a campaign song for Republican presidential candidate Dwight D. Eisenhower (1890–1969) in 1952, "I Like Ike."*

3. *"Alexander's Ragtime Band" is not actually written in ragtime; it is a march.*

★ ★ ★

Abraham Lincoln

Abraham Lincoln (1809–1865) was the second choice of many delegates to the 1860 Republican convention in Chicago. Radical antislavery delegates thought the lawyer from Illinois was too moderate; moderate Republicans worried that Lincoln, who had failed in an 1858 Senate bid, would be unelectable. Lincoln captured the nomination as the compromise candidate, the only man acceptable to all factions.

So much has been written about Lincoln—widely considered one of the greatest American presidents—that his sheer political acumen is often forgotten. Lincoln's behind-the-scenes deal making and political gamesmanship had as much to do with his success as his famously eloquent speeches. Lincoln not only won the presidency in a four-way race in 1860, he held together his fractious party during the long Civil War (1861–1865). He won the 1864 election, the first conducted in the midst of a war, despite public unease over the conflict in some parts of the country. At the time of his assassination, he was preparing for his most difficult political feat yet: finding a way to readmit the Southern states into the Union while satisfying the thirst for revenge of many of his fellow Republicans.

Lincoln's political career began in 1846, when the young Illinois lawyer served a single term in the US Congress as a Whig. His tenure was brief, largely due to his unpopular vote against the Mexican War (1846–1848). Lincoln would eventually join the Republican Party in the 1850s, following the collapse of the Whigs.

As president, Lincoln inherited a badly divided country. Many Democrats sympathized with the rebels. Even Lincoln's own generals were divided over how to attack the Confederacy, leading Lincoln to frequently change commanders until he found Ulysses S. Grant (1822–1885). Lincoln was even forced to delay the Emancipation Proclamation (1863), one of his most notable achievements, until after the morale-boosting Union victory at the Battle of Antietam (1862).

The cult of Lincoln—the tales of his hardscrabble upbringing in a log cabin, his religious zeal—did not emerge until well after his death. His success in office, amid a struggle for national survival, was often a matter of pure political brinksmanship.

ADDITIONAL FACTS

1. *The Civil War divided many American families, including Lincoln's: four of his brothers-in-law served in the Confederate army.*

2. *Lincoln's troubled widow, Mary Todd Lincoln (1818–1882), was sitting beside him at Ford's Theater when he was shot. She was declared insane in 1875, after years of erratic behavior following her husband's assassination.*

3. *Lincoln ran for the US Senate in 1858 in Illinois, losing to Democrat Stephen Douglas (1813–1861) after a series of debates that made both men nationally famous.*

★ ★ ★

Ulysses S. Grant

The most successful general of the Civil War (1861–1865), Ulysses S. Grant (1822–1885) destroyed the Confederacy by aggressively attacking the Southern army. Before Grant took command in 1864, Union strategy had been overly cautious, and, in frustration, President Abraham Lincoln (1809–1865) had fired a succession of top generals before finally putting Grant in charge.

Before the Civil War, Grant had achieved some distinction in the Mexican War (1846–1848), but he resigned from the Army afterward to pursue a string of business ventures that failed. When the war began, Grant had been reduced to working at his family's leather goods store in Illinois.

He immediately rejoined the US Army at the outbreak of war and received a prestigious leadership position in Illinois despite rumors that he was an alcoholic. Grant participated in several campaigns in Tennessee and led the successful Union siege of Vicksburg in 1863.

Impressed by his success at Vicksburg, Lincoln put Grant in charge of all Union forces in 1864. By that point, with the 1864 elections approaching, Lincoln was desperate for a general who could go on the offensive and score decisive victories over the Confederacy to reassure Union voters that the war could be won. While Grant attacked Confederate forces under General Robert E. Lee (1807–1870) in Virginia, he ordered his trusted subordinate, General William Tecumseh Sherman (1820–1891), to pursue the same aggressive strategy in Georgia.

After Lee's surrender in 1865, Grant emerged a national hero. He handily won the 1868 election running as a Republican. Grant's presidency, however, was a disaster. Marked by corruption and aimless leadership, historians consistently rank Grant's presidency as one of the worst in US history.

Near the end of his life, while dying of cancer, Grant wrote his memoirs. Published after his death, the book is considered the finest written by an American president and was a runaway bestseller in the nineteenth century. Written in concise, gripping prose, it tells the story of the Civil War from the standpoint of its greatest soldier. But the memoirs do have a considerable omission: Grant never mentions his eight years as president of the United States.

ADDITIONAL FACTS

1. *Grant's real birth name was Hiram Ulysses Grant, but the registrar at West Point listed him incorrectly as Ulysses Simpson Grant when he enrolled in 1839. Rather than correct the error, Grant decided to accept the new name.*

2. *In the preface to his war memoirs, Grant frankly admitted that he hadn't wanted to write the book but "consented for the money," which he hoped would pay off his personal debts.*

3. *The publisher of Grant's memoirs was his friend, the famous author Mark Twain (1835–1910).*

★ ★ ★

Reconstruction

The term *Reconstruction* refers to a period of twelve years between 1865 and 1877 when the federal government attempted to rebuild the Southern states that had been devastated by the Civil War. Reconstruction, however, involved much more than just physical rebuilding. Under orders from Congress, the program also sought to foster drastic social change in the South by extending new political and economic rights to ex-slaves who had been freed during the war.

In the first phase of Reconstruction, beginning in 1865, the government created an agency called the Freedman's Bureau that established schools and hospitals in the South, negotiated contracts, and mediated disputes between former slaveholders and slaves. As originally envisioned by President Andrew Johnson (1808–1875), the program was expected to be a modest, short-lived effort.

However, voters in 1866 elected a group of radical Republicans to Congress who believed Johnson's program was too weak. The Republicans wanted to use the resources of the federal government far more aggressively to help ex-slaves claim political rights. Over Johnson's opposition, they expanded Reconstruction and extended the Freedman's Bureau until 1869. The Republicans also passed the Fourteenth and Fifteenth Amendments to the Constitution, which formally granted United States citizenship and voting rights to ex-slaves.

Reconstruction was an unprecedented event in American history—a federal initiative where government authority came into direct contact with the lives of millions of ordinary Americans. Federal officials successfully registered thousands of blacks to vote, and many African-American congressmen and senators were elected from the region in the decade after the war.

Many white Southerners deeply resented Reconstruction, and federal efforts often met with violent resistance. The Ku Klux Klan, founded by ex-Confederate soldiers to oppose Reconstruction, became a powerful force across the South in the late 1860s.

Reconstruction ended abruptly in 1877, as part of the deal that resolved the contested 1876 election. With federal troops gone, white Southerners moved to undo most of Reconstruction's advances. Southern legislatures quickly imposed Jim Crow laws on blacks and erected barriers to black voting.

ADDITIONAL FACTS

1. *In addition to giving blacks the vote, the federal government barred tens of thousands of ex-Confederate officers and politicians from voting or holding office.*

2. *Despite the harsh rhetoric of Union leaders during the Civil War, most top Confederates were quietly released during Reconstruction and never tried for treason.*

3. *Whites labeled Southerners who cooperated with Reconstruction scalawags, and most of them lost their offices promptly after the withdrawal of federal troops.*

★ ★ ★

Carnegie Steel

The Carnegie Steel Company, founded by the famed industrialist Andrew Carnegie (1835–1919) in the 1870s, was the largest corporation in the United States in the late nineteenth century and a model of efficient industrial organization during the Gilded Age. After Carnegie's retirement, the company became US Steel, which was the first billion-dollar firm in the world and for decades one of the biggest companies in the nation.

Carnegie was born in Scotland and immigrated to Pennsylvania as a child. The rapidly industrializing United States of the mid-nineteenth century offered a wealth of lucrative opportunities; Carnegie dabbled in railroads, telegraphs, and oil before finally setting his sights on the steel business.

By the 1870s, Carnegie had opened the steel mills near Pittsburgh that would become the nucleus for Carnegie Steel. As a business executive, Carnegie was famous for pursuing a strategy of *vertical integration*. In addition to the mills themselves, Carnegie sought to control every step of the manufacturing process. He bought his own iron mines as well as the ships and railroads that transported his products. Carnegie was also famous for keeping wages low and suppressing union activity among his workers, most famously at the violent Homestead Strike in 1892. There, agents of the Pinkerton Detective Agency, who were hired by Carnegie's business partner Henry Clay Frick (1849–1919) to quell the protest, killed a number of workers who had gone on strike. Carnegie, who was in Scotland during the episode, stayed silently uninvolved.

Carnegie retired in 1901 and sold his business to a group of New York investors who merged it with several smaller companies to form the conglomerate US Steel. Paid an enormous fortune in gold for his stake of the business, Carnegie spent the rest of his life donating money to a variety of causes, including Carnegie libraries in thousands of towns across the United States and around the world. Although it is no longer the behemoth in the American economy that it once was, US Steel remains in business as the country's biggest steel producer.

ADDITIONAL FACTS

1. *After Carnegie's retirement, the federal government labeled US Steel a monopoly and tried unsuccessfully to break up the company under the Sherman Antitrust Act.*

2. *Pittsburgh's NFL franchise was named the Steelers in recognition of the city's long association with the steel industry.*

3. *In its beginning years of operation, US Steel accounted for 67 percent of all steel made in the United States.*

★ ★ ★

James Buchanan Eads

James Buchanan Eads (1820–1887) became the first civil engineer to bridge the Mississippi River when he completed a mile-long span between Illinois and Missouri at St. Louis in 1874. The bridge, which was the world's first made from steel and remains in use 130 years later, instantly assured St. Louis a role as a gateway of transcontinental traffic to the West. Hailed as a genius for taming the mighty Mississippi, Eads is also credited with building the Union's Mississippi River navy during the Civil War (1861–1865) and the system of jetties that made river navigation easier in the 1870s and 1880s.

Before the construction of the bridge, the Mississippi presented a formidable obstacle to transcontinental commerce. The lack of a bridge was particularly worrisome in Eads's hometown of St. Louis, which began losing trade to its rival Chicago during the Civil War.

At the time he proposed the bridge, Eads was already a national hero for his military service during the Civil War. An ardent Union supporter and an experienced Mississippi boatman, he had built seven ironclad warships at his own expense that had helped the Union keep control of the crucial waterway.

However, he had no experience building bridges. The majestic span at St. Louis would be his first, and he faced significant opposition from more-experienced engineers who insisted his plan was impossible. Further complicating the project, anxious riverboat companies insisted that Eads not block the river during the bridge's construction.

As the bridge in St. Louis neared completion, Eads began work on the other project for which he is best known, his system of jetties on the Mississippi near New Orleans. At the mouth of the river, the pace of the Mississippi slowed considerably. Eads proposed building jetties to narrow the river, which would speed the flow. Again in the face of significant nay-saying, the "tamer of the Mississippi" began construction in 1875. The project resulted in an enormous increase in river traffic. His next big project was to have been a canal across Panama, but he died before he could begin work on it.

ADDITIONAL FACTS

1. *His cousin and namesake was James Buchanan (1791–1868), the fifteenth US president.*

2. *The last freight train crossed the bridge in 1974, a century after its opening; the span is now used for a mass transit line.*

3. *During the construction of the support piers for the Eads Bridge, twelve workers died, at least three from the bends, a condition triggered by resurfacing to quickly from underwater.*

★ ★ ★

Eugene O'Neill

Generally regarded as the nation's greatest playwright, Eugene O'Neill (1888–1953) was the first American dramatist of international repute and was the recipient of the Nobel Prize for Literature in 1936 for his dark, brooding tragedies about small-time hustlers, failed marriages, drug addicts, insanity, and a gloomy range of human woes.

O'Neill was born in a hotel in New York City to James O'Neill, a successful but frugal stage actor, and Ella O'Neill, who became addicted to morphine as a result of complications during the baby's birth. Rage he felt toward his miserly father and drug-addicted mother was an emotion that would recur in many of O'Neill's plays, especially the autobiographical *Long Day's Journey into Night*, which was published only after the writer's death.

An alcoholic from an early age, O'Neill had a personal life as turbulent and tragic as his plays. He was expelled from Princeton in 1907 for poor grades and drinking, went to sea, and attempted suicide at least once before settling into a job as a newspaper reporter in New London, Connecticut. He married three times and had two sons, both of whom committed suicide later in their lives, and one daughter, Oona (1926–1991), whom O'Neill disowned after she married the actor Charlie Chaplin (1889–1977). His career eventually took off in the 1920s, but in a cruel twist of fate, he developed a debilitating tremor in his hand that prevented him from writing for the last decade of his life. O'Neill died in a hotel room in Boston; his last words, reportedly, were "Born in a goddamn hotel room and dying in a hotel room!"

O'Neill left thirty of the most original, moving plays in American history as a legacy. *The Iceman Cometh*, a play about a despondent group of barflies, published in 1939, is cited by some critics as his greatest masterpiece. In addition to his Nobel Prize, O'Neill won four Pulitzers, the most awarded to any playwright.

ADDITIONAL FACTS

1. *One of O'Neill plays,* Mourning Becomes Electra *(1931), was a reworking of the classic Greek drama* Oresteia *(458 BC) by Aeschylus (525–426 BC), which O'Neill updated and set during the American Civil War (1861–1865).*

2. *As of 2007, O'Neill remained the only American playwright to have won the Nobel Prize for Literature.*

3. *O'Neill did not want the autobiographical* Long Day's Journey into Night *published until twenty-five years after his death, but his widow, the actress Carlotta Monterey, defied his wishes and had it published in 1956, three years later.*

★ ★ ★

The Jazz Singer

Released in 1927 and starring the popular singer Al Jolson (1886–1950), *The Jazz Singer* was the first "talkie" in the history of Hollywood. The film employed a new technology that quickly revolutionized the motion picture industry. The movie, which tells the story of an aspiring jazz musician played by Jolson, was an immediate hit. Within four years, the era of silent movies was effectively over as nearly all studios rushed to embrace the talkie.

In the film, Jolson plays an Orthodox Jew who runs away from home after his conservative father disapproves of his musical career. Most of the movie is silent. But the Warner Brothers studio paid extra to record Jolson's songs in the movie, making *The Jazz Singer* the first major feature film with synchronized sound. None of the actual dialogue was recorded, except for a single prescient line spoken by Jolson: "You ain't heard nothin' yet!"

The movie's runaway success owed much to the electrifying performance of Jolson, one of the era's most well-known and versatile entertainers. Born in Lithuania, Jolson had emigrated as a child and quickly found success as a vaudeville entertainer. *The Jazz Singer* is controversial, however, because Jolson, who was white, performed in blackface, a common practice at the time that is now considered offensive.

Still, the success of *The Jazz Singer* sounded the death knell for the age of silent film. One by one, the major Hollywood studios switched from silent films to talkies, despite the huge costs then associated with the new technology. By the early 1930s, the transition was complete. Jolson remained a musical star until his death in 1950, although in films he never again matched the success of *The Jazz Singer*.

ADDITIONAL FACTS

1. The Jazz Singer *was nominated for an Oscar at the first-ever Academy Awards ceremony in 1929.*

2. *Jolson was born Asa Yoelson but anglicized his name after leaving Lithuania.*

3. *Although extremely controversial, blackface minstrel shows are still performed occasionally by Jolson impersonators, according to the* New York Times.

★ ★ ★

Confederate States of America

The government of the Confederate States of America, created by the Southern states in 1861 at the beginning of the Civil War and headquartered in Richmond, Virginia, functioned for four years as a through-the-looking-glass version of the United States. It preserved many elements of the American Constitution but explicitly protected the institution of slavery.

In early 1861, delegates from the seceding states gathered in Montgomery, Alabama, to write the Confederate constitution. Eventually, the Confederacy would include South Carolina, Mississippi, Florida, Alabama, Georgia, Louisiana, Texas, Virginia, Arkansas, Tennessee, and North Carolina. Although the Confederacy was vast in size—about a third of the US landmass—it was more sparsely populated and had far less industry than the North.

Confederate leaders based their constitution on the 1787 US Constitution and borrowed some passages verbatim, but with several major differences. In the Confederate system, the president was limited to a single six-year term. Jefferson Davis (1808–1889), a Mississippi politician, was elected the first and only Confederate president in 1861.

Leaders of the Confederacy, including Davis, believed that the South's best bet for success was winning foreign recognition, which might in turn force the North to accept a negotiated settlement recognizing Southern independence. The South was a major source of the world's cotton, and Confederate leaders hoped that the European powers would recognize the Confederacy rather than lose access to the crucial commodity. However, despite the best efforts of Confederate diplomats, no foreign countries would recognize the Confederacy.

The Confederate government, increasingly at the mercy of uncooperative state governors, proved incapable of organizing a major effort against its foe. When the Union army captured the Confederate capital of Richmond, Virginia, in April 1865, the Confederate government fled to Danville, Virginia, and had ceased to exist by the end of the month.

ADDITIONAL FACTS

1. *The Confederate government planned to mint its own coins but was so cash-strapped that it was able to produce only 504 silver half-dollars, most of which were Union coins with one side smoothed off and replaced with a Confederate logo.*

2. *The Confederate House of Representatives included a former US president, John Tyler (1790–1862), who represented Virginia.*

3. *On March 13, 1865, with the war almost lost, the desperate Confederate Congress authorized the enlistment of blacks in the Confederate army, an offer that many blacks unsurprisingly spurned.*

★ ★ ★

William Tecumseh Sherman

"War . . . is all hell."
—William Tecumseh Sherman

A deeply controversial figure, William Tecumseh Sherman (1820–1891) was one of the most successful Union generals of the Civil War (1861–1865), but he was reviled in the South for his scorched-earth tactics. Sherman's 1864 "march to the sea" destroyed much of the heartland of the Confederacy, hastening the end of the war but leaving much of Georgia in ruins.

Born in Ohio, Sherman graduated from West Point in 1840 and fought in several wars against Native American tribes early in his career. After leaving the military, he moved to Louisiana, where he took command of a small military academy and developed a personal appreciation for the South.

At the beginning of the Civil War, Confederate officials in Louisiana offered Sherman a commission in the rebel force. He refused, returning north instead to rejoin the Union army. Sherman fought bravely at the Battle of Bull Run in 1861, was promoted to general, and was eventually assigned to the staff of the Union army commander Ulysses S. Grant (1822–1885).

In Grant, Sherman found a superior who was able to make good use of his meticulous attention to detail. As Grant's star rose in the Union army, so did Sherman's. Eventually, in 1864, Grant gave Sherman overall command of Union forces in the West, with orders to break the back of Confederate military power.

After fierce fighting, Sherman's troops took Atlanta on September 1, 1864, and then began their infamous "march to the sea." The army made its way from Atlanta to Savannah, about 250 miles, sabotaging railroads and factories and pillaging the countryside. Sherman's goal was to destroy the South's ability to make war, but many Southerners saw his campaign as nothing short of barbarity.

Sherman himself saw the march as a necessary evil to force an end to the war, and he took little pleasure in the brutality of combat. A national hero after the war, Sherman declined an invitation to run for president in 1884 and died of pneumonia at age seventy-one.

ADDITIONAL FACTS

1. *The Sherman tank, the main tank used by the US Army during World War II (1939–1945), was named in honor of Sherman.*

2. *Sherman's younger brother, John, was elected to the US Senate from Ohio and authored the landmark Sherman Antitrust Act of 1890.*

3. *During their march across the South, Sherman's troops wrecked miles of railroad tracks to prevent the South from using them, bending the rails into twisted heaps nicknamed "Sherman's hairpins."*

★ ★ ★

Thirteenth, Fourteenth, and Fifteenth Amendments

In the wake of the Civil War (1861–1865), the United States Congress approved three amendments to the US Constitution—the Thirteenth, Fourteenth, and Fifteenth Amendments—that extended basic civil rights to African-Americans for the first time.

The Thirteenth Amendment, ratified in 1865, permanently abolished slavery. The amendment liberated slaves in the border states, who had not been covered by Abraham Lincoln's Emancipation Proclamation in 1863.

The Fourteenth Amendment, ratified in 1868, officially defined American citizenship for the first time and in so doing granted freed slaves citizen status. The amendment also established that all people in the United States are entitled to "due process of law."

The Fifteenth Amendment, ratified in 1870, established that the right of US citizens to vote shall not be denied "on account of race, color, or previous condition of servitude."

Northern states approved the three amendments quickly. In the South, however, opposition was strong, spearheaded by the Ku Klux Klan. In order to attain the three-quarters threshold of state ratifications required for an amendment's inclusion in the Constitution, Congress forced the states of the former Confederacy to ratify the amendments as a condition for readmission to the Union.

Of the three amendments, the Fourteenth has emerged as the most far-reaching and influential. The "due process" clause in this amendment empowered federal courts to intervene whenever judges believed civil rights were being violated by state governments. Many of the key US Supreme Court decisions expanding individual freedoms—including the decisions relating to contraception, abortion, and sodomy, among many other rights—have cited the protections contained in the Fourteenth Amendment.

ADDITIONAL FACTS

1. *Mississippi did not ratify the Thirteenth Amendment until 1995, when the state legislature symbolically approved it.*

2. *The Fourteenth Amendment also proclaimed that the United States would not pay any of the Confederacy's massive war debts, resulting in big losses for lenders in Europe who had financed the rebellion.*

3. *None of these amendments prohibited the restriction of voting rights based on sex. Women of all races had to wait until the Nineteenth Amendment was ratified in 1920 to secure their constitutional right to vote.*

★ ★ ★

J. P. Morgan

J. P. Morgan (1837–1913)—Pierpont to his friends, but Mr. Morgan to you—was the leading banker of the late nineteenth and early twentieth centuries, a titan of Wall Street who helped bankroll the massive economic growth of the Gilded Age in the late 1800s. In multimillion-dollar boardroom deals, Morgan created several of the most successful companies in American history, including General Electric and US Steel.

John Pierpont Morgan was born in Hartford, Connecticut, and began working at his father's bank after studying languages in Europe. He moved to New York and eventually founded his own bank, J. P. Morgan & Company, in 1861.

The House of Morgan, as his bank was often informally called, specialized in merging struggling or inefficient businesses to increase profits. Morgan's most famous deal was probably the creation of US Steel in 1901, which involved the merger of the Carnegie Steel Company with several other firms. The banker also funded the construction and mergers of railroads and was even called on to bail out the United States government during a gold shortage.

Due to his enormous wealth and ubiquity on Wall Street, Morgan acquired a somewhat sinister reputation. In the 1880s and 1890s, populist writers and politicians portrayed Morgan as a shady character—a dark capitalist force who controlled the government behind the scenes. After his death, control of the bank passed to his son, John Pierpont Morgan Jr. (1867–1943). J. P. Morgan & Company eventually went public and remains a major force on Wall Street.

ADDITIONAL FACTS

1. *Morgan's uncle, James Pierpont Morgan, wrote the Christmas carol "Jingle Bells."*

2. *Morgan amassed a huge art collection—including 600 medieval manuscripts—that he left in his will to the Metropolitan Museum of Art in New York.*

3. *One of the first Americans to have lightbulbs installed in his house, Morgan was fascinated by the possibilities of electricity and funded many scientific experiments.*

★ ★ ★

Los Angeles

At the encouragement of the Spanish governor of California, Los Angeles was founded in 1781 by a government-subsidized group of several dozen Spanish, Indian, black, and mixed-race settlers who trekked to the preselected site from northern Mexico. Incorporated as a US city in 1850, after Spain's loss of California to the United States in the Mexican War (1846–1848), Los Angeles remained relatively small until the late nineteenth century. The city then underwent explosive growth thanks to the arrival of the railroad, motion picture, and defense industries and the discovery of oil in the region. Today, the city nicknamed by its initials, *LA,* is second only to New York in population among American cities, with about 13 million residents living in its sprawling metropolitan region.

In the early years of its history, Los Angeles was known mostly by its reputation for violence. According to legend, "a murder a day" occurred in the city in the chaotic years after the California Gold Rush of 1848. From its founding, the multiethnic nature of the city has been a source of tension. In one of the most notorious incidents in the city's history, a rampaging white mob ran amuck in the city's Chinatown, killing nineteen Chinese residents in retaliation for the accidental death of a white person in 1871.

With the arrival of the railroad linking the city to San Francisco in 1876, new immigrants poured into Los Angeles and the city's Wild West atmosphere began to abate. The discovery of oil in 1892 brought an additional level of prosperity and thousands of new inhabitants to the city. By 1900, the population was more than 100,000. The film industry, attracted to the area's scenery and perfect weather, began migrating to LA in the 1910s. Thousands of tourists followed, many of whom decided to stay permanently.

World War II (1939–1945) created another growth boom for Los Angeles, when many aerospace firms built their factories in Southern California. Los Angeles also became one of the nation's most racially mixed cities, with large black, Asian, and Latino populations. Ethnic tension erupted into deadly riots in 1965 and again in 1992 following the acquittal of white police officers who had been videotaped beating a black man. Los Angeles surpassed Chicago as the nation's second-most-populous city between the 1980 and 1990 censuses, a position it maintains today.

ADDITIONAL FACTS

1. *In the middle of what used to be cattle country, Los Angeles was once nicknamed "Queen of the Cow Counties."*

2. *The city's original full name was* El Pueblo de Nuestra Señora la Reina de los Ángeles, *meaning* the city of our lady the queen of the angels.

3. *Although oil is no longer a major part of the Los Angeles economy, some of the original wildcat wells are still in operation, surrounded on all sides by residential neighborhoods.*

★ ★ ★

William Carlos Williams

William Carlos Williams (1883–1963), one of the leading American poets of the twentieth century, was known for his spare, detailed poems about everyday objects and events. Williams's style—direct, uninhibited, and worldly—was a major influence on Allen Ginsberg (1926–1997) and successive generations of poets. Like his contemporary Wallace Stevens (1879–1955), Williams was not able to support himself solely as a poet. To make ends meet, Williams also worked for nearly fifty years as a family physician in Rutherford, New Jersey.

Williams first began writing poetry while a student at the University of Pennsylvania medical school between 1902 and 1906. He received his MD degree in 1906 and then opened a private medical practice in New Jersey in 1910. According to the *New York Times*, few of Williams's patients were aware that their doctor was also one of the nation's leading modernist poets.

In style, Williams rejected the know-it-all complexity of contemporaries like T. S. Eliot (1888–1965) and Ezra Pound (1885–1972). The subjects of his poems were wheelbarrows, fire trucks, poor women on park benches, and the history of his home state of New Jersey. Especially in comparison to other writers of his era, Williams wrote poems that were surprisingly accessible. Unlike Eliot, for instance, whom Williams disdained, the doctor managed to complete his entire oeuvre without recourse to Sanskrit.

Williams intended his poems to leave a strong, simple image in the reader's mind. For instance, in one of his most famous poems, "This Is Just to Say," Williams apologizes for eating plums out of the refrigerator using the clipped, minimal style for which he was known:

> *Forgive me*
> *they were delicious*
> *so sweet*
> *and so cold.*

Williams regarded his medical practice as inseparable from his poetry. "One feeds the other in a manner of speaking; both seem necessary to me," he reportedly said. He retired from private practice in 1952 and lived long enough to see a new generation of poets, the Beats, claim him as a major inspiration and influence.

ADDITIONAL FACTS

1. *During his lifetime, Williams delivered more than 2,000 babies.*

2. *Although the two parted over literary issues, Williams was a friend of Pound while both were students at the University of Pennsylvania.*

3. *Williams received the National Book Award for poetry in 1950.*

★ ★ ★

Walt Disney

Walt Disney (1901–1966), one of the twentieth century's most successful entertainers and entrepreneurs, released his first animated cartoon, *Steamboat Willie*, in 1928. The eight-minute, black-and-white short, featuring an effeminate mouse named Mickey, was an instant success in the nation's theaters, in part thanks to one revolutionary feature: Unlike other cartoons in the 1920s, *Steamboat Willie* had a sound track.

Disney and Mickey's cocreator, Ub Iwerks (1901–1971), quickly produced more cartoons to fill the sudden national demand for Mickey's antics. Originally, Mickey was a somewhat mischievous character, a sort of animated Charlie Chaplin who was always getting himself into trouble. Capitalizing on the mouse's great popularity, Disney also created a comic strip version of Mickey in 1930.

Over the next decade, Disney created several other iconic cartoon characters, including Donald Duck, a cranky waterfowl, and Goofy, a talking dog. Disney's main rival, Warner Brothers studios, unveiled Looney Tunes with Porky Pig, Daffy Duck, and Bugs Bunny in the 1930s and 1940s, a period now regarded as the golden age of animation.

With the release of *Snow White and the Seven Dwarfs* in 1937, Disney moved into full-length feature films, overcoming the skepticism of many Hollywood moguls who doubted audiences would pay to see a ninety-minute cartoon. *Snow White* was an unimaginable success and remains one of the highest-grossing movies of all time. Disney went on to make a string of classic hit features, including *Dumbo* (1941), *Bambi* (1942), and *Lady and the Tramp* (1955).

After World War II (1939–1945), Disney expanded into live-action films and built his famous California theme park, Disneyland, which opened in 1955. His company, now a global media giant, continued his legacy of whimsical family entertainment after the founder's death in 1966.

ADDITIONAL FACTS

1. *Walt Disney World, the Florida theme park planned by Disney, was opened five years after Walt's death by his brother, Roy Disney.*

2. *Walt Disney was awarded the presidential Medal of Freedom in a White House ceremony in 1964.*

3. *Donald Duck appears as the school mascot of the University of Oregon in Eugene.*

★ ★ ★

Jefferson Davis

Jefferson Davis (1808–1889) was the first and only president of the Confederate States of America, the short-lived nation created by the Southern states that seceded from the United States at the beginning of the Civil War (1861–1865). As head of the Confederacy, Davis led the doomed effort to provide enough resources to his generals for a war against the more numerous and better-armed Union forces.

Davis fought in the Mexican War (1846–1848) for the United States and soon after won election as a US senator from his home state of Mississippi. When Mississippi voted to leave the Union, Davis resigned from the Senate and pledged his support for secession.

Delegates from the Southern states met in Montgomery, Alabama, in early 1861 to draft a constitution. Davis was elected to lead the new nation for a six-year term in 1861. Shortly after, the Confederate capital moved to Richmond, where it remained until the closing days of the war.

While in office, Davis tried unsuccessfully to win European recognition for the Confederacy and struggled to raise funds for the army. As the Southern war effort faltered, Davis desperately lobbied the Confederate Congress to allow blacks to enlist in the army, pleas that were ignored until it was far too late to make a difference.

After the war, Davis was arrested, indicted for treason, and held in prison for two years. Many vengeful Northerners considered Davis the personification of the rebel cause and hoped for his execution. However, he was never brought to trial, and he returned to Mississippi unrepentant for his wartime activities. To his death, Davis refused to take the oath of allegiance to the United States, an action for which he has been hailed a hero by atavistic Southerners ever since.

ADDITIONAL FACTS

1. *Davis was born in a log cabin in Kentucky only a few months before his nemesis, Abraham Lincoln (1809–1865), was born to similar circumstances.*

2. *As secretary of war under President Franklin Pierce (1804–1869) in 1854, Davis accepted the resignation of a US army captain from Ohio—Ulysses S. Grant (1822–1885).*

3. *Davis's vice president was Alexander Stephens (1812–1883), a former representative to the US House from Georgia.*

★ ★ ★

Indian Wars

In the twenty years after the Civil War (1861–1865), American settlers moved west in great numbers, seeking farmland and economic opportunity. This huge migration, facilitated by the construction of transcontinental railroads, set up an inevitable clash with the Native American tribes in the Great Plains and Southwest. Between approximately 1865 and 1890, the last pockets of armed resistance were defeated by the US Army in a series of short, bloody wars. In late 1890, the last battle between US troops and Native Americans took place in South Dakota in the Sioux village of Wounded Knee, bringing the military phase of the encounter between whites and Native Americans to a tragic close.

For decades after the Louisiana Purchase in 1803, relatively few Americans ventured into the vast new territory west of the Mississippi River. Starting in the 1860s, however, the government began offering settlers free land in the West under the Homestead Act of 1862 and encouraging railroad construction across the daunting terrain of the Rocky Mountains.

These developments posed an existential threat to the western tribes. Increasingly, railroads, telegraph lines, and barbed wire fences hemmed in the open prairie. White hunters virtually exterminated the bison, which had been a staple source of food for thousands of years. Treaties protecting tribal territory from encroachment by land-hungry white settlers were often simply ignored. Instead, Native Americans were systematically confined to reservations across the West.

Several tribes fought to prevent the seizure of their lands. In one of the most famous battles of the period, the Lakota chief Crazy Horse (c. 1844–1877) defeated General George Custer (1839–1876) at the Battle of Little Bighorn in 1876, wiping out the entire American force. In the Southwest, the Apache chief Geronimo (1829–1909) led a long fight against the US Army before surrendering in 1886.

In the end, however, the American firepower was simply too great for the tribes to overcome. The rout of Sioux warriors at Wounded Knee—some contemporaries called it a massacre rather than a battle—ended the native resistance to American expansion in the West.

ADDITIONAL FACTS

1. *Custer was a descendant of a Hessian mercenary; Hessians were the German troops sent by King George III (1738–1820) to fight against American colonists.*

2. *Custer graduated last in his class at West Point in 1861, but the army was so desperate for officers that he was given a plum job as an aide to General George McClellan (1826–1885).*

3. *After his surrender, Geronimo died in captivity at Fort Sill, Oklahoma.*

★ ★ ★

Ku Klux Klan

The Ku Klux Klan, one of the most notorious hate groups in American history, was founded in Tennessee in 1865 by veterans of the Confederate army. Over the next century, the Klan carried out thousands of attacks against blacks, immigrants, and Jews. In decline since the 1960s, the Klan still exists today as a fringe extremist group, according to the Anti-Defamation League (ADL).

Immediately after the Civil War (1861–1865), the Klan's main goal was to intimidate blacks who sought to assert their civil rights. The Klan also harassed whites who cooperated with Reconstruction. Some of the Klan's earliest killings targeted white politicians, known as *scalawags,* who collaborated with the Northern authorities

Violence aimed at blacks, however, was far more common. Specifically, the Klan used intimidation to prevent ex-slaves from voting and exercising their political rights. Wearing white hoods, Klan "night riders" terrorized blacks with random killings and whippings meant to keep African-Americans "in their place."

Klan violence grew so pervasive that President Ulysses S. Grant (1822–1885) signed emergency legislation known as the Ku Klux Klan Act in 1871 that empowered the army to pursue Klansmen and bring them to trial in federal courts. The act was successful, and Klan activity fell sharply in the 1870s.

However, the organization never completely disappeared and has experienced several revivals since Reconstruction. The largest revival came after the 1915 release of *The Birth of a Nation,* a silent movie directed by D. W. Griffith that portrayed Klansmen as heroes for resisting Reconstruction. The movie served as a potent recruiting tool for the reinvigorated Klan. In the 1910s and 1920s, the group organized and carried out hundreds of lynchings.

The Klan reappeared during the civil rights movement that began in the 1950s, and its members were implicated in some of the era's worst atrocities, including the brutal murder of black teenager Emmett Till (1941–1955) and the 1963 bombing of the Sixteenth Street Baptist Church in Birmingham, where four black girls were killed. Most recently, according to the ADL, the Klan has reemerged as an anti-immigrant and antigay organization in both the north and south.

ADDITIONAL FACTS

1. *The Klan was so strong in parts of rural South Carolina that Grant declared martial law in nine counties and declared members of the group to be "insurgents . . . in rebellion against the authority of the United States."*

2. *Future president Harry Truman (1884–1972) once applied for Klan membership but withdrew his application after the group asked him to fire his Catholic employees.*

3. *In 1991, Klan leader David Duke finished second in the Louisiana governor's race.*

★ ★ ★

John D. Rockefeller

Industrialist and robber baron John D. Rockefeller (1839–1937) founded Standard Oil, one of the greatest business juggernauts of the late nineteenth century, and became the world's first billionaire thanks to the growing demand for oil and gasoline in the early twentieth century. After his retirement, Rockefeller transferred his energies to philanthropy and became famous for giving away his fortune one dime at a time to passersby on the street.

Rockefeller was born in New York and moved to Cleveland after the discovery of oil in the region. He formed Standard Oil with several partners in 1870. In the era before the automobile created a demand for gasoline, kerosene was the company's biggest product. Thanks to Rockefeller's bare-knuckle business practices—exploiting every available legal loophole to put competitors out of business—the company became the dominant force in the oil industry by the mid-1880s. The growing power of Standard Oil was a key factor leading to the passage of the Sherman Antitrust Act in 1890.

Still, it would take another two decades for the law to catch up with Standard Oil. Thanks in part to the muckraking journalism of Ida Tarbell (1857–1944), who exposed the company's shady business practices in her 1904 book *The History of the Standard Oil Company*, public hostility to the company mounted in the early twentieth century, and the government successfully broke up the company in 1911. Several major American oil companies—including ExxonMobil, Chevron, and ConocoPhillips—were created by the breakup. Indeed, as of 2007, three of the top five corporations in the United States are descendents of Standard Oil.

By the time of the breakup, Rockefeller had retired and devoted himself to philanthropy. In addition to his infamous dimes, Rockefeller endowed numerous foundations and universities, including the Rockefeller Foundation. His descendents form one of the richest and most powerful families in the nation; Rockefellers have served as governors, as senators, and briefly, in the case of Nelson Rockefeller (1908–1979), as vice president of the United States.

ADDITIONAL FACTS

1. *One of the first casualties after the discovery of oil in Pennsylvania and the Midwest was the New England whaling industry, which quickly collapsed when kerosene replaced whale oil as a source of fuel for lamps.*

2. *The dish Oysters Rockefeller is named after the tycoon.*

3. *One of Rockefeller's philanthropic causes was the Rockefeller Institute in New York City, which later changed its name to Rockefeller University.*

★ ★ ★

Barbed Wire

The invention and mass production of barbed wire fencing beginning in 1873 changed the landscape of the American West, hastening the demise of the open range. Within several decades of its introduction, farmers had strung thousands of miles of the painful metal fencing around their homesteads, and the old cattle drives across the open prairies of the West vanished into history.

Primitive varieties of barbed wire fencing had existed since the Roman Empire but were ineffective and difficult to produce. Instead, cattlemen in the American West had to drive their herds for hundreds of miles across the prairie to prevent them from grazing crops during the planting season, an arduous trek managed by cowboys. Cowboys were also responsible for the great cattle drives of thousands of animals to depots in Kansas, where the herd would be transported by rail to slaughterhouses in distant Chicago.

Effective fencing made it possible for farmers to keep their livestock in the same location year-round, rendering cowboys obsolete. Although barbed wire was opposed by some because of the harm it caused animals—it was nicknamed "the devil's rope" by the 1890s the West was increasingly fenced in. Barbed wire also dealt a crippling blow to the Native Americans of the Great Plains by restricting the movements of the wild bison herds, which many tribes depended on for food.

In part thanks to the invention and widespread use of barbed wire to enclose the plains, the Wild West era gradually came to an end. Years later, the cowboy would be romanticized by Hollywood as a symbol of rugged American manhood overcome by the advances of modern technology.

ADDITIONAL FACTS

1. *Barbed wire was used by the military in World War I (1914–1918), adding to the misery of soldiers in the trenches.*

2. *A 700-pound monument to barbed wire in McLean, Texas, is composed of two balls of barbed wire.*

3. *Disputes over fencing occasionally led to violence, most famously in the "Johnson County war," which erupted in Wyoming in 1892 between small ranchers and big cattle companies and led to the deaths of several of the ranchers.*

★ ★ ★

The Great Gatsby

Originally published in 1925, *The Great Gatsby* is widely considered one of the greatest American novels of the twentieth century. Written by F. Scott Fitzgerald (1896–1940), the book is set in a wealthy area of Long Island, New York, and centers around a mysterious millionaire named Jay Gatsby who throws wild, lavish parties at his seaside mansion during Prohibition.

Fitzgerald had published two other novels, *This Side of Paradise* (1920), and *The Beautiful and Damned* (1922), prior to completing *Gatsby*. A product of exclusive prep schools and Princeton University, Fitzgerald frequently used the theme of money and its place in American society in his novels and short stories.

The narrator of *The Great Gatsby* is Nick Carraway, an Ivy League–educated bond dealer originally from the Midwest who moves into a house near Gatsby and befriends his mysterious neighbor. Nick attends several of Gatsby's raucous parties, where New York's young elites come to enjoy the host's seemingly inexhaustible supply of illegal liquor.

As the novel unfolds, questions grow about the source of Gatsby's great wealth, and Fitzgerald drops hints that Gatsby made his fortune in bootlegging. Nick begins to like Gatsby but realizes that his friend will never win the true acceptance by the wealthy American elite that he so desperately craves. Gatsby's failed quest for social acceptance is reflected in his doomed pursuit of Daisy Buchanan, the beautiful wife of one of Nick's rich friends from Yale.

Fitzgerald's writing style is direct and fluid, punctuated with dry wit and poignant observations. Although not an instant hit when it was published, *The Great Gatsby* was reprinted after the author's death and is now considered a classic of American literature.

ADDITIONAL FACTS

1. *The seaside mansion on Long Island believed to have been Fitzgerald's model for Gatsby's house went on sale for $28 million in 2005, according to* Forbes *magazine.*

2. *Fitzgerald spent time in France with Ernest Hemingway (1899–1961) during the 1920s; a memorable encounter between the two in a men's room is described in Hemingway's memoir,* A Moveable Feast *(1964).*

3. *Although his fiction was admired by critics, Fitzgerald was unable to support himself with his novels and moved to Hollywood in the 1930s to work on movie scripts.*

★ ★ ★

Edward Hopper

Edward Hopper (1882–1967) painted one of the most famous works of art in American history, the gloomy 1942 canvas *Night Hawks*. The painting, which shows three men and a woman at an all-night diner in an unidentified city, was the most successful work of Hopper's long and distinguished career.

Born in New York, Hopper enrolled in art school at age eighteen. His style, influenced by the Ashcan school, emphasized plain, realistic portraits of scenes from everyday life. Hopper's prosaic subjects included fire hydrants, bridges, gas stations, and people reading newspapers.

In the early twentieth century, however, Hopper's stark realist paintings were unfashionable on the art scene, and he spent the first twenty years of his career toiling in relative obscurity. To make ends meet, he painted propaganda posters during World War I (1914–1918) and even won a $300 prize for his 1918 poster *Smash the Hun*. By 1931, at age forty-nine, Hopper had sold only two of his paintings.

The Great Depression, however, caused a seismic shift in the art world and a major reappraisal of Hopper's work. Suddenly, interest among art connoisseurs in European modernism waned, while paintings that addressed the country's social problems became popular.

Night Hawks perfectly illustrates the sense of urban despair and loneliness that recurs throughout Hopper's work. The four figures in the painting each appear lost in their own thoughts and are not looking at one another. The diner is brightly lit, but the light seems harsh and artificial, in implicit contrast to the cozy glow of a fireplace.

Hopper's paintings of forlorn cityscapes have held an enduring appeal. In recognition of his lifetime achievement, shortly before his death, Hopper was one of eleven artists whose work was selected for display at the White House by First Lady Jacqueline Kennedy (1929–1994).

ADDITIONAL FACTS

1. Night Hawks *has been imitated and parodied countless times, including in the 1981 Steven Martin film* Pennies from Heaven.

2. *The painting is now on permanent display at the Art Institute of Chicago.*

3. *Following the path of most other American artists, Hopper spent four years studying in Paris and Spain in the early 1900s, but he mostly rejected European styles in his own art.*

★ ★ ★

William Seward

William Seward (1801–1872) served as secretary of state during and after the Civil War (1861–1865), becoming one of the most successful diplomats in American history by preventing foreign interference in the war and later negotiating the purchase of Alaska from Russia in 1867.

A native of New York, Seward was elected to the United States Senate in 1848 as a Whig. A leading Senate opponent of slavery, he voted against the Fugitive Slave Act and the Compromise of 1850. After the disintegration of the Whig Party in the 1850s, he joined the fledgling Republican Party, which was formed from the wreckage of the Whigs to oppose the extension of slavery.

Seward ran for president in 1856 but lost the Republican nomination to John Fremont (1813–1890). He tried again in 1860, running against a field of Republicans that included Abraham Lincoln (1809–1865). In the 1860, campaign, Seward was perceived as the more radical antislavery candidate, compared to the more moderate Lincoln. After Lincoln's victory, Seward received his cabinet post as a consolation prize.

As secretary of state, Seward had the difficult task of convincing foreign powers, especially Great Britain, then the greatest power in the world, to stay out of the Civil War. Several leading British politicians, including the prime minister, Lord Palmerston (1784–1865), initially sympathized with the Confederacy. Seward and the American ambassador in London, Charles Francis Adams (1807–1886), the son of John Quincy Adams (1767–1848), successfully lobbied the British government to remain neutral.

At the end of the war, the gang of assassins that murdered President Lincoln also intended to kill Seward. On the night of Lincoln's assassination, Seward was stabbed in his bed, but he survived. He remained secretary of state under President Andrew Johnson (1808–1875) and negotiated the purchase of Alaska from Russia for $7.2 million. Mocked as "Seward's folly" at the time, Alaska became the forty-ninth US state in 1959.

ADDITIONAL FACTS

1. *As governor of New York between 1839 and 1842, Seward took an early stand against slavery by refusing to extradite three men to Virginia, where they faced charges of helping slaves escape.*

2. *Seward's first instincts were not always very wise. In 1861, he advised Lincoln to start a war with European countries in order to promote American unity and dampen the Southern drive for secession.*

3. *At the time of the attempt on his life, Seward was wearing a neck brace from a previous injury, which may have saved his life by shielding him from the assassin's dagger.*

★ ★ ★

Spanish-American War

On the night of February 15, 1898, a massive explosion rocked the Spanish harbor of Havana, Cuba. Within seconds of the blast, an American battleship docked at the city, the USS *Maine,* was in flames. The mysterious explosion aboard the *Maine,* which Americans immediately blamed on the Spanish, killed 266 American sailors.

Two months later, taking "Remember the *Maine!*" as their rallying cry, the United States Congress declared war on Spain. The brief Spanish-American War, a decisive victory for the United States, resulted in the acquisition of the Philippines, Puerto Rico, and Guam from Spain. The war also permanently ended the Spanish presence in the New World 400 years after the voyages of Christopher Columbus.

The roots of the war far predated the sinking of the *Maine.* By the 1890s, the island of Cuba was one of a few remaining vestiges of Spain's once vast colonial holdings. Many Islanders were fed up with Spain's heavy-handed rule. Americans, mindful of their own revolution against the British, instinctively sympathized with the Cuban rebels, who had tried unsuccessfully to drive out the Spanish in 1895.

In the wake of the failed rebellion, the American press printed sensational horror stories about Spanish mistreatment of Cuban prisoners. The so-called yellow press portrayed the Spanish as monsters and agitated for American intervention in Cuba.

The *Maine* had been sent to Havana to keep an eye on the situation. Although the sinking was blamed on a mine planted by the Spanish, some modern naval experts believe the explosion was more likely caused by a coal fire aboard the ship.

The war with Spain, a withered remnant of its former self, was short and decisive. American forces landed in Cuba and Puerto Rico in the summer of 1898 and vanquished the Spanish defenders. In the Pacific, the US Navy defeated a Spanish fleet to seize control of Manila, the Philippine capital.

Under the terms of the peace treaty that ended the war later that year, the United States kept all the islands taken from Spain, establishing itself as a true global power at the dawn of the twentieth century.

ADDITIONAL FACTS

1. *Although short, the war was enormously expensive. Thousands of soldiers were called up, and while very few actually saw fighting, in total they collected millions of dollars in pensions for decades after.*

2. *The naval battle of Manila Bay resulted in no Americans killed, establishing American power in the Pacific at virtually no cost.*

3. *In all, the Spanish-American War claimed 345 men killed in combat—and 2,565 killed by disease.*

★ ★ ★

Chinese Exclusion Act

In 1882, Congress passed an unprecedented law called the Chinese Exclusion Act that was intended to prevent Chinese people from immigrating to the United States. The law—the first such prohibition aimed at a specific ethnic group—not only prohibited Chinese immigration, but also made it illegal for existing Chinese immigrants to become naturalized citizens.

Chinese laborers had begun coming to the West Coast in large numbers in the 1850s, prompted by unrest in China and lured by construction jobs in the United States. Construction of the first transcontinental railroad relied heavily on Chinese labor—about 1,000 immigrant workers died in avalanches and accidents during construction.

However, many Americans immediately developed an intense hatred for the new-comers. Western states enacted discriminatory statutes making it illegal for Asian immigrants to own property or open businesses. Convinced that Chinese immigrants constituted a "yellow peril," San Francisco and other California cities created segregated schools for Asian children.

Racial antagonism in the West mounted as people from Japan, the Philippines, and Korea began immigrating to the United States in the early twentieth century. The exclusion law was expanded to cover all Asians and reaffirmed by Congress in the Immigration Act of 1924.

The exclusion act had a particularly cruel impact on Asian-American families, making it very difficult for wives left in Asia to join their husbands in the United States. The initial 1882 law even stripped Chinese-American children born on American soil of their citizenship, although the US Supreme Court overturned this blatantly unconstitutional provision in 1898.

The United States did not eliminate the exclusion act until World War II (1939–1945), in deference to its wartime ally, China. Even then, however, the quota for Chinese immigrants was set extremely low. Indeed, Chinese immigration would not resume on a basis equitable with other groups until the mid-1960s.

ADDITIONAL FACTS

1. *The 1924 law also limited immigration from southern and eastern Europe—to exclude Italian and Polish Catholics, along with Jews—while encouraging immigration from Protestant northern Europe.*

2. *Laws forbidding Chinese-Americans from marrying whites in California were not repealed until 1948.*

3. *Many state governments tried to forbid the immigration of Chinese women, and the gender ratio of Chinese-born men to women in California was around ten men for every woman.*

★ ★ ★

Interstate Commerce Commission

The Interstate Commerce Commission (ICC), founded in 1887, was the first regulatory agency created by the federal government to rein in the power of private corporations in American life. Congress gave the ICC the authority to set railroad rates and ensure that shippers were treated fairly. Strongly opposed by the railroad industry, the ICC marked a significant change in the relationship between American business and government, as lawmakers began to move cautiously against corporate excess.

By the late nineteenth century, railroads handled the vast majority of freight. Especially in the West, shippers usually had few other options. Many farmers complained that private rail corporations abused this massive economic clout by charging exorbitant rates to captive shippers, and they demanded federal intervention. Regulating railroads became a key goal of the Progressive movement, which gained strength through the 1880s and 1890s.

The ICC represented the first attempt to establish limits on the power of the rail barons. Under the Interstate Commerce Act establishing the agency, railroads had to publish their rates and were not allowed to discriminate among shippers. Together with the Sherman Antitrust Act, passed three years later, the ICC reflected the growing opposition to unfettered laissez-faire economics.

The impact of the act was mixed. Although the ICC was able to tame some of the worst abuses of the rail companies, its powers were limited. Throughout the Progressive Era, politicians like William Jennings Bryan (1860–1925) would agitate for tighter railroad regulation and greater enforcement powers for the ICC.

In historical terms, however, the ICC was highly significant. The agency created the precedent for government regulation of business and served as a model for subsequent regulatory efforts. In the twentieth century, the scope of government intervention in private industry would expand dramatically. The ICC itself, ironically, was abolished in 1995 after the decline of railroads as a major economic force.

ADDITIONAL FACTS

1. The power of the railroads in the nineteenth-century United States was so great that when the industry divided the country into four time zones in 1883, the country had little choice but to adopt "railroad time," leading to the modern system of standard time zones.

2. The railroad industry was briefly nationalized during World War I (1914–1918), but returned to private ownership after the war.

3. Key backing for the ICC came from the Grange, a populist movement that started in the 1860s to protect agricultural interests. The Grange still exists and is now headquartered in Washington, DC, across the street from the White House.

★ ★ ★

John Muir

John Muir (1838–1914) was one of the founders of the modern conservation movement and led a successful campaign to preserve major tracts of California wilderness from human development. Muir's effort to establish Yosemite National Park would inspire similar campaigns elsewhere and helped convince President Theodore Roosevelt (1858–1919) to protect millions of acres of wilderness in the early twentieth century.

The first national park, Yellowstone, had been created by the United States Congress in 1872. Prevailing attitudes of the nineteenth century, however, had little interest in natural preservation, and for decades Yellowstone remained the sole federally protected area.

The Scottish-born Muir had immigrated to the United States as a child and moved to California after the Civil War (1861–1865). He was captivated by the rugged splendor of the Yosemite Valley, a wild stretch of a mountain range called the Sierra Nevada located east of San Francisco, during his first visit to the region in 1868. Muir climbed most of the peaks around Yosemite, and in 1889 he wrote the first proposal to protect the area from development and livestock grazing. Yosemite National Park was established by Congress in 1890, but it did not include Yosemite Valley.

Although stymied in his initial efforts to save Yosemite Valley, Muir found a powerful ally in Teddy Roosevelt, who became president in 1901. An avid hunter and outdoors enthusiast, Roosevelt passionately supported natural preservation and put millions of acres of federal land under protection. Yosemite Valley was added to Yosemite National Park in 1906, fulfilling Muir's longtime ambition.

As part of the campaign to create Yosemite, Muir in 1892 founded an organization, the Sierra Club, which would become a major political force in favor of natural preservation. For his role in leading the initial efforts to protect nature, Muir is often referred to as the father of the national park system.

ADDITIONAL FACTS

1. *Muir is featured on the back of the 2005 California state quarter.*

2. *Raised by strict, religious parents, Muir is said to have memorized the entire New Testament.*

3. *Muir's home in Martinez, California, is now preserved as a National Historic Site. A California Wilderness Preserve is also named in his honor.*

★ ★ ★

Ernest Hemingway

When the author Ernest Hemingway (1899–1961) committed suicide at his Idaho home in 1961, his death was mourned around the world. In Paris, every major newspaper put the news on the front page. In Spain, a bullfighter killed two bulls in honor of the late writer. In Hyannis, Massachusetts, President John F. Kennedy (1917–1963) issued a statement hailing the late author as "one of the great citizens of the world."

The international plaudits were a testament to Hemingway's enormous significance in twentieth-century Western literature. A larger-than-life figure thanks to his taste for guns, liquor, big-game hunting, and war, Hemingway was the rare novelist who was also a global celebrity.

Born in Illinois in 1899, Hemingway began his writing career when he went to work as a reporter for the *Kansas City Star* at age seventeen. He volunteered as a medic after the United States entered World War I (1914–1918) and later returned to Europe as a war correspondent in Greece.

Hemingway's years as a newspaper writer had a major impact on his famously direct writing style. As a reporter, he had been taught to "use short sentences. Use short paragraphs." Although Hemingway befriended many leading modernists—often coming to the aid of the famously wordy James Joyce (1882–1941) during bar fights in Paris during the 1920s—his style was economical, bracing, and simple.

Hemingway's macho persona—he was a homophobe and a well-known fan of bullfighting played a significant role in his fame. He returned to Europe during the Spanish civil war (1936–1939) and wrote arguably his most famous novel, *For Whom the Bell Tolls* (1940), based on his wartime experiences. He also covered World War II (1939–1945) and famously boasted of having "liberated" the Hotel Ritz bar in Paris after the defeat of the Nazis.

After the war, Hemingway spent time in Cuba, where his last significant novel, *The Old Man and the Sea* (1952), is set. The book, which won the Pulitzer Prize, restored Hemingway's literary reputation to its prewar heights. However, Hemingway's health declined in the 1950s, and he killed himself with a shotgun blast after receiving unsuccessful electroshock therapy for depression.

ADDITIONAL FACTS

1. *A bullfighting aficionado, Hemingway claimed to have seen 1,500 bulls killed in the ring.*

2. *The title of* For Whom the Bell Tolls *was taken from a poem by the seventeenth-century English poet John Donne (1572–1631).*

3. *Hemingway survived a plane crash in Uganda in 1954.*

★ ★ ★

Georgia O'Keeffe

Over a career spanning eight decades, avant-garde painter Georgia O'Keeffe (1887–1986) produced hundreds of lush, colorful paintings of shells, clouds, churches, bones, and flowers, a body of work that made her one of the foremost twentieth-century American artists and a lasting influence on a generation of abstract painters.

O'Keeffe was born in Wisconsin and lived in New York City for many years, but she is most closely associated with the American Southwest. The sun-scorched desert landscape near the ranch she bought in New Mexico provided the inspiration for much of O'Keeffe's best-loved art.

One of O'Keeffe's most famous paintings, *Black Iris III*, completed in 1926, provides a characteristic example of her groundbreaking style. To the viewer, the painting is immediately recognizable as a single purple flower. But in its details and color, the flower is hardly "realistic." In O'Keeffe's vivid rendering, the flower is full of undulating curves and rich, modulated shades of purple. The painting also contains fairly overt references to female anatomy, a recurring theme in O'Keeffe's work.

Starting in the late 1920s, O'Keeffe and her husband, the photographer Alfred Stieglitz (1864–1946), traveled often to New Mexico, where O'Keeffe settled permanently after his death. The haunting desert landscape and the region's distinctive adobe architecture figured in many of her later paintings.

In recognition of her contribution to American art, President Gerald Ford (1913–2006) awarded O'Keeffe the Presidential Medal of Freedom in 1977. Despite failing eyesight, she continued to work until age ninety-six, shortly before her death.

ADDITIONAL FACTS

1. *O'Keeffe worked briefly creating fruit advertisements for the Dole Company.*

2. *Her parents, Francis and Ida O'Keeffe, were dairy farmers in Sun Prairie, Wisconsin.*

3. *Before becoming famous, O'Keeffe briefly worked as an art teacher in the Amarillo, Texas, public school system.*

★ ★ ★

Andrew Johnson

In the wartime presidential election of 1864, President Abraham Lincoln (1809–1865), a Republican, selected Democrat Andrew Johnson (1808–1875) as his running mate. Johnson, a United States senator from Tennessee, had remained loyal to the Union even after his home state seceded, a decision that made him a hero in the North. By selecting a Southern Democrat as his running mate, Lincoln hoped to send a message of national unity in the midst of the Civil War (1861–1865). With public opinion buoyed by military victories over the Confederacy in late 1864, Lincoln and Johnson ended up winning by an overwhelming margin, reflecting the public's support for the president's war policies.

Johnson was picked as a symbol, but Lincoln's assassination on April 14, 1865, unexpectedly elevated him to the presidency. As president, Johnson initially pleased Republicans by promising harsh punishment for Confederate leaders. But major rifts soon opened between the headstrong Johnson and congressional Republicans. Johnson wanted the Southern states quickly readmitted to the Union, while the Republicans supported military occupation of the South and strong enforcement of civil rights laws to protect freed slaves.

The conflict between Johnson and the Republicans intensified when the president restored authority to some former Confederate officials. Johnson also fired a cabinet officer, Edwin Stanton (1814–1869), against the wishes of Congress. The acrimony between Johnson and the Republicans peaked in 1868, when the House of Representatives impeached him for violating the Tenure of Office Act, a law that prohibited Johnson from firing members of the cabinet without congressional authorization. The Senate, however, declined to convict Johnson, and the Tenure of Office Act itself was later declared unconstitutional.

Support for congressional Republicans mounted in the late 1860s, causing Johnson to lose the Democratic nomination for a second term. In 1869, he was replaced in the White House by Ulysses S. Grant (1822–1885), a Republican. Johnson briefly returned to the Senate, but died a few years later.

ADDITIONAL FACTS

1. *Johnson did not attend school and was illiterate until his twenties, when his wife, Eliza, taught him to read.*

2. *When Johnson was a young boy, his father, Jacob, died trying to save two of his wealthy employers from drowning.*

3. *Only one other president, Bill Clinton (1946–), has been impeached. The Senate has never "convicted" an impeached president, the final step under the Constitution before a president can be removed from office.*

★ ★ ★

American Imperialism

By the end of the nineteenth century, the United States was among the largest industriaized nations on earth. But unlike Great Britain, France, and other major European powers, it had a relatively puny military and no overseas empire.

Starting in the 1890s, with the Indian wars finished, many Americans argued that it was time for the United States to build up its military and begin playing a greater role in world affairs. After a century of isolationism, they felt the country needed to make itself an equal of the Europeans in global politics.

The annexation of Hawaii and the Spanish-American War, both in 1898, were two of the first examples of the new American imperialism. After the Spanish-American War, the United States suddenly had its empire: Puerto Rico, the Philippines, Guam, Samoa, and, briefly, Cuba.

Supporters cited national pride and a desire to "civilize" backward corners of the world as justifications for the new American imperialism. A famous and influential poem by Rudyard Kipling (1865–1936), "The White Man's Burden," published in an American magazine in 1899, portrayed imperialism as a selfless and altruistic effort to help "half devil and half child" peoples enjoy the benefits of Western civilization.

As might have been expected, the inhabitants of the new US possessions were somewhat less enthusiastic about American imperialism. In the Philippines, the Americans had to suppress an angry uprising of Philippine nationalists. In the United States, a strong anti-imperialist faction emerged in the 1900 election, led by Democratic presidential candidate William Jennings Bryan (1860–1925).

With the sobering experience of the Philippines, the passion for imperialism began to cool. The United States renounced control over Cuba a few years later and granted independence to the Philippines in 1946.

ADDITIONAL FACTS

1. *Kipling's poem—a call for the United States to join France and Britain as an imperial nation—was written for a US audience because of the American involvement in the Philippines.*

2. *The Virgin Islands were acquired by the United States from Denmark in 1917 for $25 million.*

3. *In a 1998 referendum, voters in Puerto Rico soundly rejected independence from the United States.*

★ ★ ★

Helen Hunt Jackson

Starting with the publication of *A Century of Dishonor* in 1881, Native American rights advocate Helen Hunt Jackson (1830–1885) called national attention to the mistreatment of indigenous peoples in the West. Her writing helped convince the United States Congress to pass laws in the 1880s intended to improve the miserable living conditions on Indian reservations. Unfortunately, however, most of those laws backfired, making reservation life even more difficult. Still, in her brief career, Jackson inspired a major reassessment of US policy toward Native Americans.

Born Helen Fiske in Amherst, Massachusetts, she married Edward Hunt in 1852 and then started writing poetry and essays after his 1863 death in a gunfire accident. She sometimes used the signature "H. H." on her pieces. Helen Hunt married William Jackson in 1875. She became interested in the plight of Native Americans in 1879 and started work on *A Century of Dishonor* that year.

The book, which Helen Hunt Jackson mailed to every member of Congress, radically challenged the fundamental self-image of many Americans. In the nineteen century, many whites believed that expansion into the West had benefited Native Americans by spreading civilization, Christianity, and modern technology. Jackson strenuously disagreed. White expansion into the West, she wrote, had led to death, disease, and the wholesale theft of tribal lands. Jackson then published *Ramona* (1884), a novel exploring anti-Indian discrimination, which she hoped would shock the nation's conscience the way Harriet Beecher Stowe's *Uncle Tom's Cabin* (1852) had galvanized opposition to slavery.

Although Jackson died of cancer in 1885, her work helped inspired the Dawes Severalty Act of 1887. The act was intended to remove Native Americans from reservation life, which many well-meaning reformers believed would ease their economic isolation and poverty. In practice, however, the act was a disaster, and it enabled whites to acquire millions of acres of reservation land.

ADDITIONAL FACTS

1. *Jackson was born in the same year as fellow Amherst native Emily Dickinson (1830–1886), and the two classmates remained friends into adulthood.*

2. *At the time of her death, Jackson was at work on a children's book about discrimination against Native Americans.*

3. *For publication in magazines and newspapers, Jackson often used a pseudonym, including "Rip Van Winkle," instead of her real name.*

★ ★ ★

Coca-Cola

John S. Pemberton (1831–1888), a Confederate war veteran and patent medicine impresario, invented Coca-Cola in Atlanta in 1886. Patent medicines—drinks or pills that claimed to have miraculous medicinal powers—were common in the United States before the government began regulating pharmaceuticals, and Pemberton hoped to market his fizzy new beverage as a "brain tonic and intellectual beverage."

The health benefits claimed by Pemberton were nonsense. However, customers in Atlanta loved his refreshing mixture of sugar, caffeine, and cocaine, and the drink sold well. In 1888, Pemberton sold the rights to his creation to an Atlanta pharmacist, Asa Griggs Candler (1851–1929), who quickly began marketing the beverage across the nation. By 1900, Coke was the most popular soft drink in most of the United States. Today, the Coca-Cola Company is the world's largest producer of soft drinks.

During the twentieth century, the company expanded around the globe, and Coca-Cola became the world's most widely recognized product. Coke is now sold in virtually every corner of the world, even North Korea. On much of Earth, the red and white Coca-Cola logo rivals the American flag as a symbol of the United States.

In the history of American business, the triumph of Coke was an early example of successful branding. Prior to the twentieth century, the modern idea of branded consumer items was basically nonexistent; customers asked for cigarettes and shoes rather than Marlboros and Nikes. In theory, brands help the public because a company needs to protect the value of its brand name by maintaining high quality. But, according to some critics, brands like Coke also harm consumers by forcing them to pay inflated prices to deflect the cost of the company's advertising and marketing.

Today, Coca-Cola remains the unrivalled king of brands. As of 2006, according to a survey by *BusinessWeek* magazine, Coca-Cola was the most valuable brand in the world, well ahead of number two, Microsoft.

ADDITIONAL FACTS

1. *Cocaine was eliminated from Coca-Cola in 1905, but the drink still contains extracts from coca leaves that are imported into the United States under special permission from the Drug Enforcement Administration (DEA).*

2. *Since 1935, Coca-Cola has been kosher.*

3. *"New Coke" was introduced in 1985 but was so unpopular that the company soon returned to its "classic" formula and logo.*

★ ★ ★

World's Columbian Exposition of 1893

To celebrate the 400th anniversary of Christopher Columbus's first voyage to the New World, the city of Chicago staged a massive world's fair in 1893 that was one of the most widely attended events of the nineteenth-century United States. More than 27 million people visited the 200 gaudy buildings erected at the sprawling fairgrounds south of downtown Chicago at a time when the total population of the United States was only about 63 million.

The fair's White City, an elaborate complex of Beaux Arts buildings designed by famed architects Frederick Law Olmstead (1822–1903) and Daniel Burnham (1846–1912), featured thousands of exhibits showcasing the industrial progress of the United States since its independence. Visitors to the fair could marvel at demonstrations of electric light, sewing machines, elevated trains, skyscrapers, and other recent American technological innovations. The Ferris wheel, which made its debut at the fair and cost the then-princely sum of fifty cents per ride, was one of the event's major attractions.

Hugely popular, the fair was a major event in American cultural history and helped fashion the modern self-image of the United States as a land of progress and optimism. The fair's 65,000 exhibits presented a triumphant history of American innovation and promised a great future for the prosperous nation. Far surpassing any world's fair held in Europe, the exposition capped off the Gilded Age of the United States with a symphony of awe-inspiring excess. For the city of Chicago, the fair marked the completion of its recovery from the devastating Great Chicago Fire of 1871.

In total, the exposition covered 633 acres, took 40,000 workers three years to build, and remained open to the public for six months. Afterward, all but two of the buildings at the site were demolished. The University of Chicago now occupies most of the area. Chicago's Museum of Science and Industry is the only major building that remains of the once-vast fairgrounds.

ADDITIONAL FACTS

1. *Chicago got its nickname "the Windy City" from a New York City newspaper editor who thought Chicagoans were a bunch of windbags with all their boasting about the fair. The rugged winds off Lake Michigan served to cement the appellation.*

2. *Chicago mayor Carter Harrison was assassinated by a disgruntled job seeker at the fair two days before it closed.*

3. *One exhibit at the fair was a map of the United States made entirely of pickles.*

★ ★ ★

William Faulkner

One of the most distinctive literary voices of twentieth-century American fiction, William Faulkner (1897–1962) wrote rich, haunting novels set in the small towns and backwoods of his native Mississippi. The winner of the Nobel Prize for Literature in 1949 for his innovative, stream-of-consciousness storytelling, Faulkner's most well-known works include *The Sound and the Fury* (1929), *Light in August* (1932), and *Absalom, Absalom!* (1936).

 Born into a prominent Mississippi family as William Falkner, the author added the *u* to his name in the 1920s before launching his literary career. He published his debut novel, *Soldier's Pay*, in 1926. Faulkner's first novels varied in subject, tone, and setting. *Mosquitoes* (1927) was a comic novel set in New Orleans, while *Sanctuary* (1931) was an attempt at pulp fiction. With the publication of *The Sound and the Fury*, however, a dense, serious tale of an unraveling Southern family, Faulkner found his literary métier.

The Sound and the Fury is told in a nonlinear fashion and can be a challenging read. Most of the story takes place in Yoknapatawpha County, a fictional Mississippi locale inspired by his hometown of Oxford, where Faulkner set many of his most famous stories and novels. In the text, Faulkner frequently departs from conventional syntax and grammar to render the thoughts and feelings of the characters. In one section, the character Quentin Compson is tormented by guilt because, among other things, his father had to sell part of the family's property to pay for his college tuition:

> On what on your school money the money they sold the pasture for so you could go to Harvard dont you see you've got to finish now if you dont finish he'll have nothing
> Sold the pasture His white shirt was motionless in the fork, in the flickering shade . . .

The great-grandson of a Confederate colonel, Faulkner explored the troubled racial history of the South and the region's class dynamics in many of his novels. His impenetrable prose style, although frequently criticized, often reflected the excruciating contradictions of the region. The Nobel Prize raised Faulkner's stature, and he went on to win two Pulitzer Prizes.

ADDITIONAL FACTS

1. *Faulkner was desperate to fight in World War I (1914–1918) but was rejected by the US Air Force; he moved to Canada and joined the Canadian Royal Air Force by posing as an Englishman.*

2. *He published a book of poetry in 1924,* The Marble Faun, *taking the title from a novel by Nathaniel Hawthorne (1804–1864).*

3. *In total, Faulkner published seventeen books set in Yoknapatawpha County.*

★ ★ ★

Dorothea Lange

On a cold, wet day in March 1936, photographer Dorothea Lange (1895–1965) was driving through California when she spotted a family camped in the mud at the side of the road. Lange pulled over, chatted with the migrant farm workers for a few minutes, and quickly snapped six pictures of the group.

A few days later, one of Lange's six black-and-white shots, titled "Migrant Mother," was wired around the world and quickly became the most famous visual icon of the Great Depression. Lange's picture, a bleak portrait of thirty-two-year old Florence Owens Thompson and two of her children, captured in a single poignant image the human misery of the nation's economic crisis. In the picture, the two children bury their heads in Thompson's shoulders while she seems to stare out wearily at the unforgiving road.

Before the Depression, Lange had worked as a conventional studio photographer in California. Starting in the mid-1930s, however, she began receiving commissions from the federal government's Resettlement Administration to document the nation's woes. Along with other well-known photographers like Walker Evans (1903–1975), Lange eventually took thousands of pictures of the homeless, breadlines, abandoned farms, and ramshackle motels in her travels across the United States.

Although journalistic in nature, Lange's Depression-era photography had a distinctive warmth and intimacy. In Lange's pictures, she managed to convey the resilient dignity of Americans affected by the Depression. For instance, although it is clear from "Migrant Mother" that Thompson's family is in dire poverty, Lange shows the mother with her head held up, her determination to persevere clear.

A compassionate ally of the downtrodden, Lange joined her friend Ansel Adams (1902–1984) during World War II (1939–1945) in photographing the plight of Japanese-Americans imprisoned at internment camps, pictures so effective they were banned by the government. Lange died in 1965, one of the most accomplished photographers in American history.

ADDITIONAL FACTS

1. *Lange was born in Hoboken, New Jersey, as Dorothea Margaretta Nutzhorn, but she adopted her mother's maiden name after her father abandoned the family.*

2. *Many of Lange's Depression-era photographs are now housed at the Library of Congress in Washington, DC, where they are accessible to the public.*

3. *The Oakland Museum in Oakland, California, owns the largest collection of Lange's prints and keeps many on permanent display.*

★ ★ ★

Victoria Woodhull

A woman well ahead of her time, Victoria Woodhull (1838–1927) achieved fame as one of the first successful female stockbrokers, the first woman to run for president of the United States, and a provocative opponent of sexual double standards in nineteenth-century American society. She was vilified in the press for her controversial support for "free love"—a euphemism for opposition to the institution of marriage—and eventually fled to England, where she died.

Born Victoria Claflin to a poor family in a small Ohio town, she married Canning Woodhull at age fourteen but divorced in her twenties. She then moved to New York City with her sister, Tennessee Claflin (1845–1923), in 1868. The two women, supported by railroad tycoon Cornelius Vanderbilt (1794–1877)—who was having an affair with Claflin and believed the sisters possessed mystical spiritual powers—started a brokerage firm on Wall Street. The business was successful, and Woodhull used the proceeds to start a newspaper, *Woodhull & Claflin's Weekly*. Among other causes embraced by the newspaper, the sisters editorialized in favor of women's suffrage, for legalized prostitution, and against mustaches on men. Despite their own backgrounds as stockbrokers, the sisters also published the first American edition of the *Communist Manifesto* in 1871.

Again drawing on her personal wealth, Woodhull ran for president in 1872. Her running mate was Frederick Douglass (1817–1895), the famous African-American civil rights advocate. Not only was Woodhull unable to vote in the race, she would not have been allowed to if she had won, since she was only thirty-four years old at the time, one year shy of the minimum age as established in the Constitution.

Fearless and utterly undeterred by the torrents of abuse she endured from mainstream Americans, Woodhull published an exposé of a prominent Protestant preacher, Henry Ward Beecher (1813–1887), whom she accused of having an affair. Her purpose was to show that while women who supported "free love" were ostracized, prominent men were promiscuous without consequence. She was prosecuted for obscenity after leveling her accusations against Beecher, and she moved to England in 1877. She started another newspaper, the *Humanitarian*, and continued supporting women's rights and other causes until her death fifty years later.

ADDITIONAL FACTS

1. *While she was in her teens, Woodhull's supposed supernatural abilities allowed her to support her family by fortune-telling.*

2. *In 1871, Woodhull became the first woman to speak before the United States Congress.*

3. *Woodhull's activities divided her fellow suffragists, some of whom, including Susan B. Anthony (1820–1906), thought she went too far and gave the women's movement a bad name.*

★ ★ ★

War of the Philippine Insurrection

In the 1898 treaty that ended the Spanish-American War, ownership of the Philippines, an archipelago in the Pacific Ocean, was transferred from Spain to the United States. Many Filipinos, who had expected independence, were outraged. A rebellion against the United States, known as the War of the Philippine Insurrection, began almost immediately after the arrival of American troops. In the brutal guerilla conflict, thousands of American troops were killed while trying to establish control over the islands. The war petered out after the capture of key rebel leaders, but quiet Philippine resistance to American rule continued.

The Philippines were colonized by the Spanish in the sixteenth century. Native Filipinos, tiring of centuries of Spanish rule, began agitating for independence in the 1880s. Rebal groups initially welcomed the Spanish-American War, hoping that the United States would back the independence movement. After the treaty, however, rebel leader Emilio Aguinaldo (1869–1964), who had battled the Spanish, simply switched targets and fought against the Americans he believed had betrayed him.

The United States, meanwhile, believed the Philippines would provide a strategic military outpost in the Pacific and a seat at the table of empires. Additionally, some Americans believed they had a responsibility to "civilize the natives." The twin motives of imperialism—paternalism and greed—combined to fuel American support for the war. Still, a significant number of Americans, led by 1900 Democratic presidential candidate William Jennings Bryan (1860–1925), opposed American involvement in the Philippines.

For American troops in the Philippines, war in the jungles of Southeast Asia was a hellish experience. Disease was rampant. Both sides were accused of serious human rights abuses and mistreatment of prisoners of war.

Two events caused the rebellion to falter. First, the Americans captured Aguinaldo, the rebellion's most charismatic leader. Second, President William McKinley (1843–1901) appointed an Ohio judge, William Howard Taft (1857–1930), as governor of the archipelago. Taft, the twenty-seventh president of the United States, significantly softened American policies toward the Philippines, giving Filipinos more say in their government and draining support for the revolt. Still, the islanders continued to press for independence until they got it—on July 4, 1946.

ADDITIONAL FACTS

1. *Opposition to the war, under the banner of the Anti-Imperialist League, included unlikely allies like steel magnate Andrew Carnegie (1835–1919), union leader Samuel Gompers (1850–1924), writer Mark Twain (1835–1910), and intellectual W. E. B. DuBois (1868–1963).*

2. *In the initial battles of the war, the Filipinos were astonished to see that unlike the Spaniards, American soldiers fought in the hot hours of daylight, making them far more formidable adversaries.*

3. *The casualties of the Philippine war were far greater than in the Spanish-American conflict that had precipitated it. In all, more than 4,000 American soldiers died in the Philippines.*

★ ★ ★

Plessy v. Ferguson

The infamous 1896 US Supreme Court decision *Plessy v. Ferguson* dealt a major blow to racial equality by permitting Jim Crow segregation in hotels, railroad cars, and schools. In the wake of the ruling, Southern states in the early twentieth century officially imposed second-class status on African-Americans through a system of legal segregation that remained in place until the civil rights movement of the 1950s and 1960s.

Plessy v. Ferguson originated in New Orleans in 1892, when a black man, Homer Plessy, was arrested after he attempted to ride in a "whites only" railroad car. In court, Plessy and his supporters unsuccessfully argued that Louisiana's segregation laws violated the Fourteenth Amendment to the United States Constitution, which required equal protection under the laws, regardless of race.

The Supreme Court upheld Plessy's criminal conviction in its 8-1 decision, holding that "separate but equal" accommodations were allowable under the Constitution. The lone dissenter, Justice John Marshall Harlan (1833–1911), wrote a lengthy and eloquent attack on the "separate but equal" doctrine:

> The arbitrary separation of citizens on the basis of race . . . is a badge of servitude wholly inconsistent with the civil freedom and the equality before the law established by the Constitution. It cannot be justified upon any legal grounds.

As Harlan predicted, *Plessy v. Ferguson* has come to be regarded as one of the most shameful rulings in the Supreme Court's history. About sixty years later, the Court overturned the *Plessy* ruling in *Brown v. Board of Education* (1954), removing the constitutional basis for segregation and leading to the eventual demise of Jim Crow laws.

ADDITIONAL FACTS

1. *After losing his case, Plessy was forced to pay a $25 fine for sitting in the whites-only car.*

2. *Justice Harlan, the sole dissenter, had been a slaveholder himself before the Civil War (1861–1865) but recanted his support for slavery afterward.*

3. *Harlan's grandson, John Marshall Harlan III (1899–1971), was also a Supreme Court justice.*

★ ★ ★

James J. Hill

"Give me enough Swedes and whiskey
and I'll build a railroad to hell."
—James J. Hill

James J. Hill (1838–1916), the builder of the Great Northern Railroad, was one of the last of the legendary nineteenth-century railroad barons. A businessman of great ambition and vision, he was nicknamed the "Empire Builder" for completing the fourth transcontinental railroad, which stretched from Chicago to Seattle across the windswept northern prairie. Hill's Great Northern was the only transcontinental railroad built without government subsidies, a testament to his legendary business acumen.

Hill was born in Ontario and eventually moved to the American Midwest. He worked in a variety of shipping and railroad businesses and purchased the St. Paul and Pacific Railroad in 1878. At the time, the railroad's grandiose name was no more than a fantasy; it served only a few towns in Minnesota and was teetering on the edge of bankruptcy. Over the next twenty years, Hill worked relentlessly to expand the company, which he eventually renamed the Great Northern.

The Great Northern crossed inhospitable territory—Idaho, North Dakota, and Montana—that had virtually no industry or white inhabitants in the late 1800s. Hill encouraged farmers to move into the areas opened up by the railroad, and he started mines and factories himself to provide business for the line. Although Hill's aggressive expansion was not without controversy—and often came at the expense of Native Americans—he is regarded by historians as a key figure in the settlement of the American Northwest. His railroad also played a decisive role in the development of Seattle, its western terminus, as a major American city.

Fifty years after Hill's death, the railroad merged with its biggest competitor, the Northern Pacific. Most of the tracks built by Hill are now owned by the Burlington Northern Santa Fe railroad, and every day dozens of freight trains roll across the route he forged over the Rocky Mountains.

ADDITIONAL FACTS

1. *An Amtrak route named in honor of Hill, the Empire Builder, runs from Chicago to Seattle along the tracks constructed by Hill in the nineteenth century.*

2. *One of Hill's engineers was John F. Stevens (1853–1943), who went on to become the chief engineer for the Panama Canal.*

3. *To build the Great Northern, Hill convinced Congress to allow him to expropriate lands from American Indian reservations.*

★ ★ ★

Frontier Thesis

In 1890, the United States government declared that the American frontier was closed. Although a few pockets of the West remained unsettled, census takers noted with little fanfare, "there can hardly be said to be a frontier line."

To historian Frederick Jackson Turner (1861–1932), a professor at the University of Wisconsin, the closing of the American frontier was an event of epochal significance. Since the arrival of the earliest European settlers, Turner pointed out, American values had been shaped by the existence of a wild frontier to their west. Now, after three centuries, it was gone.

In 1893, Turner gave a speech to fellow historians at the World's Columbian Exposition in Chicago outlining his "frontier thesis." In this celebrated lecture, he claimed that the now-vanished frontier had helped create America's sense of "freshness, and confidence, and scorn of older society"—indeed, its very identity as a youthful nation:

> This perennial rebirth, this fluidity of American life, this expansion westward with its new opportunities, its continuous touch with the simplicity of primitive society, furnish the forces dominating American character. The true point of view in the history of this nation is not the Atlantic coast, it is the Great West.

Jackson's frontier thesis would become one of the most influential ideas in the study of American history. The nation's ideology, Turner argued, was inseparably linked to its geography. The same spirit of exploration, acquisition, and rugged individualism that drove the pioneers, he said, also animated American society at large.

Although historians have since criticized many aspects of Turner's theory, it unquestionably captured the zeitgeist of its moment. The closure of the frontier worried many Americans, who feared that without new frontiers to conquer, the nation would lose its vitality. The solution, to many Americans seeking to recapture the pioneer spirit, was imperialism. The same year that Turner gave his speech, the United States overthrew the government of Hawaii, beginning a new and controversial chapter in American expansion.

ADDITIONAL FACTS

1. *A year after his death in 1932, Turner was awarded the Pulitzer Prize for* The Significance of Sections in American History.

2. *The census defined* frontier *as any area with fewer than two residents per square mile.*

3. *Turner taught at the University of Wisconsin until 1910, when he moved to a professorship at Harvard.*

★ ★ ★

Langston Hughes

"I, too, am America."
—Langston Hughes, "I, Too"

The best-known poet of the Harlem Renaissance of the 1920s and 1930s and one of the most influential African-American writers of the twentieth century, Langston Hughes (1902–1967) wrote hundreds of trenchant, poignant poems about the effects of bigotry and segregation on American blacks. Born in Missouri, Hughes lived most of his life in the Harlem neighborhood of New York City, where he was a mentor and inspiration to many other leading black writers.

In his poetry, Hughes sought to foster black pride, puncture stereotypes, and outrage his readers by telling them about the injustices of white racism. He wrote about lynching, poverty, and the inner rage of blacks confined by segregation. Hughes considered himself a people's poet and intended for his works to be read, not studied. They are direct, accessible, and often dramatic. The poem "Ku Klux," for instance, is written in the first-person voice of an African-American kidnapped by the Klan. The title of the poem is truncated, but all of Hughes's readers knew what the third word would be; likewise, the poem itself ends inconclusively, but readers understood the grim fate likely awaiting the black narrator accused of "sassin'" whites in the Deep South.

Although often dark and pessimistic, Hughes's poetry is laced with occasional flights of optimism and humor. During Hughes's lifetime, the civil rights movement made substantial progress toward equality, positive steps that were sometimes reflected in his poetry.

An eloquent champion of equality, liberation, and human dignity, Hughes has more recently been reclaimed as a gay black male icon.

ADDITIONAL FACTS

1. *Hughes's first poem was published in the* Crisis, *the NAACP magazine founded by W. E. B. DuBois (1868–1963).*

2. *Hughes briefly enrolled in Columbia University but dropped out to pursue writing. He would later graduate from Lincoln University in Pennsylvania.*

3. *Although Hughes flirted with communism in the 1930s, a time when few other political parties were willing to stand up for the rights of African-Americans, he never joined the Communist Party. Still, he was forced to testify at the McCarthy anticommunism hearings in 1953.*

* * *

The Wizard of Oz

Perhaps the most beloved children's movie in the history of American cinema, *The Wizard of Oz* was first released in 1939 and has enchanted generations of kids ever since. Although the film was not a runaway hit at the time of its initial premier, its reputation grew over the years, and dozens of the movie's most memorable lines have seeped into the fabric of American popular culture.

Based on a book by L. Frank Baum published in 1900, the movie starred actress Judy Garland (1922–1969) in the leading role as Dorothy Gale, a Kansas farm girl mysteriously transported to the magical land of Oz. The movie's first scenes, set in Kansas, were filmed in black-and-white, but the film shifts to color when Dorothy and her dog, Toto, begin their adventures in Oz.

The screenplay, a relatively faithful adaptation of Baum's book, contains some of the most famous quotes in Hollywood history. To wit:

> "I'll get you, my pretty . . . and your little dog, too!"
> "There's no place like home."
> "Toto, I've got a feeling we're not in Kansas anymore."

Music also played a major role in the film's success. The movie's sound track included the famous tune "Over the Rainbow," which won an Oscar for Best Song in 1940, has been covered by countless artists, and was recently voted the American Film Institute's best-ever song in the history of American cinema.

Although a children's movie, *The Wizard of Oz* was one of the most technologically ambitious films of its era, and it cost the MGM studio a then-astonishing $2.8 million. The film—which had five directors—employed a sound engineer to produce its sound effects, and it made extensive use of Technicolor film.

In the end, however, the singular allure of *The Wizard of Oz* owes much to Baum's whimsical story and Garland's acting. Garland, only seventeen years old when the movie propelled her to stardom, went on to act in dozens more musicals but died of a drug overdose in 1969.

ADDITIONAL FACTS

1. *The year 1939 yielded a bumper crop of classic films.* The Wizard of Oz *and* Mr. Smith Goes to Washington *were nominated for Best Picture at the Academy Awards, but they both lost to* Gone with the Wind.

2. *Terry, the dog that played Toto, acted in a dozen other films and was reportedly paid more than some of the human extras in* The Wizard of Oz.

3. *One of the original pairs of ruby slippers Garland wore as Dorothy in the movie are now on display at the Smithsonian Institution in Washington, DC.*

★ ★ ★

Rutherford B. Hayes

The election of Rutherford B. Hayes (1822–1893) as president of the United States in 1877 had far-reaching consequences for American politics and society and was particularly harmful for African-Americans. Hayes, a Republican, finished virtually tied with his Democratic opponent, Samuel Tilden (1814–1886), in one of the closest contests in American history. Behind closed doors in Washington, DC, the two parties reached a deal to resolve the disputed election. Under the terms of the pact, the Democrats reached a deal Hayes could take office, in exchange for a promise from the Republicans to end Reconstruction in the South.

For blacks, the end of Reconstruction and the removal of federal troops from the South was a disaster. After the Civil War (1861–1865), the federal government had attempted to improve the conditions in the South for blacks by enforcing civil rights legislation with military force. For the brief period between 1865 and 1877, blacks enjoyed unprecedented political power in the South, and several blacks even won election to Congress.

Many white Southerners, however, were appalled by Reconstruction and did every thing in their power to thwart racial equality. Most notoriously, some Confederate veterans formed a terrorist organization, the Ku Klux Klan, to harass blacks and intimidate federal officials.

The compromise that ended the 1877 election benefited both parties but consigned African-Americans in the South to nine decades of segregation. Hayes, meanwhile, a former Union brevet major general from Ohio, had an uneventful presidency. He retired after a single term and died in Ohio in 1893.

ADDITIONAL FACTS

1. *In 1861, after the start of the Civil War, Hayes was eager to join the action, declaring that he would "prefer to go into it if I knew I. . . was to be killed. . . than to live through and after it without taking any part."*

2. *Hayes was elected to the House of Representatives from Ohio in 1864, while on active duty, but refused to leave his post to take office until December 1865.*

3. *By tradition, Hayes and Tilden did not actively seek the presidency in 1876, leaving the actual campaigning to their staffs.*

★ ★ ★

World War I

The American entry into World War I in 1917 marked a significant milestone in the evolution of the United States into a world superpower. The war against Germany and the Austro-Hungarian Empire was the first time American troops fought in the fields of Europe. It was also the first war to make use of modern technological innovations like airplanes, tanks, and chemical weapons. Finally, the decision of US President Woodrow Wilson (1856–1924) to seek war marked a huge shift in American foreign policy away from isolationism and toward more active engagement with European and world affairs.

The war started in Europe in 1914 after the assassination of an Austrian prince, Franz Ferdinand. In retaliation for the killing, the Austro-Hungarian Empire declared war on the Balkan country of Serbia, which was suspected of harboring the assassins. From there, the war quickly spiraled into a continent-wide conflict pitting the Central Powers of Austria-Hungary, Germany, and the Ottoman Empire against the Allies of France, Italy, Great Britain, and Russia.

Initially, Wilson and the American public wanted no part in the European conflict. World War I was the first modern war, and the level of bloodshed was terrifying. Both sides deployed poison gas. In a famous poem, British soldier Wilfred Owen (1893–1918) described the horror of watching his countrymen "guttering, choking, drowning" in deadly seas of green gas. With no American interests at stake, the United States quickly declared its neutrality in 1914.

However, in 1915 German submarines began sinking American ships, which they suspected were carrying weapons to the Allies, causing American public opinion to turn against Germany. In the spring of 1917, angered by the German attacks, Wilson asked Congress to declare war on Germany, and it did so on April 6.

Most American soldiers fought in France, with a smaller contingent dispatched to Italy. American troops took part in an Allied offensive in the summer of 1918, culminating in the Second Battle of the Somme. Although French and British armies did the vast majority of the actual fighting in World War I, the entrance of the United States helped convince Germany that it would be pointless to continue. The German monarchy was overthrown, and new German leaders signed an armistice with the Allies on November 11, 1918—the day now celebrated as Veterans Day.

ADDITIONAL FACTS

1. *Fifty members of the House of Representatives voted against entering the war, including Rep. Jeanette Rankin (1880–1973) of Montana, the first woman elected to Congress, who also cast the only vote against entering World War II in 1941.*

2. *Wilson's secretary of state, William Jennings Bryan (1860–1925), was adamantly opposed to US entrance into the war, and ultimately resigned in protest.*

3. *German diplomats tried to convince Mexico to enter World War I on their side, offering to return Texas, New Mexico, and Arizona to Mexico if the United States was defeated.*

★ ★ ★

Jim Crow

The term *Jim Crow* refers to an assortment of laws adopted in many Southern states after the Civil War (1861–1865) that imposed legal restrictions on African-Americans. Jim Crow laws, which remained in effect in many states into the 1960s, covered even the most intimate aspects of everyday life. Blacks were forced to use separate waiting rooms at bus stations, separate bathrooms, and even separate drinking fountains from whites. Jim Crow also forbade blacks and whites to marry and imposed strict racial segregation in public schools.

After the end of Reconstruction in 1877, white Southerners moved swiftly to reestablish white supremacy in the South by passing a wave of segregation codes. The Supreme Court gave legal sanction to Jim Crow in its controversial 1896 *Plessy v. Ferguson* decision that sanctioned "separate but equal" facilities. Emboldened by the *Plessy* decision, southern states passed a second wave of Jim Crow laws in the first decade of the twentieth century.

Jim Crow was more than a legal system. It was also an unspoken code of racial customs and taboos. In the post–Civil War South, blacks were expected to call white men "sir," get out of the way of whites on the sidewalk, and avoid even making eye contact with white women. Black men of any age were expected to answer to "boy." This code—especially the stricture on contact with white women—was enforced by lynch mobs.

Founded in 1909, the National Association for the Advancement of Colored People (NAACP) organized to improve race relations. It would take almost sixty years, however, until the passage of the Civil Rights Act of 1964 effectively abolished Jim Crow. Laws against interracial marriage were invalidated by the 1967 Supreme Court decision *Loving v. Virginia*.

ADDITIONAL FACTS

1. *The term* Jim Crow *is thought to derive from a racist song performed by blackfaced singers that was popular in the nineteenth century.*

2. *Many white home owners placed "covenants" on their homes forbidding their sale to blacks or Jews, a practice that was deemed unconstitutional in 1948.*

3. *Professional baseball had black players until 1890 but became segregated in the wave of Jim Crow that began in the decade that followed. Another black player would not take the field in the major leagues until Jackie Robinson (1919–1972) in 1947.*

★ ★ ★

Sharecropping

The Civil War (1861–1865) ended slavery, but it did not end the demand for labor in the cotton fields of the South. Although many of the old antebellum plantations were broken up after the defeat of the Confederacy, cotton remained the region's most important cash crop. In the decades after emancipation, many African-American ex-slaves in the Deep South became trapped in the system of sharecropping, a new economic arrangement that replaced slavery as the basis of the agricultural economy throughout much of the region.

Sharecropping involved an exchange between tenant farmers and the land's owner. The farmer was given seed and supplies and allowed to live on the land, and in exchange turned over a portion of the cotton or tobacco harvest to the landlord. In theory, sharecropping gave the farmer some financial independence.

In practice, however, many tenant farmers remained in dire poverty and were locked in an insurmountable cycle of debt to their landlord. For some sharecroppers, the system represented only a marginal improvement over slavery. Indeed, many tenant farmers found themselves working for their ex-masters on the same land they had once farmed as slaves.

Unlike slavery, however, sharecropping was not confined to African-Americans. Many poor whites in the South also ended up working as sharecroppers—under equally exploitative conditions.

Dissatisfaction with sharecropping, along with omnipresent racism and Jim Crow segregation, helped fuel the great migration of African-Americans out of the South beginning in World War I (1914–1918). Sharecropping itself, however, remained a common practice well into the twentieth century. One of the most famous depictions of Southern tenant farming was *Let Us Now Praise Famous Men*, a semifictional 1941 book by writer James Agee (1909–1955) and photographer Walker Evans (1903–1975) chronicling a family of poor white sharecroppers in Alabama. Sharecropping is now virtually nonexistent in the United States.

ADDITIONAL FACTS

1. *A major catalyst for the end of sharecropping was a catastrophic Mississippi River flood in 1927, which caused many blacks to abandon the South.*

2. *The US Senate held hearings on sharecropping in 1880 and heard testimony from ex-slaves who were threatened with violence if they did not sign exploitative contracts. Still, Congress did nothing to end the abuses.*

3. *In addition to its economic unfairness, sharecropping provided an incentive to overfarm land. By the early 1900s, much of the farmland in the South was in poor condition, hurting tenant farmers further.*

★ ★ ★

Puerto Rico

Puerto Rico, one of the last remaining vestiges of the Spanish empire in the New World, became part of the United States as a result of the peace treaty that ended the Spanish-American War in 1898. Since then, the heavily populated island has struggled to define its status and identity in the modern United States. Under current law, the island is not a state and its residents do not vote in federal elections or pay taxes, but all Puerto Ricans are considered United States citizens.

European settlement of Puerto Rico began much earlier than in any other part of the modern United States. Indeed, Christopher Columbus himself "discovered" Puerto Rico on his second expedition to the New World in 1493. Spain became the world's most powerful empire in the sixteenth and seventeenth centuries and built massive fortifications to protect San Juan, the island's seaside capital. Spanish sugarcane farmers enslaved and eventually decimated the island's indigenous Arawak Indian population.

Spain's empire was eventually eclipsed by Great Britain and France, and by the nineteenth century it was in serious decline. By the time the war with the United States began, Puerto Rico and Cuba were the last two outposts of Spanish colonial rule in the Caribbean. American troops invaded both islands during the war, made short work of the Spanish defenders, and were awarded the islands in the pact ending the conflict. A 1917 act of the US Congress gave Puerto Ricans US citizenship. In 1952, Puerto Rico became a self-governing commonwealth of the United States with its own constitution approved by the US Congress.

Since then, Puerto Ricans have voted several times—most recently in 1998—to remain part of the United States and keep their unique, ad hoc legal status. Puerto Rico is the only part of the United States that fields a separate Olympic team, and it is the only US territory where Spanish is the first language of most residents. However, thousands of Puerto Ricans serve in the United States military, and at present there is little political support in Puerto Rico for changes to the island's unusual status quo.

ADDITIONAL FACTS

1. *Puerto Rico means* rich port *in Spanish.*

2. *Spanish and English are both considered official languages in Puerto Rico; the United States itself does not have an official language.*

3. *Puerto Rico's Olympic basketball team shocked the world by beating a US squad full of NBA superstars at the 2004 Summer Olympics in Athens, Greece.*

★ ★ ★

Dashiell Hammett

Author Dashiell Hammett (1894–1961) popularized the hardboiled detective fiction genre in a series of crime thrillers based on his experiences as a private detective in the 1920s. Although Hammett's creative output largely ceased after the 1930s, his novels influenced many other crime writers, including Raymond Chandler (1888–1959), and established the loner cop who plays by his own rules as a stock character in American crime movies and television.

Prior to the 1920s, the archetypal detective in fiction was Sherlock Holmes, an upright citizen who pieces together clues to put ne'er-do-wells behind bars. Hammett's detectives were different. Only slightly more ethical than the criminals they chased, his heroes cheated, bribed, and lied to solve their cases.

Hammett's most famous detective in this mold was Sam Spade, the main character of *The Maltese Falcon* (1930), who was immortalized by the tough-guy actor Humphrey Bogart (1899–1957) in the 1941 film version. The hero of most of Hammett's novels and short stories, however, was a nameless detective called the Continental Op, an operative for the Continental Detective Agency. Many of the Op's exploits were based on Hammett's own cases. For instance, in Hammett's first novel, *Red Harvest* (1929), the Op is dispatched to a violent mining town in the Rocky Mountains to investigate the murder of a newspaper publisher; Hammett himself had been stationed in Butte, Montana, during a bout of labor strife shortly after World War I (1914–1918).

The Thin Man (1934) was Hammett's last major work and one of his most beloved, featuring Nick and Nora Charles as a hard-drinking crime-solving couple. The book was the basis for a series of successful movies. Hammett himself had begun a famous romance with the playwright Lillian Hellman (1905–1984) at about the same time, an affair that would last for the rest of his life.

Hammett's politics veered sharply leftward during the 1930s in response to the author's growing concern over the spread of fascism in Europe. In the anticommunist atmosphere after World War II (1939–1945), he was imprisoned for six months for refusing to answer questions about a communist-affiliated organization of which he was a member. He lived most of his last years drinking heavily at a cottage in rural New York or with Hellman at her house on the Upper East Side of New York City. A veteran of both world wars, he is buried at Arlington National Cemetery.

ADDITIONAL FACTS

1. *After the McCarthy hearings, Hammett's books were briefly pulled from some overseas State Department libraries, until President Eisenhower (1890–1969) criticized the move as an overreaction to the author's communist sympathies.*

2. *It was Hammett's lover, Lillian Hellman, who famously refused to answer McCarthy's questions, saying she would not "cut my conscience to fit this year's fashions."*

3. *Hammett's first short story was published in 1922 by The Smart Set, a magazine edited by the famous journalist H. L. Mencken (1880–1956).*

★ ★ ★

Katharine Hepburn

The only woman to win four Academy Awards for Best Actress, Katharine Hepburn (1907–2003) played strong, no-nonsense women in a string of hit films like *The Philadelphia Story*, *The African Queen*, and *On Golden Pond*. Saucy and playful, her characters were an inspiration to independent women and a delight to moviegoers.

A graduate of Bryn Mawr, an all-women's college in Pennsylvania, Hepburn began her acting career on the stage in New York. She moved to Hollywood in 1932 but briefly returned to Broadway after a string of flops in the late 1930s. *The Philadelphia Story*, a runaway 1940 hit that also starred actors Cary Grant (1904–1986) and James Stewart (1908–1997), relaunched her movie career.

Hepburn insisted on having creative control of her own movies and was largely able to select her male costars—a Hollywood rarity. In 1942, she picked Spencer Tracy as her costar in *Woman of the Year*, beginning one of the most fabled romances in Hollywood history. Although married, Tracy began a love affair with Hepburn that would continue until his death in 1967. During that span, they would star in nine movies together.

Although a versatile actress, Hepburn's characters were usually tart, athletic, and upper-crust, much like Hepburn herself. Famous for her athletic abilities, patrician New England accent, and preternaturally straight posture, Hepburn also made it popularly acceptable for women to wear pants, complaining that skirts were uncomfortable.

Of the forty films Hepburn made during her career, she garnered Academy Award nominations for twelve of them and won Oscars for *Morning Glory* (1933), *Guess Who's Coming to Dinner* (1967), *The Lion in Winter* (1968), and *On Golden Pond* (1981). Slowed by old age, she made her final movie appearance in 1994, alongside Annette Benning (1958–) in the film *Love Affair*. A trailblazing woman and one of the best-loved actresses in Hollywood history, she died in 2003 at age ninety-six.

ADDITIONAL FACTS

1. *Hepburn is unrelated to Audrey Hepburn (1929–1993), another famous twentieth-century actress who starred in* Breakfast at Tiffany's *(1961) and* My Fair Lady *(1964).*

2. *In 2004, Cate Blanchett (1969–) won an Oscar for her portrayal of Katharine Hepburn in* The Aviator.

3. *Hepburn's older brother, Tom, killed himself when she was a teenager. Deeply saddened, Katharine adopted Tom's birthday as her own in his memory.*

★ ★ ★

William Jennings Bryan

Nebraska lawyer William Jennings Byran (1860–1925) ran for president as a Democrat three times, losing each time by a wide margin. The self-proclaimed candidate of the common man, he railed against big business and wealthy eastern financiers. Although the "Great Commoner" lost each of his elections, in the long term many of his ideas would become law, and he was deeply influential within the Democratic Party.

Bryan's start in national politics came in 1896, amid a raging debate over the gold standard. In the late nineteenth century, American currency was backed by gold, meaning that the total amount of money in circulation was linked to the quantity of gold in the government's vaults. Easterners and the middle class liked the gold standard because it offered economic stability, but the system made it difficult for farmers to repay loans. Many westerners favored moving to a silver standard, which would make money much less scarce, resulting in inflation but making it easier for them to repay debts.

It is difficult now to appreciate how heated and emotional this debate over two metals became. In his famous speech to the Democratic convention in 1896, one of the most well-known pieces of oratory in American history, Bryan thundered against the gold standard, comparing the plight of indebted farmers to the suffering of Jesus Christ himself. "You shall not press down upon the brow of labor this crown of thorns," he raged. "You shall not crucify mankind upon a cross of gold." Goldbugs, as supporters of the gold standard were called, were aghast, believing the silver standard proposed by Bryan represented nothing less than a threat to the economic foundations of the Republic.

Bryan lost to Republican William McKinley (1843–1901), an advocate of the gold standard, in an election whose turnout of 80 percent has never been matched since. Bryan ran again in 1900 and 1908, expanding his platform to criticize imperialism in American foreign policy, crusade against corporate monopolies, and support the regulation of railroad rates.

He was appointed secretary of state in 1913 but resigned in protest of World War I (1914–1918). A passionate Christian fundamentalist, Bryan, in his last act in public life, aided in the prosecution of John Scopes (1900–1970) for teaching evolution in Tennessee. He died at age sixty-five just days after the trial ended.

ADDITIONAL FACTS

1. *In 1896, Bryan was nicknamed the "Boy Orator" for his youthful looks. Twelve years later, in the 1908 campaign, his nickname was amended to the "Balding Boy Orator."*

2. *Bryan was thirty-six years old when he ran for president in 1896, only a year past the minimum age of thirty-five stipulated in the Constitution.*

3. *Bryan was the first presidential candidate to break with precedent by actively campaigning for the office. He gave 600 speeches to five million people, all without the aid of loudspeakers.*

★ ★ ★

John Pershing

John Pershing (1860–1948) led the United States Army during World War I (1914–1918). American soldiers under Pershing's command, nicknamed "doughboys," provided crucial support to the Allies in the final year of the war. Pershing's army was the first American force to fight in a European conflict. Pershing himself returned home after the war to a hero's welcome: a ticker tape parade in New York. Elevated to the highest ranks in the army, he remained on active duty until the eve of World War II (1939–1945) and was a mentor to many of the generals who commanded the second American war in Europe.

Pershing was born in Missouri and graduated from the West Point military academy in 1886. Promoted to general after the Spanish-American War (1898), Pershing led the American troops that fruitlessly searched for the Mexican bandit Pancho Villa (1878–1923) in 1916.

When the United States Congress declared war on Germany in 1917 to enter World War I, President Woodrow Wilson (1856–1924) picked Pershing to lead the American expeditionary force. Simply getting America's four million soldiers across the Atlantic Ocean proved an enormous logistical challenge, since the US Navy possessed virtually no transport ships at the time. Indeed, it would take eight months before Americans soldiers began arriving in Europe in great numbers. They made a strong impression on the French, who were astonished by the cheerful, singing American soldiers.

Arguably Pershing's most significant accomplishment on behalf of his country and his troops was to resist pressure from France and Great Britain to use American soldiers as spares in their depleted armies. Battered by three years of trench warfare and inept leadership, the French and British armies were in wretched shape.

Pershing argued with the Allied leaders to ensure that whenever possible, American troops would fight in American units. American troops saw significant action in 1918, and total US deaths amounted to 49,000 soldiers killed in action. The American troops tipped the numerical balance in Europe in favor of the Allies, and Germany agreed to an armistice on November 11, 1918, ending the war.

ADDITIONAL FACTS

1. *Pershing's military career was aided by family connections. His father-in-law, US Senator Francis Warren of Wyoming, was the powerful chairman of the Senate Military Affairs Committee.*

2. *Pershing was nicknamed "Black Jack" after commanding a regiment of black soldiers as a young lieutenant in Cuba.*

3. *Pershing was the first American general to make use of airplanes in combat. American pilots scored their first aerial victory on April 14, 1918.*

★ ★ ★

W. E. B. DuBois

African-American historian and sociologist W. E. B. DuBois (1868–1963) led the small group of young African-American intellectuals who successfully challenged black civil rights leaders to take a harder line against racial segregation in the early twentieth century. DuBois went on to edit the nation's leading civil rights journal, *Crisis*, from 1910 to 1934, publishing many of the movement's most influential essays. In his later years, disillusioned by the lack of progress toward racial equality, DuBois joined the Communist Party, moved to the African nation of Ghana, and renounced his American citizenship.

William Edward Burghardt DuBois was born in a small Massachusetts village in the Berkshire Hills and rarely encountered other African-Americans or overt racism during his childhood. A brilliant youngster, DuBois went to Fisk University in Tennessee on a scholarship.

During his summers at Fisk, he taught in local black communities and became increasingly aware of the hardships and problems that plagued Southern blacks. In many respects, his time in the South provided the foundation for his later political action.

DuBois became the first black person to receive a PhD from Harvard in 1895, where he studied under the famed philosopher William James (1842–1910). DuBois published his first book, about the international slave trade, in 1896. His most famous work, a collection of essays called *The Souls of Black Folk*, was published in 1903.

In 1895, DuBois began to write articles critical of Booker T. Washington (1856–1915), who was then considered the leader of the national African-American community. Disenchanted with Washington's failure to fight against Jim Crow, DuBois in 1905 organized the Niagara movement and in 1909 helped found the NAACP to argue more forcefully against racial segregation.

DuBois published hundreds of essays, books, novels, and newspaper articles attacking segregation. In the 1920s, he became interested in communism, traveling to the Soviet Union in 1926. DuBois eventually parted ways with the NAACP, when his communist leanings became an embarrassment to the organization. DuBois, who was born only three years after the Civil War ended, died August 27, 1963, the day before Martin Luther King Jr. (1929–1968) gave his "I Have a Dream" speech in Washington.

ADDITIONAL FACTS

1. *DuBois got his last name from a French Huguenot great-grandfather.*

2. *While editor of* Crisis, *DuBois supported World War I (1914–1918) and urged blacks to "close ranks" behind the war despite the second-class treatment endured by African-American soldiers.*

3. *DuBois never finished one of his favorite projects, called* Encyclopedia Africana, *but it was finally completed and published in 1999.*

★ ★ ★

Sherman Antitrust Act

The Sherman Antitrust Act of 1890, which was intended to prevent corporate monopolies, is regarded as one of the most important economic laws of the late nineteenth century. The act made it a crime for corporations to exercise monopolistic power in their line of business and empowered the federal government to break up companies that violated the law. Although enforcement of the law has been sporadic and sometimes controversial, the act has been a crucial tool for limiting the reach of big corporations in the American economy.

Named for Ohio senator John Sherman (1823–1900), the brother of Civil War general William Tecumseh Sherman (1820–1891), the US Congress passed the law amid growing concern over the clout of the robber barons in the United States during the Gilded Age of the late 1800s. Companies like Standard Oil had a virtual lock on their markets, and they used their dominant position to squelch smaller competitors. Senator Sherman argued that these "trusts" intrinsically harmed the consumer because without viable competition, the conglomerates had virtually no incentive to lower prices.

The law was signed by President Benjamin Harrison (1833–1901) in 1890 but not vigorously enforced until President Theodore Roosevelt (1858–1919) took office in 1901. Nicknamed the "trustbuster," Teddy Roosevelt zealously battled the trusts, beginning dozens of investigations under the Sherman Antitrust Act. The United States Supreme Court eventually upheld the government's most famous effort, a campaign to break up Standard Oil, in a 1911 ruling.

The true effectiveness of the Sherman Antitrust Act—and antitrust law in general—continues to generate heated debate among economists and politicians. Indeed, the arguments have changed little since 1890. Supporters of antitrust law argue that monopolies hurt consumers and so the government must intervene to prevent monopolies from forming. Opponents claim that antitrust laws go too far by preventing mergers that might increase efficiency. In *United States v. Microsoft*, one of the most famous recent antitrust cases, a federal judge ordered the breakup of the software company in 2000, an outcome that was eventually averted by a 2002 legal settlement in which the company agreed to change some of its business practices.

ADDITIONAL FACTS

1. *Sherman was nicknamed the "Ohio Icicle" because of his stiff, colorless personality.*

2. *One industry, Major League Baseball, enjoys a blanket exemption from antitrust law thanks to a 1922 Supreme Court ruling.*

3. *In addition to Standard Oil, the law was also used to break up the American Tobacco Company in 1911 and AT&T in 1984.*

★ ★ ★

New York City Subways

By 1900, the island of Manhattan was so overcrowded that commuting into the city was an increasingly difficult task. The patchwork system of horse-drawn streetcars and elevated trains was dangerous, congested, and unreliable, especially in bad weather. That year, to modernize the city's transportation system, New York embarked on one of the most expensive public works projects in American history, the digging of New York City's subways.

The idea of underground trains was not new. The first US subway, a short stretch of tunnel in Boston, had opened three years earlier. New Yorkers envisioned a far more ambitious network reaching every corner of their sprawling metropolis. It would take 7,700 workers four years to dig the first twenty-one miles of tunnel, which opened to passengers on October 27, 1904. Construction would continue for another thirty years, until the system measured more than 600 miles of track—far larger than any other American mass transit system.

Since their opening, New York's subways have functioned as a sort of bellwether for the city's overall condition. The system expanded rapidly before World War II (1939–1945) but languished in the 1950s and 1960s as city leaders like Robert Moses (1888–1981) concentrated on highway construction instead. By the 1970s, the subways were in disrepair, reflecting the city's crime wave and financial woes. In the 1990s, as New York's fortunes rebounded, the city began cleaning up the graffiti on railcars and buying much-needed new equipment.

Today, ridership on the New York City subways far surpasses that of any other mass transit system in the United States. Construction of the subway will continue in the twenty-first century with a planned new Second Avenue line on the city's east side.

ADDITIONAL FACTS

1. *Forty-four workers were killed in the construction of the first twenty-one miles of subway.*

2. *The original subway fare was five cents; it did not rise to a dime until 1948.*

3. *Until 1940, the operation of New York's subways was contracted out to three private companies, Interborough Rapid Transit (IRT), Independent Subway (IND), and Brooklyn–Manhattan Transit (BMT), whose initials are still seen on the walls of some subway stations in the city today.*

★ ★ ★

Zora Neale Hurston

In 1973, the contemporary writer Alice Walker went on an expedition to locate the grave of one of her heroes, the Harlem Renaissance author Zora Neale Hurston (1891–1960). Hurston had died in poverty in Florida, her seven books from the 1930s and 1940s out of print and largely forgotten. Walker was intent on saving Hurston from obscurity. The moving article Walker published in *Ms.* magazine about her search for Hurston's grave revived popular interest in the author, whose most famous book, *Their Eyes Were Watching God* (1937), was finally republished in 1978 and is now considered a classic of African-American literature.

Hurston was born in Eatonville, Florida, and came to New York in the 1920s. In addition to her novels and plays, she was a noted folklorist who traveled the South recording the oral traditions of African-Americans, a collection of which was published in 2001 as *Every Tongue Got to Confess*.

Hurston was unpopular with influential African-American literary critics of her day, however, because of her right-wing political views, hatred of communism, and aversion to protest literature. Richard Wright (1908–1960), the leading black writer of the 1930s and 1940s, wrote a scathing review of *Their Eyes Were Watching God*, calling it "counter-revolutionary." Other black writers distanced themselves from Hurston after she endorsed right wing Republican candidates following World War II (1939–1945). Hurston particularly disliked what she regarded as the self-pity of some African-American novelists; she wrote that she refused to accept "the sobbing school of Negrohood who hold that nature somehow has given them a dirty deal." Estranged from the black literary establishment, she worked as a maid and substitute teacher in Florida for the last years of her life.

Their Eyes Were Watching God is the story of a young woman named Janie Starks, whose first two marriages end unhappily but who finds happiness with her third husband. The novel focuses on Janie's interior life and relationships; it was not intended, Hurston wrote in response to her predominantly male critics, as social commentary. She wanted readers to perceive Janie as a complete character, not solely as a diminished victim of racism. Hurston is cited as a heavy influence on more recent authors like Toni Morrison (1931–) and, of course, Alice Walker (1944–).

ADDITIONAL FACTS

1. *Hurston was the only African-American student in her class at Barnard, the prestigious all-women's school in New York City.*

2. *Halle Berry (1968–) starred in a 2005 made-for-TV movie version of* Their Eyes Were Watching God *produced by Oprah Winfrey (1954–).*

3. *Hurston criticized the US Supreme Court's 1954 Brown v. Board of Education desegregation decision, which she felt undermined the tradition and importance of all-black schools.*

★ ★ ★

Woody Guthrie

Singer-songwriter Woody Guthrie (1912–1967) helped popularize the folk music genre in the 1930s and 1940s. During a career cut short by illness, Guthrie wrote more than 1,000 songs. His dry, raspy voice and angry protest lyrics railing against social injustices inspired countless imitators, including a young Bob Dylan (1941–), who visited Guthrie in the 1960s as he lay dying in a New Jersey hospital from a rare genetic brain disease.

 Oklahoma-born Woodrow Wilson Guthrie began performing country-and-western and folk songs in the mid-1930s, after spending several years aimlessly hoboing across the Depression-era United States. His angry songs about foreclosures, debts, and illness reflected the desperate poverty of the Dust Bowl. In Guthrie's famous "Ballad of Pretty Boy Floyd," for instance, he sarcastically compared the notorious robber Pretty Boy Floyd to the banks foreclosing on many farms: "Some will rob you with a six-gun / And some with a fountain pen."

In the late 1930s, Guthrie's songs began to take on a more explicitly political, left-wing bent. Guthrie moved to New York City in 1940, where he was instantly embraced by urban intellectuals thirsting for the all-American "authenticity" provided by his folk songs. That year, he wrote his most well-known song, "This Land Is Your Land." He published his best-selling autobiography, *Bound for Glory*, in 1943.

In the early 1950s, Guthrie's health began to deteriorate mysteriously. Eventually, he was diagnosed with a fatal, incurable neurological disease, Huntington's chorea, and committed to a hospital. He spent the last fifteen years of his life in misery, virtually unable to communicate after 1965. His reputation, however, only grew. During the folk revival of the early 1960s, a new generation of singers led by Dylan resurrected Guthrie's songs for a new generation of fans.

ADDITIONAL FACTS

1. *After Guthrie's death, his widow, Marjorie, set up a foundation to combat Huntington's chorea, the Huntington's Disease Society of America. There is still no cure for the rare disease. Guthrie's mother, Nora, also died of Huntington's.*

2. *Guthrie's son, Arlo (1947–), is also a prominent recording artist who racked up a number of successes during the 1960s, including the famous single "Alice's Restaurant."*

3. *The 1976 film biography* Bound for Glory *starred David Carradine (1936–) as Guthrie.*

★ ★ ★

Eugene V. Debs

Socialist candidate Eugene V. Debs (1855–1926) ran for president of the United States five times, earning hundreds of thousands of votes from supporters dissatisfied with Gilded Age American capitalism. Although Debs never won more than 7 percent of the vote, he was a crucial force in the early years of the American labor movement, and his candidacy in 1908 marked the best-ever showing for a Socialist in the United States.

Eugene Victor Debs was born in Indiana and joined a railroad union, the Brotherhood of Locomotive Firemen, at a young age. He became a union leader and published of the group's magazine, but was jailed after a strike in 1894. In prison, he began reading the works of Karl Marx (1818–1883), the founder of socialism. Shortly after his release, determined to fight for worker's rights in the political arena, Debs made his first run for the White House in 1900. He tried again in 1904, 1908, 1912, and 1920.

Few Socialists actually expected Debs to win, but they hoped to draw attention to the nation's growing economic inequalities and the party's demands for women's suffrage, an end to child labor, and safety regulations for mines and railroads. Arguably, the Socialists were successful, since all three major candidates in the 1912 election touted their commitment to labor issues first embraced by the Socialists.

Debs made his final, quixotic run for the presidency in 1920, when he was again in federal prison, this time for violating the Espionage Act. His imprisonment stemmed from a 1918 speech he gave in Canton, Ohio, attacking American involvement in World War I (1914–1918). After his fiery speech, Debs was arrested for obstructing the war effort, and the US Supreme Court upheld his ten-year jail sentence.

From behind bars, Debs won nearly a million votes and 3.4 percent of the electorate. The victor, Republican Warren G. Harding (1865–1923), pardoned Debs in 1921. His health ruined by incarceration, Debs died in 1926. Although the Socialist Party continues to field candidates for national office, none yet have approached the level of support Debs received.

ADDITIONAL FACTS

1. *Although one of the original founders in 1905 of the Industrial Workers of the World, a famous left-wing union, Debs dropped out of the organization a few years later when it did not commit to nonviolence.*

2. *In the 1908 presidential campaign, Debs's campaign train was nicknamed the Red Special.*

3. *Although permitted by his wardens to release only one written campaign statement per week in the 1920 election, Debs won 919,799 votes and finished third, behind Harding and Democrat James M. Cox (1870–1957).*

★ ★ ★

Treaty of Versailles

President Woodrow Wilson (1856–1924) set sail for France in December 1918, determined to change the world. The first president to make the six-day ocean voyage to Europe during his term in office, Wilson arrived at the peace conference in Paris with an ambitious, idealistic agenda: acceptance of the Fourteen Points, a plan for international cooperation that Wilson hoped would create a lasting peace on a continent ravaged by World War I (1914–1918).

The guiding principle of the Fourteen Points, which Wilson announced to the United States Congress during his 1918 State of the Union address, was self-determination. The defeated Ottoman and Austro-Hungarian Empires both contained many bickering nationalities. Wilson wanted these groups to choose their own futures. The Fourteen Points also envisioned free trade, free navigation of the seas, and an international body called the League of Nations to police world disputes.

Wilson's idealism, however, was considered naïve by the other victorious leaders who joined Wilson at the Paris conference. Compared to the United States, which had entered the war only in 1917, fellow Allies France, Great Britain, and Italy had suffered enormous casualties and destruction. They wanted payback and were annoyed by Wilson's idealistic rhetoric. "Mr. Wilson bores me with his Fourteen Points," the French prime minister reportedly said. "God Almighty has only ten!"

In total, Wilson spent six months in Paris—by far the longest period of time any sitting president has spent outside the United States—but failed to convince the British and French to support his proposals. The treaty, finally signed in the splendid seventeenth-century Palace of Versailles in the Paris suburbs, imposed harsh reparations on Germany and ignored many of Wilson's proposals. The Allies did agree to create a League of Nations, but when Wilson returned home, isolationists in the US Senate torpedoed even this modest achievement. Through its rejection of the Treaty of Versailles, the Senate refused to let the United States join the League of Nations that Wilson had created.

Although humiliated at home and abroad, time would vindicate many of Wilson's positions. Many historians believe that the harsh terms and crushing reparations imposed on Germany caused so much resentment that they paved the way for the rise of Adolf Hitler (1889–1945) in the 1930s and World War II (1939–1941).

ADDITIONAL FACTS

1. *In order to show Wilson the full effects of German brutality, the French invited Wilson to tour the devastated countryside. Wilson refused to go because he preferred not to prejudice the peace negotiations, which further infuriated the French.*

2. *Wilson failed to bring any prominent Republicans with him to France, a move that alienated congressional Republicans and may have contributed to their opposition to the League of Nations.*

3. *In a move freighted with historical significance, the French forced Germany to sign the treaty in the Hall of Mirrors at the Palace of Versailles, where they had surrendered to Germany in 1871.*

★ ★ ★

Susan B. Anthony

In 1906, just a month before her death, a frail Susan B. Anthony (1820–1906) took the stage at a national women's rights convention in Baltimore. After repeating one last time her lifelong goal of equal voting rights, Anthony closed her speech with an emotional tribute to her longtime colleagues in the suffrage movement. "With such women consecrating their lives," she told the delegates, "failure is impossible."

Anthony, for decades the lead organizer of the women's rights movement, had consecrated her own life to the cause from an early age. Born in Massachusetts to a Quaker family, Anthony became involved with the temperance, suffrage, and antislavery movements in the 1850s. After the Civil War (1861–1865), she devoted herself fully to the women's movement, organizing the National Woman Suffrage Association (NWSA) in 1869.

Unlike some other women's rights leaders, Anthony focused her energies almost entirely on winning the right to vote. Through the NWSA, she organized a network of thousands of activists and personally lobbied the United States Congress and state governments to enfranchise women. At the time of her death, four states had granted women the right to vote. Fourteen years after her death, the movement created by Anthony finally won passage of the Nineteenth Amendment, giving women equal voting rights nationwide.

Anthony's indefatigable energy as an organizer helped sustain the momentum for women's rights that began to build after the war. He famous, optimistic words— "failure is impossible"—would become a mantra for succeeding generations of women's rights campaigners.

ADDITIONAL FACTS

1. Some of Anthony's strong-willed nature came from her father, Daniel, who was expelled from his local Quaker church for allowing dancing in his home.

2. Anthony was arrested and fined $100 for voting illegally in the 1872 presidential election, but she refused to pay the fine.

3. Anthony backed Ulysses S. Grant (1822–1885) in the 1872 election, rather than the free-spirited first-ever female candidate, Victoria Woodhull (1838–1927), whom the prudish Anthony viewed with disdain.

★ ★ ★

Sears, Roebuck

The Sears, Roebuck catalog built the American West—literally, in many cases. On easy credit, pioneers could buy an entire mail-order house from the famed Chicago retailer, complete with cans of paint, 750 pounds of nails, and assembly instructions. A major commercial force in the late nineteenth and early twentieth centuries, the Sears mail-order catalog changed the way Americans shopped and provided affordable access to farming supplies, household goods, and the houses themselves for the first generation of settlers in the West.

Simple in concept, the mail-order catalog represented a major improvement over the rural general stores many Americans had relied on previously. By cutting out the local retailer, the mail-order firm offered significantly lower prices. Richard Sears (1863–1914) and Alvah Roebuck (1864–1948) published their first catalog, featuring only watches and jewelry, in 1888, but by 1895, the catalog was 532 pages long and included stoves, guns, bicycles, clothes, shoes, and hundreds of other wares. The passage of the Rural Free Delivery Act of 1896, which extended home delivery of the US Postal Service to rural areas, greatly expanded the company's reach and helped break the stranglehold general stores had on isolated farming regions.

By the early twentieth century, Sears, Roebuck and Co. recorded tens of millions of dollars in annual revenue from its thousands of products. Americans would buy more than 100,000 Sears houses, sold in several models with ritzy-sounding names like Maywood and Whitehall, many of which are still standing.

In historical terms, the publication of the Sears catalog was a key event in the evolution of American consumer culture. For the first time, the catalog made cheap, reliable goods available to a wide segment of the American population. Sears expanded into the retail market when it opened its first department store in 1925. The company was successful for decades, but by the 1990s it had lost its preeminent place in retailing to competitors like Wal-Mart. The famous catalog operation ceased in 1993. Nevertheless, the debut of the trailblazing Sears, Roebuck catalog is considered one of the most important commercial milestones in American business.

ADDITIONAL FACTS

1. *Sears built the tallest building in the United States, Chicago's Sears Tower, as its headquarters in 1973.*

2. *One of the items offered in the first general Sears catalog, published in 1893, was a child's doll priced at forty-five cents.*

3. *Between 1909 and 1912, the company tried unsuccessfully to sell mail-order automobiles.*

★ ★ ★

San Francisco Earthquake of 1906

The massive earthquake that struck San Francisco on the morning of April 18, 1906, nearly destroyed a major American city and is among the worst natural disasters in United States history. About 3,000 people were killed in the quake, which measured about 7.7 on the Richter scale. Until Hurricane Katrina in 2005, the San Francisco earthquake was the costliest disaster in the nation's history, and it remains the nation's deadliest earthquake.

Modern San Francisco was barely sixty years old at the time of the disaster. The city was a jumble of quickly constructed wooden buildings and overcrowded slums. Shoddy construction caused much of the quake damage; indeed, it was the fires that roared through the city in the aftermath of the tembler, rather than the quake itself, that caused the majority of the death and destruction.

At the time, the carnage in San Francisco was unprecedented in the United States and it dealt a profound shock to Americans as details spread across the country by telegraph. By the time the fires were contained four days later, about three-quarters of the buildings in San Francisco had been destroyed. The San Franciscan author Jack London (1876–1916), surveying the damage, exclaimed, "San Francisco is gone."

Fearing chaos, however, city leaders deliberately issued inaccurate statements that minimized the quake's toll. In particular, they downplayed or ignored the quake's impact on Chinatown, which was almost completely destroyed. Within a few years, much of the city had been hastily rebuilt. Today, visible traces of the earthquake are virtually impossible to find in San Francisco.

ADDITIONAL FACTS

1. *Another massive quake hit San Francisco in 1989, but fatalities were much lower, thanks in part to improved building codes.*

2. *President Theodore Roosevelt (1858–1919) declined several foreign offers of assistance, including a large donation from the empress of China.*

3. *Looting began shortly after the earthquake; the mayor issued a declaration the afternoon of the quake allowing police and US soldiers dispatched to the city to shoot miscreants on sight.*

★ ★ ★

John Steinbeck

John Steinbeck (1902–1968) wrote seventeen novels and won the Nobel Prize for Literature in 1962 in recognition of his lifetime achievement. His greatest enduring legacy, however, may be a single book Steinbeck published in 1939, *The Grapes of Wrath*. A sensitive portrait of the fictional Joads, an Oklahoma family afflicted by the Great Depression of the 1930s, the novel was an immediate sensation that outraged readers with its stark, dramatic depictions of American poverty.

Steinbeck was born in Salinas, California, and attended Stanford University. He never graduated, however, and ended up working as a handyman at a lodge near Lake Tahoe, where he wrote his first book, *Cup of Gold* (1929). The book sold only 1,500 copies, but it launched Steinbeck's literary career. A conscientious writer, he wrote prodigiously throughout the 1930s and published one of his best-known early works, *Of Mice and Men*, in 1937.

In 1938, Steinbeck began *The Grapes of Wrath*. Early in the writing process, he realized the new novel's huge potential. "If I could do this book properly it would be one of the really fine books and a truly American book," he confided to his journal. Inspired by the plight of farmworkers near his native Salinas, the novel follows the Joad family on their migration from Oklahoma, where they lost their farm to foreclosure. After many hardships, the family finally reaches California but is mistreated by farm owners. Disillusioned, the young character Tom Joad experiences a political awakening. In one of the most memorable passages in the novel, he dedicates himself to the cause of helping poor families like his own. "Wherever they's a fight so hungry people can eat, I'll be there," he says. "Wherever they's a cop beatin' up a guy, I'll be there."

Although farm owners heatedly objected to their unflattering depiction in the novel and critics called Steinbeck a communist for questioning the virtues of capitalism, *The Grapes of Wrath* was an enormous hit. A US Senate investigation provoked by the book largely backed up Steinbeck's claims about the conditions on California farms. Although he never again matched the popular success and social impact of *The Grapes of Wrath*, Steinbeck published several more novels, including *Cannery Row* in 1945 and *East of Eden* in 1952, and wrote a number of screenplays.

ADDITIONAL FACTS

1. *After* The Grapes of Wrath, *Steinbeck was wrongly believed to be a communist—even by many actual communists, whom he disappointed by enthusiastically backing American involvement in the Vietnam War (1957–1975).*

2. *Steinbeck had notoriously small handwriting; his manuscript for* The Grapes of Wrath *was only 165 pages, but the typeset book was more than 600 pages.*

3. *The title of* The Grapes of Wrath *was chosen by Steinbeck's first wife, Carol, from the song "Battle Hymn of the Republic," the words of which were written by the American reformer Julia Ward Howe (1819–1910) in 1861.*

★ ★ ★

Cary Grant

In 1931, Paramount Studios signed a handsome twenty-seven-year-old actor from England to a movie contract. Tall, tan, and debonair, with an unforgettable cleft chin, the new acquisition had all the looks of a successful leading man. But there was a problem. His name, Archibald Leach, sounded terrible. So the studio gave him a new name, and thus did Cary Grant (1904–1986) begin his incredible Hollywood career.

Born in the English port city of Bristol, Leach ran away from home as a child and joined a traveling acrobatic troupe, where he learned stilt walking and other carnival tricks. He toured extensively in England and hit the vaudeville circuit in the United States for the first time in 1920. He also appeared in a number of stage musicals before making the leap to the silver screen.

In an ironic twist on his humble beginnings, in Hollywood Grant was often cast as a suave, upper-crust gentleman. He starred as an upright captain alongside legendary film tart Mae West (1892–1980) in his first leading role, *She Done Him Wrong*, in 1933. In an era of strict censorship, West famously teased Grant, "Why don't you come up sometime and see me?"—a line that some considered scandalously suggestive at the time.

Over his long career, Grant was nominated for an Academy Award as Best Actor twice—for his leading roles in *Penny Serenade* (1941) and *None but the Lonely Heart* (1944)—and almost all of his more than 70 movies were commercial successes. He played in thrillers like *North by Northwest* (1959) and lighter fare like *The Philadelphia Story* (1940). He often performed his own stunts, drawing on his acrobatic training, and he never played a "bad guy" in any of his films.

Grant retired in 1966 and obstinately refused huge offers to return to the screen. He was awarded a lifetime achievement Oscar in 1970.

ADDITIONAL FACTS

1. *Although he often played a breezy, happy-go-lucky character on screen, in real life Grant suffered from depression and was treated with LSD before the drug was criminalized.*

2. *Grant became an American citizen in 1942.*

3. *Grant had a turbulent personal life and was married five times.*

★ ★ ★

Theodore Roosevelt

Theodore Roosevelt (1858–1919) was the twenty-sixth president of the United States and is widely considered one of the most influential politicians of the early twentieth century. Elected as vice president in 1900, Roosevelt took office in 1901 after the assassination of President William McKinley (1843–1901). Roosevelt was re-elected in 1904 on the Republican ticket. Roosevelt's progressive views on economic issues eventually caused him to leave the GOP, however, and he ran unsuccessfully for a third term in 1912 as a third-party candidate.

Born to a prominent New York family, Roosevelt was already nationally famous as a historian and war hero before his election as vice president. He had written several well-received books and led a cavalry unit called the "Rough Riders" during the Spanish-American War.

In office, Roosevelt's image of youthful vigor—he was an avid hunter and outdoorsman—made him enormously popular. In domestic affairs, Roosevelt embraced many progressive causes, including stricter enforcement of antitrust laws to break up corporate monopolies. He also signed legislation creating thousands of square miles of national parks.

On the international front, Roosevelt entered the White House at a time when the United States was pondering its role in world affairs as the new century dawned. As president, Roosevelt enthusiastically backed the expansion of American military power. Under the credo "speak softly and carry a big stick," Roosevelt expanded the size of the Navy and took on the role of world statesman by serving as a mediator in foreign conflicts. He also backed the construction of the Panama Canal, an enormous undertaking with both economic and military benefits.

After leaving the White House in 1909, Roosevelt became disenchanted with his hand-picked successor, William Howard Taft, whom he viewed as too conservative, and ran for president against Taft and Democrat Woodrow Wilson (1856–1924) in 1912. Roosevelt survived an assassination attempt during one of his campaign speeches but lost to Wilson.

ADDITIONAL FACTS

1. *The teddy bear was named after Roosevelt following a famous incident on a hunting expedition when he refused to shoot a bear cub.*

2. *Roosevelt was the first president to invite an African-American, Booker T. Washington (1856–1915), to dine at the White House; the invitation was issued in 1901.*

3. *Roosevelt, later running for president as the candidate of the Progressive Party, was shot by a would-be assassin at a campaign rally on October 14, 1912, but delivered his speech anyway. His Democratic opponent in that year's election, Woodrow Wilson (1856–1924), stopped campaigning for ten days in deference until Roosevelt was able to resume his campaign.*

★ ★ ★

Lend-Lease Act

At the beginning of World War II in 1939, US President Franklin D. Roosevelt (1882–1945) sympathized with the British in their fight against Adolf Hitler's Nazi Germany. However, popular and congressional opposition to American involvement in the new war was strong. With sad memories of World War I (1914–1918) still fresh, many Americans wanted no part in another bloody European war.

But the British, standing virtually alone against Hitler's war machine, were desperate for help. Even if the United States wouldn't enter the war, Roosevelt decided, it could still provide the British with ships and ammunition. In March 1941, Roosevelt convinced the US Congress to pass the Lend-Lease Act, which allowed Roosevelt to "lend" supplies to Great Britain while remaining technically neutral in the war against Germany.

In Britain, news of the Lend-Lease Act was met with elation. British Prime Minister Winston Churchill (1874–1965) called the law "Hitler's death warrant." Within three hours of the bill's signing, the United States had transferred twenty-eight ships to the Royal Navy, the first of what would be billions of dollars in aid.

The bill's isolationist opponents feared that the Lend-Lease Act would put the United States on an irreversible course to war. They were correct: in the summer and fall of 1941, the official neutrality of the United States faded into outright military support for Britain. American ships transporting war supplies to Britain traded fire with German submarines, and American marines were sent to Iceland to relieve British forces there.

That December, Germany's ally Japan attacked Pearl Harbor in Hawaii, and the United States finally entered the war. For the rest of the conflict, American convoys of food, weapons, and supplies steamed across the Atlantic. In total, the "arsenal of democracy" exported more than $50 billion in aid to its allies during the war.

ADDITIONAL FACTS

1. *In a symbolic move, the Lend-Lease Act was numbered House Resolution 1776 when it was introduced into Congress.*

2. *After the war, attempts to collect repayment of the "loans" to Britain and the Soviet Union proved controversial. In all, the United States spent $50 billion and got about $8 billion back. In 1994, Russia began to pay off the Lend-Lease debts of the former Soviet Union, which had refused to do so. Britain repaid its last Lend-Lease debts in December 2006.*

3. *Roosevelt and Churchill had a personal connection—they were seventh cousins.*

★ ★ ★

Lynching

For nearly a century after the Civil War (1861–1865), mob killings of African-Americans, usually by hanging, remained a relatively common occurrence in the South. These lynchings, often extremely gruesome, were intended to terrorize and intimidate the black population and maintain white supremacy. Local authorities rarely stopped lynch mobs or punished their leaders, lending the practice the government's tacit support.

In total, about 3,500 African-Americans were lynched in the reign of terror between the Civil War and 1960, according to records kept by Tuskegee University. Victims were typically young black men suspected of contact with a white woman. Although lynching occurred across the nation, the vast majority were in rural areas of the Deep South. The local Ku Klux Klan often, although not always, organized the lynch mobs.

Lynching, a homegrown American form of terrorism, was unimaginably barbaric. Since the purpose of the attack was to make an example of the victim and intimidate other blacks, the bodies of victims were often burned, dismembered, castrated, and then shown to the public. Graphic photographs of the practice often show smiling whites next to the charred remains of their victim.

In her famous song about lynching, "Strange Fruit," the African-American singer Billie Holiday (1915–1959) described the savage ritual:

> Southern trees bear strange fruit,
> Blood on the leaves and blood at the root,
> Black bodies swinging in the southern breeze,
> Strange fruit hanging from the poplar trees.
> Pastoral scene of the gallant south,
> The bulging eyes and the twisted mouth,
> Scent of magnolias, sweet and fresh,
> Then the sudden smell of burning flesh.

Since state courts in the South rarely punished members of lynch mobs, civil rights groups repeatedly asked Congress to make lynching a federal crime. President Franklin Roosevelt (1882–1945) declined to push antilynching legislation in the 1930s out of fear of alienating southern Democrats whose support he needed in Congress to pass his New Deal program of economic reforms during the Great Depression. The federal government finally began pursuing lynch mob members after World War II (1939–1945), and the number of lynchings declined precipitously.

ADDITIONAL FACTS

1. *A moving—and graphic—compilation of lynching photos can be found at www.withoutsanctuary.com.*

2. *The worst year of lynchings was 1892, when 231 were recorded.*

3. *The term "lynching" probably originated with Charles Lynch, a Virginia planter of the 1700s who led mobs of his neighbors in attacks against British sympathizers and others who plundered their property.*

★ ★ ★

Wright Brothers

On a windy December day in 1903, the brothers Orville Wright (1871–1948) and Wilbur Wright (1867–1912) invited spectators to a remote beach at Kitty Hawk, North Carolina, for a peek at their engine-powered flying machine. Few took the pair of eccentric Ohio inventors seriously. Only five witnesses braved the cold weather to watch their twelve-second flight, the first successful demonstration of an invention that would have a profound effect on the twentieth century—the airplane.

The Wright brothers were born in the Midwest to a strict, religious father. In the early 1890s, they went into business together running a bicycle shop in Dayton, Ohio, and began manufacturing their own line of bicycles in 1895. Seeking a new challenge, the duo began their experiments with aeronautics in 1899.

By the late nineteenth century, when the Wrights first entered the field, many of the basics of flight were understood by physicists. Building a practical, engine-powered flying machine, however, had proved elusive in both Europe and the United States. With little formal education, the Wrights began reading aeronautics treatises and testing their own designs at Kitty Hawk in 1900. Using extensive trial-and-error methods, they developed a primitive steering mechanism and designed a contoured wing that would keep the aircraft aloft.

The flight of the Kitty Hawk airplane marked the beginning of the age of flight. Forming a company to manufacture the invention, the Wrights sold several planes to the US Army, which had grasped their military promise of flight after overcoming initial skepticism. However, the Wrights themselves never managed to profit greatly from their famous creation. Wilbur died of typhoid fever in 1912, and Orville sold the brothers' company in 1915.

ADDITIONAL FACTS

1. *The Kitty Hawk airplane made three more flights after its first one on December 17, 1903; the best lasted 59 seconds and covered 852 feet.*

2. *It is believed that only five of the roughly 300 bicycles manufactured by the Wrights are still in existence; they are considered priceless collectibles.*

3. *Army Lieutenant Thomas O. Selfridge became the first airplane accident fatality on September 17, 1908, when a plane piloted by Orville Wright experienced propeller problems and crashed in a field. Selfridge died of a fractured skull several hours later.*

★ ★ ★

Pine Ridge

The isolated American Indian reservation at Pine Ridge, South Dakota, is neither the largest nor the most populous reservation in the United States. Because of its uniquely tragic history, however, Pine Ridge has become one of the most notorious symbols of the plight of Native Americans in the twentieth century. Belonging to the Lakota Sioux tribe, the 2.2-million-acre reservation remains one of the poorest places in the nation and a reminder of the scarred history of the American West.

Modern Indian reservations were first created in the 1850s as a homeland for tribes evicted from the Southeast. The federal government typically forced tribal groups onto remote and undesirable tracts of land that had been bypassed by white settlers. The Sioux, inhabitants of the northern Great Plains, were the last tribe to offer significant military resistance to American expansion; the massacre of Sioux civilians at Wounded Knee in 1890 is often cited as the last armed clash between Native Americans and the US Army in the frontier period.

For many Native Americans, life on the reservation—already challenging due to poverty, isolation, alcoholism, and the hostility of their white neighbors—has been further complicated by harmful federal policies of the nineteenth and twentieth centuries. Starting in the 1880s, the federal government's policy toward Native Americans encouraged assimilation and the breakup of communal lands, which undermined efforts to maintain ancient tribal cultures into the twentieth century. Although the government eventually abandoned the assimiliationist policies, they continue to cause resentment.

Anger toward the federal government culminated in 1973 at Pine Ridge with a seventy-one-day standoff between the FBI and members of the American Indian Movement, an activist group that occupied Wounded Knee to protest federal neglect and mistreatment. The occupation, which put Wounded Knee back in the headlines nearly a century after the massacre, ended only after two Indians and two federal agents were killed. The reservation remains one of the poorest places in the nation, with rates of unemployment, infant mortality, and suicide that greatly exceed national averages.

ADDITIONAL FACTS

1. *One of the most famous books ever written about American Indians, Dee Brown's* Bury My Heart at Wounded Knee *(1970), takes its name from the site of the 1890 massacre.*

2. *President Bill Clinton (1946–) became the first sitting president to visit the reservation in 1999.*

3. *Bison, long the staple food of the Sioux, were nearly exterminated by whites but reintroduced to the Pine Ridge reservation in 2004.*

★ ★ ★

Gone with the Wind

One of the best-selling American novels of the twentieth century, *Gone with the Wind* (1936) by Margaret Mitchell (1900–1949) is an epic tale of an aristocratic Georgia family's hardships during and after the Civil War (1861–1865). The book quickly became a cultural phenomenon, winning the Pulitzer Prize for fiction and inspiring the hugely popular 1939 film version.

Highly sentimental and melodramatic, *Gone with the Wind* follows the travails of the O'Haras, a rich plantation-owning family, during and after the war. Deprived of their slaves following emancipation and forced to pay taxes on their plantation, the O'Haras are reduced to working for a living, much to the chagrin of the main character, the beautiful and bratty Scarlett O'Hara.

Along with its immense popularity, the novel has been controversial for decades because of its fond depiction of slavery and blatant use of offensive racial stereotypes. For instance, at one point Scarlett compares African-Americans to "apes."

The novel was a product of the "lost cause" romanticism embraced by many Southerners of Mitchell's generation. In the early twentieth century as memories of the war faded, many Southern writers recalled the antebellum and Confederate eras with great nostalgia that minimized or denied the evils of slavery. Mitchell herself had contributed to the lost cause literature by penning worshipful profiles of Confederate generals that were published during the 1920s in newspapers in her native Atlanta.

Gone with the Wind, however, was the only novel Mitchell would ever complete. She began work on a sequel but was killed in an automobile accident in Atlanta. The book is still in print and garners strong sales. A parody of the book's rampant racism, *The Wind Done Gone*, was published in 2001.

ADDITIONAL FACTS

1. *The movie's most famous line—"Frankly, my dear, I don't give a damn"—was taken almost verbatim from Mitchell's novel.*

2. *In an indication of its continued popularity, a hardcover edition issued for the book's fiftieth anniversary in 1986 was a New York Times bestseller.*

3. *A sequel authorized by Mitchell's estate,* Scarlett, *written by Alexandra Ripley (1934–2004) was published in 1991 to scathing reviews. Still, it sold 2.5 million copies.*

★ ★ ★

Ansel Adams

In 1916, a San Francisco teenager named Ansel Adams (1902–1984) arrived in Yosemite National Park on a sightseeing trip. For the fourteen-year-old Adams, a precocious boy with an artistic bent, the tour would be a life-changing experience. Captivated by the rugged splendor of Yosemite, the trip sparked Adams's lifelong quest to capture the scenery of the American West on camera.

Over the next fifty years, Adams returned repeatedly to Yosemite Valley, where he made some of the most memorable nature photographs in American history. He also traveled through the national parks of the West, taking pictures of mountains, lakes, and soaring desert vistas. At the time of his death, the *New York Times* called Adams the most famous photographer in the United States.

Indeed, Adams's trademark artistic style is instantly recognizable. His black-and-white photographs are unusually crisp and detailed. They rarely show people, houses, or any other sign of human presence. The composition of his photos, which encompass huge mountains beyond any human scale, seem to suggest both the awesome majesty of nature and the loneliness of the wilderness.

An ardent environmentalist, Adams explicitly linked his photography to conservation efforts in the West. He joined the Sierra Club at age seventeen, shortly after his first trip to Yosemite, and served on the group's board of directors for decades. His photographs helped build awareness of the natural beauty of the West and also the threat posed by pollution and lumbering. In an appropriate tribute to one of the best-loved American artists, a peak in California's Sierra Nevada was named for Adams after his death.

ADDITIONAL FACTS

1. *In his youth, Adams was trained as a classical pianist and made a living playing music before hitting it big with photography.*

2. *In 1944, in protest of the internment of Japanese-Americans, Adams published a book of photographs from one of the camps titled* Born Free and Equal.

3. *He was friends with the painter Georgia O'Keeffe (1887–1986) and was often a guest at her home in Taos, New Mexico.*

★ ★ ★

Woodrow Wilson

President Woodrow Wilson (1856–1924) led the United States to victory in World War I (1914–1918), the first American war fought on European soil, but failed to realize his idealistic goal of creating a durable international peace following the conflict.

Born in Virginia and raised in small towns across the South, Wilson was deeply affected by his boyhood memories of carnage from the Civil War (1861–1865). When World War I broke out in Europe in 1914, Wilson initially proclaimed American neutrality. However, the United States entered the war three years later on the side of Great Britain, France, and Italy.

From the beginning, Wilson infused his argument for war with a sense of high moral purpose. The purpose of fighting, he said, was not just to protect American interests but to destroy the old tyrannical empires of Europe and bring freedom to the world. Wilson outlined this vision in his famous Fourteen Points, an idealistic list of goals for the postwar world that included decolonization, disarmament, and the establishment of international bodies to prevent future conflicts.

After the Allied victory, however, those goals proved impossible to realize. At the lengthy treaty negotiations in Paris, many of Wilson's suggestions were simply ignored by his country's war allies. Over Wilson's objections, the Treaty of Paris harshly punished Germany, leading to widespread anger and resentment among the German people.

As a concession to Wilson, the treaty did endorse his cherished idea of an international League of Nations, a forum for countries to air their differences in a peaceful fashion. However, in a cruel twist for Wilson, isolationists in the United States Senate refused to accept the treaty, thus preventing US membership in the League of Nations. Shortly after returning from Paris in 1919, Wilson suffered a stroke. He died not long after departing the White House in 1921.

ADDITIONAL FACTS

1. *In 1919, Wilson vetoed the act establishing Prohibition, but Congress overrode his veto, and alcohol was banned in the United States between 1920 and 1933.*

2. *Wilson's wife, Ellen (1860–1914), died in the middle of Wilson's first term, in August 1914. He remarried sixteen months later to Edith Bolling Galt (1872–1961).*

3. *Two US presidents, Wilson and Dwight Eisenhower (1890–1969), served as the president of an Ivy League college before their election to the White House. Wilson led Princeton for eight years, and the university later named an institute at the school after him.*

★ ★ ★

Pearl Harbor

The Japanese bombing of Pearl Harbor in the US territory of Hawaii on December 7, 1941, triggered the belated entrance of the United States into World War II (1939–1945). In the short term, the Pearl Harbor bombing was a massive military setback for the United States. Twelve American warships were sunk and many others were badly damaged, and a staggering 2,403 service members lost their lives in the sneak attack. It would take months for the United States military to regroup from Pearl Harbor and begin attacking the Japanese in the Pacific. In the long term, however, the Pearl Harbor bombing was a serious Japanese mistake. As the historian Samuel Eliot Morison wrote, "One can search military history in vain . . . for an operation more fatal to the aggressor."

Prior to the attack, relations between the United States and imperial Japan had deteriorated throughout the 1930s. Japan was ruled by a militaristic elite bent on expanding the nation's influence throughout Asia, especially in China, which Japanese troops had invaded in 1931. Leading Japanese politicians, including its prime minister, General Hideki Tojo (1884–1948), regarded the United States as an obstacle to Japanese ambitions in the region. The United States, meanwhile, restricted the export of oil and military supplies to Japan. The two countries edged toward war in the summer and fall of 1941.

Although American military officials knew a sneak attack was possible amid worsening relations with Japan, commanders at Pearl Harbor were taken by surprise at 7:55 a.m. on December 7, when the first Japanese warplanes appeared in the skies over Hawaii. Almost immediately, a well-aimed Japanese bomb hit the battleship USS *Arizona*, causing massive loss of life among its crew. Of the battleships berthed at Pearl Harbor, four were sunk and the rest heavily damaged, dealing a significant blow to the Pacific Fleet. Fortuitously, all three American aircraft carriers in the Pacific were at sea on the morning of the attack and escaped damage.

The national response to Pearl Harbor was overwhelming. Before Pearl Harbor, some Americans still favored neutrality in World War II. But the attack by Japan aroused the public's wrath, and Americans quickly united behind the war. Cries of "Remember Pearl Harbor" resonated deeply with the American people, who were particularly enraged by the sneaky nature of the bombing.

ADDITIONAL FACTS

1. *After Pearl Harbor, not only the United States but also a number of Latin American countries declared war on Japan. Together with the British and Soviet empires, the forces arrayed against the Axis powers led by Germany suddenly amounted to roughly half the world's population.*

2. *Two of the surviving ships from the Pearl Harbor attack, the* Pennsylvania *and the* Nevada, *were later used as test targets for atomic bombs in the waters near Bikini Atoll in the Pacific.*

3. *The Japanese premier who ordered the Pearl Harbor bombing, General Tojo, was captured by the Americans after the war and hanged as a war criminal in 1948.*

★ ★ ★

Ellis Island

Ellis Island, located in the middle of New York Harbor near the Statue of Liberty, was the gateway to the United States of America for more than twelve million immigrants between 1892 and 1954. At its peak in 1907, the facility handled more than a million new arrivals, most of them immigrants from Italy, Ireland, and eastern Europe. In an era when virtually anyone could become an American citizen—except the Chinese—this massive infusion from Europe changed the face of the United States.

By law, only the poorest immigrants, those who had crossed the Atlantic in the third-class "steerage" section of the ship, were required to go through inspections at Ellis Island. Passengers who could pay for first- or second-class accommodations, officials reasoned, were not expected to cause problems.

For about 98 percent of immigrants, the inspections at Ellis Island were a mere formality, lasting an average of three to five hours. However, a small number were refused entry to the United States for medical reasons or because immigration officials suspected they would become "wards of the state." These unlucky few were deported back to their home countries, giving Ellis Island its nickname, "Island of Tears."

The first two decades of the twentieth century witnessed the highest levels ever of immigration to the United States and helped create the image of the country as a "nation of immigrants." The arrival of so many poor immigrants from predominantly Catholic countries, however, also provoked a backlash. In 1924, the US Congress limited immigration from southern and eastern Europe, and the number of immigrants arriving at Ellis Island plummeted sharply. Ellis Island remained open until 1954, when a Norwegian sailor was the last immigrant processed there. Now a national park, Ellis Island has been partially restored to its former glory, and the public is welcome to visit the Ellis Island Immigration Museum housed in the renovated main building.

ADDITIONAL FACTS

1. *Ellis Island immigrants included comedian Bob Hope (1903–2003) and director Frank Capra (1897–1991).*

2. *According to the federal government, more than 40 percent of the current American population is descended from Ellis Island immigrants.*

3. *The island was named after Samuel Ellis, its owner in the 1770s.*

★ ★ ★

Samuel Gompers

Samuel Gompers (1850–1924), the founder of the American Federation of Labor (AFL), is considered one of the fathers of the American labor movement. A cigar maker by trade, Gompers formed the AFL in 1886 to fight for higher wages, job security, and workplace safety during the Gilded Age. Union organizers in the late nineteenth century had few legal protections and faced considerable hostility, and often violence, from owners, but Gompers successively moved unions into the nation's economic mainstream and enlisted millions of new workers into the labor movement.

Gompers was born in London, went to work rolling cigars with his father at age ten, and immigrated to New York City with his family at age thirteen. He joined his first union, the United Cigar Workers, in 1864, when only fourteen.

At the time, the American labor movement was still in its formative stages. However, the glaring inequalities of the Gilded Age led to a far more confrontational generation of unionists. Despite the massive wealth created by the Industrial Revolution, wages actually fell throughout the 1870s, and ruthless tycoons like Andrew Carnegie (1835–1919) aggressively opposed their workers' efforts to organize.

Gompers rose through the ranks of the cigar-makers' union and helped form an umbrella group of unions, the Federation of Organized Trades and Labor Unions, in 1881. The group was reorganized into the AFL in 1886, and Gompers was elected the first president. The union pushed for higher wages, eight-hour workdays, and legal protection for the right to unionize.

During his nearly forty years at the helm of the AFL, Gompers worked to expand the union while containing the more radical elements in his movement. Gompers opposed violence and was leery of socialism; his perceived moderation led to the creation of several rival unions, including the famous International Workers of the World. By working within the system, Gompers became a force within the Democratic Party, and he was an advisor to President Woodrow Wilson (1856–1924) on labor issues during and after World War I (1914–1918). By the time of Gompers's death, the AFL had three million members—a vast increase from 50,000 in 1886.

ADDITIONAL FACTS

1. *Gompers played a minor role at the Versailles peace conference that ended World War I, helping to found an international labor group.*

2. *The AFL merged with the second biggest union umbrella group, the Congress of Industrial Organizations (CIO), in 1955.*

3. *American entrance into World War I divided labor leaders; Gompers supported the war and worked to deliver union support for Wilson's war effort.*

★ ★ ★

Annexation of Hawaii

In 1893, a contingent of 162 United States Marines from the USS *Boston* landed in Hawaii and overthrew Queen Liliuokalani, the local ruler. Five years later, the Pacific archipelago was officially annexed to the United States. The American takeover of Hawaii is often cited as the first major episode of American imperialism and a precursor to the expansionist foreign policy of the United States in the early twentieth century.

Before 1887, Hawaii was ruled by an absolute monarchy based in the Iolani Palace in Honolulu. A revolution in that year, backed by European and American businessmen on the islands, limited the ruler's powers but left the monarchy intact. Queen Liliuokalani (1838–1917), who inherited the throne after the death of her brother, King Kalakaua (1836–1891), antagonized Europeans and some indigenous Hawaiians by attempting to restore the monarchy's dictatorial powers.

The exact circumstances of Queen Liliuokalani's overthrow on January 17, 1893, are disputed. However, a congressional investigation launched later that year concluded that the American ambassador to Hawaii, John L. Stevens (1820–1895), had improperly summoned the marines into a sovereign country and forced the queen to abdicate. US President Grover Cleveland (1837–1908), who opposed the annexation of Hawaii and was more sympathetic to native rights than many of his contemporaries, proposed a compromise that would put the queen back on her throne in exchange for amnesty for the coup planners. Liliuokalani wanted the plotters executed and refused the offer.

With the archipelago's status in limbo, a Republic of Hawaii was formed the next year. In 1896, a pro-annexation candidate, William McKinley (1843–1901), was elected to the White House. With Cleveland out of the way, the islands were annexed as a United States possession in 1898. Hawaii became a US territory in 1900 and then a US state in 1959. In a 1993 resolution on the 100th anniversary of the coup, the US Congress and President Bill Clinton (1946–) officially apologized for overthrowing Liliuokalani.

ADDITIONAL FACTS

1. *The first people to live in Hawaii arrived about 2,000 years ago from Polynesia.*

2. *The first European to visit Hawaii was British navy captain James Cook (1728–1779), who arrived in 1778 and named them the Sandwich Islands in honor of an English noble, the Earl of Sandwich.*

3. *Hawaii is not the westernmost point in the United States; the western tip of Alaska's Aleutian Islands extends farther west.*

★ ★ ★

Richard Wright

Richard Wright (1908–1960) was the first African-American novelist to achieve widespread critical acclaim and commercial success with his 1940 book, *Native Son*. The novel, a harrowing story of a black Chicagoan named Bigger Thomas who is arrested after accidentally killing a white woman, was the first book by an African-American author selected for the Book-of-the-Month Club, and it sold hundreds of thousands of copies. Wright's commercial success made him an extremely influential figure in American literature, and he used his influence to challenge black writers to inject more social realism into their fiction. His autobiography *Black Boy* (1945), released after the author went into self-imposed exile in France, was also a bestseller.

 Wright was born in poverty on a plantation in Natchez, Mississippi, the grandson of slaves. His father abandoned the family when Wright was five, and he was raised by other relatives. During the great migration of Southern blacks to the North in the early 1900s, Wright moved first to Memphis and later to Chicago. He published his first book, a collection of short stories that was based on his Mississippi upbringing, called *Uncle Tom's Children*, in 1938.

For Wright, politics and literature were inseparable. He had joined the Communist Party in 1932, and he heeded the party's insistence that writers use fiction as a vehicle for social criticism and agitation. Wright is one the most famous authors of "protest literature" in American history, and he used his literary criticism to attack authors like Zora Neale Hurston who did not root their novels in social protest. Wright's approach has been criticized by other authors, however, including Hurston, who wanted to place a greater emphasis on storytelling and felt less concerned with politics. The backlash against Wright's unstintingly political literature grew in the 1950s after he quit the Communist Party and moved to Europe.

ADDITIONAL FACTS

1. *A successful Broadway version of* Native Son *was produced in 1941 under the direction of Orson Welles (1915–1985).*

2. *Wright himself starred as Bigger Thomas in a film version of the book made in Argentina in 1951.*

3. *His 1953 novel* The Outsider *was praised in France as the first American existentialist novel.*

★ ★ ★

Casablanca

Casablanca, a motion picture starring Humphrey Bogart (1899–1957) and Ingrid Bergman (1915–1982), was released in 1942, in the midst of World War II (1939–1945). The movie, set in the African port city of Casablanca, won three Academy Awards, including the Oscar for Best Picture, and is one of the best-loved films of the twentieth century. War movie, love story, and comedy rolled into one, the film produced some of Hollywood's most memorable and oft-quoted lines, including "Here's looking at you, kid," "Round up the usual suspects," and "I think this is the beginning of a beautiful friendship."

The filming of the movie began in 1941, before the United States had actually entered World War II. As many critics have pointed out, the plot of the movie, which centers on European refugees stranded in Casablanca on their way to the United States, was wildly implausible. Based on a play called *Everybody Comes to Rick's*, the script contains numerous factual inaccuracies and inconsistencies—none of which have detracted from the film's lasting sentimental appeal.

Most of the movie is set within Rick's Café Americain, an expatriate hangout owned by the world-weary and cynical Rick Blaine, played by Bogart. Bergman plays an old flame of Rick's who reenters his life unexpectedly. The cast also includes memorable performances by Peter Lorre (1904–1964) as a small-time forger, Sydney Greenstreet (1879–1954) as Casablanca's criminal kingpin, and Claude Rains (1889–1967) as the city's corrupt French police chief.

Warner Brothers, the studio that made *Casablanca*, had no inkling that the movie would be such an enormous success. The directing of the film by Michael Curtiz, who won an Oscar as Best Director, is thoroughly conventional. But the combination of the buoyant script, Bogart's tough-guy acting, and a famous emotional climax produced one of Hollywood's most enduring films ever. As the film critic Roger Ebert has written, "the greatness of *Casablanca* was largely the result of happy chance."

ADDITIONAL FACTS

1. *A 1990 remake,* Havana, *starring Robert Redford (1937–) and directed by Sydney Pollack (1934–), was nominated for two Oscars.*

2. *There is no such thing as a "letter of transit," a plot device that was invented by the screenwriters.*

3. *The grandson of one of the screenwriters, Philip G. Epstein (1909–1952), is Boston Red Sox general manager Theo Epstein (1973–).*

★ ★ ★

Jane Addams

Social worker, Nobel Peace Prize winner, and pacifist leader Jane Addams (1860–1935) organized volunteer efforts in the slums of Chicago in the 1890s and early 1900s, drawing attention to the horrors of urban poverty, and later spearheaded domestic opposition to the United States' entering World War I (1914–1918). Her famous 1910 book *Twenty Years at Hull House* exposed to a wide audience the rampant malnourishment, alcoholism, and health problems in American cities. Urban reformers, influenced by Addams, successfully pushed for government programs to clean up the Dickensian conditions in many American slums. Later in life, Addams became a vocal leader of the antiwar movement, an extremely unpopular stance at the time. In recognition of her volunteer efforts and antiwar work, she won the Nobel Peace Prize in 1931.

 Born in Illinois, Addams was the daughter of a local Republican politician who had been an ally of Abraham Lincoln in state politics. Addams was a lifelong Republican and regarded Lincoln and her politician father as personal heroes. Addams and a friend, Ellen Starr, founded Hull House, a community center in Chicago, in 1889. Inspired by a similar experiment in England, the purpose of Hull House was to help struggling families in the city's worst slums. The center provided medical care, kindergarten classes, and meeting space for clubs. Eventually it expanded to include an art gallery, coffeehouse, gym, library, and museum.

Addams's work at Hull House made her a national celebrity and a moral authority on the nation's social ills. As a result of her fame, she became a leader in national efforts to improve prisons and education.

When World War I began, Addams actively campaigned against American entrance into the war. Her efforts made her so unpopular that she was expelled from the Daughters of the American Revolution. Horrified by the war, Addams became an assistant to Herbert Hoover (1874–1964) in his campaign to distribute food supplies in Europe, and she later endorsed Hoover in his 1928 bid for the presidency.

ADDITIONAL FACTS

1. *Although Addams was a Republican, she broke ranks with the party to second the nomination of Theodore Roosevelt (1858–1919) at the 1912 Progressive Party convention.*

2. *Among her many accomplishments is that Addams convinced government leaders in Chicago to create a juvenile court in 1899, allowing children accused of crimes to be tried separately from adults.*

3. *Addams was the first woman to be granted an honorary degree from Yale.*

★ ★ ★

World War II on the Home Front

The period of American involvement in World War II (1941–1945) was a time of enormous sacrifice for the American people. As millions of soldiers fought in Europe and the Pacific, the public was asked to endure unprecedented hardships, including rationing of food, gas, rubber, metal, and other supplies. The experience of the war would leave a profound mark on American society and helped to set the stage for many of the social changes that would accelerate in the 1950s and 1960s.

Widespread mobilization began immediately after the Japanese attack on Pearl Harbor in 1941. In all, a total of about 15 million men entered the Armed Forces during the conflict, and about 400,000 American service members were killed in Europe and Asia.

At home, the war placed huge demands on American workers. To fill the jobs left vacant by men who joined the Armed Forces, many women entered the workforce for the first time. The famous "Rosie the Riveter" poster is one of the most well-known icons that reflected the new role women played in society during the war. The demand for labor at factories in the North also fueled the migration of African-Americans out of the South, a demographic shift known as the "Great Migration."

Indeed, the effect of World War II on race relations was far-reaching. Wartime required whites and African-Americans to work and fight alongside each other to an unprecedented degree. At home, many Americans became painfully aware of the deep contradiction of fighting bigotry abroad while permitting Jim Crow segregation in the United States.

With Europe in ruins at the end of World War II, the United States was left as the most powerful nation on earth. At home, the experience of the war helped plant the seeds of the civil rights and feminist movements, which would gain force in the second half of the twentieth century.

ADDITIONAL FACTS

1. *Congress allowed women to join the regular US Army for the first time in World War II. Although they did not serve in combat roles, sixteen women were killed in action during the war and eighty-three were taken prisoner.*

2. *The commissioner of Major League Baseball offered to suspend the league for the duration of the war, but President Franklin D. Roosevelt (1882–1945) insisted the games be played for the sake of national morale.*

3. *American troops in World War II were the first generation with access to modern medicine, including blood transfusions and penicillin, resulting in a sharp decrease in noncombat deaths.*

★ ★ ★

Niagara Movement

The Niagara movement was a series of conventions held by African-American civil rights advocates in the early twentieth century that led to the establishment of the National Association for the Advancement of Colored People (NAACP), now the nation's oldest and largest civil rights group.

Organized by W. E. B. DuBois (1868–1963), the Niagara movement embraced much more aggressive goals than existing civil rights groups, demanding an immediate end to Jim Crow segregation and promising "persistent, manly agitation" against racism.

In July 1905, when the thirty-two delegates to the first Niagara convention met, Booker T. Washington (1856–1915) was the reigning African-American civil rights leader. Washington, the head of the Tuskegee Institute in Alabama, had largely accepted segregation as inevitable, and he focused his energies on building strong African-American institutions. For instance, Washington had convinced wealthy white philanthropists to fund hundreds of segregated schools for blacks in the South.

The young DuBois had emerged as a major critic of Washington, whom he derided as the "Great Accommodator" for his acceptance of segregation, in the 1890s. At the first Niagara meeting, DuBois and the other delegates released a statement that did not mention Washington by name but was loaded with veiled criticisms. "We refuse to allow the impression to remain that the Negro-American assents to inferiority, is submissive under oppression and apologetic before insults," the statement said.

Four years later, after establishing dozens of branches across the country, members of the Niagara movement founded the National Association for the Advancement of Colored People (NAACP). The NAACP would define the agenda of the African-American civil rights community for decades to come. Although considered radical in 1905, the Niagara movement's emphasis on ending segregation would soon become the goal of the mainstream civil rights movement.

ADDITIONAL FACTS

1. *In a symbolic gesture, DuBois held the second Niagara movement meeting in Harpers Ferry, West Virginia, the site of John Brown's failed 1859 effort to spark a slave uprising.*

2. *Although initially all Niagara members were black, DuBois invited several whites to join the group at its second meeting. When the NAACP was founded three years later, most of its executive board was white.*

3. *The Niagara movement took place against the backdrop of a spike in lynchings beginning in the 1890s, an era historians have identified as the worst period of race relations in American history since the Civil War (1861–1865).*

★ ★ ★

Milton Hershey

In 1907, philanthropist and chocolate tycoon Milton Hershey (1857–1945) unveiled his most famous creation: the Hershey's Kiss, a small, conical piece of milk chocolate wrapped in foil. One of the most popular candies in American history, the success of the Kiss helped Hershey build what was once the world's largest chocolate factory in his company town of Hershey, Pennsylvania.

Hershey was born on a farm in Pennsylvania and raised in the Mennonite church, a strict pacifist sect. He was apprenticed to a local candy maker after completing the fourth grade, and he started his own caramel company in 1883. In 1900, he sold the caramel company to devote his energies to milk chocolate, which was then a relatively new delicacy that was not widely marketed in the United States. The Hershey's chocolate bar debuted that year.

For a corporate titan in the age of robber barons, Hershey was an unusual boss. The town of Hershey, which he built, was a model of city planning, meant to create a town where workers would be happy to live, rather than a faceless suburb built on the cheap. Influenced by his religious beliefs, he donated all of his stock in the company to fund educational programs for orphans. Hershey lived in the town for the rest of his life. A modest man, he eventually donated even his house.

Today the Hershey company remains a Fortune 500 company, although it is no longer the world's largest chocolatier. The town of Hershey is still a tourist attraction, both for the amusement park located there and for the distinctive smell of chocolate that wafts through streets designed by the company's famous founder.

ADDITIONAL FACTS

1. *The two main roads in Hershey are called Chocolate and Cocoa Avenues.*

2. *Hershey and his wife, Catharine, were unable to have children of their own and instead founded a school for orphans.*

3. *Hershey's Kisses were wrapped by hand until 1921, when a wrapping machine was introduced. Today's wrapping machines can cover up to 1,300 Kisses a minute.*

★ ★ ★

Panama Canal

The Panama Canal, a fifty-one-mile waterway across the Isthmus of Panama that connects the Atlantic and Pacific Oceans, opened to shipping in 1914 after a decade of construction. Although it was not built on United States soil, the Panama Canal was mostly an American project, and its completion remains one of the most dazzling feats of engineering ever undertaken. The United States retained control over the canal until 1999, when it was returned to Panama.

Prior to the opening of the canal, ships sailing from San Francisco to New York had to travel around the southern tip of South America, a long and dangerous voyage. Plans to dig across Panama had been discussed for centuries, and French engineers had attempted to construct a canal as recently as the 1880s. However, the dense Panamanian jungle, deadly diseases such as malaria and yellow fever, and the massive amounts of equipment and personnel required eventually doomed the French project.

For US President Theodore Roosevelt (1858–1919), completing the canal was a major commercial and military goal. With technological improvements, he felt the Americans could succeed where France had failed. However, the government of Colombia, which controlled Panama at the time, was hesitant to allow American involvement. In a controversial move, the United States then launched a scheme to support Panamanian independence in exchange for permission to dig the canal.

The ploy worked. Panama, which had attempted a number of unsuccessful uprisings against Colombia since the 1830s, revolted once more, this time with US support, and became independent in 1903. Within a month, the United States received permission from the new government of Panama to complete the canal. Roosevelt's meddling in Panama launched a period of far more aggressive American intervention in Latin American affairs. This interventionist policy, known as the "Roosevelt corollary," would eventually prove extremely unpopular with many Central Americans.

With the political obstacles cleared, all that remained was to construct the canal itself. The remains of the French canal—basically, a giant ditch—formed the starting point for the Americans. Engineers would eventually spend $352 million over ten years to complete the project; more than 5,000 workers died of disease or accident. When it was completed, the canal drastically slashed travel time between the Atlantic and Pacific Oceans, strengthened US naval power, and signaled the grand scale of American ambitions in the twentieth century.

ADDITIONAL FACTS

1. *The first ship to traverse the canal, on August 15, 1914, was SS* Ancon, *a passenger vessel.*

2. *Until 1999, the United States exercised control over the canal and surrounding areas; Americans in the area were referred to as Zonians.*

3. *Builders used 102 steam shovels on the canal project, one of which has been preserved by the Smithsonian Institution.*

★ ★ ★

Arthur Miller

Arthur Miller (1915–2005) was one of the most respected playwrights of modern American theater. He wrote seventeen plays, including several scripts that are now considered classics: *Death of a Salesman* (1949), *The Crucible* (1953), and *A View from the Bridge* (1955). Miller enjoyed unusual celebrity for an American playwright, in part because of his high-profile stance against McCarthyism during the 1950s and in part because of his infamous, rocky marriage to movie sex symbol Marilyn Monroe (1926–1962).

Born on the Upper West Side of New York City, Miller grew up wealthy. The Great Depression ruined his father's business, however, forcing the family to move; many of Miller's plays reflected his family's traumatic experiences during the 1930s.

Miller put himself through college at the University of Michigan by winning undergraduate theater prizes. His first Broadway play, however, *The Man Who Had All the Luck*, failed after a handful of performances. Miller's breakthrough finally came in 1947 with the production of *All My Sons*, a drama about corruption in the military that garnered two Tony Awards, including Best Play.

The most famous of Miller's plays, *Death of a Salesman*, was produced in 1949, and the play's main character, a traveling salesman named Willy Loman, has become one of the best-known creations in American theater. The play depicts Loman as he becomes increasingly delusional and despondent after failing as a businessman. Often interpreted as a savage criticism of the American Dream, the play ran for hundreds of performances and won both the Tony and the Pulitzer Prize in 1949.

Miller's next play, *The Crucible*, was a retelling of the 1692 Salem witch trials, in which twenty suspected witches were executed. The play was as a thinly veiled commentary on the anticommunist hysteria of the 1950s. In 1956, Miller was summoned before the House Un-American Activities Committee chaired by Senator Joseph McCarthy (1908–1957) of Wisconsin, where he famously refused to "name names" of other playwrights involved with the Communist Party.

Also in 1956, Miller married film actress Marilyn Monroe. The marriage was short-lived, however, and the two divorced shortly before Monroe's death from a drug overdose in 1962. Miller remained active in politics and continued to write, but never matched his creative output of the 1950s; his last hit play was *The Price* in 1968.

ADDITIONAL FACTS

1. *Before the success of* All My Sons, *Miller worked a variety of odd jobs, including one feeding mice used in medical experiments.*

2. *Before Miller, Monroe had been married to New York Yankees slugger Joe DiMaggio (1914–1999).*

3. *Active in the antiwar movement during the Vietnam era, Miller was a delegate from Connecticut to the 1968 Democratic National Convention.*

★ ★ ★

Citizen Kane

Often named the best motion picture in American history by movie buffs, *Citizen Kane*, starring and directed by Orson Welles (1915–1985), tells the story of a dying newspaper tycoon and his mysterious last word, "rosebud." Upon the release of *Citizen Kane* in 1941, Welles was immediately hailed as a genius by critics, but the film flopped at the box office. In *Citizen Kane*, Welles pioneered the use of *deep focus,* a photographic technique in which everything in a frame remains in focus, and he also employed highly creative sound and editing techniques.

The black-and-white movie begins at the giant, secluded estate of Charles Foster Kane, whose character was loosely based on the real-life publishing magnate William Randolph Hearst (1863–1951). As Kane is dying, reporters hear him mutter the word "rosebud," setting off a frantic search through his past to discover its elusive meaning.

In the course of their investigation, the reporters, played by members of a New York theater troupe called the Mercury Players, revisit Kane's rise to fame and fortune amid the cut-throat world of early twentieth-century American business. Although based partially on Hearst, the character of Kane is also based somewhat on Welles himself, a vain, egotistical genius with a self-destructive tendency.

The Wisconsin-born Welles had become famous in 1938, at the tender age of twenty-three, for his radio adaptation of the 1898 science fiction novel *The War of the Worlds* by British author H. G. Wells (1866–1946). The performance was so realistic that it caused widespread panic among radio listeners who missed the disclaimer at the beginning of the broadcast and feared that aliens from Mars had actually invaded New Jersey.

Impressed by his success in radio, the movie studio RKO gave Welles an usual amount of freedom to make *Citizen Kane* however he saw fit. After the commercial failure of the movie, however, Welles struggled with studio bosses for the rest of his career. He directed several more critically acclaimed films, including *Touch of Evil* (1958), an adaptation of Shakespeare's *Othello* (1952), and *Falstaff* (also called *Chimes at Midnight,* 1966), a film based on several Shakespeare plays, but never again was allowed the unfettered freedom to make a movie like *Citizen Kane*.

ADDITIONAL FACTS

1. *Hearst was so infuriated by* Citizen Kane *that he offered the studio $800,000 not to release it.*

2. Citizen Kane *was originally titled simply* American.

3. *In the movie, Kane's estate is called Xanadu; the real-life Hearst had a seaside mansion in California named San Simeon.*

★ ★ ★

Warren Harding

Warren G. Harding (1865–1923) has the dubious distinction of finishing last in most polls of presidential greatness. Elected to the White House in 1920, he lasted three scandal-plagued years before his sudden death from a stroke in 1923. Of himself, Harding supposedly said, "I am not fit for this office and never should have been here."

Born in Ohio, Harding made his fortune in the newspaper business before getting involved with Republican politics in 1899. He was elected to the United States Senate from Ohio in 1914 and won the GOP's presidential nomination in 1920. Promising a return to normalcy after World War I (1914–1918), Harding won the election in a landslide.

As president, Harding raised eyebrows by hosting poker nights and drinking parties at the White House at a time when alcohol was illegal. He also filled his cabinet with unqualified cronies from Ohio, several of whom were later caught abusing their offices.

The most famous example of corruption during Harding's tenure was the Teapot Dome scandal. In the scandal, Harding's secretary of the interior, Albert Fall (1861–1944), was caught accepting bribes from oil companies in exchange for lucrative leases on federal lands in the West. In the fallout from the scandal, Fall became the first cabinet officer sentenced to prison for official misconduct. He went to jail in 1929.

Although President Harding himself was never accused of corruption, and some of his defenders claimed his weakness was simply trusting old friends, he was criticized for using poor judgment in his selection of government officials.

In 1923, with new wrinkles of the scandal beginning to emerge in Washington every day, Harding got as far away from the capital as he could, paying a visit to Alaska. On his way back, Harding stopped in San Francisco, where he fell ill and died on August 2, 1923.

ADDITIONAL FACTS

1. *The Teapot Dome scandal took its name from a parcel of land in Wyoming that had been leased to cronies for oil drilling without a competitive bid.*

2. *In 1884, Harding bought a tiny Ohio newspaper, the* Marion Star, *which he turned into a profitable enterprise that also provided a platform for his political career.*

3. *Harding's home state of Ohio was nicknamed the Mother of Presidents, having produced eight presidents. However, since Harding, no Ohioan has been elected president.*

★ ★ ★

Bataan Death March

After the defeat of American forces in the Philippines in 1942, 76,000 soldiers taken prisoner by the Japanese were forced to march across the island under horrifying conditions in a gruesome wartime atrocity known as the Bataan Death March.

Japan had invaded the lightly guarded American territory of the Philippines toward the beginning of World War II, just after the 1941 attack on Pearl Harbor, and cornered the combined American and Filipino force led by General Douglas MacArthur (1880–1964). Boxed in on every side at the tip of the Bataan Peninsula, the soldiers on the island ate ponies, lizards, and monkeys to survive. President Franklin D. Roosevelt (1882–1945), who considered MacArthur too important to lose in a hopeless battle, ordered him to Australia. Several weeks later, on April 9, 1942, the tattered remnants of the defending army finally surrendered to the Japanese. For the American military, the surrender of the Philippines was one of the lowest points in the early stages of the war, before the tide began to turn against imperial Japan.

On the sixty-five-mile march that ensued, the American and Filipino prisoners were given no food or water and killed if they lagged too far behind. By some estimates, about 10,000 of the soldiers taken captive died en route to the prison camps.

After forces led by MacArthur reconquered the Philippines on July 5, 1945, the US military hunted down the Japanese officers responsible for the atrocity. The Japanese commander accused of organizing the death march, Masaharu Homma (1887–1946), was tried as a war criminal and executed by firing squad, although doubts over his guilt surfaced later. April 9, the anniversary of the surrender, is now a national day of remembrance in the Philippines.

ADDITIONAL FACTS

1. *The American public only learned about the Bataan Death March three years after the fact, when American prisoners escaped from the Japanese and exposed the atrocity.*

2. *Although Homma was executed for the crime, evidence later emerged that one of his underlings, Colonel Masanobu Tsugi, was probably directly responsible for the march.*

3. *The unlucky commander of US forces after MacArthur's departure from the Philippines, Lieutenant General Jonathan M. Wainwright (1883–1953), became the highest-ranking officer captured by the Axis and spent more than three years in captivity. After the war, he was promoted to full general and received the Medal of Honor.*

★ ★ ★

Margaret Sanger

In the early twentieth century, it was illegal in most states to publish information about birth control, and the vast majority of American women had little or no access to contraceptives. Starting in 1914, birth control advocate Margaret Sanger (1879–1966) waged a long, lonely battle against censors and hostile church leaders to legalize contraception and provide women with information about their reproductive choices. Although still considered controversial for her embrace of eugenics, Sanger's lifelong commitment to empowering women made her one of the pivotal figures in the history of twentieth century medicine and women's rights.

Sanger's belief in *birth control*—a term that she invented—stemmed from her personal experiences as a nurse tending poor women in the slums of New York City. Unplanned and unwanted pregnancies, Sanger felt, robbed women of control of their own lives and forced them to resort to dangerous and illegal back-alley abortions. In 1914, Sanger started a newsletter, *The Woman Rebel*, to spread information about birth control.

The newspaper immediately fell afoul of censors, who considered the publication obscene, and Sanger was forced to flee to England to avoid arrest. She returned in 1916, and the charges against her were dropped. Later that year, she opened the nation's first birth control clinic in Brooklyn and became a leading spokesperson for nationwide efforts to repeal anti-contraception laws. In 1921, Sanger founded the Birth Control League, which became the Planned Parenthood Federation in 1942. In the late 1920s, she also became a supporter of eugenics, a controversial theory that social ills could be eliminated through selective breeding and the sterilization of "undesirables."

Throughout her career, Sanger was frustrated by the scarcity of birth control options for women. As early as 1912, she had dreamed of a "magic pill" that could be used for contraception. In search of better options, Sanger helped finance medical research that led to the invention of the birth control pill, which received FDA approval in 1960. Shortly before Sanger's death, the United States Supreme Court invalidated laws against birth control in its landmark *Griswold v. Connecticut* (1965) decision, fulfilling one of her lifelong goals.

ADDITIONAL FACTS

1. *In her youth, Sanger saw her mother die at age fifty after eighteen pregnancies, including seven miscarriages.*

2. *Because it was illegal to sell contraceptives in the United States, most were marketed under euphemisms, most commonly "feminine hygiene."*

3. *The diaphragm was the most reliable form of birth control available to women in the early twentieth century, but it had to be smuggled in from abroad.*

★ ★ ★

William Randolph Hearst

Press baron William Randolph Hearst (1863–1951) may be most famous today as the model for Charles Foster Kane in the 1941 movie *Citizen Kane*. During his lifetime, however, Hearst was one of the most powerful men in the country, capable of influencing public opinion and even starting a war by using the chain of major metropolitan newspapers under his ownership. Hearst, along with rival Joseph Pulitzer (1847–1911), invented the modern American newspaper business and built the first successful newspaper conglomerates.

 Hearst was born in California to a wealthy father who had made his fortune in mining. The young Hearst attended Harvard but was expelled after sending personalized chamber pots to his professors as a prank. He took over a small San Francisco newspaper, the *Examiner*, that was owned by his father. By adopting an unapologetically populist tone, Hearst turned the *Examiner* into the city's leading rag.

Hearst soon expanded into other markets. He bought a newspaper in New York City, the *Journal*, in 1895, which put him in direct competition with Pulitzer's *World*. At a time when papers were the dominant source of news for most Americans, the two vied for readers in the nation's biggest city by improving production quality and printing ever more outrageous and titillating articles. The tabloid-style journalism of the era is known as "yellow journalism," a name derived from the Yellow Kid, a popular comic-strip character that appeared in both papers.

The most notorious example of Hearst's yellow journalism came during the run-up to the Spanish-American War (1898), when the *Journal* and the *World* both printed lurid stories about supposed Spanish atrocities. The articles inflamed public opinion and may have contributed to the US decision to go to war.

In 1941, he tried unsuccessfully to stop the release of *Citizen Kane*, but the unflattering portrayal of the fictional Kane in the movie now dominates Hearst's public image. Hearst Newspapers remains under the ownership of William Randolph Hearst's heirs today and publishes the *San Francisco Chronicle*, the *Houston Chronicle*, and many magazines.

ADDITIONAL FACTS

1. *One of Hearst's granddaughters, Patty Hearst (1954–), was kidnapped in 1974 by the Symbionese Liberation Army, a domestic terrorist group, and participated in bank robberies after being brainwashed by the organization. She served prison time, but her sentence was commuted by President Jimmy Carter (1924–).*

2. *Hearst briefly employed Stephen Crane (1871–1900), the author of* The Red Badge of Courage *(1895), as a war correspondent.*

3. *One of Hearst's most well-known features was* Krazy Kat, *by the cartoonist George Harriman (1880–1944), which ran for decades and is regarded as one of the most influential newspaper comic strips ever.*

★ ★ ★

Yankee Stadium

Arguably the most famous sporting venue in the nation, Yankee Stadium opened in 1923 as the home to the New York Yankees major league baseball team. At the time of its construction, the stadium was the largest ballpark in the nation and was regarded as an architectural marvel for its three-tiered design. In the decades since, dozens of championships have been decided on the field of Yankee Stadium, in both baseball and professional boxing, making it one of the most fabled locations in all of American sport.

When it first opened, the stadium was considered a major gamble by the Yankees' ownership. In the early 1920s, the future of professional spectator sports in the United States seemed uncertain at best, due to a game-fixing scandal involving the 1919 Chicago White Sox that had tarnished major league baseball's reputation. In addition, New York had three professional baseball teams—the Yankees, the Dodgers, and the Giants—and some critics wondered how the Yankees planned to fill 58,000 seats at their new park in the Bronx.

However, thanks to the star power of Yankees slugger George Herman "Babe" Ruth (1895–1948) and baseball's rebounding popularity during the Roaring Twenties, Yankee Stadium was a huge success and inspired a wave of imitators. In addition to its role as the home field of the Yankees, the stadium was home to several of history's biggest boxing matches, including the first-round victory of American pugilist Joe Louis (1914–1981) over the German fighter Max Schmeling (1905–2005) for the heavyweight belt in 1938, a bout that acquired geopolitical overtones due to Nazi dictator Adolf Hitler's support for Schmeling.

In a historical context, the success of Yankee Stadium presaged the growing popularity of sports as mass entertainment in the twentieth century. Starting in the 1920s, radio and television broadcasts made baseball accessible to a huge audience and turned players like Ruth—who became known as "the Bambino"—into national stars. By the end of decade, Ruth was making a higher salary than even President Herbert Hoover (1874–1964). (As Ruth explained, "I had a better year than him.") Many cities now build a stadium or arena as the anchor of their downtown. Yankee Stadium itself, however, is scheduled to be torn down after the 2008 baseball season, fifteen years shy of its centennial.

ADDITIONAL FACTS

1. *Yankee Stadium is sometimes referred to as "The House That Ruth Built" for the Bambino's role in the team's success during the 1920s and 1930s.*

2. *Wrigley Field, the home of the Chicago Cubs, and Boston's Fenway Park are the two oldest ballparks in the major leagues: Fenway Park opened in 1912 and Wrigley Field in 1914.*

3. *Schmeling was reportedly displeased with his portrayal as an Aryan superman in Nazi propaganda during the 1930s, and he supported Louis financially after World War II. The German boxer died a few months shy of his 100th birthday.*

★ ★ ★

Tennessee Williams

The playwright Tennessee Williams (1911–1983) was born in Mississippi and grew up in an extremely troubled home. His father was a shoe salesman who abused Williams's mother, and his sister, Rose, suffered from schizophrenia. His traumatic childhood provided the grist for many of Williams's works—now among the most well-known American plays of the twentieth century—that probe the crippling emotional problems of star-crossed Southern protagonists.

One of Williams's early plays, *The Glass Menagerie*, which premiered in 1945, is typical of his so-called Southern gothic style. Set in Depression-era St. Louis, the play unfolds in the small apartment of Amanda Wingfield, whose husband had abandoned her and their two children, Tom and Laura, long before the action begins. Despite her poverty, Amanda considers herself a proper Southern lady and hopes to introduce her shy and disabled daughter to a respectable "gentleman caller."

Although he wrote more than thirty full-length plays beginning in 1930s, *The Glass Menagerie* was Williams's first major success. Several other hit plays soon followed, including *A Streetcar Named Desire* in 1947 and *Cat on a Hot Tin Roof* in 1955, both of which won Pulitzer Prizes for drama. Themes of poverty, religion, and sex, along with the tragic figure of the "faded Southern belle," appear frequently in Williams's plays, seemingly inspired by the long-suffering women in his family and his own difficult upbringing.

In adulthood, Williams struggled with drugs and alcohol, and many critics believe the quality of his plays deteriorated later in life. At a time when even Broadway was hesitant to fully accept homosexuality, his private life became the subject of gossip and ridicule. In 1983, a month away from his seventy-second birthday, Williams died in New York after choking on a bottle cap in his hotel room.

ADDITIONAL FACTS

1. *Nicknamed "Tennessee" for his Southern drawl, Williams legally changed his name from Thomas in 1939.*

2. *The original 1947 stage production of* A Streetcar Named Desire *starred Marlon Brando (1924–2004) and featured Karl Malden (1912–), both of whom went on to act in the 1951 movie version. Malden and Vivien Leigh (1913–1967) each won an Academy Award for their role in the film.*

3. *There are still streetcar lines in New Orleans, but none go to the Desire neighborhood.*

★ ★ ★

Humphrey Bogart

The epitome of cool masculinity to a generation of American men, Humphrey Bogart (1899–1957) achieved his most lasting fame playing gangsters, cowboys, detectives, and broken-hearted lovers in the golden age of Hollywood. Immortalized thanks to his role as the embittered club owner Rick Blaine in the 1941 film *Casablanca*, Bogart went on to win the 1951 Best Actor Oscar for *The African Queen*, which costarred Katharine Hepburn (1929–1993).

Born in New York to a prosperous family, Bogart began acting in the early 1920s after he was expelled from prep school. Moderately successful, he moved to Hollywood in 1930 and was cast in dozens of gangster films, one of the decade's most popular genres.

In 1941, Bogart's breakout year, he played a private detective, Sam Spade, in *The Maltese Falcon*. An adaptation of the acclaimed 1930 novel by Dashiell Hammett (1894–1961), *The Maltese Falcon* showcased Bogart's trademark sardonic wit and hard-boiled cynicism. Like Rick Blaine, Bogart's Sam Spade professed not to care about anyone but himself, but as the movie unfolds the audience learns he also has a hidden, sensitive side.

A bona fide celebrity after *The Maltese Falcon* and *Casablanca*, Bogart made headlines in 1945 by marrying Lauren Bacall (1924–), his much-younger costar from *To Have and Have Not* (1944). He also became involved with politics, protesting the tactics of the House Un-American Activities Committee, a government inquisition that sought to root out the alleged communist menace in Hollywood. Bogart starred in *The Treasure of the Sierra Madre* in 1948 and made his last major film, *The Caine Mutiny*, in 1954.

Tragically, Bogart died at age fifty-seven of throat cancer after many years of heavy smoking. His legend, however, has only grown with the years. In 1999, he was named the twentieth century's number one male star by the American Film Institute.

ADDITIONAL FACTS

1. *Bacall and Bogart costarred in two other films,* The Big Sleep *(1946) and* Key Largo *(1948).*

2. *Bogart was parodied posthumously in the movie* Play It Again, Sam *(1972), written by and starring Woody Allen (1935–).*

3. *A stretch of West 103rd Street in New York City, near where Bogart grew up, was named after the actor in 2006.*

★ ★ ★

Calvin Coolidge

Nicknamed "Silent Cal" for his shy, taciturn personality, Calvin Coolidge (1872–1933) was sworn in as president of the United States in 1923 following the death of President Warren G. Harding (1865–1923). Reelected to a full term in 1924, Coolidge presided over the economic boom of the Roaring Twenties and left office just before the stock market crash of 1929 that would trigger the Great Depression.

Coolidge was born in Vermont and later moved to Massachusetts, where he was elected governor in 1918. As governor, the Republican Coolidge received acclaim for quashing a 1919 strike by Boston police officers. Nationally famous after breaking the strike, Coolidge was chosen as Harding's running mate on the Republican ticket in the 1920 election.

Harding's death in 1923, as he returned from a vacation in Alaska, ended a scandal-plagued administration. Indeed, Coolidge's first task in the White House was to undo the damage of his predecessor, a job for which he was well suited. In contrast to the poker-playing, tobacco-chewing Harding, who had associated with a gang of disreputable characters, Coolidge's image as an upstanding New Englander helped restore public confidence in the presidency.

In office, Coolidge governed as a conservative, vetoing several spending proposals he considered excessive and avoiding government interference with the economy. Coolidge's hands-off approach to the economy, combined with his actions during the Boston police strike and a legendary quotation that the "business of America is business," have led to his reputation as a pro–big business, antilabor stalwart. Although Coolidge certainly shared the antiunion views of many of his fellow Republicans, he was a pragmatist above all else, governing with a light touch.

After the tragic death of his son in 1924 following an injury in a tennis game, Coolidge became distraught and gradually lost his passion for politics. The presidency, he remarked, suddenly seemed inconsequential after such a loss. Coolidge decided not to seek another term, issuing a typically terse one-sentence statement to the press: "I do not choose to run for President in 1928." He handed off the presidency to Herbert Hoover (1874–1964) and returned to Massachusetts, just in time to miss the cataclysm of the Great Depression.

ADDITIONAL FACTS

1. *When President Harding died in office, Coolidge was visiting his family in Vermont. He was administered the presidential oath of office by his father, a notary, at 2:47 a.m. before returning to Washington, DC.*

2. *Coolidge was buried in his hometown of Plymouth Notch, Vermont, where his family's homestead has been re-created for tourists.*

3. *Coolidge is the only president born on the Fourth of July.*

★ ★ ★

D-Day

The Allied invasion of Normandy on the northern coast of France the morning of June 6, 1944, was the largest amphibious military assault of World War II (1939–1941) and the beginning of the end of Nazi tyranny in Europe. Directed by the American general Dwight D. Eisenhower (1890–1969), the D-day invasion involved troops from a dozen countries and about 5,000 boats, the largest war armada ever assembled. Allied casualties on the five Normandy landing beaches were heavy, but the Germans were caught off guard and could not repulse the invasion. From Normandy, the Allies quickly attacked the Nazis across the rest of France and marched triumphantly down the Champs-Élysées in Paris less than three months later, on August 26, 1944.

The Allies had begun planning an invasion of continental Europe in 1942. The logistics of getting enough troops and equipment across the stormy English Channel were daunting.

Eisenhower originally scheduled D-day for June 5 but postponed the invasion because of bad weather. Although German intelligence warned that an attack was imminent, Nazi leaders did not believe the Allies would actually attempt an invasion on June 6 because of stormy weather and high winds.

Eisenhower and his staff had selected five beachheads for the landing forces and given them code names. The Americans were given the responsibility for Omaha and Utah beaches. Despite landing in the wrong place on Utah beach, the invasion there went relatively smoothly. Omaha, however, was another story. The cloudy weather made it difficult for Allied bombers to provide air support, and the soldiers defending the beach were among the German army's best. Within a few hours, American casualties at Omaha beach totaled about 2,000 troops killed or wounded.

After seizing the coast on June 6, the battle moved inland, to the farmhouses, country lanes, and quiet hedgerows of the Normandy region of France. Over the next several weeks of brutal combat, the Allies established air and ground superiority in the region, allowing thousands more Allied troops and equipment to land in France. Within a year of the D-day landing, Hitler was dead and the war in Europe was over.

ADDITIONAL FACTS

1. *The D-day invasion was a massive logistical undertaking, and not just for the combat forces. In anticipation of the invasion, the US Army hired and secretly trained 4,500 new cooks to prepare food for the troops once they reached France.*

2. *The underground French Resistance, according to US Army estimates, amounted to more than 200,000 partisans in 1944 and played a crucial role in sabotaging the Germans. By the day after D-day, the Resistance had cut twenty-six French railroad lines, severely impairing Germany's ability to rush more troops to Normandy.*

3. *The German general responsible for the Normandy defenses, Erwin Rommel (1891–1944), committed suicide later that year after he was implicated in a failed plot to assassinate Hitler.*

★ ★ ★

Nineteenth Amendment

With thirty-nine simple words, the Nineteenth Amendment to the Constitution extended full voting rights to women. The amendment, ratified in 1920, was the culmination of decades of agitation for equal rights by feminist groups that began with the Seneca Falls Convention in 1848.

The amendment, in its entirety, proclaimed:

> The right of citizens in the United States to vote shall not be denied or abridged by the United States or by any State on account of sex.
> Congress shall have power to enforce this article by appropriate legislation.

Prior to the passage of the amendment, twenty-eight states had already granted voting rights to women. Wyoming—the Equality State—entered the union in 1890 with equal voting rights, the first state to enfranchise women. Illinois became the first state east of the Mississippi River to extend suffrage to women, which it did in 1913. By 1919, most western states and New York had also enfranchised women. Several big states, however, including Virginia, Massachusetts, and Pennsylvania, refused.

The fate of the constitutional amendment was uncertain until the last minute. As recently as 1915, the US House of Representatives had defeated a similar proposal. The support of President Woodrow Wilson (1856–1924), who campaigned for the amendment beginning in 1918, proved crucial to its passage.

Both the House and the US Senate approved the amendment in 1919, and the states rushed to ratify it in time for women to participate in the 1920 presidential election.

By the time of the amendment's passage, many of the founders of the women's rights movement—including Lucretia Mott (1793–1880), Elizabeth Cady Stanton (1815–1902), and Susan B. Anthony (1820–1906)—were dead. In just seventy years, though, their movement had turned the notion of women's suffrage from a laughingstock into reality. As Carrie Chapman Catt (1859–1947), another suffragist leader, said, "When a just cause reaches its flood tide, whatever stands in the way must fall before its overwhelming power."

ADDITIONAL FACTS

1. *Catt formed the League of Women Voters in 1920 to help educate newly enfranchised American women about politics.*

2. *Beer companies and saloon owners were the biggest political opponent of women's suffrage, fearing that women would vote for bans on alcohol. As it turned out, Prohibition was approved in 1919 without women's votes.*

3. *In news accounts of the time, the Nineteenth Amendment was referred to as the "Anthony amendment," a testament to the lasting influence of Susan B. Anthony, who had died thirteen years earlier.*

★ ★ ★

Triangle Shirtwaist Factory

A deadly fire at the Triangle Shirtwaist Factory in downtown New York City on March 25, 1911, killed 146 garment workers and prompted the passage of several workplace safety laws in the early twentieth century. The fire, a seminal event in the history of American labor, still ranks among the nation's worst industrial disasters.

Located on the top three floors of a ten-story building next to Washington Square, the Triangle factory was a sweatshop that employed mostly young immigrant Jewish and Italian women to sew cotton shirts. On the day of the fire, the sweatshop's owners, Max Blanck and Isaac Harris, had barricaded the doors shut to prevent theft. When the fire broke out, sparked by a cigarette tossed onto a pile of cloth, the women on the ninth floor found themselves trapped in an inferno. Unable to use the building's rickety fire escape, many leapt out the ninth-floor windows to their death.

Pictures and accounts of the devastating tragedy traumatized New York and led to an immediate public outcry. Families of the victims demanded justice, but a jury eventually acquitted Blanck and Harris of wrongdoing at trial. The State of New York launched an investigation into the garment industry and eventually proposed a long list of workplace safety reforms—including a ban on smoking in factories, regular fire drills, and mandatory installation of sprinklers—many of which became law. Other states also tightened their safety laws in response to the carnage.

Triangle was hardly the only sweatshop in New York, and the fire hastened the unionization of the garment industry and the American workforce in general. The fire is still commemorated in New York every year on March 25.

ADDITIONAL FACTS

1. *The building, at 23-29 Washington Place, is now part of the campus of New York University.*

2. *Although acquitted in their criminal trial, Blanck and Harris lost a civil case and were forced to pay compensation of $75 per victim to the families.*

3. *Prior to the fire, Triangle Shirtwaist was already notorious for its opposition to unions; the company had refused to sign a collective bargaining agreement after a strike in 1910, even after many other garment companies acceded to union demands.*

★ ★ ★

Empire State Building

Erected in just over a year, the 103-story Empire State Building was the tallest skyscraper in the world when it opened in 1931, a distinction it would hold for four decades. Located in midtown Manhattan, the giant edifice is one of the best-known buildings in the world and one of the most distinctive features of New York City's iconic skyline.

A milestone of efficient construction, the building was finished in record time. Its frame—58,000 tons of steel rising 1,250 feet into the sky—took only twenty-three weeks to complete. On average, about four and a half stories per week were added to the structure, which cost a total of $24.7 million.

Coming during the Great Depression, the project was a welcome source of employment for the city's workforce and an uplifting accomplishment for the nation as a whole. As the author E. B. White (1899–1985) wrote, the Empire State Building "managed to reach the highest point in the sky at the lowest moment of the Depression." On May 1, 1931, President Herbert Hoover (1874–1964) officially opened the building by turning on its lights for the first time.

The art deco–style skyscraper immediately became an international icon. It made one of its first and most famous movie appearances two years later in the blockbuster film *King Kong*. It has featured in countless movies since—including a *King Kong* remake in 2005—often as the target of disgruntled or misunderstood aliens.

Despite its immense popularity, the building was never a great commercial success. At the time of its construction, a docking station for zeppelins was built atop the structure, but it was never used. With the destruction of the World Trade Center towers in 2001, the Empire State Building regained its status as the city's tallest building, and about four million tourists visit its observation deck every year.

ADDITIONAL FACTS

1. *Counting its spire, the building is 1,454 feet tall.*

2. *The building did not have air-conditioning until 1950.*

3. *More than three tons of garbage are generated by the Empire State Building's occupants every day.*

★ ★ ★

Wallace Stevens

Wallace Stevens (1879–1955) lived a double life. Beginning in 1916, he worked as an executive at the Hartford Insurance Company by day, eventually becoming a senior vice president for fidelity and surety claims at the large Connecticut firm. By night, he was one of the leading modernist poets in the United States, eventually winning a Pulitzer Prize for the dazzling, idiosyncratic poems he wrote in his spare time. The two careers virtually never intersected; during his lifetime, Stevens feared that too much publicity for his poetry would hamper his business career. His abstract poems, for their part, certainly never discussed insurance.

Stevens was born in Pennsylvania and attended Harvard, where he first tried his hand at poetry. However, his literary career did not flourish until much later in life. As a late bloomer—and in many other respects—Stevens defied the conventional expectations for poets. His personal life was unspectacular and, apart from one drunken brawl with Ernest Hemingway (1899–1961) in Key West, produced little controversy. He mostly led the quiet, bourgeois life of an insurance executive and disdained the bohemian pretensions of the literary scene. He distrusted left wing politics and was often uncomfortable among fellow writers.

His work, however, has been of lasting influence on twentieth century poets. Like T. S. Eliot (1888–1965), Stevens wrote in an abstract, enigmatic style that can be difficult to decode. Unlike Eliot, however, Stevens wrote poems that are often upbeat, even joyful in tone. Stevens bent and shaped the English language into new forms; in one famous poem, "The Emperor of Ice-Cream" (1923), apparently set at a fairground, he writes of a "roller of big cigars" whipping "in kitchen cups concupiscent curds."

In addition to "The Emperor of Ice-Cream," some of Stevens's best-known works include "Sunday Morning" (1923), "Anecdote of the Jar" (1923), and the long poem *Auroras of Autumn* (1950), which is considered his masterpiece by some critics. Stevens's poems, especially "Sunday Morning" and *Auroras of Autumn*, address themes of death, nature, and the spiritual uncertainties of an increasingly post-Christian society.

ADDITIONAL FACTS

1. *Stevens worked briefly as a reporter after his college graduation, covering politics for the* New York Tribune.

2. *Stevens hated reading poetry aloud and once explained, "I am not a troubadour and I think the public reading of poetry is something particularly ghastly."*

3. *He learned he had won the Pulitzer Prize in 1955 while at a Hartford hospital; he died three months later.*

★ ★ ★

Alfred Hitchcock

Master of suspense Alfred Hitchcock (1899–1980) directed dozens of hit Hollywood thrillers, including the classic films *Strangers on a Train* (1951), *Vertigo* (1958), *North by Northwest* (1959), *Psycho* (1960), and *The Birds* (1963), among the scariest and most gut-churning movies in American cinema.

Born in England, Hitchcock made several successful movies in his home country—including *Blackmail* (1929; the first British feature film with sound), *The Thirty-Nine Steps* (1935), and *The Lady Vanishes* (1938)—before moving to Hollywood in 1939. His first American film, *Rebecca* (1940), was a noirish adaptation of the 1938 mystery novel by the British writer Daphne Du Maurier (1907–1989) that earned him the first of his five Academy Award nominations (though he never won the Oscar).

For the most part, Hitchcock's films were psychologically intense but never especially violent. As a director, he disdained gore for its own sake. Instead, Hitchcock built layer upon layer of suspense by depicting the swirling fears and dangers that drove his characters to the brink of disaster.

To build suspense, Hitchcock's movies often used a notorious plot device he called a *MacGuffin.* A MacGuffin, according to Hitchcock, is the object everyone in a movie wants. For instance, in *North by Northwest,* all the main characters are chasing a stash of secret microfilm. The audience never learns what's on the microfilm—or why anyone wants it in the first place—but its existence provides a justification for an otherwise improbable plot. Never overly troubled by the plausibility of his movies, Hitchcock turned to this basic plot structure repeatedly with great success.

One of the most recognizable personas in Hollywood history—the *New York Times* described the baldish, 300-pound director as a "pixieish gargoyle"—Hitchcock and his dark, sinister films remain extremely powerful influences on makers of horror and action movies.

ADDITIONAL FACTS

1. *Hitchcock gave himself a small, nonspeaking cameo in most of the films he directed. For instance, in* Strangers on a Train, *he is seen boarding the train carrying a musical instrument.*

2. *Although Hitchcock became an American citizen in 1955, he was given an honorary knighthood by Queen Elizabeth II (1926–) in 1980, shortly before his death.*

3. *Alfred Hitchcock lives on in syndicated television as well as film. His half-hour* Alfred Hitchcock Presents *mystery series originally aired from 1955 to 1962 and then was expanded into* The Alfred Hitchcock Hour, *which ran from 1962 to 1965.*

★ ★ ★

Herbert Hoover

On October 29, 1929, the stock market in New York tumbled 12 percent, the third consecutive day of massive losses on Wall Street. The magnitude of the sudden downturn was unprecedented. The crash of 1929 abruptly ended a decade of economic prosperity and caused millions of Americans to lose their savings in the ensuing Great Depression.

Politically, the main casualty of the crash was Herbert Hoover (1874–1964), the Republican president who was quickly overwhelmed by the crisis and drubbed by Franklin D. Roosevelt (1882–1945) in the 1932 election.

Prior to the Depression, Hoover enjoyed a reputation as a capable administrator, and even a national hero for his efforts to provide food relief to starving Europeans during World War I (1914–1918). He was nicknamed the "Great Humanitarian" for organizing the wartime United States Food Administration. Prior to his wartime service, he was a successful mining engineer.

Hoover entered politics in the 1920s, serving in the cabinets of both Warren G. Harding (1865–1923) and Calvin Coolidge (1872–1933) as secretary of commerce. With the economy roaring, Hoover was the natural choice for the 1928 Republican presidential nomination.

Initially, Hoover hoped the 1929 crash would be a short-term downturn. He authorized a few relief programs and urged state governors to start public works projects to give unemployed workers jobs. But his response to the Depression was far too restrained and did little to solve the massive economic problems afflicting Americans. Soon, bitter critics began referring to slums filled with people who had lost their homes as *Hoovervilles*, a cruel gibe indeed for the Great Humanitarian.

In the election of 1932, Hoover lost in a landslide, even in his home state of California, and carried only a few states in New England, then a Republican bastion.

After the presidency, though, Hoover did not retreat from public life, instead becoming an elder statesman of the Republican Party. He reprised his role as a food relief organizer after World War II (1939–1945), touring Europe on behalf of President Harry Truman (1884–1972) and suggesting ways to improve the American relief effort.

ADDITIONAL FACTS

1. *Both Herbert Hoover and his wife, Lou Henry Hoover (1874–1944), spoke Mandarin, a language they learned while Hoover was working as a mining engineer in China in the late 1890s.*

2. *Hoover was the first president born west of the Mississippi. He was born in West Branch, Iowa.*

3. *Hoover was a graduate of the first class of Stanford University.*

★ ★ ★

Iwo Jima

One of the fiercest battles of World War II (1939–1945) took place in 1945 on the tiny island of Iwo Jima, a barren speck of land in the middle of the Pacific Ocean that housed a strategically important Japanese military base. Combined American and Japanese deaths in the monthlong battle, waged at times in hand-to-hand combat, rose to almost 30,000 troops—6,821 Americans and about 21,000 Japanese—before the Americans finally emerged victorious.

The American amphibious assault on Iwo Jima began February 19, 1945. At that point, the war in Europe was nearly over, as American and Soviet forces poured across the German border and rushed toward Berlin. In the Pacific theater, however, there appeared to be no end in sight.

American military commanders wanted to capture Iwo Jima to knock out a radar installation on the island, which had no civilian residents at the time of the battle, that was helping the Japanese detect American bombers before they reached mainland Japan. As an added benefit, Allied commanders thought, capturing Iwo Jima would give American warplanes an emergency landing strip in case of trouble on their missions.

The Japanese military leaders understood the strategic importance of the island and instructed the Japanese commander on the island, Tadamichi Kuribayashi (1891–1945), to hold the outpost at all costs. His 21,000 men burrowed a maze of caves in the side of the island's dormant volcano, Mount Suribachi, and waited for the American onslaught they knew was coming. True to their orders, by the end of the battle nearly all of Kuribayashi's soldiers were dead.

Although the commanders and soldiers at Iwo Jima had no way of knowing it, the American victory there would be one of the last Allied victories of the war. In the summer of 1945, President Harry Truman authorized the use of the atomic bomb against Japan, in part because he feared that an invasion of the Japanese home islands would amount to a thousand Iwo Jimas. The Japanese surrendered on August 14, 1945, and the cinder-strewn island of Iwo Jima remained an American military outpost until it reverted to Japanese control in 1968.

ADDITIONAL FACTS

1. *Iwo Jima means* sulfur island *in Japanese.*

2. *The famous Pulitzer Prize–winning picture of US Marines raising the flag on Iwo Jima was taken by Joe Rosenthal, a photographer for the Associated Press.*

3. *The 2006 movie* Letters from Iwo Jima, *directed by Clint Eastwood (1930–), was based on letters sent home by Japanese soldiers preparing for the battle.*

★ ★ ★

Marcus Garvey

One of the leading black nationalists in the United States of the twentieth century, Jamaican-born Marcus Garvey (1887–1940) rallied thousands of African-Americans behind his plans to launch a mass migration back to Africa. Between 1916, when he first arrived in the United States, and 1927, when he was deported back to Jamaica, the charismatic Garvey created a black pride movement that claimed up to six million followers. Although his plans fizzled, Garvey's emphasis on racial pride, unity, and self-reliance had a major influence on later black nationalists, including Malcolm X (1925–1965).

Garvey's political agenda, which he expounded to rapt audiences at Madison Square Garden and Carnegie Hall in the early 1920s, was twofold. In the long term, he hoped to lead an exodus back to Africa, and he opened serious negotiations with the West African nation of Liberia to create a Garveyite colony on the continent. In the short term, Garvey wanted to create strong black-owned businesses in the United States. He founded the United Negro Improvement Association, which was an international self-help organization. His followers financed efforts to create black steamship lines, restaurants, factories, publishers, and grocery stores.

Although many of these businesses were successful, the steamship line, Black Star, failed, and after a subsequent federal investigation, Garvey was imprisoned for mail fraud in 1925. He was deported to Jamaica two years later and never returned to the United States.

With his riveting speeches, Garvey tapped a growing sense of disillusionment among African-Americans in the early twentieth century. After the Civil War (1861–1865), many civil rights advocates had optimistically predicted a quick end to racism. But fifty years later, hatred and discrimination against blacks were as deeply entrenched as ever. To Garvey and his followers, the time for waiting was over—a message that would continue to resonate among black nationalists long after Garvey's death.

ADDITIONAL FACTS

1. *Both of Malcolm X's parents were members of Garvey's movement, and Garvey's writings had a deep influence on the Black Muslim leader.*

2. *Garvey was nearly barred by the FBI from reentering the United States in 1921, but one of his followers bribed a corrupt Harding administration official to give Garvey a visa.*

3. *Garvey survived an assassination attempt in October 1919 when his secretary—later his wife, Amy Ashwood (1897–1969)—fought off the attacker.*

★ ★ ★

Henry Ford

The biggest automaker of the early twentieth century, Henry Ford (1863–1947) made his fortune on the success of the Model T, which first went on sale in 1908. Ford's Model T was a milestone of both automotive design and efficient factory organization. The car was built on a moving assembly line, which enabled mass production and greatly increased the output of Ford's plants. It was sold at modest prices that were affordable to most middle-class Americans.

Ford was born in Dearborn, Michigan, and worked as a mechanic before starting the Ford Motor Company with several partners in 1903. Most of his initial factories were located in or near Dearborn, making Michigan the center of the American automotive industry.

In addition to Ford's use of the assembly line, he was also noted for offering his factory workers a forty-hour workweek, shorter than the norm at that time, and a then-unprecedented daily wage of $5. Paying his workers well, Ford believed, would attract the best mechanics, encourage productivity, and give his employees enough cash to buy a Ford automobile themselves. Admirers dubbed his business philosophy *Fordism*, and it was influential among industrialists worldwide.

One of the most famous American entrepreneurs of the twentieth century, Ford is also among the most controversial. Despite his professed concern for his workers, Ford steadfastly resisted unions and was the last major Detroit automaker to sign a union contract. Moreover, beginning in World War I (1914–1918), Ford took a series of increasingly bizarre political stances. He said he believed the war had been caused by a sinister coterie of Jewish bankers, and he opposed American involvement. After the war, he became an outspoken anti-Semite and published an American edition of *The Protocols of the Elders of Zion*. His anti-Semitic writings were admired by Adolf Hitler (1889–1945), whose Nazi government awarded the automaker one of its highest honors. Ford initially opposed World War II (1939–1945), again blaming the conflict on a cabal of Jewish bankers, but later backed the war effort and happily sold military vehicles to the US Army.

ADDITIONAL FACTS

1. *The Model T was not discontinued until 1927 and during its heyday was the most popular model of car in the United States.*

2. *Ford was so rabid in his anti-Jewish beliefs that he had 500,000 copies of an anti-Semitic pamphlet printed and sent to Ford dealerships for free distribution to customers.*

3. *Ford is one of the villains in the 1932 novel Brave New World, by British author Aldous Huxley (1894–1963), which envisions a dystopian future in which Fordism has replaced religion and Ford himself is regarded as a messiah.*

★ ★ ★

Golden Gate Bridge

An international architectural icon, the Golden Gate Bridge in San Francisco was the longest and tallest suspension bridge in the world when it opened in 1937. The bridge was the first suspension bridge to cross a stretch of ocean, rather than a river or lake; cold, fog, high winds, and rapid ocean currents made construction of the span especially vexing for the bridge's ambitious engineers. The graceful, orange span is considered both an engineering and aesthetic wonder, and it is often said to be the most recognizable and most photographed bridge in the world.

Golden Gate is the name for the relatively narrow strait that connects the Pacific Ocean with San Francisco Bay. Massive amounts of seawater surge through the choppy narrows, a body of water that could be crossed only by ferry for most of San Francisco's history. The width of the turbulent strait and the difficult geography on both sides made conventional bridges impossible.

Plans to span the Golden Gate had been discussed since the 1860s but dismissed as impractical. Joseph Baermann Strauss (1870–1938), an Ohio-born engineer and amateur poet with a penchant for grand, sweeping projects, first presented his design to the city in 1921. The initial presentation began a sixteen-year odyssey to finance and build the structure, which was opposed by a wide variety of environmental groups and San Francisco citizens worried about its steep cost and impact on ocean vistas.

Mindful of the safety hazards of building in San Francisco's windy climate, Strauss was determined to make the Golden Gate Bridge the safest in history, requiring his workers to wear hard hats and erecting a safety net. Ten workers died during construction, which was considered a relatively light toll by the standards of the 1930s. The bridge opened in 1937—in true San Francisco fashion, the festivities began with the sounding of a foghorn—but Strauss, exhausted by the effort, died of a stroke within a year of the bridge's completion.

ADDITIONAL FACTS

1. *The Golden Gate Bridge is considered one of the seven engineering wonders of the modern world by the American Society of Civil Engineers; it is one of only two American structures on the list. The other is the Empire State Building in New York City.*

2. *The bridge figured prominently in the James Bond movie* A View to a Kill *(1985), in which Roger Moore (1927–) and Christopher Walken (1943–) were seen fighting atop the span, with a combustible zeppelin hovering nearby.*

3. *The cables used for the Golden Gate Bridge were built by the firm of John Roebling and Sons, whose namesake had designed the Brooklyn Bridge about fifty years earlier.*

★ ★ ★

Alfred Kinsey

Biologist Alfred Charles Kinsey (1894–1956) provoked a firestorm of controversy in the United States following World War II (1939–1945) after publishing two groundbreaking studies of human sexual behavior known collectively as the Kinsey Reports. The books, *Sexual Behavior in the Human Male* (1948) and *Sexual Behavior in the Human Female* (1953), were the first scientific investigations of human sexuality, and they confronted many intimate subjects formerly considered taboo. Based on his confidential interviews with tens of thousands of Americans, Kinsey concluded that adultery, masturbation, and homosexuality were far more prevalent in American society than had been believed.

 Kinsey was born in New Jersey and attended Bowdoin College in Maine, where he studied biology. After finishing his doctorate at Harvard, Kinsey published books on insects and plants, but became interested in the largely unexplored field of human sexuality in the 1930s. He was named director of the Institute for Sexual Research at Indiana University, where he began conducting and compiling thousands of interviews for his two famous reports.

When they were first released, Kinsey's findings created an enormous uproar, and Kinsey was viciously attacked by conservatives upset by his reports. Among his other conclusions, Kinsey reported that 26 percent of married women had extramarital affairs by their fortieth birthday and that 50 percent of husbands cheated on their wives at some point in their life. He also found that homosexuality was far more widespread than most Americans wanted to believe—about 10 percent of men were categorized as homosexuals in Kinsey's surveys and fully 37 percent of all male respondents reported at least one homosexual experience in their lifetime.

Despite the backlash against Kinsey, his reports were widely read by an inquisitive public and became cultural landmarks. The first book sold 200,000 copies within two months; the second landed Kinsey on the cover of *Time* magazine. By forcing Americans to confront the surprising realities of human sexuality, Kinsey is widely credited—or blamed—for helping to liberalize American attitudes toward sex.

Kinsey died several years later at age sixty-two after a bout of pneumonia. Although conservative groups continue to gripe about Kinsey's findings, his reports have had a deep impact on changing American attitudes toward sex.

ADDITIONAL FACTS

1. *Each interviewee in Kinsey's research was asked 300 to 500 questions about his or her sex life.*

2. *Kinsey joined the Boy Scouts in 1911 and only two years later achieved the top rank of Eagle Scout.*

3. *Liam Neeson (1952–) starred in a 2004 movie about Kinsey's life titled* Kinsey.

★ ★ ★

Marlon Brando

Beginning with his brilliant performance as the angry husband Stanley Kowalski in the 1951 film version of *A Streetcar Named Desire*, Marlon Brando (1924–2004) electrified Hollywood in a series of trailblazing roles. Although his eccentric personal life and legendary moodiness hampered Brando's career, he is almost universally regarded as one of the greatest male movie actors ever.

The son of an insecticide salesman and an alcoholic mother, Brando was born in Nebraska and suffered through an unhappy childhood. He was sent to military school, where he first began acting, but was expelled before graduation. He moved to New York City in 1943, where he worked at a number of menial jobs to pay for his acting classes.

In New York, Brando learned an unconventional acting technique known as *method acting*, which requires the actor to connect his or her role with personal life experiences. Drawing on his own painful past, Brando became a master of this technique.

Brando's first big break came when director Elia Kazan (1909–2003) picked him for the male lead in the stage version of *Streetcar*, a play written by Tennessee Williams (1911–1983). He won a Best Actor Academy Award nomination for the film but lost the Oscar to Humphrey Bogart (1899–1957) for his role in *The African Queen*.

Suddenly famous, Brando acted in an astonishing range of roles in the 1950s. He played Marc Antony in Shakespeare's *Julius Caesar* in 1953. The same year, he played the rebellious leader of a biker gang in *The Wild One*. (In one scene, asked what he was rebelling against, Brando's character famously replied, "What've you got?") He won an Oscar in 1954 for his sensitive portrayal in *On the Waterfront* of Terry Malloy, a dimwitted ex-boxer who famously insisted he "coulda been a contender."

Brando's career began to teeter in the 1960s, when his unusual personal habits began taking a toll on his work. He refused to memorize lines, demanded exorbitant paychecks, and lost his sex-symbol image when his weight ballooned to 300 pounds.

His career revived, however, in 1972 when he played Vito Corleone in *The Godfather*. His last great role, as a psychotic army officer in Vietnam, came in the classic 1979 film *Apocalypse Now*, which reunited him with director Francis Ford Coppola (1939–), who also directed *The Godfather*.

ADDITIONAL FACTS

1. *Brando demanded—and received—top billing and $3.7 million to portray Jor-El, Superman's father, in the 1978* Superman *movie, although he was on-screen for only a few minutes.*

2. *At the 1973 Oscar ceremony, he refused his Academy Award for Best Actor in* The Godfather *to protest Hollywood's unflattering depiction of Native Americans in films.*

3. *Brando parodied himself in the 1990 Mafia movie* The Freshman, *which also starred Matthew Broderick (1962–).*

★ ★ ★

Franklin D. Roosevelt

Elected in 1932 at the lowest point of the Great Depression, President Franklin Delano Roosevelt (1882–1945) put the United States on the road to recovery with his New Deal economy and then led the country through World War II (1939–1945). Roosevelt died in office just weeks before the final defeat of Germany and Japan. FDR, as he was commonly known, was the only president to serve more than eight years, and the public and historians rank him as one of the top presidents in American history for his military and economic achievements.

Born in New York, Roosevelt belonged to the same upper-crust family as President Theodore Roosevelt (1858–1919). He broke with the Republican Roosevelt clan in 1910, however, by running for office as a Democrat. Roosevelt served as secretary of the navy for President Woodrow Wilson (1856–1924), a Democrat, where he met his British counterpart, a young member of Parliament named Winston Churchill (1874–1965), with whom he would work closely during World War II.

While vacationing with his wife, Eleanor (1884–1962), in 1921, FDR was stricken with polio, a debilitating disease that paralyzed his legs. Despite his disability, Roosevelt challenged Herbert Hoover for the presidency in 1932, promising sweeping economic reforms if elected. Despite dire economic conditions, Roosevelt gave a famously optimistic speech at his inauguration, declaring that "the only thing we have to fear is fear itself."

Within months, FDR had embarked on a program that would fundamentally change both the federal government and the office of the presidency. The New Deal greatly expanded the federal government's role in the economy and in the everyday lives of Americans. New Deal programs established a minimum wage, Social Security, and protections for labor unions. Roosevelt mastered the use of mass media by communicating with the public in his famous fireside radio chats, establishing a personal relationship with them unlike any previous president had had.

In 1940, Roosevelt broke with tradition by seeking a third term, and he was elected handily. Although in poor health, Roosevelt ran again successfully in the wartime election of 1944, but he died shortly after his fourth inauguration of a cerebral hemorrhage on April 12, 1945.

ADDITIONAL FACTS

1. *Roosevelt's landslide electoral college victory in 1936, 523 votes to only eight for Republican Alf Landon (1887–1987), was the most lopsided since the election of George Washington in 1789.*

2. *One of the blemishes on Roosevelt's record was his decision not to support antilynching legislation out of fear of losing the support of Southern Democrats.*

3. *FDR and Eleanor were fifth cousins; her last name was already Roosevelt when they married.*

★ ★ ★

Atom Bomb

Before dawn on August 6, 1945, an American B-29 bomber named the *Enola Gay* departed from an air base on the remote Pacific island of Tinian. The plane, piloted by Colonel Paul Tibbets (1915–), carried a fearsome cargo. After six hours aloft over the Pacific, the twelve-man crew of the *Enola Gay* reached its intended target, the bustling Japanese port city of Hiroshima. From 26,000 feet in the air, shortly after 8:00 a.m., Tibbets unleashed the world's first atomic bomb.

In an instant, the bomb incinerated downtown Hiroshima. About 140,000 Japanese were killed, and the city was turned into a smoldering wasteland. Nicknamed "Little Boy," the atom bomb was like nothing ever seen in the history of warfare. The bombing, followed three days later by another atomic strike against the city of Nagasaki, forced Japan to give up and thus brought World War II to an end. On August 10, 1945, Emperor Hirohito (1901–1989) ordered the Japanese military to surrender rather than endure any more of the terrible atomic onslaughts.

More than sixty years later, the fateful decision by US President Harry Truman (1884–1972) to use the atom bomb remains extremely controversial. American planners knew tens of thousands of civilians would be killed in the bombing but went ahead anyway. Around Hiroshima and Nagasaki, civilians continue to suffer debilitating diseases caused by radiation.

However, most Americans, including President Truman, argued that in the case of the atomic bomb, the ends justified the means. Only by terrifying the emperor into surrender could the Americans avoid an invasion of the Japanese home islands, which Truman's generals forecast would cost hundreds of thousands of American and Japanese lives. "Dropping the bombs ended the war, saved lives, and gave the free nations a chance to face the facts," Truman wrote later, defending his decision.

Tibbets harbored no doubts about his critical role in world history. In 2005, a reporter in Ohio asked him if he would drop the bomb again under similar circumstances. "Hell, yeah," he replied.

ADDITIONAL FACTS

1. *Even before the introduction of the atomic bomb, American bombing was taking a terrible toll on Japan. An earlier firebombing of Tokyo burned 84,000 people to death and destroyed 250,000 homes.*

2. *Two days after the first atom bomb was dropped, the Soviet Union, sensing Japan's imminent defeat, finally declared war on Japan, just in time to reap the rewards of the Allied victory in Asia.*

3. *Truman's plan B, had he decided against using the atomic bomb, was a November 1945 invasion of the Japanese mainland.*

★ ★ ★

Scottsboro Boys

On March 25, 1931, nine African-American teenagers were arrested on a freight train in Paint Rock, Alabama, and charged with rape and assault. Two weeks later, after two white women testified that the young men had raped them in a boxcar, eight of them were convicted by all-white juries in nearby Scottsboro and sentenced to die in the electric chair.

Almost immediately, serious questions about the alleged crime began to emerge, and the fate of the condemned men—soon dubbed the "Scottsboro Boys" by the press—became a lengthy courtroom saga that exposed the injustices of Alabama's racially biased criminal justice system.

At the time of the arrest, the nine men and the two alleged victims were on their way to Memphis to look for work. The case against them began to unravel when one of the victims, Ruby Bates (1913–1976), changed her story after the trial and said that no rape had actually occurred on the train.

In the North, doubts about the guilt of the defendants, combined with objections to the speed of the trial and the draconian verdicts, aroused major concerns among civil rights advocates. A communist-affiliated labor group asked Samuel Leibowitz (1893–1978), a well-known New York defense attorney (who was not a communist), to defend the accused on appeal.

Leibowitz, a Jewish attorney who was one of the era's most famous defense lawyers, argued that the exclusion of blacks from the jury in Alabama had denied the Scottsboro Boys a fair trial. He eventually took the case to the Supreme Court, which sided with the accused and overturned the guilty verdicts.

Alabama retried the men, and several were again sentenced to death or given long prison terms, despite Bates's recantation of her accusations. Leibowitz, the target of growing anti-Semitic hostility in the South, eventually had to take himself off the case to avoid hurting his clients.

In all, the case of the Scottsboro Boys had no happy ending. Some of the men were still in prison in the late 1940s. By 1950, four were paroled, nearly twenty years after a crime that may never have occurred.

ADDITIONAL FACTS

1. *After retracting her story, Bates had to flee Alabama. She died in Washington State in 1976.*

2. *One of the Scottsboro Boys, Haywood Patterson (1913–1952), escaped from prison in 1947 and fled to Michigan. He was captured there as a fugitive, but Michigan's governor refused to extradite him back to Alabama.*

3. *The incident was one of the inspirations for the Pulitzer Prize–winning novel* To Kill a Mockingbird *(1960) by Harper Lee (1926–).*

★ ★ ★

Federal Reserve

In 1913, the United States Congress approved two pieces of economic legislation that would become milestones in twentieth-century American life. The first was a constitutional amendment permitting the federal government to levy an income tax. The second created the Federal Reserve System, also called the Fed, a central government banking system that has grown into one of the most powerful economic institutions in the United States.

As envisioned by its founders, the Fed had a twofold purpose. First, it was charged with managing the huge assets of the United States government, including the proceeds from the new income tax. Second, it was meant to regulate the financial industry as a whole by setting interest rates and banking policies. Congress hoped that the Fed could prevent the kinds of cyclical banking panics that had periodically damaged the American economy throughout the nineteenth century.

The creation of the Fed resulted from a bipartisan consensus that effectively ended one of the most contentious political debates in American history. Since the election of President Andrew Jackson (1767–1845) in 1828, the Democratic Party had opposed the concept of a central bank as a boon to wealthy bankers; as late as 1912, party stalwart William Jennings Bryan (1860–1925) still opposed the Fed, but he was overruled by Democratic President Woodrow Wilson (1856–1924).

For average Americans, the impact of the Fed's creation was evident in their wallets. Every US dollar bill is now labeled *Federal Reserve Note*. In theory, the first bills issued by the Fed were backed by gold and could be redeemed for bullion. Now, however, the dollar is a *fiat currency*, meaning that it is backed by nothing and has value only because the Fed says it does.

In its modern form, the Federal Reserve has enormous power to manage the American economy and has occasionally come under fire for its policies. By design, the Fed is largely independent of the federal government and is sometimes accused of prioritizing stability over economic growth or reducing unemployment.

ADDITIONAL FACTS

1. *The United States was taken off the gold standard in 1933, and for several decades it was illegal to own gold as an investment.*

2. *Although the $100 bill is the highest-denomination bill printed by the Fed today, in the past it has issued currency worth up to $100,000 in face value.*

3. *The Fed has twelve branch offices scattered across the United States, which were established partly as a political compromise to avoid the impression the bank was purely intended for New York City financiers.*

* * *

Los Alamos

Located on a remote plateau northwest of Santa Fe, New Mexico, the town of Los Alamos was a secret for the first several years of its existence. Once an ancient Native American community, the isolated site was selected by the US Army to house a group of scientists who designed and built the world's first atomic bomb during World War II (1939–1945). Today, Los Alamos National Laboratory is one of the world's biggest physics and engineering research institutions in the world.

Early research on the atomic bomb was carried out throughout the United States. To centralize the project in a single location, head researcher J. Robert Oppenheimer (1904–1967) picked Los Alamos in 1942. The military officer in charge of what was code-named the Manhattan Project, Major General Leslie R. Groves (1896–1970), insisted on total secrecy. During the war, Los Alamos would not appear on maps, and the mysterious activities on the mesa were referred to only as Project Y. Mail had to be sent to a post office box in Santa Fe, and the town would not be allowed to have its own post office until 1947.

Eventually thousands of scientists would gather secretly in Los Alamos, including some of the most brilliant minds of the twentieth century. After three years of frenzied research, the scientists completed the first atomic bomb, which was tested in Alamogordo, New Mexico, on July 16, 1945. The scientists were painfully aware of the destructive force they were about to unleash on the world. After the successful test, one of Oppenheimer's assistants famously said to his boss, "Now we are all sons of bitches."

Nuclear research and testing continued in New Mexico during the Cold War of the mid- to late 1900s, although Oppenheimer and many other scientists eventually quit. The town's existence was revealed to the public after two atomic bombs were dropped on Japan in August 1945. Los Alamos is now one of the largest cities in New Mexico and home to an internationally famous government research center.

ADDITIONAL FACTS

1. Los Alamos *means* the poplars *in Spanish.*

2. *One of the scientists at Los Alamos, Klaus Fuchs (1911–1988), was a German-born Soviet spy who passed nuclear secrets to the Soviet Union. Based on the American design, the Soviet Union tested its own atomic bomb in 1949.*

3. *The town had its own high school, where world-famous physicist Edward Teller (1908–2003) taught an after-school class on advanced physics.*

★ ★ ★

Saul Bellow

Saul Bellow (1915–2005) was a Canadian, Quebec-born, who became famous as one of the most astute chroniclers of twentieth-century American urban life in novels including *The Adventures of Augie March* (1953), *Henderson the Rain King* (1959), and *Herzog* (1964). Bellow won the Pulitzer Prize for *Humboldt's Gift* (1975) and the 1976 Nobel Prize for Literature for lifetime achievement. Bellow's novels—comic on one page, deeply philosophical on the next—are considered among the finest examples of American literature of the late twentieth century.

When he was nine years old, Bellow moved with his family to Chicago, the city that would be the setting for many of his novels. He graduated from Northwestern University, was rejected by the US Army during World War II (1939–1945) for health problems, and wrote his debut novel, *Dangling Man*, in 1944. Nine years later, Bellow published *The Adventures of Augie March*, his first hit and still one of his most celebrated novels. Set in Chicago during the Great Depression of the 1930s, the book chronicles the exploits of its blustering hero as he careens from job to job searching for his calling in life.

In addition to his novels, Bellow was a prolific essayist, playwright, and short story writer; he even covered the 1967 Arab-Israeli war for *Newsday*. He taught at several universities, most famously at the University of Chicago, where he was a faculty member of the school's Committee on Social Thought.

Later in life, Bellow developed a reputation as a contrarian and provocateur. He was unsparing in his criticism of authors he disliked, and he enjoyed jousting with left-wing and feminist literary critics. By Bellow's own description, he was widely regarded as "an elitist, a chauvinist, a reactionary and a racist—in a word, a monster." He continued teaching until his seventies, long after his books had made him wealthy, and published his last novel, the well-received *Ravelstein* (2000), at age eighty-five.

ADDITIONAL FACTS

1. *Before launching his literary career, Bellow worked briefly for Encyclopaedia Britannica, penning entries on great books.*

2. *Although rejected by the army in World War II, Bellow had more luck with the merchant marines; by the time he was accepted, however, the war was over.*

3. *Bellow almost died in 1994 after eating a tainted fish during a Caribbean vacation; he included the experience in Ravelstein.*

★ ★ ★

The Honeymooners

Although short-lived, the CBS TV comedy *The Honeymooners*, which aired between 1955 and 1956, was one of the most successful and influential shows in the early years of television. Developed by comedian Jackie Gleason (1916–1987), who played main character Ralph Kramden, the show ranked third on *TV Guide*'s all-time list of best television shows, published in 2002, even though only thirty-nine episodes of the program were ever recorded.

Television was invented in the 1920s and 1930s, but TV sets did not go into mass production until after World War II (1939–1945). Although color TV technology was available, the early networks all broadcast most of their shows in black-and-white.

The Brooklyn-born Gleason, a former cabaret comic, first debuted the *Honeymooners* characters in short sketches for DuMont, a long-vanished television network that once competed with NBC, CBS, and ABC. He eventually moved to CBS, where the half-hour version of the show began airing October 1, 1955.

The show featured Gleason as Kramden, a bus driver, and Audrey Meadows (1926–1996) as his wife, Alice. Art Carney (1918–2003) played one of their neighbors in a Bronx apartment building, sewer worker Ed Norton, who was, to many viewers, the show's most endearing character. Most of the show's plots involved Kramden and Norton, who are portrayed as ordinary blue-collar boobs—instead of the upper-middle-class families portrayed on most TV shows at the time—getting mixed up in get-rich-quick schemes and kvetching about their wives.

Despite its enormous ratings, Gleason and CBS discontinued it after only one year. A pioneer of the sit-com genre, the show influenced television writers for decades. Reruns of the show still air in syndication, a testament to its lasting impact on the medium.

ADDITIONAL FACTS

1. *Gleason was famously rotund but felt his roly-poly figure made him funnier.*

2. *In one of his last appearances, Gleason appeared alongside Tom Hanks (1956–) in the forgettable 1986 movie* Nothing in Common.

3. *Gleason was nominated for an Academy Award in 1961 for his role as the real-life pool shark Minnesota Fats (1913–1996) in* The Hustler.

★ ★ ★

Huey Long

Among the most colorful figures in American political history, Louisiana politician Huey Long (1893–1935) emerged as one of the strongest opponents of President Franklin D. Roosevelt (1882–1945) during the Great Depression of the 1930s. Although both men were Democrats, Long considered Roosevelt too moderate in his response to the nation's economic crisis. The textbook definition of a populist, Long favored massive redistribution of wealth, a version of socialism far more radical than Roosevelt's New Deal programs. Long was making plans to challenge Roosevelt for the presidency in 1936 when he was assassinated. The alleged shooter, a doctor named Carl Weiss, was killed by Long's bodygaurds in the incident.

Long, nicknamed "the Kingfish," was initially supportive of Roosevelt's New Deal. As Louisiana governor, he had enthusiastically backed public works projects in his home state, where bridges and buildings named after Long are still common. But as it became clear that Roosevelt's reforms would not offer far-reaching aid to the poor, Long began to champion a more radical alternative.

The popularity of Long illustrates the pressure Roosevelt was under during the Depression and the degree to which many Americans of the time had lost faith in capitalism. Although Roosevelt was later embraced by the Left, his New Deal was often conservative and cautious in the context of the 1930s, eschewing both the radicalism of Huey Long and the anti-Semitism of Northern rabble-rousers like radio broadcaster Father Charles Coughlin (1891–1979).

Part of Long's reputation rests on his personality and reputation for bare-knuckle politics, which partly inspired the main character in the classic novel *All the King's Men* (1946) by Robert Penn Warren (1905–1989). Long was undoubtedly corrupt. Accounting for the public works projects he brought to Louisiana was often unorthodox or nonexistent. Like most other Southern politicians of his era, he enthusiastically supported segregation.

On September 8, 1935, Long was shot and killed at the Louisiana state house in Baton Rouge. Long's premature death has left many intriguing what-ifs for historians. Roosevelt was reelected in 1936, without a serious challenge from the Left.

ADDITIONAL FACTS

1. *Long's last words were reportedly, "God, don't let me die. I have so much to do."*

2. *Long's younger brother, Earl K. Long (1895–1960), served three terms as governor of Louisiana in the 1940s and 1950s.*

3. *After Long was assassinated, his widow, Rose McConnell Long (1892–1970), won a special election to fill his seat in the US Senate.*

★ ★ ★

United Nations

The victorious Allies created the United Nations (UN) in 1945 in an effort to foster world peace and prevent another cataclysmic conflict like World War II (1939–1945). The organization, headquartered in New York City, now includes representatives from virtually every nation in the world. More than sixty years after its founding, the United Nations remains the premier international forum for resolving disputes, although critics complain that it gives the World War II victors unfair influence in a world that has changed greatly since 1945.

President Franklin D. Roosevelt (1882–1945) coined the term *United Nations* in 1942 to describe the international coalition against Nazism. As the Allies neared victory, delegates from fifty nations gathered in San Francisco in 1945 to sign a formal agreement creating the body. The UN was intended to replace the defunct League of Nations, which had proved powerless to prevent the outbreak of the war.

The various agencies of the United Nations govern international telephones, decolonization, even postage. But the most well-known part of the United Nations is the Security Council, a board of fifteen countries that is responsible for maintaining world peace. The principal Allies from World War II—the United States, Russia (then the Soviet Union), the United Kingdom, France, and China—hold permanent seats on and veto power in the Security Council. In recent years, India, Japan, and other populous countries have lobbied for permanent membership.

The UN's record in international peacekeeping is mixed. Arguably, the fact that the Cold War of the late 1900s never broke out into actual war proves that the system worked. However, critics have charged that the international body has been slow to respond to emerging world threats like nuclear proliferation and terrorism. Since the UN's establishment, successive American presidents from both political parties have sought to reform the body to make it more effective in the twenty-first century.

ADDITIONAL FACTS

1. *The United Nations compound, on the East Side of New York City, is considered foreign territory.*

2. *Traditionally neutral Switzerland did not join the United Nations until 2002.*

3. *The United Nations considered Philadelphia, Boston, and San Francisco before picking New York City as its permanent home in 1946.*

★ ★ ★

Internment Camps

In the aftermath of Japan's 1941 Pearl Harbor bombing, US President Franklin D. Roosevelt (1882–1945) authorized the military to imprison more than 100,000 Japanese-American civilians in internment camps scattered across the United States. One of the most controversial actions of World War II, internment was justified by the US military as a necessary precaution to prevent Japan from recruiting spies or saboteurs from among the Japanese-American population. More than forty years later, the US Congress and President Ronald Reagan (1911–2004) officially apologized to surviving internees for the violation of their civil liberties.

The internment order, which Roosevelt approved about three months after the United States entered the war, ordered Japanese citizens and Japanese-Americans on both coasts to report to the authorities for relocation. They were transferred to ten camps located in isolated parts of the country, where most would remain in spartan barracks for the rest of the war.

Some Japanese-Americans attempted to resist internment. Fred Korematsu (1919–2005), a California shipyard worker who didn't want to be separated from his non-Japanese girlfriend, challenged the order but lost a pivotal US Supreme Court ruling in 1944. "When under conditions of modern warfare our shores are threatened by hostile forces," the Court ruled in the Korematsu decision, "the power to protect must be commensurate with the threatened danger."

During the war, patriotic Japanese-Americans fought with distinction in the US Army even while their families sat in internment camps. The 442nd Regimental Combat Team, an all-Japanese-American US Army regiment, was one of World War II's most decorated army units.

In 1988, Congress apologized for internment and paid $20,000 each to all surviving internees. Korematsu was awarded the Presidential Medal of Freedom and died in 2005, shortly after filing amicus curiae briefs before the Supreme Court arguing against the imprisonment without charge of American citizens in the "war on terror."

ADDITIONAL FACTS

1. *One young internee, Norman Mineta (1931–), was later a cabinet official for President Bill Clinton (1946–) and President George W. Bush (1946–).*

2. *Through World War II, internment of foreigners was viewed as a routine part of war; German-Americans were interned in camps during both World War I (1914–1918) and World War II (1939–1945).*

3. *US senator Daniel Inouye (1924–) of Hawaii was an officer in the 442nd Regimental Combat Team.*

★ ★ ★

Louis B. Mayer

In 1918, film producer Louis B. Mayer (c. 1882–1957) moved to California, joining the rest of the fledgling movie industry in its exodus to Los Angeles. On the West Coast, Mayer became the head of the era's biggest studio, MGM (Metro-Goldwyn-Mayer), where he played a leading role in the creation of the Hollywood studio system and the modern entertainment industry.

Mayer was born in Ukraine, which was then a province of imperial Russia. His original given name was Lazar. His family fled to Canada to escape anti-Semitism when he was a child. Mayer eventually ended up in Boston, where he established himself as a film distributor to the nickelodeons—movie theaters that charged a nickel for admission—that were just beginning to emerge in New England in the early twentieth century. Mayer made his initial fortune distributing the 1915 blockbuster *The Birth of a Nation*.

By the end of the World War I (1914–1918), most major film companies had settled in Los Angeles, drawn by weather that was ideal for filming. Two years after making his fortune, Mayer joined the migration west.

MGM was founded in 1924, and Mayer was named the studio head, a position he would hold for the next three decades. In an era of studio "bosses," Mayer wielded enormous power over the entire moviemaking process at MGM: he signed talent, picked scripts to produce, and managed production budgets. Mayer moved aggressively to sign Hollywood's biggest names, including Greta Garbo (1905–1990) and Joan Crawford (1905–1977), to MGM contracts. He also oversaw the studio's transition from silent to talking films in the late 1920s.

By the beginning of the Great Depression, MGM was the nation's biggest movie studio, responsible for dozens of films distributed to American theaters every year. Mayer was highly conservative in his political views and cultural tastes, and he preferred uplifting movies with positive, patriotic messages. For example, MGM released such classics as *The Wizard of Oz* (1939), *Gone With the Wind* (1939), and *The Philadelphia Story* (1940).

Mayer was forced out in 1951 after MGM suffered several consecutive years of box-office flops, marking the end of the formative era in Hollywood history.

ADDITIONAL FACTS

1. *Mayer usually went by "L. B."*

2. *An ardent Republican, Mayer was offered the ambassadorship to Turkey by President Herbert Hoover (1874–1964) but declined the invitation.*

3. *Mayer was the highest-paid executive in the United States in 1936, with a salary of more than $1 million a year.*

★ ★ ★

The Pentagon

Built in less than eighteen months during World War II (1939–1945), the Pentagon is the world's largest office building and a granite icon of American military might. More populous than many small cities, the giant structure holds more than 25,000 workers in its five concentric tiers. An embodiment of the American military establishment, the Pentagon was one of the targets of the September 11, 2001, terrorist attacks.

The Pentagon was first proposed in 1941, as America's entrance into World War II appeared imminent. Its purpose was to consolidate a dozen different War Department offices scattered across Washington, DC, under a single roof. The Pentagon's simple design was a function of practicality and efficiency; President Franklin D. Roosevelt (1882–1945) wanted a building that could be constructed quickly without spoiling the views from the adjoining Arlington National Cemetery. The blueprint was designed so that no two points in the building would be more than a seven minute walk apart.

After the Allied victory in World War II, the Pentagon emerged as a symbol of American global military dominance in the Cold War. The term *The Pentagon* entered the language as shorthand for the United States Department of Defense, which has been headquartered in the building since its creation in 1947.

During the Vietnam War, the Pentagon became a locus for antiwar protests, including an infamous march on the building chronicled in the Pulitzer Prize–winning book *The Armies of the Night* (1968) by Norman Mailer (1923–). Although protesters failed to levitate the building through the force of their collective will, as planned, the demonstration did mark an early indication of souring public opinion on the war.

More recently, 184 people were killed at the Pentagon during the 2001 terrorist attacks. The building was quickly rebuilt, and evidence of the damage is virtually undetectable today.

ADDITIONAL FACTS

1. *Each of the building's five sides is 921 feet long, roughly the same as the height of the Eiffel Tower.*

2. *The Pentagon is located in Virginia, across the Potomac River from Washington, but it has a District of Columbia zip code.*

3. *There are 691 water fountains scattered throughout the corridors of the Pentagon.*

★ ★ ★

Ralph Ellison

The literary acclaim of author Ralph Ellison (1913–1994) rests almost entirely on *Invisible Man* (1952), the sole novel he published during his lifetime. The story of an unnamed African-American protagonist and his struggle to find his identity as a black man in American society, *Invisible Man* won the National Book Award for fiction in 1953 and endures as one of the century's greatest novels.

Ellison was born in Oklahoma City and attended the Tuskegee Institute on a music scholarship for three years. He moved to New York City in the 1930s, where he befriended Harlem Renaissance writers Langston Hughes (1902–1967) and Richard Wright (1908–1960), who encouraged his early literary efforts.

A perfectionist, Ellison toiled over *Invisible Man* for seven years. Autobiographical in many respects, the story follows the path of an idealistic young African-American man who wins a scholarship to an all-black college modeled on Tuskegee. He is kicked out of college for reasons he does not understand, however, and moves to New York, where he struggles to fit in with both the fractious black community and the white mainstream. He discovers that despite his efforts, white American society refuses to see him as an individual. "I am invisible, understand, simply because people refuse to see me," the narrator declares.

The novel was an immediate sensation and went on to sell millions of copies. Ellison took creative writing positions on the faculty of New York University, the University of Chicago, Rutgers, and Yale, and he began work on a second novel. However, the manuscript was lost in a fire at his house in 1967, and he was forced to start over. Meticulous in his literary craft, Ellison worked slowly but steadily on the new book, writing more than 2,000 pages, until a few weeks before his death in 1994, but he was unable to finish it. The novel, titled *Juneteenth,* was finished by an editor and published in 1999.

ADDITIONAL FACTS

1. *Ellison's full name was Ralph Waldo Ellison; he was named after the transcendentalist writer Ralph Waldo Emerson (1803–1882).*

2. *Ellison served as a cook in the merchant marine during World War II.*

3. *Too poor to buy a ticket, Ellison traveled to college in Alabama by hopping freight trains.*

★ ★ ★

Miles Davis

The most acclaimed jazz master of the late twentieth century, trumpeter Miles Davis (1926–1991) pushed the genre in new directions by incorporating *fusion* styles inspired by rock, funk, and electronic music into traditional jazz. An artist of wide-ranging tastes who spent decades at the pinnacle of the music world, Davis collaborated with legends ranging from Charlie Parker (1920–1955) to Quincy Jones (1933–) during his long career.

Davis was born in Alton, Illinois, and moved to New York City in 1944 to attend the prestigious Julliard School of Music. He soon dropped out, however, and began playing gigs with Parker's band. Davis launched a solo career later in the 1940s and soon won a recording contract.

New York in the 1950s was home to a thriving jazz scene, including legends like Charles Mingus (1922–1979) and Thelonious Monk (1917–1982), a generation that introduced a new level of sophistication to jazz music. The era's musicians are also credited with introducing the elusive concept of *cool* to American culture. With his fashionable clothes and suave personality, Davis himself practically defined hip; one of his first albums released, in 1957, was titled *Birth of the Cool*.

In 1959, Davis released the album widely regarded as his masterpiece, *Kind of Blue*. One of the best-selling jazz records of all time, the album showcases Davis's languid, lyrical trumpet solos as well as the talented backup band he assembled in the late 1950s. He released another seminal album, *Sketches of Spain*, in 1960.

Unlike some jazz purists, Davis was fascinated by the new musical styles of the 1960s, including the British Invasion bands. He began to incorporate elements of rock into his music, an unorthodox style sometimes referred to as fusion jazz. Davis even planned a collaboration with Jimi Hendrix (1942–1970), although the rock guitarist died before the project came to fruition. Davis released the groundbreaking fusion album *Bitches Brew* in 1970, which became an immediate hit.

Davis was plagued by drug problems for much of his adult life, and he temporarily retired for health reasons in the 1970s. He recovered in the 1980s and released a Grammy-winning antiapartheid album, *Tutu*, in 1986, shortly before his death.

ADDITIONAL FACTS

1. *Davis guest starred on an episode of the TV series* Miami Vice *in 1985.*

2. *To the consternation of jazz purists, Davis recorded a jazz version of the Michael Jackson (1958–) song "Human Nature" in 1985.*

3. *Davis won a posthumous Grammy Award in 1992 for the album* Doo-Bop, *a collaboration with rapper Easy Mo Bee.*

★ ★ ★

Harry S Truman

Harry S Truman (1884–1972) ascended to the White House after the death of President Franklin D. Roosevelt in April 1945. Truman was elected in his own right in 1948 in an extremely close race, but his popularity plummeted during the Korean War (1950–1953), and he did not seek another term in 1952.

In domestic affairs, Truman, a Democrat, proposed a set of welfare and employment policies known as the Fair Deal, but Republicans in the United States Congress blocked most of them and forced Truman to accept new restrictions on labor unions. Truman desegregated the military by executive order in 1948, a crucial civil rights milestone.

However, it was foreign policy in the wake of the World War II (1939–1945) that dominated Truman's presidency. With large parts of Europe and Asia in ruins, the United States was suddenly thrust into the role of the world's biggest military power.

The great question facing Truman was how strong a stand to take against communism. Under dictator Joseph Stalin (1879–1953), the Soviet Union had occupied much of Eastern Europe after the war and installed puppet communist regimes.

Some factions within Truman's own Democratic Party, led by former vice president Henry Wallace (1888–1965), favored a soft-line policy toward the Soviets, who had fought side by side with US forces during the recently ended war. On the other hand, Truman also faced pressure from the Right, urging him to attack the Soviets immediately to end communist domination of Eastern Europe.

In the end, Truman took the middle road, an approach that would become known as the Truman Doctrine. The United States would not try to topple existing communist regimes, Truman declared in a policy first outlined in 1947, but would actively seek to thwart future communist expansion.

The Korean War tested the limits of Truman's policy and ultimately caused the Democrats to lose the White House. In 1952, with no end to the fighting in sight, the Republican candidate, Dwight D. Eisenhower (1890–1969), won the election by promising to end the conflict. However, the Truman Doctrine remained the basic guiding force for American foreign policy for the remainder of the Cold War between the United States and the Soviet Union into the 1980s.

ADDITIONAL FACTS

1. *Truman is the last United States president who did not graduate from college.*

2. *As FDR's vice president, Truman had not been told about the atomic bomb program and had to decide whether to drop the bomb on Japan only a few weeks after learning of its existence.*

3. *Truman's middle initial, S, does not actually stand for anything.*

★ ★ ★

GI Bill

World War II (1939–1945) required the largest mobilization of armed forces in American military history. Near the end of the war, the United States Congress passed the GI Bill of Rights to help returning veterans readjust to civilian life. The GI Bill, one of the most successful government programs in history, paid college tuition and subsidized mortgages for millions of soldiers, reflecting a new sense of what the American government owed those who served in uniform.

After the Civil War (1861–1865) and World War I (1914–1918), Congress had provided pensions and modest aid to soldiers and their widows and had also built retirement homes for veterans. Still, many crippled by war injuries or psychological damage from combat—felt their government had abandoned them. This dissatisfaction culminated in the Bonus March in 1932, during the Great Depression, when more than 20,000 World War I veterans marched on Washington, DC, demanding immediate payment of a war bonus that they had been promised. In a low point of his presidency, Herbert Hoover (1874–1964) was forced to call out the army to chase angry crowds of veterans out of the capital.

The GI Bill, passed in 1944 and signed into law by President Franklin D. Roosevelt (1882–1945), promised a far more active role for government in helping soldiers reenter civilian life. In addition to the education benefits, soldiers could also receive low-interest loans for buying a house and generous unemployment benefits while they looked for a job. In all, more than two million soldiers used their education benefits after World War II, causing a massive increase in college enrollment nationwide.

In addition, the government greatly expanded the medical care available for veterans after World War II and the Vietnam War (1957–1975). In 1988, President Ronald Reagan (1911–2004) created the cabinet-level Department of Veterans Affairs to manage the chain of hospitals, financial assistance, retirement facilities, and cemeteries for soldiers. Today the GI Bill remains the centerpiece of the federal government's commitment to veterans and a significant force for giving the disadvantaged access to a college education.

ADDITIONAL FACTS

1. *GI, the famed nickname for American soldiers, does not actually stand for anything and is not official government terminology. The official name of the GI Bill was the Servicemen's Readjustment Act.*

2. *The act provided unemployment insurance for returning soldiers who couldn't find work, but in the booming postwar economy, far fewer GIs than expected needed the help.*

3. *President Roosevelt, hoping to avoid a repeat of the Bonus Army fiasco, had first proposed a GI bill during the 1930s as part of the New Deal, but Congress did not approve the program.*

★ ★ ★

Military Desegregation

During World War II, minority soldiers fought with distinction in segregated military units, including the famous all-black Tuskegee Airmen and the all-Japanese-American 442nd Regimental Combat Team. The heroism demonstrated by black soldiers in the war made continued discrimination in the military increasingly indefensible, and in 1948 President Harry Truman (1884–1972) signed Executive Order Number 9981, fully integrating the armed forces.

Truman's order ended a century of second-class treatment for African-Americans in the military. Although hundreds of thousands of black soldiers had enlisted in the Civil War (1861–1865), World War I (1914–1918), and World War II (1939–1945), they were often kept in segregated barracks. While the army appointed a handful of black officers, the navy and marines did not commission an African-American until the closing days of World War II. Black units fighting in Europe often received secondhand equipment and inadequate training.

The military desegregation order also had ramifications that extended beyond the battlefield. In an era when virtually all American men were subject to the draft, the military was an important social institution. In the Korean War (1950–1953), which began two years after Truman's order, thousands of white soldiers would fight alongside black ones and learn to regard them as comrades.

In the years since Truman's order, the military has transformed into one of the most racially diverse institutions in American society and has played a leading role in promoting acceptance of integration. About forty years later, a black general, Colin Powell (1937–), led American forces to victory in the 1991 Gulf War.

ADDITIONAL FACTS

1. *Many top officers, including World War II hero Omar Bradley (1893–1981), opposed desegregation as being bad for morale, but Truman ignored them.*

2. *In total, more than one million blacks served in World War II, making up about 10 percent of the entire United States force.*

3. *Truman's pro–civil rights stance enraged the so-called Dixiecrat wing of the Democratic Party, which abandoned him in the 1948 election.*

★ ★ ★

Shepherd-Towner Act

The Shepherd-Towner Act, a health-care law approved by the United States Congress in 1921, was one of the first steps in the creation of the modern welfare state. Although modest by contemporary standards, the grants for poor mothers and children authorized by the bill represented one of the first concerted national efforts to construct a social safety net. The act, which sponsored wellness care for mothers and newborn babies, expired in 1929, but would serve as a model and precedent for the social welfare programs enacted during the Great Depression of the 1930s.

At the beginning of the twentieth century, infant mortality in the United States approached 20 percent. For every 1,000 babies born in 1900, for instance, 165 died before reaching their first birthday. Many families lacked awareness of fundamental hygiene and could not afford doctors or a hospital delivery for their babies.

The Shepherd-Towner Act, one of the key reforms of the Progressive Era, stemmed from the advocacy of urban reformers like Jane Addams (1860–1935). It was also, not coincidentally, passed by the first Congress elected with women's votes following the Nineteenth Amendment's ratification in 1920. During the years the law remained in effect, thousands of nurses funded by the federal government visited pregnant women across the nation, offering education on basic child-care techniques. Along with other progressive reforms, the law had a far-reaching impact; by 1930, infant mortality was less than 80 per 1,000 and would continue to fall.

The passage of the act signaled a shift in attitudes about welfare that would accelerate during the Great Depression. Prior to Shepherd-Towner, aid to the poor was widely perceived by the American public as the function of private charities or local governments. However, the Depression overwhelmed these traditional sources of "relief." As a result, the federal government greatly expanded its role in the welfare system, creating Social Security and many employment programs. The welfare state expanded still further in the 1960s thanks to the Great Society programs championed by President Lyndon B. Johnson (1908–1973).

ADDITIONAL FACTS

1. *Congress passed the act amid fears that newly enfranchised women would vote strictly based on gender; those fears dissipated after it became clear in the 1920s that women voted along much the same lines as men.*

2. *Because it involved the federal government in child care, the Shepherd-Towner Act was controversial; one Ohio medical journal inveighed against what it called the "federal, detached, impersonal, expensive and paternalistic system" created by the act.*

3. *The League of Women Voters was a major force behind the bill and convinced legislatures in every state but Connecticut, Illinois, and Massachusetts to provide matching funds.*

★ ★ ★

Levittown

The bedroom community of Levittown, New York, was built in 1947 to house American veterans returning home from World War II (1939–1945). Considered one of the first modern suburbs, Levittown was the template for thousands of housing subdivisions that led to profound demographic and cultural changes in postwar American society.

After the war, the United States faced an unprecedented housing shortage. Millions of returning veterans wanted to get married and start a family but encountered difficulty in finding an affordable place to live. The GI Bill guaranteed veterans low-interest housing loans, but housing was so scarce that many were unable to use them.

To capitalize on the massive demand for housing, the construction firm of Levitt and Sons bought a defunct potato farm on Long Island in New York and announced plans to build 2,000 homes. Within days, the houses had all been rented, many of them to ex-GIs. The company mass-produced the homes, which kept costs low but produced street after street of identical houses.

Levittown was a huge success, and the Levitts rapidly expanded the community to meet demand. By 1948, their army of workers was completing thirty new homes a day. In 1950, family patriarch William Levitt (1907–1994) was featured on the cover of *Time* magazine. The firm also built suburbs in New Jersey and Pennsylvania, making the word *Levittown* synonymous with *suburb*.

With the growth of the suburbs, the American population began to melt away from city centers, a major demographic shift. Cars quickly replaced trains as the most popular form of transportation, and city planners like New York's Robert Moses (1888–1981) built new expressways to carry suburbanites to their jobs in the city. The exodus to suburbia intensified in the 1960s with the "white flight" of the middle class from strife-torn urban areas. Levittown, the prototypical suburb, now boasts a population of about 50,000—more than many small cities.

ADDITIONAL FACTS

1. *Most of the early homes in Levittown were built without a basement to save time and money.*

2. *Beginning in 1950, Levitt homes came with a TV set preinstalled.*

3. *The Levitts refused to sell to African-Americans, and the suburb is still about 95 percent white.*

★ ★ ★

James Baldwin

In 1956, three years after his critically acclaimed debut novel, *Go Tell It on the Mountain*, author James Baldwin (1924–1987) released a second novel, *Giovanni's Room*. The novel surprised many of Baldwin's readers. Unlike *Go Tell It on the Mountain*, a story about an African-American teenager and his tyrannical father, the main characters in *Giovanni's Room* were white. And, far more controversially, they were gay. In the novel, the two main characters engage in a homosexual love affair at the Paris apartment belonging to one of the men.

First as a black man in the United States, then as an American expatriate in France, and always as a gay man in a hostile world, Baldwin was a perpetual outsider. He was born in the Harlem neighborhood of New York City and grew up in an intensely religious household ruled by a cruel stepfather who disapproved of his artistic ambitions. Baldwin was mentored by several Harlem Renaissance writers, especially Richard Wright (1908–1960), but later broke with Wright and moved to France. *Go Tell It on the Mountain* was highly autobiographical and explored the contradictory role of religion in African-American life as both the glue holding the community together and a cruel, repressive force.

Baldwin published *Giovanni's Room* long before such frank discussions of homosexuality were considered mainstream, and the book received a puzzled, lukewarm response. Despite Baldwin's dedication to the civil rights movement in the 1960s, his writing on homosexuality caused many leaders of the movement to keep their distance from him. In a later interview in the *New York Times Book Review*, Baldwin acknowledged that he had spent most of his literary career as a "maverick"—"in the sense that I depended on neither the white world nor the black world," he said.

In addition to his fiction, Baldwin published many articles and an influential book of autobiographical essays, *Notes of a Native Son*. In the opinion of some critics, including the poet Langston Hughes (1902–1967), Baldwin's essays were superior to his fiction. "He is much better at provoking thought in the essay than he is in arousing emotion in fiction," Hughes wrote. Baldwin died at age sixty-three at his home in France; his funeral in New York City was attended by many leading writers, including Toni Morrison (1931–), Maya Angelou (1928–), and Amiri Baraka (1934–).

ADDITIONAL FACTS

1. *Baldwin was made a commander of the Legion of Honor in 1986 by the French government.*

2. *The title of* Go Tell It on the Mountain *was inspired by a well-known religious spiritual.*

3. *Baldwin participated in the 1963 civil rights march in Washington, DC, that was the setting for Martin Luther King Jr.'s "I Have a Dream" speech.*

★ ★ ★

Chuck Berry

Singer and guitarist Chuck Berry (1926–) is one of the most influential musicians in American history, a rock pioneer imitated by countless stars. He also was one of the most high-profile victims of the extreme racism African-American performers were subjected to in the 1950s.

Born in St. Louis, Charles Edward Anderson Berry listened to blues and swing music on the radio as a child and began singing and playing guitar at parties in high school. In 1944, however, Berry and several friends were arrested for robbery in Kansas City and sentenced to ten years in juvenile prison. Berry was released after three years, married, and got a job at an automobile plant in his hometown.

In the early 1950s, Berry joined a blues band and began to play gigs at nightclubs in St. Louis. The trio flourished, largely thanks to Berry's energetic stage presence. A born entertainer, Berry quit his factory job and soon became the leader of the band.

In 1955, during a trip to Chicago, Berry cut his first record for Chess Records, the single "Maybellene." The song, half rock and half country, was an instant hit, selling a million copies and reaching number one on the *Billboard* R&B chart. Berry was cheated out of two-thirds of the royalties, however, in his first bitter taste of the music industry's racist treatment of African-American stars.

More big hits followed, including "Roll Over Beethoven," "Brown Eyed Handsome Man," "Johnny B. Goode," "School Days," and "Rock and Roll Music." Many of his songs, particularly "Roll Over Beethoven," became rock standards that were covered by countless other artists.

Berry was imprisoned again in 1961 after being convicted by an all-white jury on dubious charges of transporting a minor across state lines for the purpose of prostitution. While Berry was in jail, the Beatles and Rolling Stones achieved huge commercial success in the United States with songs heavily influenced by Berry. Although both of these British bands idolized Berry, he would develop a lifelong animosity toward Stones guitarist Keith Richards (1943–), once allegedly punching him backstage at a concert.

Berry continues to perform and is now recognized as one of the founders of rock and roll. In a testament to Berry's influence, the late Beatle John Lennon (1940–1980) once said, "If you tried to give rock 'n' roll another name, you might call it Chuck Berry."

ADDITIONAL FACTS

1. *Berry's last hit was the ribald 1972 single "My Ding-A-Ling," which is about exactly what it sounds like it's about.*

2. *One of Berry's songs, "You Never Can Tell," was used on the sound track of the 1994 movie* Pulp Fiction.

3. *The Chuck Berry song "School Days" was covered by the* Simpsons *TV show character Bart Simpson on a novelty album in 1990.*

★ ★ ★

Dwight D. Eisenhower

Both political parties asked war hero Dwight D. Eisenhower (1890–1969) to run for president after World War II (1939–1945), and he chose the Republicans in 1952. As president, between 1953 and 1961, Eisenhower enjoyed historically high public approval ratings and presided over a thriving economy after ending hostilities in the unpopular Korean War (1950–1953). Eisenhower's amiable, pragmatic personality reflected a nation eager to get back to business after the upheavals of the war.

As a general in World War II, Eisenhower lacked the flamboyance and outsize ego of colleagues like George Patton (1885–1945) and Douglas MacArthur (1880–1964), but his quiet managerial talent propelled him to the top of the ranks. He brought the same traits—outwardly unassuming but adept at working behind the scenes—to the presidency.

In foreign affairs, Eisenhower's presidency was dominated by the continuing Cold War with the Soviet Union. He ended the fighting in Korea but approved controversial CIA-sponsored coups against the governments of Iran and Guatemala. In 1957, during Eisenhower's presidency, the Soviet Union launched its first Sputnik satellite, setting off the space race.

On the domestic front, Eisenhower's presidency coincided with the first stirrings of the major social changes that would accelerate in the 1960s. Civil rights first reemerged as a major national issue after the US Supreme Court ordered school desegregation in the *Brown v. Board of Education* decision in 1954. While no trailblazer on civil rights, Eisenhower firmly supported *Brown* and sent troops to Little Rock, Arkansas, in 1957 to force local authorities to comply with the ruling by admitting black students.

Eisenhower, who had shown little interest in politics until his run for the presidency, had little zeal for partisan combat, and his presidency was an age of comparative political peace on Capitol Hill. His most famous and lasting domestic initiative, the multibillion-dollar National Highway System, enjoyed wide bipartisan appeal.

ADDITIONAL FACTS:

1. *Eisenhower graduated sixty-first in his class of 164 cadets at West Point.*

2. *In the New Hampshire primary of 1952, Eisenhower did not campaign because he was still on active military service.*

3. *Eisenhower's likeness was on the dollar coin between 1971 and 1978.*

★ ★ ★

Cold War

The Cold War (1945–1991) was the international contest between communism and democracy during the last half of the twentieth century. During this era, the foreign policy of the United States was mostly driven by the desire to stop the spread of communism. Although the Cold War had a strong military dimension and trillions was spent on weaponry, the war was more a clash of ideas and a battle for the hearts and minds of people increasingly connected by technology. The collapse of the Soviet Union in 1991 marked the end of the Cold War, although communist governments still remain in Cuba, North Korea, and elsewhere.

The roots of the conflict date back to 1917, when the autocratic Russian czar was overthrown and replaced by the world's first communist leader. The Union of Soviet Socialist Republics (USSR) rapidly expanded its industrial base but also murdered millions of its citizens in purges and government-instigated famines. Although the United States and the USSR were allies against Nazi Germany in World War II (1939–1945), both sides regarded the other with suspicion, and relations quickly soured after the defeat of the Nazis.

After Germany's surrender, it was unclear how the United States would respond to the USSR's growing power. The Red Army had liberated several countries in Eastern Europe from the Nazis and installed communist puppet governments in Poland, Hungary, and East Germany, among others. In 1947, US president Harry Truman (1884–1972) promulgated the Truman Doctrine. While tacitly recognizing existing communist governments, Truman said the United States would actively oppose any further efforts to spread communism.

The Cold War was not without controversy. The ill-fated US involvement in Vietnam stemmed from the desire to stop communism from spreading in Asia. The United States also frequently backed authoritarian anticommunist governments in foreign countries. The tension between supporting democracy and opposing communism proved a difficult balance for Cold War presidents and foreign-policy makers.

The Cold War effectively ended in 1989, when jubilant crowds of young Germans destroyed the Berlin Wall in a wave of anticommunist revolutions in Eastern Europe. The Soviet hammer-and-sickle flag was lowered over the Kremlin in Moscow for the last time on December 25, 1991.

ADDITIONAL FACTS

1. *The term* third world *dates from the Cold War period and refers to nations that were neither part of the capitalist first world nor of the communist second world.*

2. *Germany, which had been split into the two nations of East and West Germany after World War II, reunited on October 3, 1990. The postwar Allied occupation of Germany officially ended in 1991.*

3. *At a speech in Missouri in 1946, former British prime minister Winston Churchill coined the term* iron curtain *to refer to the divide between communist Eastern Europe and the democratic West that emerged after World War II.*

★ ★ ★

Brown v. Board of Education

The 1954 United States Supreme Court decision *Brown v. Board of Education of Topeka, Shawnee County, Kansas* outlawed racial segregation in American public schools—one of the single most important and controversial decisions in the Court's history. The *Brown* decision provoked an enormous outcry in the South but set the stage for the civil rights movement and the demise of Jim Crow laws.

Prior to *Brown*, the Court had sanctioned segregation in its notorious 1896 decision *Plessy v. Ferguson*. Emboldened by the *Plessy* precedent, Southern states had imposed strict racial segregation in their school systems. While theoretically black and white schools were "separate but equal," in practice schools for whites were nearly always better funded and equipped.

The *Brown* case originated in Topeka, Kansas, where a group of African-American parents filed a class-action lawsuit challenging the city's segregated elementary schools. The NAACP agreed to take their case and assigned lawyer Thurgood Marshall (1908–1993) to represent the parents when the Supreme Court heard arguments in late 1953.

A few months later, the Court released its unanimous decision, holding that "separate educational facilities are inherently unequal." Topeka was ordered to desegregate its elementary schools. *Plessy v. Ferguson*, after nearly sixty years, was overturned.

In the South, lawmakers immediately grasped the huge implications of the *Brown* ruling and promised "massive resistance" if the federal government sought to integrate Southern schools. In 1957, President Dwight D. Eisenhower (1890–1969) sent federal troops to Arkansas to integrate Little Rock High School in a show of force that demonstrated the government's resolve to enforce the Court's order.

The *Brown* decision did not end segregation overnight, but it provided an enormous boost to civil rights advocates. Martin Luther King Jr. (1929–1968), in praising the Supreme Court's ruling, said, "It served to transform the fatigue of despair into the buoyancy of hope."

ADDITIONAL FACTS

1. *Topeka's Monroe Elementary School, the focus of the Brown ruling, became a national historic site in 1992.*

2. *The US government, concerned about its image abroad during the Cold War, filed a brief on behalf of the families, explaining that segregation in the South was "a source of constant embarrassment to this government in the day-to-day conduct of its foreign relations."*

3. *In the South, some towns closed their school districts rather than allow integration.*

★ ★ ★

Stock Market Crash of 1929

On the morning of Thursday, October 24, 1929, the Dow Jones Industrial Average crumbled. Stocks had gone up virtually without interruption since World War I (1914–1918), but the day that became known as Black Thursday wiped out billions of dollars in investments in a few hours. By lunchtime, the first suicides of speculators had been reported. The market actually regained some of its value in the afternoon of Black Thursday, but the next day the slide resumed. The following week, amid increasingly panicked trading, the market lost 13 percent on Monday and another 12 percent on Tuesday. By 1932, when the market bottomed out, the Dow had lost almost 90 percent of its value.

The five days of the stock market crash of 1929 were perhaps the single most traumatic events in the economic history of the United States up to that point. Compared to other crashes like the Panic of 1837 and the Panic of 1873, the losses on Wall Street in October 1929 were far greater in magnitude and affected almost every sector of the market. Additionally, during the prosperous 1920s, many average Americans had invested their savings in stocks, making the impact much more real and devastating for them than previous financial downturns had been.

Economists continue to debate the exact cause of the crash. In essence, analysts agree that the overheated market of the 1920s had pushed speculative stocks to unsustainable levels. The stock bubble had been fueled by unrealistic expectations and easy credit; when stocks collapsed, the banking industry was left holding millions of dollars in worthless loans. As a consequence of the crash, the entire banking industry was nearing insolvency by 1933.

The stock slide destroyed public confidence in the markets and wiped out the life savings of many Americans. Whether Black Thursday "caused" the Great Depression, however, is a matter of some dispute; the crash may have only reflected the same underlying economic forces that would cause the mass unemployment and business losses of the 1930s. The crash eventually led the United States Congress to impose stricter regulation on Wall Street. Stocks would not return to their pre–Black Thursday levels until the mid-1950s.

ADDITIONAL FACTS

1. *The biggest one-day percentage decline in stock market history was October 19, 1987, when the market fell by more than 20 percent.*

2. *At the time of the 1929 crash, stock market information was transmitted by the ticker tape machine; trading volume during the crash was so heavy that the machine often fell hours behind.*

3. *Under current New York Stock Exchange rules, trading is halted if the Dow declines more than 10 percent, a measure designed to prevent cataclysmic collapses like the 1929 crash.*

★ ★ ★

Las Vegas

The gambling mecca of Las Vegas was constructed after World War II (1939–1945) by mobsters, who transformed the dusty desert town into a worldwide symbol of fun and debauchery. With a population of about 550,000 today, Las Vegas is the biggest American city that was founded in the twentieth century.

Las Vegas was originally named by Spanish travelers before the United States acquired the territory in the Mexican War (1846–1848). *Las Vegas* means *the meadows* in Spanish. For decades, however, the area was mostly uninhabited. The United States Army built Fort Baker there in 1864, and it was connected by railroad in 1905. The city was officially founded by charter in 1911, although its population remained small. The State of Nevada legalized casino gambling in 1931, but it would be another fifteen years before Las Vegas became a major destination.

In 1946, the turning point in the city's history, the first big casino opened in Las Vegas. Built by Los Angeles gangster Bugsy Siegel (1906–1947), the Flamingo actually lost money at first, leading to Siegel's execution by his investors. Within a few years, however, the casino was a stunning success, and other organized crime figures moved to the city's famous Las Vegas Strip to open more casinos.

By the 1960s, Vegas, as it was familiarly called, was a thriving boomtown. Elvis Presley (1935–1977), Frank Sinatra (1915–1998), and other singers performed in Vegas casinos, making the city an all-purpose entertainment capital. (The city now calls itself "The Entertainment Capital of the World.") The influence of organized crime, meanwhile, was curtailed by city reformers.

To many writers, the explosive growth of Las Vegas and its unapologetic pursuit of human pleasure made the city an irresistible symbol of the United States in the twentieth century, both for bad and for good. In one of the most famous literary portrayals of the city, *Fear and Loathing in Las Vegas,* author Hunter S. Thompson (1937–2005) described the city as the last bastion of the American dream but also an icon of consumerism and conformity in modern American life.

ADDITIONAL FACTS

1. *Prostitution is legal in some Nevada counties, but not in Las Vegas.*

2. *Siegel's downfall was depicted in the 1991 movie* Bugsy, *which starred Warren Beatty (1937–) as the legendary gangster.*

3. *The US military tested atomic bombs for decades at a location near Las Vegas.*

★ ★ ★

Vladimir Nabokov

Although he lived in the United States for only about twenty years, Russian author Vladimir Nabokov (1899–1977) wrote several of the finest American books of the twentieth century, including his shocking 1955 novel *Lolita*, the story of a pedophile and his infatuation with a twelve-year-old girl that is widely considered one of the greatest novels ever written in the English language.

Nabokov was born into an extremely wealthy Russian family in the czarist capital of St. Petersburg, where he was raised in an atmosphere of aristocratic privilege. The family was forced to flee Russia after the outbreak of the communist-led Russian Revolution in 1917, and Nabokov would never return to his homeland. The family ended up in Berlin, where Nabokov wrote nine novels in Russian. Just before the outbreak of World War II in 1939, he fled to the United States, where he switched to writing in English.

In addition to his literary pursuits, Nabokov was an accomplished entomologist. After coming to the United States, he was made a curator of a science museum at Harvard, and he is credited with discovering several new species of insects, including one known as Nabokov's satyr (*Cyllopsis pyracmon nabokovi*). During his summers, he took long road trips across the United States to catch butterflies; his experience staying in roadside motels would figure prominently in *Lolita*.

With its main theme of pedophilia, *Lolita* has been controversial virtually since the day it was released. Nabokov was rejected by four publishers before he could find one willing to print the novel. It was banned by many libraries and labeled "highbrow pornography" by a *New York Times* reviewer. The novel follows the disturbing story of its narrator, a European expatriate named Humbert Humbert, who becomes enamored of a twelve-year-old girl named Dolores Haze, whom he lovingly refers to as "Lolita."

The proceeds from *Lolita* gave Nabokov financial independence, and in 1959 he moved to Switzerland with his wife. He spent the last seventeen years of his life in a luxury hotel on the shores of Lake Geneva, where he wrote several more novels in English, including *Pale Fire* (1962) and *Ada* (1969), also considered masterpieces.

ADDITIONAL FACTS

1. *Nabokov held teaching positions at Stanford, Wellesley, Harvard, and Cornell; one of his students at Cornell was the author Thomas Pynchon (1937–).*

2. *For the screenplay adaptation of* Lolita, *Nabokov was nominated for an Academy Award in 1962.*

3. *Nabokov's father was assassinated in Berlin in 1922 for his anticommunist views.*

★ ★ ★

Jasper Johns

One of the most well-known living American painters, Jasper Johns (1930–) achieved fame at an early age with his abstract portraits of numbers, beer cans, flags, and mysterious blank spaces. In recent years, paintings by Johns reportedly have fetched $80 million at auction, stunning prices that are testament to his enduring appeal.

Born in Georgia in 1930, Johns grew up in South Carolina, served a brief stint in the US Army, and then moved to New York in 1953 to complete one of his most famous works, *Target with Four Faces,* at age twenty-five. Like many of his other paintings, *Target with Four Faces* has no obvious meaning. It shows four orange human faces, their eyes obscured, above a large, menacing blue and yellow target. The painting evokes fear and paranoia, and critics have interpreted it as a commentary on McCarthyism, homophobia, or even atomic weapons.

By the early 1960s, Johns was a leader of the American art scene and an inspiration to pop art innovators like Andy Warhol (c. 1930–1987). Other famous works by Johns include canvases largely made up of a single color, such as *White Flag* (1955), a monochromatic painting of the American flag that sold for $20 million in 1998. Johns's works are highly abstract and rarely show human figures or identifiable objects.

By his thirtieth birthday, Johns was one of the most prominent artistic forces in the United States. His paintings and prints have been displayed prominently at the Metropolitan Museum of Art in New York City, the Smithsonian Institution, and around the world. At the same time, Johns is an occasional lightning rod for critics who decry what they see as the difficulty and obscurity of modern art.

ADDITIONAL FACTS

1. *Some critics have speculated that Johns's interest in flags derives from one of his ancestors, Sergeant William Jasper (1750–1779), a hero of the American Revolution.*

2. *In the 1970s, Johns illustrated a book by the famously difficult Irish writer Samuel Beckett (1906–1989), Fizzles.*

3. *Johns appeared in 1999 in cartoon form, as himself, on an episode of the animated TV show* The Simpsons.

★ ★ ★

Earl Warren

The chief justice of the United States Supreme Court during the civil rights era, Earl Warren (1891–1974) wrote many of the key court rulings that ended racial segregation in the South, in the process becoming the most controversial and influential American jurist since John Marshall (1755–1835).

Warren, a former California governor and attorney general, was selected by President Dwight D. Eisenhower (1890–1969) in 1953 to lead the high court. Eisenhower had defeated Warren in the race for the 1952 Republican presidential nomination but gave him the Court appointment as a consolation prize.

Almost immediately after his US Senate confirmation, Warren surprised his fellow Republicans by writing the first in a series of surprisingly liberal Supreme Court decisions. The first landmark case decided by the Warren Court, *Brown v. Board of Education* (1954), overturned a sixty-year-old precedent allowing segregation in public schools. Later, in the 1960s, the Warren Court declared that accused criminals must be provided with an attorney and informed of their rights—now known as *Miranda rights* after the name of that 1966 case, *Miranda v. Arizona*—among other decisions extending new rights to the accused.

Warren's decisions made him an extremely polarizing figure during the tumultuous 1960s. To liberals, he was a hero. Conservatives, on the other hand, deeply resented the Warren Court's rulings on crime, which they felt handcuffed law enforcement in a decade marked by riots and urban unrest. The *Brown* decision earned him deep enmity in the South, where many cities resisted orders to desegregate. Eisenhower, for one, described the appointment of Warren as the biggest mistake he made in his eight-year presidency. Warren retired from the Supreme Court in 1969.

ADDITIONAL FACTS

1. *After the assassination of President John F. Kennedy (1917–1963), Warren chaired the Warren Commission that concluded that Lee Harvey Oswald (1939–1963) had acted alone in killing the president.*

2. *Warren's father, Matt, was the victim of a gruesome unsolved murder in 1938, while Earl Warren was running for California attorney general.*

3. *Warren established such a reputation for integrity that during his first run for statewide office in 1938, he had the endorsement of the Republican, Democratic, and Progressive Parties.*

★ ★ ★

Korean War

The Korean War (1950–1953) was among the largest conflicts in recent American history but has been so overshadowed by World War II (1939–1945) and the Vietnam War (1957–1975) that some veterans' groups have dubbed it "the forgotten war." In the conflict, nearly a half million Americans fought and 33,686 died defending South Korea from communist invasion. After 1951, the war became increasingly unpopular with the American public, and President Dwight D. Eisenhower (1890–1969) agreed to a cease-fire that remains in effect today.

The roots of the war date back to 1910, when imperial Japan invaded the Korean peninsula and abolished the centuries old Korean monarchy. The brutal thirty-five-year Japanese occupation ended only with Japan's defeat in World War II. After Japan's surrender, the Soviet army occupied the peninsula north of the 38th parallel while the Americans occupied the south.

When the United States and the Soviet Union withdrew in 1949, they left behind two countries, communist North Korea and pro-Western South Korea. Both North and South claimed to want reunification, but only on their own terms. On June 25, 1950, weary of negotiations, the North Koreans crossed the 38th parallel, invading South Korea. Within weeks, president Harry Truman (1884–1972), ordered American troops to South Korea to aid in the country's defense.

By late 1950, the allies had successfully repulsed the North Korean invasion and crossed the 38th parallel into North Korean territory. The setbacks for the North Koreans alarmed the communist Chinese leader Mao Zedong (1893–1976). Worried that he would be next if the Americans defeated North Korea, Mao brought China into the war in the fall of 1950. China's entrance into the war was a serious blow to the allies and promised to prolong the conflict indefinitely.

The two sides continued the inconclusive fighting for the next two years. In the 1952 US presidential election, Eisenhower promised to seek an end to the war and was elected to carry out that promise. In the cease-fire, both sides agreed to return to the original border of the 38th parallel. However, a peace treaty was never signed and they remain technically at war. Thousands of American troops remain in South Korea today. North Korea, still ruled by communists, is one of the most militarized nations on earth and is widely regarded as an unpredictable threat to world peace.

ADDITIONAL FACTS

1. *The wartime leader of North Korea, Kim Il-sung (1912–1994), remained in power until his death, and then he was succeeded by his son, Kim Jong-il (1942–).*

2. *Initially, the commander of American forces in Korea was World War II hero General Douglas MacArthur (1880–1964), but he was replaced in 1951 after a falling-out with President Truman.*

3. *Although South Korea and the United States contributed the vast majority of United Nations forces in the war, the coalition included troops from many countries, including Colombia, Ethiopia, and Turkey.*

★ ★ ★

Montgomery Bus Boycott

The Montgomery bus boycott of 1955–1956 was one of the first major events of the organized civil rights movement in the United States. During the yearlong boycott, African-Americans in the city of Montgomery, Alabama, refused to ride municipal buses until the city abolished Jim Crow rules that required blacks to sit in the back of the bus. The successful, nonviolent protest made a national celebrity of its organizer, a local pastor named Martin Luther King Jr. (1929–1968).

Nicknamed "the Cradle of the Confederacy," Montgomery was a rigidly segregated city in 1955. On the city's buses, the law required blacks to sit only in the back of the bus. Additionally, if the white section of the bus was full, blacks had to give up their seats to make room for white riders.

On the evening of December 1, 1955, a black seamstress named Rosa Parks (1913–2005) was riding home from work on a crowded bus when the driver ordered her to give up her seat for a white man. Parks, also a secretary for the local chapter of the NAACP, quietly but firmly refused and was arrested. The next day, King announced his call for a boycott.

During the boycott, blacks in Montgomery organized carpools or walked to work rather than taking the bus. A few whites in the city supported the boycott by giving rides to workers in need. The city's bus lines, deprived of the revenue from black customers—who accounted for about 70 percent of the bus system's ridership—suffered huge financial losses. City officials had King arrested, but the move backfired by drawing national attention to segregation in Montgomery.

Finally, in the summer of 1956, a US district court ruled that Montgomery's bus laws were unconstitutional. The city and the state appealed the verdict to the US Supreme Court, but when the Supreme Court sided with the lower court in November 1956, King triumphantly called an end to the boycott.

The Montgomery bus boycott made heroes of King and Parks and drew national attention to Southern segregation. King used Montgomery as a template for subsequent nonviolent protests of segregation across the South in the late 1950s and early 1960s.

ADDITIONAL FACTS

1. *On her death in 2005, Rosa Parks became the first woman to lie in state at the United States Capitol.*

2. *The white backlash against the boycott was intense, and King's house was firebombed by the local Ku Klux Klan.*

3. *Another black woman in Montgomery, Claudette Colvin (1939–), had refused to give up her seat earlier in 1955. Civil rights leaders considered launching their campaign then but decided that a single, pregnant fifteen-year-old was the wrong symbol for the cause.*

★ ★ ★

Great Depression

Lasting between roughly 1929 and late 1941, the Great Depression was the worst economic crisis in American history. By any measure—the stock market, the unemployment rate, or wage levels—the Depression was a disaster of unprecedented scope and severity. The downturn triggered some of the most far-reaching economic reforms in American history, including a minimum wage, Social Security, new legal protections for unions, and much tighter regulation of Wall Street. Although the worst of the Depression was over by 1935, the economy remained feeble until World War II created an enormous economic stimulus that finally allowed American manufacturing to recover.

The cause of the Great Depression, which spread from the United States to most of the world like a global virus, is the subject of continuing debate. The shortsighted economic policies of the 1920s may have contributed to the collapse by creating an economy sustained by credit. Some scholars believe the Federal Reserve deserves blame, too, for failing to pursue wise monetary policies. The international gold standard—the prevailing monetary system after World War I (1914–1918)—is also often assigned some of the blame.

Whatever its causes, the Depression had a devastating social impact. The unemployment rate surpassed 24 percent; agricultural exports fell by half, putting many farmers out of business. Images of hoboes roaming the railways in search of work and breadlines on American streets added to the sense of gloom and despondency. Meanwhile, corporate revenues plummeted, and the stocks market lost most of its value.

After his election in 1932, President Franklin D. Roosevelt (1882–1945) proposed a set of reforms called the New Deal. At his request, Congress allocated billions of dollars for public works projects to put the unemployed to work. Roosevelt established Social Security, a public pension system. Various reforms to Wall Street, including the Glass Steagal Act of 1933, were intended to prevent financial arrangements prevalent during the Roaring Twenties that were blamed for the Depression. The unemployment rate fell in the mid-1930s but peaked again in 1938; the job market didn't recover until World War II.

ADDITIONAL FACTS

1. *Many New Deal reforms remain in place; one such program, the Federal Deposit Insurance Corporation (FDIC), guarantees savings accounts under a certain limit (usually $100,000) to prevent small investors from losing their savings if a bank goes out of business.*

2. *Gross national product, or GNP, a measure of economic output, fell nearly 25 percent during the Depression, by far the greatest decline in American history.*

3. *The Smoot-Hawley Tariff Act of 1930, which imposed a high tax on imports, is also blamed for the Great Depression by some economists who assert that it cooled international trade.*

★ ★ ★

Robert Moses

One of the most influential and controversial builders of the twentieth century, Robert Moses (1888–1981) shaped much of the New York City skyline by constructing hundreds of parks, bridges, highways, and housing developments in the nation's largest city. Although he never held elected office, Moses remained in positions of power within the city and state bureaucracy for about five decades and steered thousands of his pet projects to completion. In the process, however, Moses bulldozed many old New York neighborhoods, moves that alienated many city residents and continue to shape his historical legacy.

Moses was born in Connecticut and moved to New York City to earn his PhD in political science at Columbia University. After earning his degree in 1914, he began his political career as an idealistic reformer, writing reports on ways to improve the effectiveness of city and state government in New York. By 1924, most of his reform plans were gathering dust, but Moses had forged several key political connections. That year, he was installed as chairman of the New York State Council of Parks, beginning his career as a builder and planner.

Over the course of his long career, Moses ordered the construction of 416 miles of highways, 658 playgrounds, and dozens of swimming pools. He also built New York's Triborough Bridge, Verrazano Narrows Bridge, and West Side Highway. Arrogant and ambitious, Moses was a master of bureaucratic politics, a talent that enabled him to ram through hundreds of controversial projects even in the face of overwhelming opposition. Where neighborhoods lay in the way of his projects, Moses had them torn down. Like many other city leaders across the United States in the 1950s and 1960s, Moses was convinced that New York needed "urban renewal," which to him meant clearing away much of the city for gigantic housing developments and highways.

In 1974, after Moses had retired, journalist Robert Caro published a devastating biography, *The Power Broker*, which exposed many of Moses's backroom shenanigans and won that year's Pulitzer Prize. Although Moses continues to find many admirers, his style of grandiose urban renewal projects has largely fallen out of favor in American cities.

ADDITIONAL FACTS

1. *Moses ran for elected office only once, losing the 1934 New York governor's race by the widest margin in the state's history.*

2. *One of Moses's first major projects was Jones Beach on Long Island, which he intended as a getaway for the city's working class.*

3. *Although notorious for building hundreds of miles of highways, Moses never learned how to drive a car.*

★ ★ ★

Allen Ginsberg

Poet, jester, and political agitator Allen Ginsberg (1926–1997) was the guiding spirit of the Beat generation and the author of "Howl," one of the twentieth century's most well-known poems. A critic of American conformity, consumerism, and foreign policy, Ginsberg's poems expressed in vivid, jarring language the disillusionment of many Americans in the Cold War era.

Ginsberg was born into a Jewish family in Newark, New Jersey. His mother, Naomi, who suffered from mental illness and paranoia, would figure in several of his most famous poems, including the elegy he wrote after her death, "Kaddish for Naomi Ginsberg (1894–1956)." A gifted student, Ginsberg attended New York's Columbia University on a scholarship.

In the 1940s, the Columbia campus was home to several founders of the nascent Beat movement, including Jack Kerouac (1922–1969), the author of *On the Road* (1957), and William S. Burroughs (1914–1997), the author of *Naked Lunch* (1959). Beat literature questioned mainstream American middle-class values and celebrated individual liberty, nonconformism, and self-expression.

Ginsberg's "Howl," published in 1956 after he moved to San Francisco, is one of the most well-known texts of the Beat generation. In the poem, Ginsberg laments the self-destruction of many of his friends and peers. As Ginsberg saw it, they had been destroyed for challenging the oppressive norms of American culture. The poem famously begins:

> I saw the best minds of my generation destroyed by madness, starving hysterical naked,
> dragging themselves through the negro streets at dawn looking for an angry fix;
> Angel-headed hipsters burning for the ancient heavenly connection to the starry dynamo in the machinery of the night.

The poem's graphic discussions of drug use, homosexuality, and suicide made it highly controversial; the federal government initially sought to block distribution of the book under obscenity laws. After a protracted court battle, a judge allowed the poem to be published.

The censorship battle over "Howl" helped make Ginsberg a celebrity, and he was a constant fixture at political protests in the 1960s. He lived in New York City with his longtime partner, the Beat poet Peter Orlovsky (1933–), until his death from cancer.

ADDITIONAL FACTS

1. *According to the* New York Times, *Ginsberg's favorite Chinese food dish was steamed flounder in ginger sauce.*

2. *Ginsberg is mentioned in the lyrics to John Lennon's antiwar anthem "Give Peace a Chance."*

3. *The epicenter of the Beat community in San Francisco, City Lights Bookstore, is still open for business in the North Beach neighborhood of the city.*

★ ★ ★

Elvis Presley

Elvis Aaron Presley (1935–1977), the King of Rock and Roll, popularized the genre in the mid-1950s and recorded chart toppers including "Heartbreak Hotel," "Don't Be Cruel," "Hound Dog," and "Jailhouse Rock." Considered a brash, rebellious sex symbol when he began his career in 1954, Presley had an immediate influence on American and world music. The Beatles, Bob Dylan (1941–), and the Rolling Stones would all credit Elvis as a major inspiration.

Presley did not, however, invent rock and roll. The distinctively American musical style, built on a driving backbeat, guitar chords, and heavy percussion, was developed by African-American performers in the 1940s and 1950s, particularly Chuck Berry (1926–), Bo Diddley (1928–), Fats Domino (1928–), and B. B. King (1925–).

Born in Mississippi, Presley learned to sing at his church and developed an appreciation for the "race music" he heard sung by blacks. In 1948, his family moved to Memphis, Tennessee, where Presley caught the attention of Sam Phillips (1923–2003), the owner of Sun Records, a local recording label. Phillips believed that a good-looking white performer singing black musical styles had major business potential, and he signed Presley to a recording contract in 1954.

Presley's runaway success surpassed Phillips's wildest dreams, but it also created lingering bitterness among some of the African-American inventors of rock. Bo Diddley, in a 2003 interview with the *New York Times*, vented, "What gets me is when my white brothers started playing guitars and sounding like us, and folks said that Elvis started rock 'n' roll . . . Well, let me tell you Elvis ain't started a damn thing. I love Elvis, Elvis was great, I love what he did. But he came three years after me." Presley himself, however, was always quick to note his debt to African-American performers.

A string of successful movies—Presley appeared in thirty-three films during his lifetime—helped boost the singer's popularity. His career was put on hold in 1958, however, when he was drafted into the US Army and stationed in Germany. After his return in 1960, he was never quite able to recapture the magic of his earliest recordings.

In 1977, after years of drug abuse, Presley collapsed at his Graceland mansion in Memphis. The mansion later opened as a monument to the first American rock star.

ADDITIONAL FACTS

1. *Elvis's ex-wife, Priscilla Presley (1945–), played a lead role in the* Naked Gun *detective spoof movie trilogy (1988, 1991, 1994).*

2. *His daughter, Lisa Marie Presley (1968–), has been married four times, including to the singer Michael Jackson (1958–) in 1994 and to the actor Nicholas Cage (1964–) in 2002. Each of those marriages ended in divorce within two years.*

3. *Presley's 1968 single "A Little Less Conversation" was rereleased in the United Kingdom in 2002 with a techno beat and became a number one hit.*

★ ★ ★

George Wallace

Alabama governor George Wallace (1919–1998) led the political opposition to the civil rights movement in the United States, running for president three times on a platform of maintaining racial segregation in the South. The depth of Wallace's support was so great that he swept the Deep South in the election of 1968. Despite Wallace's bigoted views on blacks, he remained a perennial force in Alabama politics and finished his last term as governor in 1987.

A lifelong Democrat, Wallace entered politics when the South was still a stronghold for the party. With the backing of the Ku Klux Klan, a potent influence in state politics, he won his first election as governor of Alabama in 1962. In the election, he promised to "stand up for Alabama" by confronting federal efforts to force the state's schools to accept blacks. Wallace's first appearance in the national limelight came several months later, on June 11, 1963, when he infamously followed through on a promise to "stand in the schoolhouse door" in an unsuccessful effort to prevent African-American students Vivian Malone (1942–2005) and James Hood (1945–) from enrolling at the all-white University of Alabama.

When Wallace ran for president in 1968 on his newly invented American Independent Party ticket, he was universally scorned by the mainstream American political establishment. But he received national support, polling well even in pockets of the North where some white voters were upset by federal court orders to bus black students into their high schools. He was elected governor of Alabama again in 1970.

During his 1972 presidential run, Wallace entered the Democratic primaries rather than pursue another third party run. After polling well in early contests, he was shot in an assassination attempt that paralyzed Wallace's legs and derailed his candidacy. But he was elected governor of Alabama in 1974. Wallace ran for president one last time, in 1976, but pulled out of the race and endorsed fellow Democrat Jimmy Carter (1924–).

By the mid-1970s, segregation was fading into history, vanished from the schools and lunch counters of Dixie and repudiated by the rising generation of Southern leaders like Carter. Wallace, the last of a breed of white Southern politicians, eventually apologized for his support of segregation.

ADDITIONAL FACTS

1. *Wallace's running mate in the 1968 election was retired Air Force general and nuclear weapons enthusiast Curtis LeMay (1906–1990), famous for his role in the firebombing of Tokyo during World War II (1939–1945) and the inspiration for the character Buck Turgidson in the 1964 film* Dr. Strangelove.

2. *Wallace may be most familiar to Americans born after 1970 as a prominent character in the 1994 movie* Forrest Gump. *In the movie, actor Tom Hanks is digitally inserted into the famous videotape of Wallace's stand in the schoolhouse door.*

3. *Wallace's shooter, Maryland truck driver Arthur Bremer (1950–), was convicted in Maryland and given a sixty-three-year jail sentence.*

★ ★ ★

Bay of Pigs

In 1959, a guerilla fighter named Fidel Castro (1926–) overthrew the dictatorial government on the island nation of Cuba. The country's loathed ex-leader, Fulgencio Batista (1901–1973), fled to Europe. Castro and his rebels, including the famed revolutionary Che Guevara (1928–1967), promised they would hold free, democratic elections on the island.

At first, the American administration of President Dwight D. Eisenhower (1890–1969) welcomed Batista's overthrow. A few months after taking power, Castro visited Washington, DC, for a long chat with Vice President Richard Nixon (1913–1994), who was impressed by the Cuban leader's charisma.

However, within months, Eisenhower soured on Castro and authorized a secret CIA program to undermine Cuba's new government. At the same time, Castro increasingly embraced communist-tinged rhetoric and policies. In late 1959, he decided to eliminate private property in Cuba. The Soviet Union began actively supporting Castro in 1960. To date, the free elections Castro promised have not been held.

Eisenhower's successor in the White House, John F. Kennedy (1917–1963), reauthorized the covert anti-Castro efforts after he took office in 1961. The plan hatched by the CIA called for training and equipping a group of Cuban exiles to invade Cuba and drive Castro out of power.

On April 17, 1961, the invasion force landed at a beach on the southern coast of Cuba known as Bahía de Cochinos—the Bay of Pigs. Despite months of CIA training, the invasion quickly turned into a debacle. Pummeled by the well-prepared Cuban defenders, few of the ships carrying the invasion force were even able to make land.

The Bay of Pigs was a national embarrassment for the United States. American diplomats initially denied a role in the failed raid, but on April 21, Kennedy went on national television to accept responsibility for the fiasco. "There's an old saying that victory has a hundred fathers and defeat is an orphan. What matters," Kennedy said, is that "I am the responsible officer of the government."

The invasion was a serious setback for the United States. American hostility convinced Castro to seek a tighter alliance with the Soviet Union, thus creating a communist outpost a mere hundred miles from Florida. The next year, the Soviets tried to base nuclear weapons on the island, sparking the Cuban missile crisis that nearly led to war.

ADDITIONAL FACTS

1. *One of the CIA operatives trained for the Bay of Pigs, Virgilio Gonzalez (c. 1925–), later participated in the 1972 break-in at the Watergate complex that triggered the political scandal of the same name.*

2. *Castro had several of the Bay of Pigs invaders executed, and the rest were released to the United States several years later in exchange for food aid.*

3. *In the aftermath of the invasion, CIA director Allen Dulles (1893–1969) was forced to resign.*

★ ★ ★

Betty Friedan

Feminist author and organizer Betty Friedan (1921–2006) sparked the modern women's rights movement with the publication of her famous 1963 book *The Feminine Mystique*, which criticized the strictures placed on women in American society.

Betty Naomi Goldstein was born in Illinois. She graduated from Smith, a prestigious all-women's college, in 1942, and briefly studied psychology at the University of California at Berkeley. She gave up her academic career, however, and married a New York theatrical producer, Carl Friedman, in 1947. He later dropped the *m* from their last name.

As a suburban housewife in the 1950s, Betty Friedan began to notice that many young mothers her age were despondent, despite their material prosperity. Raising children and keeping a neat home, to Friedan and many other women, proved stifling and unfulfilling. In *The Feminine Mystique*, Friedan referred to this sense of creeping malaise as the "problem that has no name."

> *The problem lay buried, unspoken, for many years in the minds of American women. It was a strange stirring, a sense of dissatisfaction, a yearning that women suffered in the middle of the twentieth century in the United States. Each suburban wife struggled with it alone. As she made the beds, shopped for groceries, matched slipcover material, ate peanut butter sandwiches with her children, chauffeured Cub Scouts and Brownies, lay beside her husband at night—she was afraid to ask even of herself the silent question—"Is this all?"*

The book struck a nerve among millions of American women by giving voice to their frustrations, and it was a huge success. After its publication, Friedan would go on to help found the National Organization for Women (NOW, established in 1966) and several other feminist groups, lobbying against gender discrimination, unequal pay in the workplace, and restrictions on abortion.

ADDITIONAL FACTS

1. *As president of NOW, one of Friedan's first projects was a campaign to stop airlines from requiring "stewardesses"—female flight attendants—to resign once they reached age thirty-two.*

2. *She divorced her husband in 1969.*

3. *In the 1970s, concerned by what she regarded as the growing radicalism of the feminist movement, Friedan split with her former allies, whom she dismissed as the "bra-burning, anti-man, politics-of-orgasm school" of feminism.*

★ ★ ★

Minimum Wage

The federal minimum wage, enacted in 1938, was one of the most important of the New Deal programs signed by President Franklin D. Roosevelt (1882–1945) during the Great Depression. The United States Congress approved the first minimum wage of 25 cents an hour only after rancorous debate; one Alabama newspaper predicted "chaos" and the "destruction" of the region's economy if Southern textile factories were forced to raise their pay. As Roosevelt hoped, however, the minimum wage had an immediate impact on the American economy, raising the income level of about 750,000 workers while causing minimal job losses. Raised repeatedly in the seven decades since, the minimum wage is now widely considered one of the government's fundamental economic guarantees to workers.

At the time the bill first passed, wages in the United States varied widely by region and industry. Southern textile mills were particularly notorious for their low hourly pay, while in other parts of the country, such as California, most workers already made more than 25 cents an hour. Roosevelt proposed the minimum wage law partly as a matter of simple economic fairness but also as a way to give consumers more money to pump back into the economy, which, in 1938, was still struggling to shake off the Depression.

The law that contained the minimum wage bill, the Fair Labor Standards Act, also introduced a slew of other worker protections, including a ban on child labor and a requirement that employers pay time-and-a-half wages for hours worked in excess of forty per week. Modified several times since its first passage, the minimum wage bill is one of the main legacies of the New Deal and continues to regulate how American workers are treated by their employers. The minimum wage reached $1 in 1956 and has been raised periodically over the years. Under legislation signed into law in 2007, the minimum wage went up to $5.85 and was scheduled to rise further in increments through 2009 to reach $7.25. In recent years, however, many individual states have raised the minimum wage beyond the federal minimum—replicating the regional imbalances that helped spur the passage of the act in the first place.

ADDITIONAL FACTS

1. *Challenged by employers, the constitutionality of the minimum wage law was upheld by the US Supreme Court in 1941.*

2. *Farm owners initially were exempt from the minimum wage, but protections for agricultural workers were added in the 1960s.*

3. *An exemption in the law allows restaurant owners to pay much lower wages to servers on the theory that they will make up the difference in tips.*

★ ★ ★

Interstate Highways

In 1919, a young lieutenant colonel in the United States Army led a 3,251-mile expedition of eighty-one vehicles from Washington, DC, to San Francisco. The convoy, crawling across rough dirt roads, muddy trails, and barren deserts, completed its mission in what was then a record time for a transcontinental road trip: sixty-two days.

The officer was Dwight D. Eisenhower (1890–1969). Thirty-five years later, as president of the United States, Eisenhower would ask the US Congress to create a system of modern, limited-access interstate freeways to replace the treacherous roads he remembered from his cross-country trip. Built at enormous expense, Eisenhower's interstate highways would enable the growth of suburbs, slash driving times between the coasts, and change the way Americans travel.

Before Eisenhower signed the interstate legislation in 1956, the road network in the United States was a patchwork of state-constructed highways. The German autobahn system, which began being constructed in 1934 and had impressed Eisenhower during World War II (1939–1945), served as an inspiration for the new US federal system. "The old convoy had started me thinking about good, two-lane highways, but Germany had made me see the wisdom of broader ribbons across the land," Eisenhower later explained. To convince Congress to fund highway construction, Eisenhower and his allies in the automobile industry cast better roads as a national security project that would help the army move its convoys in the event of nuclear war.

Measuring 42,793 miles, the federal interstate highway system cost $111 billion over thirty-five years, making it by far the biggest public works project in the nation's history. Eisenhower, along with many historians of his administration, considered the interstate system his greatest domestic accomplishment. However, critics complain that the interstate system destroyed cities by tearing apart downtowns and that the billions of federal dollars spent on roads amounted to a massive subsidy to the road-building and automobile industries. Nevertheless, the highway system was officially completed in 1991.

ADDITIONAL FACTS

1. *In 1990, the system was officially renamed the Dwight D. Eisenhower System of Interstate and Defense Highways in recognition of the president's role in creating the highways.*

2. *The interstate system is partially funded with the proceeds from a federal gas tax, which in 2007 was 18.4 cents per gallon.*

3. *Eisenhower signed the bill June 29, 1956, while at Walter Reed Army Medical Center recovering from intestinal surgery.*

★ ★ ★

Lorraine Hansberry

Playwright Lorraine Hansberry (1930–1965) authored *A Raisin in the Sun* (1959), the first Broadway play written by an African-American. The play quickly became a landmark in theater history and inspired a generation of black writers and thespians. In 1961, *Raisin* was also made into a successful movie starring Sidney Poitier (1927–), and later a musical. Sadly, Hansberry wrote only one more play, *The Sign in Sidney Brustein's Window* (1964), before her death from cancer a few months shy of her thirty-fifth birthday.

A Raisin in the Sun, based on Hansberry's own Chicago upbringing, follows the fortunes of a working-class African-American family, the Youngers, who unexpectedly receive a $10,000 insurance payout after the death of their father. Each member of the family has different dreams for what to do with the money, and the play largely follows the family's fight over how to spend it.

The play's evocative title takes its name from "Harlem," a poem by Langston Hughes (1902–1967) that succinctly explains the Younger family's predicament:

> *What happens to a dream deferred?*
> *Does it dry up*
> *like a raisin in the sun?*
> *Or fester like a sore—*
> *And then run?*

Although *A Raisin in the Sun* tells a timeless story, it is firmly rooted in the unique experiences of the post–World War II generation of African-Americans. For Hansberry's generation, whose parents had moved out of the South during the great migration, a middle-class life finally seemed within reach—and with it, a whole new set of agonizing challenges and dilemmas.

More than forty years after the death of its author, *A Raisin in the Sun* remains one of the best-loved and most-performed modern American plays and was revived on Broadway in 2004.

ADDITIONAL FACTS

1. *Rapper Sean "Diddy" Combs (1969–) starred in the 2004 revival of* Raisin. *One unkind reviewer wrote that he acted "like a high school sophomore."*

2. *Hansberry inspired the song "Young, Gifted and Black," which has been recorded by Nina Simone (1933–2003) and Aretha Franklin (1942–).*

3. *Before* Raisin, *Hansberry had complained that most Broadway plays written by whites depicted African-Americans as one-dimensional "cardboard" characters.*

★ ★ ★

Leonard Bernstein

Musical polymath Leonard Bernstein (1918–1990) was the leading American classical music conductor and composer of the late twentieth century, renowned for his symphonies and leadership of the New York Philharmonic. In addition to his classical work, Bernstein wrote the musical *West Side Story* and dozens of other pieces of popular music for Broadway, making him one of the most versatile and successful American composers since George Gershwin (1898–1937).

Born in Massachusetts to a Ukrainian immigrant family, Bernstein was a piano prodigy at an early age. He graduated from Harvard in 1939 and then struggled to land a steady job in the music industry during World War II (1939–1945). He eventually won a position as an assistant conductor with the New York Philharmonic in 1943.

Like Gershwin, Bernstein was drawn to both the European classics and American popular music. As a conductor, he favored works by Gustav Mahler (1860–1911), Wolfgang Amadeus Mozart (1756–1791), and Franz Joseph Haydn (1732–1809), giants of the European classical tradition. Bernstein wrote two full-length symphonies, Symphony no. 1, *Jeremiah* (1944), and Symphony no. 2, *The Age of Anxiety* (1949).

Bernstein was no less adept at writing popular music, as exemplified by his Broadway musicals *Peter Pan* (1950), *Candide* (1956), and *West Side Story* (1957). He also scored *On the Waterfront*, the classic 1954 movie starring Marlon Brando (1924–2004). Fast becoming an international musical celebrity, Bernstein was officially put in charge of the New York Philharmonic in 1957.

A liberal Democrat who supported the civil rights movement and hired the Philharmonic's first black member, violinist Sanford Allen, Bernstein was also a friend and backer of the Kennedy family. Following the assassination of President John F. Kennedy in 1963, Bernstein wrote a Catholic Mass that was performed at the opening of the John F. Kennedy Center in Washington.

Enthusiastic and energetic on stage, Bernstein broke with many conventions as a conductor. He paced the stage, gesticulated wildly, and occasionally got so carried away by the music that he fell over during performances. Bernstein continued conducting until a few months before his death from smoking-related lung problems.

ADDITIONAL FACTS

1. *Bernstein was the first American to conduct at La Scala, the famed opera house in Milan, Italy.*

2. *He refused to accept an honor from the administration of George H. W. Bush (1924–) in 1989 in protest of what he regarded as government censorship of art exhibits dealing with the AIDS crisis.*

3. *On Christmas Day in 1989, Bernstein conducted Beethoven's Ninth Symphony—featuring the "Ode to Joy"—in Berlin to celebrate the demolition of the Berlin Wall.*

★ ★ ★

John F. Kennedy

Massachusetts politician John F. Kennedy (1917–1963) became the first non-Protestant president of the United States, serving three years in the White House before his tragic assassination in Dallas, Texas, on November 23, 1963.

Kennedy was born on May 29, 1917, in Brookline, Massachusetts, and attended Harvard, where he was a member of the freshman swimming team. His athletic experience proved useful during World War II (1939–1945), when as a naval officer he survived the sinking of his boat, PT *109*, by swimming to a nearby island with ten fellow crew members.

After the war, Kennedy was elected to the United States House of Representatives and then the US Senate. Family connections—both of his parents came from influential Massachusetts Irish Catholic political families—hastened his meteoric rise in the state's rough-and-tumble politics.

In the 1960 election, Kennedy faced tremendous obstacles. Many Americans were hesitant to vote for a Catholic candidate and had to be assured that Kennedy's first loyalty was to the United States, not the Vatican. In addition, the Republican candidate, Vice President Richard M. Nixon (1913–1994), was expected to capitalize on the popularity of the incumbent, Dwight D. Eisenhower (1890–1969).

Kennedy pulled off the upset, however, thanks to his personal charisma in televised debates and to dubious vote counting in Illinois. Compared to his opponent, the dark and brooding Nixon, Kennedy appeared handsome and optimistic on television.

Kennedy's inauguration in 1961 represented a generational turning point. Forty-three years old at the time he was sworn in on January 20, 1961, Kennedy was the youngest person ever elected to the White House.

In foreign affairs, the Bay of Pigs fiasco and the Cuban missile crisis dominated Kennedy's presidency, while civil rights struggles at home preoccupied Kennedy and his brother, Attorney General Robert F. Kennedy (1925–1968).

Coming in the midst of the Cold War, the Kennedy assassination was a national crisis. A single assassin, Lee Harvey Oswald (1939–1963), was arrested several days later, but he was murdered before he could come to trial for the killing.

ADDITIONAL FACTS

1. *While Kennedy was the youngest person ever elected president, Theodore Roosevelt (1858–1919) remains the youngest president ever to take office. Teddy Roosevelt was forty-two when his predecessor, William McKinley (1843–1901), was assassinated and Roosevelt assumed the presidency.*

2. *Kennedy is the only president who has won a Pulitzer Prize, an honor he was awarded in 1956 for his book* Profiles in Courage.

3. *The presidential jet,* Air Force One, *was purchased in 1962 by Kennedy.*

★ ★ ★

Vietnam War

The Vietnam War (1956–1975) cost the United States the lives of 58,000 soldiers and resulted in defeat at the hands of communist North Vietnam. The United States had entered the war gradually in the early 1960s, hoping to defend the government of South Vietnam from the communists. However, the ineffective South Vietnamese government had flimsy popular support and collapsed shortly after the United States withdrew from the war in 1973. Unpopular at home, the conflict in Vietnam provoked the most powerful antiwar movement in American history and was, arguably, the first war "lost" by the United States.

The roots of the Vietnam War trace back to Vietnam's colonial occupation by France. After World War II (1939–1945), Vietnamese rebels began battling the French, hoping to achieve independence. Their leader, Ho Chi Minh (1890–1969), declared himself a communist, but nationalist opposition to foreign occupation, rather than enthusiasm for Marxist doctrine, was the foundation of his popular support.

The French left Vietnam in the 1950s, and the country split into North and South. Ho Chi Minh's communists took power in the North, while the weak government based in the city of Saigon controlled the South. Many Vietnamese hoped for a united country and regarded Ho Chi Minh as a hero. During the 1960s, the North and South fought an increasingly bitter war.

The foreign policy of the United States, based on the Truman Doctrine, stressed the need to contain communism. Because North Vietnam was officially communist and received aid from the large communist powers China and the Soviet Union, US presidents John F. Kennedy (1917–1963) and then Lyndon B. Johnson (1908–1973) followed the doctrine's reasoning that the United States needed to prevent a communist takeover, which they feared would lead to a "domino effect" of other countries in Southeast Asia adopting Marxism.

The war failed. Where the White House saw a clash between communism and capitalism, the Vietnamese saw a struggle for national liberation. Amid giant protests at home and international opprobrium, President Richard Nixon (1913–1994) in 1969 initiated a gradual troop withdrawal as the fighting continued. The United States withdrew its last combat troops in 1973. The war ended in 1975 with the fall of Saigon. Fears that the fall of Vietnam would lead to the spread of communism in Asia proved unfounded. The United States restored diplomatic relations with communist Vietnam in 1995.

ADDITIONAL FACTS

1. *Measured in tons, the US Air Force dropped more bombs on North Vietnam than the entire Allied forces had dropped against the Axis in World War II.*

2. *American allies Australia, New Zealand, Thailand, and the Philippines also contributed forces to the Vietnam War.*

3. *Only two US senators, Democrats Wayne Morse (1900–1974) of Oregon and Ernest Gruening (1887–1974) of Alaska, voted against the 1964 Gulf of Tonkin resolution that authorized the war.*

★ ★ ★

Malcolm X

One of the most controversial African-American civil rights leaders, Malcolm X (1925–1965) advocated a far more radical response to white racism than did the more mainstream Martin Luther King Jr. (1929–1968). While King preached nonviolent resistance to segregation and envisioned the two races living peacefully side by side, Malcolm X labeled all whites evil and derisively referred to King as "Reverend Dr. Chickenwing."

Malcolm X was born Malcolm Little in Omaha, Nebraska, the son of a Christian minister. His parents were both active members of the United Negro Improvement Association founded by Marcus Garvey (1887–1940). His father died under violent circumstances—ruled a suicide—and his mother was committed to a mental institution when he was twelve. Malcolm Little drifted across the country, eventually ending up in Boston, where he was arrested for burglary and sent to prison in 1946.

While in prison, he converted to Islam and abandoned his "slave name" in favor of Malcolm X. He was released from prison in 1952 and became an organizer for the Nation of Islam, sometimes called the Black Muslims, a fringe Muslim offshoot group that supported creating all-black schools and businesses and minimizing interaction with whites.

Under Malcolm X's leadership, the group grew in popularity, eventually claiming 100,000 members. In the early 1960s, Malcolm X achieved notoriety for railing against white "devils" and suggesting that the assassination of President John F. Kennedy (1917–1963) was a case of "chickens coming home to roost." However, in 1964, he broke with the Nation of Islam to start his own Black Muslim group, the Muslim Mosque. He went on a pilgrimage to the Islamic holy city of Mecca that year, a trip that changed many of his beliefs; on his return, he embraced Sunni Islam, a traditional branch of the faith followed by most Muslims, and renounced his earlier beliefs about the inherent evil of whites.

His conversion to mainstream Islam outraged the Nation of Islam, and a few months after his return, Malcolm X was assassinated as he stepped to the podium to deliver a speech at a theater in Manhattan. Three men with connections to the Nation of Islam were convicted of the murder.

ADDITIONAL FACTS

1. *While a petty criminal in the Harlem neighborhood of New York City in the 1940s, Malcolm X went by the nickname "Detroit Red," a reference to his brown-red hair.*

2. *After returning from Mecca, Malcolm X changed his name once more, to El Hajj Malik El-Shabazz; after his death, his widow went by Betty Shabazz (1936–1997).*

3. *Malcolm X collaborated with the author Alex Haley (1921–1992) on his best-selling memoir, The Autobiography of Malcolm X, which was published in 1965, after his death.*

★ ★ ★

Military-Industrial Complex

President Dwight D. Eisenhower (1890–1969), in his farewell address to the nation in 1961, offered a warning to his compatriots. With the Cold War at full tilt, he cautioned Americans not to allow the needs of the defense industry to dictate the nation's foreign policy. Eisenhower called this corrupt nexus between policymakers and arms manufacturers the "military-industrial complex," a memorable phrase that quickly entered the political lexicon and has been hotly debated ever since.

In Eisenhower's view, as long as the United States was a military superpower, "the potential for the disastrous rise of misplaced power exists and will persist." The permanent defense establishment needed international tension to continue turning profits, he said, regardless of whether conflict was actually in the national interest. As Eisenhower explained,

> Until the latest of our world conflicts [World War II], the United States had no armaments industry. American makers of plowshares could, with time and as required, make swords as well. But now we can no longer risk emergency improvisation of national defense; we have been compelled to create a permanent armaments industry of vast proportions. . . .
>
> This conjunction of an immense military establishment and a large arms industry is new in the American experience. The total influence—economic, political, even spiritual—is felt in every city, every State house, every office of the Federal government. We recognize the imperative need for this development. Yet we must not fail to comprehend its grave implications. Our toil, resources and livelihood are all involved; so is the very structure of our society . . ."

Coming from a hero of World War II (1939–1945), Eisenhower's warning about the military-industrial complex could not be dismissed as the conspiratorial ravings of a left-wing crank. Few presidential speeches have had such a lasting influence; Eisenhower's warning to remain wary of the defense industry resonated for the rest of the Cold War and beyond.

ADDITIONAL FACTS

1. *After the presidency, Eisenhower retired to a 189-acre farm near the Civil War battlefield of Gettysburg, Pennsylvania.*

2. *Adding to Eisenhower's concerns in 1961 was the previous year's election of Democrat John F. Kennedy (1917–1963) to succeed him in the White House. Eisenhower reportedly called JFK a "whippersnapper" and regarded him as incompetent.*

3. *After Eisenhower's death, an aircraft carrier was christened in his honor by his widow, Mamie Eisenhower (1896–1979).*

★ ★ ★

St. Lawrence Seaway

Constructed jointly by Canada and the United States, the St. Lawrence Seaway provided an improved all-water passage between the Great Lakes and the Atlantic Ocean, opening ports in both countries to huge increases in international trade. When it opened in 1959 after five years of construction, the 114-mile seaway between Montreal, Quebec, and Ogdensburg, New York, replaced the Erie Canal as the main conduit of oceangoing commerce to and from the nation's industrial heartland.

Unlike the Erie Canal, the route from the Great Lakes to the Atlantic was not a single contiguous project. Canadian and American engineers built sections of the St. Lawrence Seaway in piecemeal fashion beginning in the nineteenth century. The Welland Canal, which connected Lake Ontario and Lake Erie on the Canadian side of Niagara Falls in 1829, formed the linchpin of this patchwork system. By World War II (1939–1945), however, many of these sections were too narrow for modern shipping, and the section between Montreal and Lake Ontario remained a gap in the waterway.

Discussed for decades, the seaway was resisted by railroad companies, which feared competition. After the war, however, the two governments resolved to complete the water route to the Atlantic by building a modernized system of canals, locks, and artificial channels deep enough for large ships. The US Congress approved American participation in the project in 1954.

When it was completed, the waterway allowed a freighter to travel from as far away as Duluth, Minnesota, to Montreal and onward to the Atlantic, bypassing both Niagara Falls and the rapids on the St. Lawrence River. Befitting its economic importance and symbolic value as a monument of international cooperation, the seaway was opened by US President Dwight Eisenhower (1890–1969) and Canada's head of state, Queen Elizabeth II (1926–), in a ceremony on June 26, 1959.

ADDITIONAL FACTS

1. *About 6,500 residents of the Lake Ontario region had to be permanently relocated as a result of changing water levels caused by the project.*

2. *The seaway closes during the winter, when ice makes navigation of the route impossible. It usually reopens in mid-March.*

3. *An icebreaker, D'Iberville, was the first boat to traverse the entire length of the seaway in 1959.*

★ ★ ★

Silent Spring

Silent Spring, written by marine biologist Rachel Carson in 1962, was one of the most influential nonfiction books of the twentieth century and is generally credited with jump-starting the modern American environmental movement by exposing the dangers of toxic pesticides.

Carson, born in Pennsylvania in 1907, worked for the US Bureau of Fisheries for fifteen years and wrote her first book on marine life in 1941. Her 1951 book *The Sea Around Us* won the National Book Award and established Carson's reputation as an eloquent explainer of complex science to general audiences. After the book's success, she quit her government job to devote herself to writing.

Although Carson spent most of her life in Maryland, she summered in Maine, where she became disturbed by the rapid disappearance of the state's rugged seashore to human development. Carson's first two books were largely apolitical, but watching the pristine Maine coast disappear helped turn her into a champion of land conservation.

Silent Spring, which took Carson four years to write, combined her expert understanding of chemistry and biology with a sharp attack on chemical companies and the government. In the book, Carson claimed that pesticides like DDT were killing birds—potentially leading to a "silent spring"—and endangering human health, too. Her book was immediately attacked by the pesticide industry, but virtually all of her research was soon vindicated, and DDT is now banned in the United States.

Carson died of cancer in 1964, but her book has had an enormous and continuing impact. Prior to *Silent Spring*, the environmental movement was largely defined by support for land conservation. By exposing the corporate malfeasance poisoning the atmosphere, Carson focused the environmental movement on pollution, a new emphasis that led to the passage of major antipollution laws in the 1960s and 1970s.

ADDITIONAL FACTS

1. *Carson never saw the ocean until she was twenty-two years old, during a visit to the Marine Biological Laboratory in Woods Hole, Massachusetts.*

2. *In 1980, she was posthumously awarded the Presidential Medal of Freedom.*

3. *Carson was nicknamed "Ray" by her friends.*

★ ★ ★

Bob Dylan

Over a career spanning more than forty years, singer-songwriter Bob Dylan (1941–) has written many of the best-known American songs of the twentieth century, including "Blowin' in the Wind" (1963), "The Times They Are A-Changin'" (1964), and "Like a Rolling Stone" (1965). Although Dylan will forever be associated with the '60s, when he burst onto the music scene as the purported voice of his generation, he continues to tour and record. Dylan's 2006 album *Modern Times* debuted at the top of the *Billboard* album chart in the United States, giving him the distinction of being the oldest artist to enter the charts at number one.

Born Robert Allen Zimmerman in Duluth, Minnesota, Dylan grew up in a middle-class Jewish household. As a teenager in the 1950s, he was a fan of early rock-and-roll pioneers like Little Richard (1932–) and Buddy Holly (1936–1959), and he learned to play guitar in several short-lived garage bands he formed with classmates. Zimmerman later changed his last name to Dylan, after the Welsh poet Dylan Thomas (1914–1953), and dropped out of college after one year to start a music career in New York City.

Dylan arrived in New York in the midst of an upswing of interest in traditional American folk songs. His first album, 1962's *Bob Dylan*, included arrangements of folk standards like "House of the Rising Sun" and "Man of Constant Sorrow," as well as a few of Dylan's compositions. The album garnered praise, but it was Dylan's second album, *The Freewheelin' Bob Dylan* (1963), that made him a star. The album included the song "Blowin' in the Wind," which quickly became an anthem of the civil rights movement and earned Dylan an invitation to perform at the 1963 rally where Martin Luther King Jr. (1929–1968) gave his famous "I Have a Dream" speech.

Dylan released several more albums in the early 1960s, nearly all of which are considered masterpieces. The press proclaimed Dylan the "voice of youth," a label that made him uncomfortable. In the mid-1960s, to the chagrin of some of his fans, Dylan famously "went electric," abandoning folk music in favor of his first love, rock.

Since the 1960s, Dylan has largely moved away from sweeping political statements in favor of introspective songs about love and relationships. The poignant 1975 album *Blood on the Tracks,* released after a messy divorce, is considered the major classic of Dylan's post-1960s career. Dylan has also been on an "endless tour" for the last two decades.

ADDITIONAL FACTS

1. *Dylan won an Academy Award in 2001, his first, for his song "Things Have Changed" in the movie* Wonder Boys.

2. *Dylan released the first volume of his autobiography,* Chronicles, *in 2004.*

3. *In a somewhat self-serving selection,* Rolling Stone *magazine named "Like a Rolling Stone" its number one all-time rock-and-roll single in a 2004 ranking, ahead of the number two single, "Satisfaction," by—you guessed it—the Rolling Stones.*

★ ★ ★

Martin Luther King Jr.

Jim Crow segregation—the practice of confining African-Americans to inferior schools, hotels, even bathrooms—ended in the South during the 1950s and 1960s thanks to a grassroots civil rights movement led by a Baptist minister, Martin Luther King Jr. (1929–1968). King organized many of the most effective political protests against segregation and became the most visible and eloquent explainer of the movement's goals. He won the Nobel Peace Prize in 1964; at age thirty-five, he was the youngest person ever to receive the award.

After World War II (1939–1945), segregation came under increasingly harsh national scrutiny, despite efforts by white Southern politicians to preserve it. President Harry Truman (1884–1972) desegregated the military shortly after the war, and major league baseball began fielding black players in 1947.

Still, segregation remained deeply entrenched in the daily lives of both blacks and whites in cities and small towns across the South. King's first major campaign, to desegregate public buses, began in 1955 in Montgomery, Alabama. The Montgomery bus boycott catapulted the twenty-six-year-old King to fame. He appeared on the cover of *Time* magazine in 1957 and later chronicled his successful protest in his 1958 book, *Stride Toward Freedom*.

Influenced by the philosophy of the great independence leader Mohandas Gandhi (1869–1948) of India and the American writer Henry David Thoreau (1817–1862), King adopted a nonviolent approach to political protest, in contrast to the frequent violence of his Southern white opponents. Aware of the dangers he faced, King said, "If physical death is the price that I must pay to free my white brothers and sisters from a permanent death of the spirit, then nothing can be more redemptive."

As the civil rights movement began to defeat segregation in the mid-1960s, King expanded his political agenda beyond civil rights to include support for antipoverty programs and opposition to the war in Vietnam. However, on April 4, 1968, King was murdered at a motel in Memphis, Tennessee. After an international manhunt, James Earl Ray (1928–1998) was arrested in London, where he had fled after the shooting. In 1983, President Ronald Reagan (1911–2004) signed legislation creating a federal holiday in honor of King's birthday. It has been observed annually since 1986, on the third Monday in January, near King's birthday of January 15. The only other American to be so honored was George Washington (1732–1799).

ADDITIONAL FACTS

1. In 1948, King graduated with a sociology degree from Morehouse College in Atlanta, one of the nation's most prestigious black colleges. He had entered at age fifteen.

2. Among his other accolades, King won a posthumous Grammy Award in 1970 for his spoken-word recording Why I Oppose the War in Vietnam.

3. King's assassin, James Earl Ray, died in prison in 1998.

★ ★ ★

Vietnam Protest Movement

The Vietnam War (1957–1975) provoked the largest and most successful anti-war movement in American history. Huge demonstrations in Washington, DC, combined with nationwide resistance to the military draft, helped turn public opinion against the war in Indochina. With popular support evaporating, United States combat troops left Vietnam in 1973.

No American war, of course, has been fought without vocal public opposition. New England states protested the War of 1812 to no avail. The writer Henry David Thoreau (1817–1862) went to jail rather than pay his taxes in protest of the Mexican War (1846–1848), and in the midst of the Civil War (1861–1865), massive draft riots broke out in New York City.

But those efforts pale in comparison with the protests mounted in the late 1960s. Regular protests on college campuses and symbolic gestures like the burning of draft cards reflected the popular opposition. In essence, opponents of the war argued that it was an unnecessary and immoral intrusion into the affairs of another country.

Sensing the popular mood, Republican presidential candidate Richard M. Nixon (1913–1994) ran in 1968 promising to bring American troops home from Vietnam. He narrowly defeated the Democratic candidate, Vice President Hubert Humphrey (1911–1978), who was hurt by his association with the war's chief architect, President Lyndon B. Johnson (1908–1973).

It took Nixon five years to deliver on his pledge, and during that time antiwar protests continued unabated. One of the most famous incidents of the period occurred in 1970 at Kent State University in northeastern Ohio, where National Guard troops shot and killed four unarmed demonstrators. The incident inflamed opposition still further.

However, the protests also created a lasting backlash. Some Americans regarded the demonstrators as overprivileged, long-haired brats unwilling to make the sacrifices for their country that previous generations had. The end of the war left the electorate deeply polarized. Indeed, a central legacy of the protest movement has been a yawning cultural divide.

ADDITIONAL FACTS

1. *The famous circular peace sign used by Vietnam-era protestors is believed to derive from a symbol first used by the antinuclear movement in England in the early 1960s.*

2. *Several Guardsmen accused of the shootings at Kent State were indicted in 1974, but the charges were later dismissed.*

3. *Amid criticism that young men were being forced to fight and die for their country but not allowed to vote, the Twenty-Sixth Amendment to the US Constitution was ratified in 1971, lowering the voting age from twenty-one to eighteen.*

★ ★ ★

Civil Rights Act of 1964

A major achievement in the struggle for racial equality, the Civil Rights Act of 1964 outlawed segregation and discrimination on the basis of race, religion, or gender. The law, which the US Congress passed and President Lyndon B. Johnson (1908–1973) signed over the strident opposition of powerful Southern senators, abolished Jim Crow and led to profound social and political reforms across the nation.

By 1964, the civil rights movement had scored a string of victories in local campaigns across the South, such as the Montgomery bus boycott and the successful protests against segregated lunch counters in Birmingham, Alabama. To build on these successes, President John F. Kennedy (1917–1963) proposed a major civil rights bill in the summer of 1963 to ban segregation nationwide. After Kennedy's assassination, Johnson continued to push for the bill despite the opposition of many his fellow Southern Democrats.

In the spring of 1964, Southern lawmakers mounted an eighty-three day filibuster in the US Senate in a last-ditch effort to prevent passage of the bill. The filibuster eventually failed, but every Southern senator except one, Ralph Webster Yarborough (1903–1996) from Texas, along with a handful of Northern senators, voted against the bill. President Johnson invited civil rights movement leader Martin Luther King Jr. (1929–1968) to the White House to watch him sign the bill into law.

Politically, the passage of the Civil Rights Act ended a century of Democratic domination of the South. Enraged by Johnson's backing of the bill, Southern whites turned against the Democratic Party in droves. In the 1964 presidential election, the Deep South backed a Republican candidate—Senator Barry Goldwater (1909–1998) of Arizona—for the first time since the Civil War (1861–1865). But Johnson was reelected anyway.

The Civil Rights Act of 1964 represented the biggest expansion of civil rights since the passage of the Fifteenth Amendment in 1870. Along with the Voting Rights Act of 1965, the law spelled the end of legally sanctioned segregation.

ADDITIONAL FACTS

1. As of 2007, only one opponents of the 1964 act—West Virginia Democrat Robert C. Byrd (1917–)— remained in the US Senate.

2. The filibuster was broken on June 10, 1964—the only time the Senate successfully broke a filibuster of civil rights legislation.

3. Johnson was aware of the political damage the bill would do to the Democrats, and he ruefully remarked after signing the legislation that "we have lost the South for a generation."

★ ★ ★

IBM

Arguably the most important invention of the twentieth century, computers have no single creator. The technology was developed by hundreds of scientists across the globe over several decades. However, the firm most closely associated with bringing computer technology into the mainstream during the 1950s was IBM, which remains one of the world's biggest makers of information technology.

IBM—which stands for International Business Machines—was a behemoth of mid-twentieth-century American business. Founded in 1911 and originally a manufacturer of adding machines and punch card equipment, the company made its first computer in 1944. The computer, called the Harvard Mark I, weighed five tons and took about six seconds to complete a multiplication problem. By the end of the decade, after significant refinements to the design, the company began manufacturing computers for business use.

The growing use of computers in the postwar era laid the groundwork for major shifts in the military and business worlds. Computers allowed for the organization of massive amounts of information, greatly improved productivity, and helped create the giant white-collar corporations of the late twentieth century. For the military, computer technology allowed development of far more sophisticated weaponry like "smart bombs."

IBM played the leading role in this transition and was the company most often associated with the computer age by the public. A national icon, it was nicknamed "Big Blue" for the conservative dress code imposed on its employees. IBM's image was not altogether positive. To some Americans, computers were an ominous invention that threatened to depersonalize society by empowering faceless machines. The killer computer in Stanley Kubrick's 1968 movie *2001: A Space Odyssey*, for instance, was named HAL—*H-A-L* immediately preceding the letters *I-B-M* in the alphabet.

Despite its success in the 1950s and 1960s, IBM made two major miscalculations that hurt the company. First, IBM assumed that the biggest profits were to be made in computer hardware, not software, and allowed a West Coast start-up called Microsoft to grab the market for business applications. Second, Big Blue was caught off guard by the development of the personal computer in the 1980s. Although IBM began marketing its PC in 1981, cheaper "IBM clones" that used the same microprocessors and software soon flooded the market. IBM's losses mounted, and many observers questioned the company's viability until a turnaround in the 1990s.

ADDITIONAL FACTS

1. IBM "unbundled" hardware and software in 1969, a momentous decision that gave rise to the software industry.

2. One of IBM's innovations was the floppy disk, which it invented in 1971.

3. In 1997, an experimental supercomputer designed by IBM called Deep Blue defeated chess champion Garry Kasparov (1963–) in a famed six-game match in New York City.

★ ★ ★

Trans-Alaska Pipeline

In 1968, a century after the United States purchased Alaska from Russia, massive oil reserves were discovered off the state's northern coast. Following the discovery, President Richard M. Nixon (1913–1994) authorized the construction of the Trans-Alaska Pipeline through the frigid northern reaches of Alaska to connect the new oil wells with the port of Valdez on the Pacific coast. The 800-mile pipeline was a boon for Alaska's economy and also one of the most challenging engineering projects of the twentieth century.

Most of Alaska's oil is located on icy Prudhoe Bay, an extremely remote area on the Arctic Ocean with few inhabitants. At the time oil was discovered, no roads linked the pristine region with the outside world.

Initially, some environmental and Native Alaskan groups lobbied against the pipeline, claiming construction would damage the fragile arctic ecosystem. The political climate, however, was not in their favor. In 1973, oil prices spiked as a result of instability in the Middle East, causing an energy crisis in the United States. Nixon, hoping the estimated ten billion barrels of crude oil in Alaska would help end the nation's dependence on foreign oil, signed legislation in 1973 fast-tracking the project in the name of national security.

The pipeline, which was completed in less than three years at a cost of $8 billion, required workers to battle subzero weather conditions in an earthquake-prone part of the Arctic. When it opened in 1977, the pipe wound across thirty-four rivers and three mountain ranges.

The discovery of oil in Alaska has been a huge plus for the forty-ninth state's economy and its residents (a share of the state's oil revenues are distributed every year to each Alaskan). Initial estimates of 10 billion barrels proved too low, and the region continues to pump about a million barrels a day. Still, Alaska's oil fell far short of fulfilling Nixon's dream of "energy independence" for the United States.

ADDITIONAL FACTS

1. *Designed to resist earthquakes, the pipeline survived a 2002 earthquake measuring 7.9 on the Richter scale without major damage.*

2. *A barrel of oil cost roughly $3 in 1973, before the energy crisis; the price now frequently tops $60.*

3. *As of 2007, the United States imported roughly 63 percent of its oil, according to the Department of Energy; Alaska provides about 5 percent of the country's overall oil.*

★ ★ ★

Hunter S. Thompson

Among the leading nonfiction writers of the 1970s, Hunter S. Thompson (1937–2005) wrote one of his generation's most famous books, the hallucinogenic odyssey *Fear and Loathing in Las Vegas* (1971). An inspiration to many writers for his wild, inventive prose, Thompson published several more books before committing suicide in 2005 at his secluded mountain compound near Aspen, Colorado.

Thompson was born in Kentucky and served briefly in the Air Force, where he dabbled in sportswriting for a base newspaper. After leaving the military, he moved to New York City, where he was fired from a variety of journalism jobs in quick succession. Thompson's big break came in 1966, when he published his first book, *Hell's Angels: The Strange and Terrible Saga of the Outlaw Motorcycle Gangs*, which was based on hundreds of interviews with gang members and produced rave reviews and respectable sales.

Hell's Angels was written in relatively conventional journalistic form. Not until 1970 did Thompson debut the unorthodox "gonzo" style for which he became legendary. Although difficult to define, gonzo journalism involved Thompson inserting himself fully into the story, often while under the influence of illegal drugs, and writing about the ensuing mayhem in the first person. The most famous example is *Fear and Loathing in Las Vegas,* a lightly fictionalized account of a drug-fueled trip that Thompson took to Las Vegas with a friend in 1970, which was first published in two parts in *Rolling Stone* magazine in 1971 and quickly released as a book.

Fear and Loathing in Las Vegas won instant acclaim and was followed in 1972 by *Fear and Loathing on the Campaign Trail '72,* an account of the 1972 presidential contest between Republican Richard Nixon (1913–1994), whom Thompson openly despised, and Democrat George McGovern (1922–).

Thompson became increasingly reclusive in the 1980s. He published *Better Than Sex* in 1994 and *Kingdom of Fear,* a searing attack on the administration of George W. Bush (1946–), in 2003. Disillusioned by the state of American politics and in increasingly bad health, Thompson killed himself with a shotgun blast to the head. In accordance with the author's wishes, Thompson's funeral ended when his cremated remains were fired from a cannon into the Colorado mountains.

ADDITIONAL FACTS

1. *Thompson was the inspiration for the beloved* Doonesbury *comic strip character Uncle Duke.*

2. *Johnny Depp (1963–) played Thompson in the 1998 movie version of* Fear and Loathing in Las Vegas. *Bill Murray also played the gonzo journalist in* Where the Buffalo Roam *(1980).*

3. *Although he rarely contributed to the magazine after the 1970s, Thompson was listed as chief of the National Affairs Desk on the* Rolling Stone *masthead until his death.*

★ ★ ★

Andy Warhol

Painter Andy Warhol (c. 1928–1987) shot to prominence in the 1960s for his glitzy pop art portraits of giant soup cans, world-famous celebrities like Marilyn Monroe (1926–1962) and Mao Zedong (1893–1976), and bottles of Coca-Cola. A shrewd self-promoter, Warhol quickly turned himself into a celebrity in his own right and was the godfather of New York's bohemian artistic community during the 1960s.

The son of a Pennsylvania coal miner and construction worker, Warhol moved to New York in 1949 and began working as an illustrator for magazines and advertisers. Although highly successful as a commercial artist, Warhol craved to make a name for himself on the art scene.

Warhol's breakthrough came in 1962, when he exhibited his famous portraits of Campbell's soup cans at a Los Angeles gallery. The gigantic paintings of the ubiquitous red-and-white cans typified both Warhol's work and the emerging pop art genre. Pop art, a vividly colorful style heavily influenced by comic books and advertisements, celebrated the iconic and the famous even while mocking the superficiality of American popular culture.

By 1965, Warhol was a major sensation in the art world. Over the next ten years, he made screen prints of celebrities ranging from Elvis Presley (1935–1977) to Jimmy Carter (1924–), as well as dozens of stylized self-portraits. Warhol was infatuated with fame—both his own and that of others—and worked assiduously to craft his own sensational reputation.

Warhol's New York studio, nicknamed the Factory, soon became a notorious hangout for Warhol groupies, avant-garde musicians, and artistic wannabes. This world of glamour and glitz, however, had a dark and violent side. One of Warhol's deranged fans, Valerie Solanas (1936–1988), shot and nearly killed Warhol at the Factory in 1968. Warhol returned after several years' recovery but died in 1987 after a hospital bungled the treatment of Warhol's gall bladder infection.

ADDITIONAL FACTS

1. Warhol produced an exhibit for a children's museum in Rhode Island in 1985 and insisted that the paintings be hung only a few feet above the floor, where only kids could look at them directly.

2. Warhol's last name was originally Warhola, but he changed the spelling after moving to New York.

3. Warhol's shooter, who said her murder attempt was a strike against male oppression, served three years in prison.

★ ★ ★

Lyndon B. Johnson

The thirty-sixth president of the United States, Lyndon Johnson (1908–1973) took office after the assassination of President John F. Kennedy (1917–1963). A Democrat, Johnson was elected in a 1964 landslide victory over Republican Barry Goldwater (1909–1998). Johnson did not run for reelection in 1968, instead returning to his home state of Texas.

Two major issues—the Vietnam War (1957–1975) abroad and civil rights at home—dominated Johnson's turbulent five years in the White House. As president, LBJ, as he became known, signed the Civil Rights Act of 1964 and the Voting Rights Act of 1965, two landmark pieces of federal civil rights legislation that outlawed discrimination against African-Americans and removed the legal barriers that had prevented black citizens from voting. In addition, Johnson signed legislation greatly expanding the federal benefits available to citizens—the so-called welfare state. Medicare, Medicaid, and federal assistance to public schools all date back to the LBJ presidency.

Still, it was the unpopular conflict in Vietnam that eventually forced Johnson to retire from the White House in 1968 and has clouded his legacy ever since. American involvement in Vietnam began under President Kennedy, but Johnson and his headstrong secretary of defense, Robert McNamara (1916–), greatly increased the American military presence in Southeast Asia in the name of preventing the spread of communism.

With casualties mounting, American public opinion began to turn against the war in the mid-1960s. Johnson responded by deploying even more troops. He initially planned to run again in 1968, but polled so poorly in early Democratic primary states that he was forced to abandon his candidacy.

Johnson remains a deeply polarizing politician in both the domestic and foreign policy arenas. Liberals applaud his Great Society programs expanding the welfare state, while conservatives see them as the quintessence of government waste. Likewise, LBJ is still harshly criticized for expanding American involvement in Vietnam.

ADDITIONAL FACTS

1. *Among the other civil rights milestones achieved during his administration, Johnson appointed the first black cabinet secretary, Robert C. Weaver (1907–1997), and the first black US Supreme Court justice, Thurgood Marshall (1908–1993).*

2. *Johnson won the Texas Democratic primary in his first race for the US Senate by a scant eighty-seven votes, earning him the sarcastic nickname "Landslide Lyndon."*

3. *McNamara later regretted his Vietnam strategy and wrote the book* In Retrospect: The Tragedy and Lessons of Vietnam *(1995). The subsequent film* The Fog of War: Eleven Lessons from the Life of Robert S. McNamara *(2003) won an Oscar for Best Documentary Feature.*

★ ★ ★

Military Draft

For most of its history, the manpower of the United States Army in times of war was supplied by a draft that forced military-age men to serve in the armed forces. The abolition of the draft in 1973 and the subsequent creation of an all-volunteer army reflected a significant shift in the way American wars are fought and the way American society relates to the military.

American attitudes toward the military have varied over time, reflecting the country's changing values. The Founders, including George Washington (1732–1799), regarded standing armies and navies with deep suspicion. Rather than fund an army, which reminded many Americans of monarchial oppression, the early United States depended on state-organized volunteer militias for its defense.

However, conscription became necessary during the Civil War (1861–1865), when the country ran short of soldiers. The Civil War–era draft was patently unfair, allowing the wealthy to buy their way out of service for a fee. It was also extremely unpopular and sparked draft riots in New York City in 1863.

The draft was reinstated during both World War I (1914–1918) and World War II (1939–1945) and remained in effect during the Cold War and until 1973. For a generation of American men, dealing with local draft boards became a rite of passage. Singer Elvis Presley (1935–1977) and boxer Muhammed Ali (1942–) were infamously drafted at the pinnacle of their fame. Presley was inducted into the army in 1958 and served two years, primarily in Germany, but Ali, drafted in 1967, refused to serve during the Vietnam War (1957–1975).

Although much reformed since the Civil War, the Vietnam-era draft was riddled with unfairness. Rich and connected men often won deferments. Indeed, the unpopularity of the draft contributed to the resistance to the war.

The current all-volunteer army also has detractors, who feel the nation should share equally in the sacrifice of military service. Several Democratic members of Congress routinely introduce legislation to reinstate the draft, although the proposals never attract more than a handful of votes.

ADDITIONAL FACTS

1. *Although unused since the Vietnam era, the bureaucracy for the draft remains in place, and all American men are required to register with Selective Service at age eighteen in case conscription is reinstated.*

2. *The US Supreme Court ruled in 1981 that it was legal to exempt women from the draft.*

3. *During wartime, men who could prove a religious or moral objection to all war, not just the war being fought, could avoid military service by earning classification as a "conscientious objector."*

* * *

Cesar Chavez

The most famous Mexican-American civil rights leader in United States history, Cesar Chavez (1927–1993) campaigned tirelessly for the rights of poor Hispanic farmhands in California and organized the first major labor union for migrant agricultural workers in 1965. Millions of Americans, appalled by the low wages and abusive working conditions on California farms exposed by Chavez and his union, joined a grape boycott in the late 1960s that forced growers to meet major union demands.

Born in rural Arizona, Chavez learned to farm on his family's small ranch during the worst years of the Great Depression. In 1937, the family lost their property to foreclosure, and for the next several years they traveled across the West looking for work harvesting grapes, carrots, melons, and cotton. Chavez joined the US Navy in 1946 and then returned to California, settling in the San Joaquin River valley, a major agricultural center.

At the time, conditions for migrant farmworkers like Chavez were abysmal. Paid less than $1.50 an hour, they received no benefits or job security, were subject to arbitrary pay cuts, and were often exposed to toxic pesticides. Past efforts to unionize the farmhands, most of them Mexican-Americans or Filipinos, had failed.

In 1958, Chavez formed the National Farm Workers Association union (in 1972 renamed the United Farm Workers of America and commonly called the UFW). As a union leader, Chavez devoted his life to the cause and accepted only a $5-a-week salary. The union's most notable success came in 1968, when Chavez asked Americans to boycott table grapes from the San Joaquin valley until growers recognized the union. The boycott was a huge success—about 17 million Americans stopped buying grapes—and in 1970, planters were forced to sign union contracts.

To Chavez, the purpose of the union was not solely economic. By demanding that growers respect the basic human dignity of their Hispanic workers, he was a hero and inspiration to a marginalized sector of American society.

ADDITIONAL FACTS

1. *Because his family moved so often in search of work, Chavez attended thirty-eight different elementary schools before dropping out for good after the eighth grade.*

2. *President Bill Clinton (1946–) awarded Chavez a posthumous Medal of Freedom, one of the nation's highest civilian honors, the year after his death.*

3. *California made Chavez's birthday, March 31, an official state holiday in 2000.*

★ ★ ★

McDonald's

Under the leadership of its founder, Ray Kroc, the fast-food chain McDonald's changed the way Americans eat. Starting in 1955, Kroc (1902–1984) assembled a global empire of inexpensive restaurants famous for their golden arches logo, speedy service, and food of questionable healthfulness. By the time Kroc died, he had built McDonald's into the country's biggest restaurant chain and a global symbol of American cuisine.

The first McDonald's opened in San Bernardino, California, in 1940 as a hot dog stand and barbecue place. Its owners, Dick and Mac McDonald, eventually sold the business to Kroc, a franchisee. By locating his restaurants in the growing American suburbs and advertising relentlessly, Kroc made the chain one of the most visible brands in the country.

The basic conceptual innovation of McDonald's was to apply the assembly-line logic of automaker Henry Ford (1863–1947) to food. Unlike its competitors, McDonald's originally did not make food to order. Kroc placed his emphasis on speed, efficiency, and quantity, for many years, the McDonald's billboard displayed the number of burgers the chain had sold as it climbed into the billions.

McDonald's has been highly controversial, especially in its foreign incarnations. In many countries, McDonald's is regarded warily as an American interloper. Domestically, McDonald's has been criticized for its low wages and high-fat food, which is sometimes blamed for the nation's ongoing obesity crisis.

Nevertheless, the company remains highly profitable and served as an inspiration for almost all the modern chain restaurants that now dominate American dining.

ADDITIONAL FACTS

1. *Original prices at the first McDonald's were fifteen cents for a hamburger, ten cents for french fries, and twenty cents for a milkshake.*

2. *McDonald's parent company also operates the Chipotle Mexican Grill chain and owned Boston Market until 2007.*

3. *Ray Kroc owned the San Diego Padres major league baseball team for the last ten years of his life.*

★ ★ ★

Love Canal

The federal government was forced to evacuate parts of Niagara Falls, New York, in 1978 after the discovery of toxic levels of pollution in the Love Canal section of the city. Dominating national news, the evacuation of Love Canal was a major environmental tragedy that alerted many Americans for the first time to the dangers lurking in industrial sites in their neighborhoods. In the wake of Love Canal, the government started an effort, still ongoing, to clean up the toxic legacy of the industrial age at factory sites across the nation.

Beginning in the 1920s, Love Canal was used as a toxic waste dump by chemical companies. Then, in 1953, the owner filled in the sixteen-acre site and sold it to the city, which built about 100 homes and an elementary school on the property. The working-class residents who moved into Love Canal had no idea their homes were built on top of leaking drums of deadly chemicals, including cancer-causing benzene. For decades, babies born in Love Canal had higher-than-average levels of birth defects and miscarriages, and the cancer rate in the community was extremely high.

When researchers finally pieced together the clues connecting the waste dumps with Love Canal's health problems, President Jimmy Carter (1924–) declared Love Canal a federal emergency area in the summer of 1978. The school on the site was demolished, and some residents were evacuated. Eventually, the government reimbursed hundreds of residents who were forced out of the neighborhood, most of which was then bulldozed.

In 1980, motivated by Love Canal, the United States Congress passed the Comprehensive Environmental Response, Compensation, and Liability Act, more commonly known as Superfund, which provided federal funds to clean up the most hazardous polluted sites. More than 1,000 locations across the United States—from nail factories in Massachusetts to abandoned mines in Montana—were placed on the list in an effort to protect the public from public health emergencies like Love Canal.

ADDITIONAL FACTS

1. Originally, chemical companies were taxed to pay for Superfund cleanups, but now the cleanups are paid for by taxpayers at large.

2. Part of the Love Canal area was declared safe and reopened for construction in the 1990s.

3. The neighborhood was named for William T. Love, a nineteenth-century entrepreneur who wanted to build a canal bypassing nearby Niagara Falls that would generate hydroelectric power.

★ ★ ★

Thomas Pynchon

Thomas Pynchon (1937–) is among the most critically acclaimed contemporary American authors, known for his byzantine, incomprehensible novels and reclusive lifestyle. He has written six books over about four decades, from *V.* in 1963 to *Against the Day* in 2006. Pynchon's influence is huge, and he is considered one of the leading postmodern writers in American literature.

A recluse, few details of Pynchon's life are known. Born in Glen Cove, New York, he served in the US Navy, graduated from Cornell University in 1959, and worked briefly for Boeing as an engineer. His first book, *V.* was a literary sensation for its provocative symbolism—what does *V.* really stand for?—and his writing style; it won him the Faulkner First Novel Award in 1963. *The Crying of Lot 49*, his most widely read book, was published in 1966.

Next came his famous, 760-page epic, *Gravity's Rainbow* (1973). A landmark of twentieth century American fiction, the novel starts in the late stages of World War II (1939–1945), during the German rocket bombardment of London, and continues beyond Germany's surrender into the war-torn landscape of continental Europe. *Gravity's Rainbow* has divided critics for more than three decades; it won the National Book Award in 1974 but the same year was dismissed as "unreadable, turgid, overwritten, and obscene" by the Pulitzer Prize committee. Pynchon's writing contains countless references to obscure songs, calculus equations, comic books, movies, and other cultural ephemera, and many readers rely on a concordance to decipher the book.

After the publication of *Gravity's Rainbow* and the controversy that surrounded the book, Pynchon literally disappeared, his whereabouts unknown for most of the next two decades. He resurfaced in 1990 with the publication of *Vineland*, a slightly more accessible story of burnt out ex-hippies in Northern California. He published *Mason & Dixon* in 1997. This novel is a retelling of the story of Charles Mason (1728–1786) and Jeremiah Dixon (1733–1779), the British surveyors who mapped the Mason-Dixon line between Pennsylvania and Maryland in the 1760s. In Pynchon's fictionalized account, which he wrote in archaic English to mimic the style of the eighteenth century, the two men encounter many of the Founding Fathers in their travels, including Benjamin Franklin and George Washington.

ADDITIONAL FACTS

1. *Pynchon was a passing acquaintance of Bob Dylan (1941–), on whom one of the minor characters in* V. *is based.*

2. *Like Nathaniel Hawthorne (1804–1864), one of Pynchon's ancestors was a judge at the Salem witch trials.*

3. *According to legend, Pynchon wrote the first draft of* Gravity's Rainbow *in longhand on graph paper.*

★ ★ ★

The Godfather

The Godfather, a film directed by Francis Ford Coppola (1939–) and released to critical acclaim in 1972, was a huge hit that launched the movie career of Al Pacino (1940–) and cemented the legendary reputation of Marlon Brando (1924–2004), who won that year's Academy Award for Best Actor for his portrayal of the aging Mafia kingpin Vito Corleone. The movie itself won the Best Picture Oscar.

The epic, three-hour movie, set in the 1940s and 1950s, follows the fortunes of the Corleone crime family in New York City's bloody mob wars. Based on the best-selling 1969 novel of the same title by Mario Puzo (1920–1999), *The Godfather* features characters loosely inspired by actual mob figures from the "Five Families" that ruled New York's criminal underworld.

In addition to Brando and Pacino, the movie starred James Caan (1940–) and Robert Duvall (1931–) in supporting roles. All four were nominated for Oscars for their performances.

Although the dark, atmospheric cinematography of *The Godfather* is outstanding, critics credit the bravura acting performances of Brando and Pacino for transforming *The Godfather* into a timeless classic. The *New York Times*, reviewing the movie in 1972, immediately recognized the film's accomplishment, calling it "one of the most brutal and moving chronicles of American life ever designed within the limits of popular entertainment."

The film is not without detractors. Some critics have argued that *The Godfather* romanticized organized crime and fostered negative stereotypes of Italian-Americans. Still, the film nearly always finished at the top of lists of the century's greatest American movies, second only to *Citizen Kane* (1941) in the estimation of many critics.

ADDITIONAL FACTS

1. *The film's major competitor at the Oscars was* Cabaret *(1972). It won Best Director (Bob Fosse, 1927–1987), Best Actress (Liza Minnelli, 1946–), and Best Supporting Actor (Joel Grey, 1932–).*

2. *Part of* The Godfather *was shot on Sicily, the Italian island considered the birthplace of the Mafia.*

3. *The Godfather, Part II (1974) also won the Academy Award for Best Picture.*

★ ★ ★

Richard M. Nixon

"When the President does it, that means it is not illegal."
—Richard Nixon

Richard M. Nixon (1913–1994) was the thirty-seventh president of the United States and the first to resign from office. The scandal that drove him from the White House, Watergate, overshadowed the rest of Nixon's career. Before Watergate ended his presidency, Nixon was a highly successful figure who won the popular vote in the 1972 election by the widest margin in American history.

Born in California in a small Quaker community, Nixon was a bright and ambitious student who graduated third in his class at Duke Law School. He returned to California in 1946 and beat an incumbent Democrat in a race for the House of Representatives, an upset victory that impressed national Republicans. GOP presidential candidate Dwight D. Eisenhower (1890–1969) picked Nixon as his running mate in 1952, catapulting the thirty-nine-year-old representative to national prominence. They won both that election and the next, in 1956.

Nixon ran for president in 1960 to succeed Eisenhower but lost the race to Democrat John F. Kennedy (1917–1963). When he ran again in 1968, the Democrats were badly divided over foreign policy, and Nixon won the election on a platform promising an American troop withdrawal from Vietnam.

Domestically, Nixon made modest reforms to the welfare state programs started by President Lyndon Johnson (1908–1973) and created a few of his own, including the Environmental Protection Agency, a new office to safeguard the environment. In foreign affairs, he made a famous trip to China in 1972, restoring American diplomatic relations with the communist nation.

Nixon sought a second term in the 1972 election. The Democratic candidate, George McGovern (1922–), won only one state, Massachusetts, in one of the worst showings in American history, giving Nixon a landslide victory. But after details of Nixon's involvement in the Watergate scandal began to emerge in 1973 and 1974, Congress began to consider impeachment. Sensing the inevitable, Nixon resigned August 9, 1974. His vice president, Gerald Ford (1913–2006), was sworn in as president.

ADDITIONAL FACTS

1. The faculty at Nixon's alma mater, Duke Law School, voted against giving him an honorary degree.

2. In 1968, Nixon's daughter Julie (1948–) married David Eisenhower (1948–), grandson of Dwight D. Eisenhower.

3. Nixon's resignation had a disastrous impact on his Republican Party, which lost forty-nine seats in the House of Representatives in the 1974 congressional elections.

★ ★ ★

Iran Hostage Crisis

When Iranian militants invaded the United States embassy in Tehran in 1979, taking fifty-two American diplomats hostage, the incident sparked an international crisis that severely damaged the administration of President Jimmy Carter (1924–) and marked the first prominent clash between the United States and the Islamic world. After 444 days of captivity, the hostages were finally released unharmed on January 20, 1981, the day Carter left office. However, American relations with Iran have remained frosty ever since.

The roots of the Iranian hostage crisis stretch back to 1953, when American and British spies organized a coup against a popular Iranian prime minister. In his place, they installed the shah, a hereditary monarch whose regime became increasingly repressive over the next two decades. In the middle of the Cold War, the United States continued to support the anticommunist shah, enraging Iranians who chafed at his authoritarian rule.

In the late 1970s, Islamic fundamentalists led by a radical cleric, Ayatollah Ruhollah Khomeini (c. 1900–1989), began agitating against the shah, who fled from Iran and eventually was admitted into the United States for medical treatment in October 1979. Angry that the United States had admitted the shah instead of sending him back to Iran for trial and certain execution, followers of the ayatollah burst into the American embassy in November 1979 and seized the hostages.

The Carter administration was divided over how to respond. The United States first imposed economic sanctions and cut diplomatic ties. Then in April 1980, the president ordered a military raid to rescue the hostages, but it failed. The shah died in July 1980, but the Iranian captors held on to the hostages in further protest of US policies. Carter's inability to win the release of the hostages would cost him the 1980 election, which he lost to Ronald Reagan (1911–2004). The Iranians finally released the hostages in January 1981, minutes after Reagan took the oath of office.

However, the relationship between the United States and Iran remained hostile. The Reagan administration supported Iraq, ruled by Saddam Hussein (1937–2006), in the bloody Iran-Iraq war between 1980 and 1988, and it sought to counter growing Iranian influence in the Islamic world.

ADDITIONAL FACTS

1. *In recognition of their hardships, each hostage was given a free lifetime pass to major league baseball games when they returned to the United States.*

2. *Despite promises to take a tough line against the ayatollah, the Reagan administration later illegally sold weapons to Iran in order to finance its own secret operations in Latin America, an action that became known as the Iran-contra affair.*

3. *Many Americans tied yellow ribbons around the trunks of trees in a gesture of support for the hostages, beginning a tradition that would be resurrected during the Gulf War (1991) and in other times of crisis.*

★ ★ ★

Thurgood Marshall

A renowned civil rights lawyer, Thurgood Marshall (1908–1993) was the first African-American appointed to the United States Supreme Court. President Lyndon Johnson (1908–1973) made the appointment in 1967. Over the next twenty-four years, Marshall was a stalwart supporter of affirmative action and racial equality and an opponent of the death penalty.

Born in Baltimore, Maryland, Marshall opened his first law office in the midst of the Great Depression of the 1930s, when he filed successful challenges to Maryland's segregation statutes. He soon joined the legal staff of the National Association for the Advancement of Colored People (NAACP) and launched a series of court challenges to segregation in colleges and universities across the South. This effort culminated in 1954 with Marshall's most famous victory, the *Brown v. Board of Education* Supreme Court decision outlawing segregation in public schools.

President John F. Kennedy (1917–1963) named Marshall to a federal appeals court seat in 1961, over the objection of Southern senators who vehemently objected to his past civil-rights work. After Marshall's elevation to the Supreme Court, he often sided with other liberal justices remaining from the Warren Court era. In his first ten years on the bench, Marshall was in the majority on decisions decriminalizing abortion and allowing the private possession of pornography.

However, as the court moved to the right in the 1970s, Marshall frequently found himself on the losing end of controversial decisions. Marshall strongly supported affirmative action, and he criticized a 1978 Supreme Court decision that curtailed racial quotas meant to reserve spaces in college classes for African-Americans. Marshall also fought against the death penalty, which was reintroduced in the United States in 1976 over his objections. In failing health, the legal hero of the civil-rights movement resigned from the Court in 1991 and died two years later.

ADDITIONAL FACTS

1. The name Thurgood came from Marshall's grandfather, who had made up the name Throughgood when he joined the Union Army in the Civil War (1861–1865).

2. Marshall dissented in 25 of his last 112 Supreme Court cases.

3. Baltimore's international airport was renamed in Marshall's honor in 2005.

★ ★ ★

ARPAnet

In the heyday of the military-industrial complex during the Cold War of the late twentieth century, a secretive office at the Pentagon called the Advanced Research Projects Agency (ARPA) was in charge of developing cutting-edge technology for use by the military. Flush with defense funds, ARPA funded an array of futuristic research, including a project that began in 1962 to link computers to one another across the country. The result, seven years later, was a primitive network called ARPAnet, the ancestor of the modern Internet. ARPAnet officially shut down in 1990, but the Internet that continues today is built on many of the technologies first developed for the defense agency.

In the 1960s, relatively few high-powered computers existed, and they were scattered among college campuses. Military planners hoped to use the ARPAnet system to link these distant computers together to make research faster and easier. ARPAnet went operational in 1969, and the first e-mail was sent across the network in 1971 by Ray Tomlinson (1941–), an American computer programmer. For its first twenty years, the Internet would remain primarily a text-based network.

The Internet's roots as a military project reflected the vast sums lavished on defense during the Cold War. Whatever else the faults of the military-industrial complex may have been, money spent by the Pentagon on research often resulted in useful new civilian technology. The Internet, which separated from the defense network in the 1980s, is perhaps the best example of an unexpected benefit arising from Cold War–era defense spending.

Throughout the 1980s, the network continued to develop but its use was still mostly limited to computer nerds. Then in 1991, a British computer programmer, Tim Berners-Lee (1955–), developed *hypertext markup language* (HTML), which made the network much more user-friendly by linking words in one computer file to those in another, enabled the use of graphics, and for the first time made the net widely accessible to the public. The hypertext portion of the Internet became known as the World Wide Web, which in turn provided the impetus for the Internet revolution of the 1990s. Now accessible on computers in virtually every corner of the globe, the Web has hugely increased business productivity and speeded up global communications.

ADDITIONAL FACTS

1. Tomlinson first used the @ symbol for e-mail in 1971.

2. The "ownership" of the Internet remains subject to a contentious and confusing debate; at present, the US Department of Commerce retains some control over it and the issue of so-called top-level domain names like ".com" and ".net."

3. The first Internet connection in 1969 was between computers at Stanford University and the University of California at Los Angeles.

★ ★ ★

Provincetown

The sunny oceanside village of Provincetown, Massachusetts—where the Pilgrims first set foot in the New World in 1620—later attracted pilgrims of a different sort as one of the first towns in the United States to openly welcome gays and lesbians. The picturesque town at the tip of Cape Cod has been at the vanguard of the gay rights movement since the 1970s and is now considered one of the vacation capitals of gay Americans.

English settlers first colonized the area in the early eighteenth century, attracted by the rich fisheries that gave the cape its name. After the American Revolution, many Portuguese immigrated to Provincetown and other coastal New England towns, where they gradually came to dominate the fishing industry.

In the twentieth century, however, the fishing industry fell into decline, and the town was reborn as a center for the arts. Many playwrights, including Eugene O'Neill (1888–1953) and Tennessee Williams (1911–1983), were involved in the village's burgeoning artistic scene.

The town's association with the gay rights movement began in the early twentieth century, at a time when gays and lesbians faced rampant harassment and ostracism in most American cities. Provincetown welcomed gay tourists, many of whom bought property in the town. Today, the city is overwhelmingly gay during the summer tourist season, when the movement's symbolic rainbow flag flutters above many homes and shops.

In 2004, Massachusetts made national headlines by becoming the first state to permit gay marriage. Hundreds of gay weddings have been held in "P Town," which to many observers symbolizes the growing acceptance of equal rights for gays and lesbians in the United States.

ADDITIONAL FACTS

1. *The area of Provincetown facing the Atlantic Ocean is closed to development as part of the Cape Cod National Seashore.*

2. *Provincetown is at the eastern end of US Route 6, a transcontinental road that stretches 3,652 miles to Long Beach, California.*

3. *Mostly a summer resort, the town has only about 4,000 permanent residents, compared to 50,000 during the summer.*

* * *

Alex Haley

The publication in 1976 of *Roots: The Saga of an American Family*, by journalist Alex Haley (1921–1992), was a major literary phenomenon and it is one of the most commercially successful books ever written by an African-American author. An autobiographical story of Haley's quest to trace his family's origins in Africa, the book sold five million copies in its first three years in print and was made into an enormously popular TV miniseries.

Haley was born in New York and spent most of his childhood in Tennessee. He served for twenty years in the United States Coast Guard, spanning World War II (1939–1945) and the Korean War (1950–1953), and took a job at *Playboy* magazine in 1959 after leaving the military. In 1965, he published *The Autobiography of Malcolm X*, which he had begun several years earlier based on interviews for *Playboy* with the black nationalist leader. The book has sold more than six million copies to date, and it made Haley a household name.

His next project, *Roots*, took Haley more than ten years to research and involved trips to three continents in search of clues about his ancestry. Starting with only a few scraps of oral history passed down from his family, Haley was eventually able to trace his lineage back to a small village in the West African nation of Gambia, where one of his ancestors had been kidnapped and sold into slavery. Haley based the book closely on his own family but fictionalized certain elements; the book won a Pulitzer Prize and topped national bestseller lists for weeks. In a time before VCRs and TiVo, millions of people in 1977 stayed home night after night for a week to tune in to the *Roots* saga on network TV.

The runaway success of *Roots* reflected the growing desire among African-Americans in exploring their genealogical background and writing about their past, seeking to reclaim the history of black Americans. Although Haley would be criticized for certain elements of the story, the book proved deeply moving and inspirational to millions of readers. Haley died of a heart attack before he could complete a planned second novel about slavery.

ADDITIONAL FACTS

1. *The Coast Guard created a new military position especially for Haley—chief journalist—which he held for the last seven years of his military career.*

2. *The author Harold Courlander (1908–1996) sued Haley in 1978, alleging that Haley had lifted some passages of* Roots *verbatim from Courlander's novel* The African. *The case was settled out of court after six weeks.*

3. *The last episode of the* Roots *miniseries, which aired on ABC in 1977, is the third-highest-rated TV program ever, behind the series finales of* M*A*S*H *and* Dallas, *respectively.*

★ ★ ★

Michael Jackson

Michael Jackson (1958–), nicknamed the King of Pop, is the most popular recording artist on the planet. His 1982 hit album, *Thriller*, is the best-selling record of all time.

Born in Gary, Indiana, Jackson was a major star by age five as the lead singer of the Jackson 5, a boy band consisting of Michael and four of his brothers: Jackie (1951–), Tito (1953–), Jermaine (1954–), and Marlon (1957–). The band scored big hits on the Motown recording label with songs such as the 1970 chart toppers "ABC" and "I'll Be There."

Widely regarded as the most talented of the five, Michael Jackson began his solo career in the early 1970s, while still a teenager. *Off the Wall*, his breakthrough 1979 album produced by Quincy Jones (1933–), became a mammoth global hit on the strength of its title track and the tune "Don't Stop 'Til You Get Enough."

Thriller, however, was a global entertainment sensation utterly without precedent. Hit singles from the album include "Billie Jean," "Beat It," and the title track, "Thriller." The album featured duets with other major stars, including former Beatle Paul McCartney (1942–)and distinguished hair-metal guitarist Eddie Van Halen (1955–). Music videos of the album's hit singles were played repeatedly on MTV and helped define that emerging genre.

The success of *Thriller* made Jackson the most popular musician of the 1980s and earned him an invitation to the White House to meet President Ronald Reagan (1911–2004). In 1985, at the peak of his fame, he cowrote with Lionel Richie (1949–) the charity single "We Are the World" to raise funds for famine relief in Africa. Jackson went on to release two more hit albums, *Bad* (1987) and *Dangerous* (1991).

And then Jackson started getting weird. Rumors emerged that he slept in a special, pressure-controlled chamber to prevent aging. His skin color and facial structure changed inexplicably. He bought an old amusement park in California that he turned into his own private hideaway called Neverland Ranch, and he began inviting prepubescent children to the ranch for sleepovers.

In 2005, with his musical career in decline, Jackson was tried on child molestation charges stemming from his Neverland slumber parties. His trial resulted in acquittal. Jackson temporarily moved to the island kingdom of Bahrain in the Persian Gulf to escape publicity but later returned to the United States.

ADDITIONAL FACTS

1. Michael Jackson was married to Lisa Marie Presley (1968–) from 1994 to 1996 and then to Debbie Rowe (1958–) from 1996 to 1999. He reportedly fathered two children with Rowe and a third with a woman of undisclosed identity.

2. Jackson bought the rights to half the catalog of the Beatles in 1985.

★ ★ ★

Watergate

In early 1972, United States president Richard M. Nixon (1913–1994) appeared to be headed for easy reelection in the November presidential campaign. The famously paranoid Nixon White House, however, was in no mood to take any chances. On June 17, 1972, five burglars hired by the Republicans running Nixon's reelection campaign were arrested breaking into Democratic Party headquarters at the Watergate building complex in Washington, DC, where they were trying to install telephone wiretaps to monitor Nixon's rivals.

At first, the arrest of the Watergate burglars attracted relatively little attention. The local newspaper, the *Washington Post*, assigned two lowly metro reporters, Bob Woodward (1943–) and Carl Bernstein (1944–) to cover the break-in. However, as the two investigated the case, it became apparent that the Watergate burglars had mysterious connections to high-ranking Republican officials.

That fall, running against Democrat George McGovern (1922–), Nixon rolled to a landslide victory. The Watergate criminal investigation, however, was only then starting to pick up steam. In early 1973, the burglars were linked to two top White House aides, H. R. Haldeman (1926–1993) and John Ehrlichman (1926–1999). Both were forced to resign and eventually went to prison.

By mid-1973, the unfolding Watergate scandal dominated the headlines and had the Nixon administration reeling. One by one, top officials were implicated in the scandal and forced to step down to face criminal charges. The central question gripping the nation was whether President Nixon himself had been aware of—or perhaps had even ordered—the break-ins.

Publicly, Nixon proclaimed, "I am not a crook," and maintained that he had had nothing to do with Watergate. However, in 1974, the US Supreme Court ordered Nixon to turn over secret audiotape recordings of his White House conversations that proved he knew far more about the break-in than he had acknowledged in public and also that he had conspired to cover up the burglary.

The tapes proved to be the last straw that doomed Nixon. In the summer of 1974, the US House of Representatives began considering articles of impeachment against him for his Watergate role. With many fellow Republicans against him, Nixon resigned on August 9, 1974, rather than face almost certain removal from office.

ADDITIONAL FACTS

1. *The June 17, 1972, break-in at the Watergate was actually the second GOP burglary of the building; three days earlier the operatives had broken in without being detected.*

2. *Woodward and Bernstein wrote a best-selling book about their investigation,* All the President's Men, *that was published in 1974 and made into a popular movie of the same title in 1976.*

3. *The secret source who tipped off the* Washington Post *to many aspects of the Watergate scandal, nicknamed "Deep Throat," was finally unmasked as former FBI official W. Mark Felt (1913–) in 2005.*

★ ★ ★

Gulf War

On August 2, 1990, the army of Iraq launched a surprise invasion of its tiny Persian Gulf neighbor, Kuwait. The Kuwaiti defenders, badly outgunned, surrendered within hours. Five months later, however, after Iraqi dictator Saddam Hussein (1937–2006) repeatedly ignored demands by the international community to withdraw his forces from oil-rich Kuwait, American and allied forces liberated the country and restored its pro-American monarchy in the brief Gulf War.

In the wake of the Iraqi invasion, the administration of US President George H. W. Bush (1924–) feared Hussein's next step would be to send his troops into Saudi Arabia, a long-standing American ally and the world's largest oil producer. A successful Iraqi invasion of Saudi Arabia, they feared, would seriously alter the balance of power in the Middle East and embolden a dictator they considered a dangerous maniac. Although Saudi Arabia's absolute monarchy collected billions of dollars in oil revenues, it had virtually no military to defend itself.

To protect Saudi Arabia, Bush hastily assembled an international coalition that was dispatched to the Persian Gulf in the fall of 1990. The American contingent alone amounted to half a million troops, the largest foreign combat force sent abroad since the Vietnam War (1957–1975). In addition, Bush warned Hussein that unless Iraqi troops left Kuwait by mid-January 1991, the allies would force them out.

The Gulf War began shortly after the January deadline passed. Militarily, the war proved to be a tremendous mismatch. Although the Iraqi army seemed large and powerful on paper, it stood no chance against the smart bombs, night vision goggles, and advanced weaponry of the United States and its allies. The war showcased the gigantic strides in military technology the United States had made since the Vietnam War. Allied casualties were light—378 dead, compared to tens of thousands of Iraqis.

After making short work of the Iraqi invasion force in Kuwait, American commanders briefly crossed the border into Iraq. However, Bush and his defense secretary, Dick Cheney (1941–), decided against continuing on to Baghdad. Removing Hussein from power, they felt, would create chaos in the country and turn allied troops from liberators of Kuwait into occupiers of Iraq. Unfortunately, their worries proved prescient. Hussein would remain in power until the United States invaded in 2003, removing the dictator but sparking a bloody and ongoing civil war.

ADDITIONAL FACTS

1. *The great World War II–era battleships USS Missouri and USS Wisconsin both performed their last active-duty combat missions during the Gulf War, bombarding Iraqi forces in Kuwait and Iraq.*

2. *The war resulted in an ecological catastrophe for the Persian Gulf region, when Iraq dumped hundreds of thousands of tons of oil into the gulf and many oil wells were set on fire, spewing dangerous smoke into the atmosphere.*

3. *Although expensive, most of the financial cost of the Gulf War was repaid by Kuwait and Saudi Arabia, with other contributions coming from Germany and Japan, nations that did not send troops.*

★ ★ ★

Stonewall

The Stonewall riot, a three-day protest in 1969 against police harassment of gays and lesbians in New York City, is considered the founding event of the gay rights movement. Stonewall's anniversary is now celebrated around the world as Gay Pride Day.

Before the late 1960's, homosexuality was widely considered a psychiatric disorder and a public menace. In New York and most other major cities, the police regularly raided gay bars and arrested gays on indecency charges.

"Gay bars were frightening," one patron recalled years later in the *New York Times*. "You never knew what might happen, especially with police raids. The cops treated customers like scum."

The Stonewall Inn, a gay bar at 53 Christopher Street in New York's bohemian Greenwich Village neighborhood, was the target of one such raid on the early morning of June 28, 1969. Although many of the patrons of the bar had endured police raids before, that night they fought back, throwing bricks, coins, and beer cans at the officers. The ensuing melee soon spilled out onto nearby streets, where clashes with police continued for several days after.

In the wake of Stonewall, gay and lesbian rights groups became far more aggressive, demanding an end to police harassment and demeaning antigay laws.

By the early 1970s, New York and other American cities would stop many of the worst indignities imposed on gays, including the notorious raids, and major medical organizations would stop labeling homosexuality as a disorder. In the three decades since then, civil rights groups have successfully expanded legal protections for gays and lesbians, including the addition of sexual orientation to many anti-discrimination statutes. Modern gay rights groups continue to draw inspiration from the men and women at the Stonewall Inn who took a dramatic stand against discrimination and harassment.

ADDITIONAL FACTS

1. *The federal government added the Stonewall Inn to the National Register of Historic Places in 1999, on the thirtieth anniversary of the Stonewall rebellion.*

2. *Although laws against gay sex were rarely enforced, they remained on the books in many states until they were ruled unconstitutional in a 2003 Supreme Court decision, Lawrence v. Texas.*

3. *In 2004, Massachusetts became the first US state to allow gays to wed. Several European countries, South Africa, and Canada have also extended marriage rights to gays. Some religious groups have battled against gay marriage in the United States, however, and dozens of states have passed laws explicitly banning gay marriage.*

★ ★ ★

Enron

The collapse of the Enron Corporation in 2001 triggered one of the most significant business scandals in recent American history and resulted in several major changes to corporate law. Although litigation and criminal investigations related to Enron's shady financing were still ongoing as of 2007, the historical significance of the company's bankruptcy is already evident from the raft of new business legislation imposed on US corporations after Enron's downfall.

Enron, founded in 1985 by Texas business executive Kenneth Lay (1942–2006), initially specialized in natural gas pipelines and transmission lines for electricity. During the 1990s, Enron generated billions of dollars in profits by expanding into the market for *derivatives*. A derivative is a financial instrument that can be used to lessen risk. In essence, a derivative is a tradable contract to pay a certain price for a good or service at a future date; derivatives are often purchased to lock in a price for vital goods like oil or electricity.

During the 1990s, flush from its success in derivatives trading, Enron was widely considered a model of cutting-edge corporate management. However, the company's financial records came under scrutiny in 2001, and it quickly emerged that executives at the company had overstated Enron's earnings by several hundred million dollars and set up deceptive shell companies to hide Enron's huge losses. Stunningly, the Fortune 500 company collapsed within a few weeks toward the end of 2001. Many employees of the Houston-based firm lost their life savings, which had been invested in Enron stock in the company's 401(k) retirement plan, and top executives were soon arrested for fraud. Arthur Andersen, the firm that handled Enron's accounting, went out of business as a result of its association with the disgraced company.

In the wake of the Enron scandal and a similar accounting scandal at WorldCom, a telecommunications company, the United States Congress approved the Sarbanes-Oxley Act, a law that is meant to create greater transparency in corporate accounting and make executives personally responsible for their companies' financial statements. The law, signed by President George W. Bush (1946–) in 2002, represented a renewed effort by the government to tighten regulations on American businesses. However, corporate executives continue to complain about the cost of complying with Sarbanes-Oxley, and the law's future remains uncertain.

ADDITIONAL FACTS

1. *The home of the Houston Astros, Enron Field, was renamed Minute Maid Park after the company's collapse.*

2. *Lay, Enron's founder, died in July 2006, a few months before he was due to be sentenced for fraud. Jeff Skilling (1953–), the company's CEO at the time of the collapse, was sentenced to twenty-four years in prison.*

3. *The Enron collapse was explained in the Oscar-nominated 2005 documentary feature film* Enron: The Smartest Guys in the Room.

★ ★ ★

Hurricane Katrina

One of the deadliest natural disasters in American history, Hurricane Katrina struck Louisiana and Mississippi in 2005, killing about 1,800 people and destroying much of the historic city of New Orleans. As of 2007, hundreds of thousands of people remain displaced from their homes as a result of the devastating storm. In monetary terms, Katrina caused more damage—estimated at around $80 billion—than any other disaster in the nation's history.

The storm, a Category 5 hurricane—the strongest possible on the scale, classified as "devastating"—formed in the Atlantic Ocean and hit New Orleans on August 29. Although most city residents had obeyed an order to evacuate, thousands remained in their homes. Others fled to the Superdome, a New Orleans football stadium that had been opened to the public as an emergency shelter.

When it struck, Katrina was one of the strongest storms ever to reach land in the United States. Wind speeds of more than 120 miles per hour were reported across coastal Louisiana and Mississippi, and massive flooding occurred across the region.

The aftermath of the storm, however, caused more deaths than the hurricane itself. Levees at a lake in New Orleans were breached, and 80 percent of the city was inundated with floodwater. Live television coverage beamed around the world captured images of city residents on their roofs—for some, the only part of their home that remained above water. Many of the storm's victims were poor, elderly, and African-American residents who had not been able to flee. Supplies at the Superdome were exhausted, and after chaos erupted there, the stadium quickly became a symbol of government dysfunction during the crisis. The head of the Federal Emergency Management Agency, Michael D. Brown (1954–), was forced to resign as a result of the agency's inept response to the disaster.

The historical significance of Hurricane Katrina may be too early to assess. Politicians from both major political parties have vowed to rebuild New Orleans, but the city's population remains significantly lower and many residents have yet to return to the city.

ADDITIONAL FACTS

1. *In recognition of the devastation caused by the storm, the name Katrina has been removed from the list of possible future hurricane names.*

2. *As a result of evacuations, the population of the entire state of Louisiana declined by about 5 percent between 2005 and 2006.*

3. *In a reprise of the American response to the 1906 San Francisco earthquake, the United States declined many foreign offers of assistance—including medical assistance offered from nearby communist Cuba.*

★ ★ ★

Toni Morrison

The American writer to most recently win the Nobel Prize for Literature, novelist Toni Morrison (1931–) was honored in 1993 for her rich, complex novels such as *Song of Solomon* (1977) and *Beloved* (1987) that, in the words of her award citation, have "given the Afro-American people their history back, piece by piece."

Morrison was born Chloe Anthony Wofford in Lorain, Ohio. In 1958, she married Harold Morrison; they divorced in 1964. As Toni Morrison, she wrote her first novel, *The Bluest Eye* (1970), while teaching at Howard University. The main character of the novel, which is set in Depression-era Ohio, is a black girl named Pecola who yearns for blue eyes like the white child movie star Shirley Temple (1928–).

Like most of Morrison's work, the novel takes an unflinching look at American society, dealing frankly with themes of child abuse and racism. After publishing *The Bluest Eye*, Morrison wrote *Sula* in 1973 and *Song of Solomon*, one of her most highly regarded works, in 1977.

By the time Morrison published *Beloved* in 1987, she was already considered one of the leading American novelists. *Beloved*—the story of an African-American escaped slave named Sethe who kills her baby rather than allow her to be taken back into slavery—was a literary sensation, winning the 1988 Pulitzer Prize for fiction and solidifying Morrison's critical reputation.

Morrison's writing style, influenced by William Faulkner (1897–1962), is often nonlinear and fragmentary. For instance, the narration of *Beloved* jumps between the 1850s and 1870s, often with little or no warning. Indeed, the wandering time frame reflects the major themes of the novel: the difficulty of dealing with traumatic memories and the crushing psychological damage caused by slavery.

After winning the Nobel Prize, Morrison released *Paradise* in 1998 and *Love* in 2003, both of which received enthusiastic reviews. She recently retired from a professorship at Princeton University but continues to write and publish. A 2006 poll of prominent authors in the *New York Times Book Review* named *Beloved* the top American novel of the last twenty-five years, a testament to Morrison's standing within contemporary American literature.

ADDITIONAL FACTS

1. *Morrison wrote a 1986 play,* Dreaming Emmett, *about the murder of Emmett Till (1941–1955).*

2. *A movie version of* Beloved *was made in 1998 starring Oprah Winfrey as Sethe.*

3. Beloved *was based on the true story of Margaret Graner, an escaped slave who killed one of her children in 1851 to keep him from being taken back into slavery.*

★ ★ ★

The Simpsons

First aired in 1989 on the Fox television network, the animated sitcom *The Simpsons* topped *Time* magazine's ranking of the twentieth century's best television shows and is generally considered one of the best-ever American TV series. Globally popular, new episodes of *The Simpsons* are still being made as of 2007, and the show is also widely broadcast in syndication.

The show was created in the late 1980s by cartoonist Matt Groening (1954–) and Hollywood screenwriter James L. Brooks (1940–). Many of the characters in the Simpson family were named after Groening's relatives. Although a cartoon, from its very beginning *The Simpsons* was much edgier than many of its live-action competitors. The show frequently holds authority figures in the fictional town of Springfield up for ridicule, and it often mocks television itself.

The Simpson family—Homer, Marge, Lisa, Bart, and Maggie—and the show's numerous supporting characters, like convenience store clerk Apu Nahasapeemapetilon and villainous nuclear power plant owner Charles Montgomery Burns, have become cultural mainstays familiar to many Americans. But did you know:

* One of the voice actors in *The Simpsons*, Harry Shearer, also appeared in the 1984 cult film *This is Spinal Tap*.
* Before *The Simpsons*, Groening created a print comic strip named *Life in Hell* that featured talking rabbits.
* *The Simpsons* began as a series of crudely drawn shorts on *The Tracey Ullman Show* on Fox in 1987.
* The word "D'oh," often uttered by Homer Simpson, has been inducted into the *Oxford English Dictionary* as an annoyed exclamation.
* After a national competition in the summer of 2007, the small town of Springfield, Vermont, was selected as the "official" hometown of *The Simpsons*.

The show has won countless Emmy Awards, and a highly anticipated movie version was released in 2007.

ADDITIONAL FACTS

1. Eight-year-old Lisa Simpson, the irritating, self-righteous middle child in the family, became a vegetarian in a 1995 episode of the show that featured former Beatle and vegetarian Paul McCartney (1942–).

2. The program is broadcast around the world dubbed in local languages, although in Muslim countries it is edited to remove the show's rampant references to alcohol.

3. Tony Blair (1953–), the former prime minister of the United Kingdom, appeared in cartoon form as a guest star on the show in 2003.

★ ★ ★

Ronald Reagan

Ronald Reagan (1911–2004) entered the White House in 1981, pledging to renew American pressure on the Soviet Union. His hard-line policy against the Soviets ultimately resulted in Reagan's crowning legacy, the collapse of Communism shortly after he left office. Reagan's domestic record, however, was mixed. To his supporters, Reagan's tax cuts and deregulation of many large industries strengthened the foundations of the American economy. Detractors point out the massive national debt run up by his administration, bills that the nation continues to pay twenty years later.

Reagan grew up in Illinois and graduated from Eureka College in 1932 before moving to California to begin his acting career. In the golden age of Hollywood, Reagan starred in a number of popular films, achieving his most lasting cinematic fame for his portrayal of legendary Notre Dame football player George "The Gipper" Gipp. At the time, Reagan considered himself a Democrat, and voted for Franklin D. Roosevelt.

As his film career faded, Reagan's interest in national politics grew, and he began to lose faith in the Democratic Party. His staunch opposition to communism and support for free-market economic theories found favor with a growing conservative movement in the 1960s. He officially changed parties, famously declaring, "I didn't leave the Democratic party, the party left me." Reagan ran for governor of California in 1966 and defeated an incumbent Democrat.

In the late 1960s and early 1970s, Reagan's Republican Party was dominated by traditionalist Midwestern and northeastern Republicans like Gerald Ford, who became president after the resignation of President Nixon. Reagan represented a more ideologically conservative wing of the party and challenged Ford for the party's 1976 presidential nomination. Although Reagan lost, that campaign laid the challenge for his successful 1980 campaign for the GOP nomination.

As president, Reagan sharply increased military spending, passed several tax cuts, and increased the American arsenal of nuclear weaponry. The Soviets tried to keep pace with the American military build-up, and historians believe the pressure on their economy contributed to the collapse of the Soviet Bloc in 1989 under Reagan's successor, George H. W. Bush (1924–).

ADDITIONAL FACTS

1. *One of Reagan's first jobs after graduating from college was as a broadcaster of Chicago Cubs games for an Iowa radio station, WOC.*

2. *Reagan served five terms as the president of the Screen Actor's Guild, a union for Hollywood actors, during the 1940s and 1950s, and is the only union member elected president of the United States.*

3. *At 69 in 1980, Reagan was the oldest man elected president.*

★ ★ ★

Index

★ ★ ★

★ ★ ★

★ ★ ★

★ ★ ★

★ ★ ★

* * *

★ ★ ★

★ ★ ★

★ ★ ★

Image Credits

★ ★ ★